THE CATALOG OF BOAT CATALOGS

A Comprehensive Listing of over 500 Boat and Nautical Accessory Catalogs

Researched and Compiled

by

Janet C. Gilmore

the writing works

Seattle, Washington

THE CATALOG OF BOAT CATALOGS. Copyright © 1983 by The Writing Works. All rights reserved. Printed in the United States of America. No part of this book may be used or reproduced in any manner whatsoever without written permission from the publisher.

FIRST EDITION

Designers
Cover: Jessica Fields
Interior: Ronn Talbot Pelley

LIBRARY OF CONGRESS
CATALOGING IN PUBLICATION DATA

Gilmore, Janet Crofton, 1949-
The catalog of boat catalogs.

Includes index.
1. Boats and boating—Catalogs. I. Title.
VM321.G49   1983   623.8′223′0294   83-12342

ISBN 0-916076-63-6

Published by
The Writing Works
417 East Pine Street
Seattle, Washington 98122

THE WRITING WORKS IS A PART OF THE CONE-HEIDEN GROUP

CONTENTS

INTRODUCTION

A guide to marine equipment companies that sell boats and related equipment, this volume is aimed primarily at the person who wishes to purchase, build, maintain, repair, or outfit a small boat under 35 feet, whether it be a power-, sail-, or rowboat, workboat, sportsfisher, pleasure boat, or competitive racer. A lengthy enough review of each firm's offerings as well as its literature has been provided in order to help boaters locate desired items, procure helpful publications, and choose the companies with which they would like to do business.

The inclusion of a company in this catalog is not meant as an endorsement of that company. However, time constraints, space limitations, and a lack of knowledge have invariably resulted in the exclusion of some companies. Exclusions should not be interpreted to mean that a particular company is not a valuable source of boating and nautical goods and services.

USING THIS CATALOG

A sense of humor is often needed in guides such as this because, regretably, businesses do shift with the times. Do keep in mind that firms will change addresses and phone numbers—even names.

Listings have been organized into as many categories as possible to help the reader find products easily from the table of contents. The location of an entry depends on the firm's primary offerings, but since many companies offer merchandise that would fit into several categories, cross-references appear at the end of each section. The index can be used to find specific items. Within sections, a company using a personal name in its title, A. L. Don, for example, is listed according to the last name, while in the index such a title appears under both the first and last names.

Where more than one phone number is listed for a company, the first is generally a customer service number; additional numbers, and most of the toll free numbers, are ONLY for making orders. Use the ordering numbers to obtain catalogs and other literature, but NOT to make detailed inquiries about products, prices, and services.

When price lists or order forms are mentioned specifically in an entry's heading, they must be specially requested when ordering the firm's literature. An asterisk (*) placed to the left of a manufacturer's name indicates that items must be ordered through the company's dealers and distributors except in unusual cases.

OBTAINING CATALOGS

The quickest way to obtain a company's literature is to request it over the phone. Mail is the slower method of soliciting catalogs. If the literature is free, a postcard simply requesting it will do. If the literature costs, send a check, secondly a money order or bank draft, to have a record of the transaction.

PLACING ORDERS

To make ordering by mail more enjoyable and successful, various experts suggest following these helpful practices and procedures:

1. Check a product's photo or illustration carefully against the description. If you find any discrepancies, make inquiries directly to the company before ordering. In the case of a product not manufactured by the company selling it, you may write for a free copy of any manufacturer's guarantee that may cover it.

2. Read carefully the company's guarantees regarding products, pricing, delivery time, refunds, and returns. Compare prices carefully, taking into account shipping charges. Do not hesitate to make inquiries before ordering to confirm prices and guarantees.

3. Follow ordering instructions carefully and print your order legibly, for many mail-order misunderstandings arise from incomplete ordering information, unclear handwriting, and failure to read or understand the directions or catalog descriptions.

4. Allow for the appropriate amount of time to elapse to receive your order. How you place the order and pay for it, how quickly the company can process the order, and how the order is shipped should all be taken into account.

5. Check carefully the merchandise ordered upon receipt. If damaged, notify the deliverer, not the supplier. If otherwise unsatisfactory, review the company's guarantees, follow carefully the instructions for returns and refunds, rewrap the merchandise securely, and return it insured.

Remember, mail order is a quick and easy way of procuring those goods and services needed to build, repair, maintain, or outfit your boat. The catalogs and informational literature to be obtained from the companies listed here will provide you with valuable information and endless hours of exciting reading.

1. BOATS: PLANS, KITS, COMPLETE OR PARTIALLY COMPLETED BOATS, AND MODELS

Canoes
Kayaks
Inflatables
Rowing Shells
Whitehalls
Sailboats
Rowing Boats
Power Boats
Hovercraft
Ice Boats
Pontoon Boats
Sailboards
Commercial Boats
Workboats
Utility Skiffs
Yachts
Cruisers
Multihulls
Houseboats
Scale Models
Half-Models

Easy Rider Canoe and Kayak Company   Rugged canoe of Uniroyal's Royalex ABS material takes pounding of whitewater in stride.

Canoes, Kayaks, Inflatables, and Accessories

THE ADIRONDACK MUSEUM
Blue Mountain Lake, New York 12812
(518) 352-7311

Pamphlet, 12 pages; Order form. Free.

This booklet represents the Museum's offerings of books, prints, and boat plans pertinent to the Adirondacks. At $1 apiece, the 17¾" x 22½" plans of Rushton sailing and paddling canoes, a Rushton guideboat, and a John Blanchard guideboat ($2, 24" x 36") are mainly for decorative and informational purposes and do not give detailed instructions. Among the books briefly described are some regarding fishing, hunting, boating, and camping in the Adirondacks, and, notably, Durant's *The Adirondack Guide-Boat, The Naphtha Launch,* and Manley's *Rushton and His Times in American Canoeing.* Small photographs picture the prints available ($4.50 each) of Adirondack scenes (some hunting and fishing) of the late 1800s by A. F. Tait, Winslow Homer, and other artists.

ALLAGASH CANOES
Riverside Associates, Inc.
Francestown, New Hampshire 03043
(603) 547-2738

Three pamphlets, 3 pages each; Price list. Free.

Each pamphlet offers photos, lists specifications, and describes the features, design, construction, and performance of one of 3 Riverside canoes—a multilaminate Royalex whitewater/flatwater wilderness river touring model with hardwood rails and inwales (15'8", 17'3"; 65#, 75#); a hunting/fishing sports canoe constructed of fiberglass with integral keel, reinforced with fiberglass-covered hardwood ribs, and fitted with foam flotation and wooden gunwales, seat frames, decks, and carrying yokes (13', 16'; 58#, 73#); and a family recreational canoe with integral keel, fabricated with a hand-layup of fiberglass mat and woven roving, and fitted with foam flotation and wooden gunwales, seat frames, decks and carrying yoke (13', 15'8"; 58#, 73#). All canoes feature woven cane seats. Listed on the price sheet but not described are a balsa-core fiberglass "Guide" canoe and a variety of accessories—Maine Guide paddles, car-top carriers, a hardwood motor mount (3 hp), and a life vest.

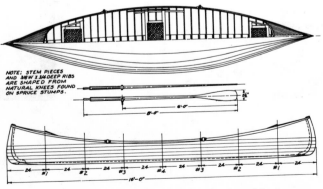

The Adirondack Museum Laker.   Diagram and line drawing of the Saranac Laker.

APPALACHIAN BOATS
T & B Plastics Corporation
Box 32, Isthmus Road
Rumford, Maine 04276

Pamphlet, 4 pages; Accessory and price list. Free.

With this literature, Appalachian Boats briefly advertises, with scant photographs, its 100% woven fiberglass canoe, in 14' and 16' models, which incorporates a rugged keel and flat bottom, aluminum gunwales, ash cross pieces, and hand-caned seats of ash. Deep, wide, and self-righting, the boats are built to provide outstanding stability for hunting, fishing, and family recreation. There is a five-year warranty on defects in materials and workmanship. Sponsons, motor mounts, carrying yokes, and hand-formed 5' to 5'6" ash paddles with pear-shaped grips and 7" blades are also available.

APPLE LINE COMPANY
146 Church Street
Amsterdam, New York 12010
(518) 843-4465

Catalog, 19 pages; Order form. Free.

Apple Line offers 15 kayak models (10' to 17'), 13 C-1 models (10' to 14'), 9 C-2s (15' to 16'5"), and 19 open canoe models, in economy, standard, duraflex, wilderness, or ultilite fiberglass layups. Open canoes come with foam flotation, while covered canoes and kayaks require additional flotation. All boats are available as kits (discount off price of completed boat), but minimal instructions are supplied, purchase of a builder's manual is recommended, and shipment of kit boats is discouraged. The catalog presents specifications, minimal side- and top-view profiles, and a very brief description of each boat. The various layups, options, and kit information are also briefly described, and a page of illustrated boat terms is given. A color brochure is in the works, and a catalog may eventually be available for the firm's line of sailing craft which includes a 10' dinghy, 14' scow, 18' catamaran, and blue water sailing yachts, many of which are still in the developmental stage. The firm offers lessons and safety clinics in addition to building boats and helping customers choose the right boat.

BLACK RIVER CANOES
P.O. Box 537
167 Railroad Street
LaGrange, Ohio 44050
(216) 355-4293

Booklet, 14 pages; Price list. Free.

This booklet presents a fairly technical general description of Black River canoes—their design, construction materials, and hardware—along with specifications and descriptions of 3 standard (15' to 18', 55# to 73#), 2 lightweight (10' to 13', 22# to 36#), and 5 performance models (14' to 18', 29# to 69#) in fiberglass. The price list shows that the 5 performance models are available also in Kevlar, and 2 of them are offered additionally in a heavier Kevlar construction. Also included are a glossary illustration of a canoe, and short articles discussing the nature of canoes, comparing canoe designs and construction materials (especially Kevlar), and giving advice on buying a recreational canoe. Black River offers a lifetime warranty on its workmanship.

THE BLUE HOLE CANOE COMPANY
Sunbright, Tennessee 37872
Catalog, 18 pages; Price list. Free. Booklet, 7 pages; Brochure, 5 pages; Poster. All free upon request.

Blue Hole's catalog presents a history of the company, gives a general description of its canoes, their manufacture, and the Royalex/ABS material of which they are made, and furnishes specifications, drawings, photos, and descriptions of 2 models of whitewater canoes (16′, 17′; 70#, 78#), and one model river cruising canoe (17′6″, 85#). The 16′ whitewater and 17′6″ cruising canoes are available with wood trim, special seatings, and brass hardware. Also included is a discussion of outfitting craft with various flotation devices and spray covers for rough river usage. Specially-designed knee brace, knee pad, and anchor pad kits, touring seats, T-shirts, belt buckles, and Extra-Sport life vests are also described. The booklet offers guidelines for evaluating and selecting a canoe; the brochure explains preventive maintenance and simple repair procedures for Blue Hole canoes; and the poster illustrates features of Blue Hole canoes and recommended accessories for the whitewater canoeist.

CALIFORNIA RIVERS
P.O. Box 468
21001 Geyserville Avenue
Geyserville, California 95441
(707) 857-3872
Catalog, 18 pages; Order form; Various promotional sheets for "Kiwi Kayak." Free.

Featuring "Dragonfly Designs" canoeing, kayaking, and rafting accessories, the California Rivers catalog provides generous descriptions and large photos of each item available: Kiwi, Perception, Tamiak, and Whitewater Boats kayaks; Blue Hole, Mad River and Old Town canoes; Barum and Sea Eagle inflatables; Carlisle, Iliad, Mohawk, Nona, and Sawyer paddles; spray skirts and seat cushions; air and float bags; floats; knee pads, anchor pads, back pads, helmets and liners; back packs, storage bags and pouches; pumps, repair supplies and kits; car-top carriers; jackets, knickers, socks, and shoes; bandanas, hats, T-shirts, belts, and a variety of river camping and running miscellany, books, and games. California Rivers also offers canoe and kayak trips, classes, and rentals (mostly in northern California), which are also described. Prices for kayaks and canoes must be specially requested since they are not listed in the catalog due to fluctuations throughout the year.

CANOE MAGAZINE
Highland Mill
Camden, Maine 04843
(207) 236-9621
Buyer's guide, 40 pages (published each November). $2.

Canoe magazine's Buyer's Guide details the products of nearly every major canoe, kayak, and rowing shell manufacturer in the business, listing the dimensions, materials, construction, weight, and current retail price for each boat in a manufacturer's line. Also included are brief reviews of new models, and short articles on how to choose canoes and kayaks. A mail-order form is provided for purchasing canoe-building plans, T-shirts, and belt buckles from *Canoe*. The Buyer's Guide contains numerous advertisements and order forms for obtaining canoe/kayak equipment and catalogs.

The Blue Hole Canoe Company   Whitewater canoe.

CANOE SPECIALISTS
Midwest Region:
Blackhawk Outfitters
937 N. Washington
Janesville, Wisconsin 53545
(608) 754-2179
Northeast Region:
Curtis Enterprises
4587 Clay Street
Hemlock, New York 14466
(716) 367-3165
Catalog, 28 pages; Price and order sheets (4). $1.

Articles appear throughout the catalog explaining canoe selection, materials, features, and nomenclature, and prefacing catalog sections on solo canoes, wilderness trippers and tripping gear, fast cruisers and accessories, family fun canoes, wood canoes, paddles, and canoe equipment. Good photos and descriptions represent most of the canoes and equipment offered, which are compared and reviewed within the pertinent sections. In addition to Beaver, Freedom, Galt, Grumman, Lotus, Mackenzie birchbark, Mad River, Old Town, Phoenix, Sawyer, Stowe, and E. M. White (Island Falls) canoes, Canoe Specialists makes available 2 solo canoes in fiberglass or wood strip (13′8″, 15′6″; 36#, 24#), a tripper canoe in fiberglass or Kevlar (17′, 68#), or wood strip (17′, 58#), and a family fun Royalex canoe (17′1″, 75#). Also available are Carlisle, Clement, Gillespie, Grey Owl, Iliad, Kruger, McCann, Mohawk, Sawyer, and Shaw and Tenney paddles; waterproof gear, flotation, and camera bags; rescue bags and life vests; portage yokes, car-top carriers (including Canoe Specialists' brand), and motor mounts; sail rigs, sliding seats, and knee and foot braces; repair kits for various hull materials; and much outdoor equipment —tents, packs and sacks, sleeping bags and mattress pads, camp stoves, lanterns, lights, and knives. A list of current canoeing books and periodicals in stock is furnished upon request; some voyageur prints and books on wooden canoes are available through the catalog.

CASCADE OUTFITTERS
P.O. Box 209
Springfield, Oregon 97477
(503) 747-2272

Catalog, 38 pages; Order form. Free.

Cascade Outfitters offers the quickest possible service and thoroughly tested river equipment: Avon, Campways, Maravia, Wind River inflatable rafts and packages; raft frames, materials, oars, pumps, inflators, and accessories; Eddyline and Perception kayaks, Cherokee and Sea Eagle inflatable kayaks, and Blue Hole, Grumman, and Lincoln canoes; kayak and canoe paddles; PFDs, wetsuits, spray skirts, float bags, and foot braces; car-top carriers; helmets, paddle jackets and sweaters among other river clothing, and waterproof gear bags; cooking and camping equipment; rafting, kayaking, and river-guide books; T-shirts and personalized scrimshaw. The river equipment catalog includes a lengthy discussion of the materials, designs, and constructions of inflatable rafts and the company's own raft frames; information regarding choosing a kayak, canoe, and paddles; and full descriptions of specific brands and kinds of river equipment as well as the individual items offered. The company builds custom equipment and welcomes customer advice in its on-going development of new products.

CLARK CRAFT BOAT COMPANY
16 Aqua Lane
Tonawanda, New York 14150

Catalog, 46 pages; Inserts; Order form. $1.

This catalog presents a general explanation of the kinds of catalogs, and boat, frame, paint, and hardware kits available. Photos and often lengthy descriptions cover the variety of products offered including canoe and kayak accessories such as paddles, sail rigs, seats, footbraces, spray skirts, life vests and carrying yokes; powerboat racing accessories, hardware kits, and boat seats; plywood, lumber, lumber kits, and fastenings; fiberglass cloth, epoxy and polyester resins, resin colors, foam, paint, thinner, brushes and rollers. Photographs of canoe and kayak construction and advice regarding the selection of canoe, kayak, and construction material are provided along with descriptions of the canoes and kayaks for which there are plans or kits: plans for 16 models (11′ to 17′6″ singles and doubles) fabric-covered kayaks, plans or kits for 6 plywood kayaks (10′ to 16′) some with fibershield sheathing option, a plan for a 16′ canvas-covered canoe, and kits and some plans for a 16′ foam-fiberglass canoe, 14′ and 16′ prelaminated sectional fiberglass canoes with square-stern option, and 4 plywood canoes including a square-sterner (13′6″ to 17′6″). Some of these boats may be purchased complete if the customer will pick up the finished product at the factory. The catalog also includes inserts on

"Armor-poxy" coatings and wood saturation, discussions of fiberglass materials and construction, and short descriptions of wood, aluminum, steel, fiberglass, and ferrocement constructions covered in books that Clark Craft sells.

Cascade Outfitters.

CLASS VI WHITEWATER
3994 South 300 West #8
Murray, Utah 84107
(801) 261-1875

Brochure, 7 pages. Free.

Class VI kayaks are constructed of Kevlar and various high performance synthetic materials vacuum-molded in a new high elongation vinylester matrix. This "HEC" laminate is over 35% lighter than plastic boats and more impact-resistant than S-glass/Kevlar counterparts; it is available in five layups. Only 3 kayak models are offered (12′8″ to 13′1″), as well as a durable paddle with aircraft aluminum shaft and blades with composite foam cores, graphite and unidirectional glass skins, and P-Tex protectors in slalom or asymmetrical shapes. Protective and paddling clothing, spray skirts and cockpit covers, float bags and rescue lines, Mitchell paddles, knee braces, and glue are also available. The brochure provides an explanation of HEC construction, and furnishes descriptions of the accessories and each kayak's design and handling characteristics; specifications and top/side-view photos are also given for each boat. Each kayak is so carefully fitted to the customer that "a Class VI fit is seldom interchangeable."

COLORADO KAYAK SUPPLY
P.O. Box 291
Buena Vista, Colorado 81211
(303) 395-2596/6798

Catalog, 64 pages; Order form. Free.

Embellished with a detailed index, this catalog is packed with good photos (some color, some quite spectacular) and good descriptions of the full range of high quality equipment offered for the whitewater enthusiast: 5 "Colorado Rivermachine" kayaks of various volumes in light, heavy, or expedition weight Kevlar/S-glass constructions (12′9″ to 13′2″), and Perception's Mirage, Quest, and Eclipse kayaks; Carlisle, Harmony, Iliad, Mitchell, Nimbus, and new Norse paddles; flotation/ storage bags, foam beams, and a variety of helmets, PFDs, wetsuits and accessories, paddling suits and garments, polypropylene underwear, comfortable but functional camping wear, Slumberjack sleeping bags, Therma-rest mattresses, SierraWest tents, Tekna knives, safety equipment and flashlights, camping cookware and miscellaneous boater's supplies and accessories including waterproof boxes and bags; Yakima carriers, Quick-N-Easy roof racks, and nylon rope; and numerous whitewater manuals and guidebooks. Also described and available are many boatbuilders' supplies — Kevlar, S-glass, E-glass, and nylon fabrics, tapes, resins, pigments, related compounds, and repair materials. Professionally run river trips are occasionally offered.

CREESPOON MANUFACTURING
P.O. Box 1357
Berkley, Michigan 48072
Pamphlet, 2 pages; Order form. Free.
Creespoon at present only offers twin yokes, constructed of aluminum and placed on the horns of a backpack frame, for easily portaging a canoe. The pamphlet describes and illustrates the yokes, available in ¾″ or 1″ sizes depending on pack frame, and explains how to mount and balance a canoe using the yokes.

THE DAGGER COMPANY
P.O. Box 132
Long Creek, South Carolina 29658
(803) 647-6958
Information sheet. Free.
Without photographs, Dagger's sheet provides detailed descriptions of its standard and custom construction canoe and kayak paddles. Strong, lightweight, excellent in feel, and "incomparably beautiful," the standards feature oval shafts of ash-spruce-ash laminate, and blades either of cedar-spruce-willow-basswood with hickory edges or white pine sandwiched in an epoxy-fiberglass matrix and tipped with inlaid aluminum. The canoe paddle comes in even lengths between 54″ and 62″; the kayak paddle up to 214 cm, and the blade includes 90 degree feathering. For custom paddles, the customer may specify shaft and blade sizes, layup (extra-strong, standard, or extra-light) and in the kayak paddle, feathering angle other than 90 degrees; the customer's name is permanently laminated on the blade at no extra charge. The custom shaft is an oval laminate with epoxy-dynel sleeve, and the blade consists of a multiple softwood laminate edged with steam-bent hickory sandwiched in an epoxy-fiberglass matrix and tipped with inlaid aluminum.

DENVER QUALITY VINYL
3885 Forest Street
Denver, Colorado 80207
(303) 388-4608
Pamphlet, 8 pages; Order form. Free.
This pamphlet describes and illustrates in detail Denver Quality Vinyl's line of vinyl flotation bags for canoes and kayaks, and water/airtight storage bags, including a double-wall inflatable bag for fragile articles like cameras and binoculars. All bags are fitted with patented watertight double-seal closures and non-rusting fasteners and reinforcements. Storage bags, which can also be used for flotation, additionally feature lap seams and heavy duty grommets for strength. Both standard and split flotation bags are available, Denver Quality Vinyl only sells directly to the customer to keep prices down; quantity discounts are available. The firm welcomes suggestions and comments on its products.

DUNN'S CUSTOM-BUILT KAYAKS
8991 Gowanda State Road
Eden, New York 14057
(716) 992-3941
Informational sheets (2). Free.
Dunn's literature shows photos of one custom kayak built in skin on wood frame, another in foam-fiberglass sandwich construction, and another which can be built in fiberglass and Kevlar. Prices, specifications, construction details, and a list of accessories and options are furnished only for the 17′ model available in fiberglass or Kevlar and weighing about 40#. Its bottom consists of a four-ply layup of 10 oz. fiberglass cloth, while the deck is composed of a three-ply layup. In addition to foam flotation, foot braces, Henderson hatches, spray skirts, and laminated wood paddles, options include hand-drawn decorations and a hand-lettered name.

EASY RIDER CANOE AND KAYAK COMPANY
P.O. Box 88108, Tukwila Branch
15666 West Valley Highway
Seattle, Washington 98188
(206) 228-3633
Four brochures, 4 pages each; Accessory catalog, 12 pages; Buyer's Guide, 8 pages; Various price and order sheets. Free.
Easy Rider offers a wealth of literature regarding 32 models of canoes, kayaks, and rowing shells. The Buyers Guide provides photos and generous descriptions of 4 open Royalex canoes (15′8″ to 18′6″), 8 open fiberglass canoes (13′ to 18′6″), 3 decked fiberglass canoes (16′6″ to 18′6″), 2 single (14′9″, 17′) and 3 double cruising kayaks (16′8″ to 18′6″), and 2 rowing shells (17′, 18′6″), giving advice about selection and discussing the use of several models including the shells. A companion selection guide sheet lists design specifications for 30 boats, comparing them in terms of solo and tandem paddling; use on small or large lakes, Puget Sound, the ocean, easy or wild rivers, expeditions; accommodation for extra gear, motor, sail, or rowing. Another sheet depicts and describes 4 models of fiberglass slalom competition kayaks (13′2″, 32#) and 3 fiberglass slalom competition canoes (13′2″ to 15′, 32# to 48#). Single promotional sheets with ample photos are available on a new cruising kayak (17′) with optional rowing shell gear, and a square-sterned sports canoe (15′).

One promotional brochure provides color photos of a variety of models and the Easy Rider plant. Another brochure compares the fiberglass, Royalex, Kevlar/ graphite, and custom Kevlar materials used in Easy Rider boats. Another brochure contrasts sizes, designs, and the use of some options, while yet another brochure relates a six-month round-trip Seattle-Ketchikan kayak expedition. The accessory catalog describes and pictures a multitude of equipment, some Easy Rider's own brand: paddles, seats, foot braces, tracking fins, rudders, pads, straps, spray skirts, dust covers, flotation, storage, and dry bags, protective clothing and life vests, motors, motor mounts, sailing rigs, rowing seats and oars, car racks, carrying yokes, boat carts, repair kits and supplies. The Royalex canoes can be purchased in kit or shell form, thus saving off regular prices. With the exception of the 9′8″ fiberglass surf kayak all Royalex and fiberglass boats can be custom built in Kevlar.

EDDYLINE KAYAK WORKS
8423 Mukilteo Speedway
Mukilteo, Washington 98275
(206) 743-9252

Informational sheets (5); Order and price sheets. Free.

A sheet covers each of 4 seagoing touring kayaks—a short lightweight version (16′, 38# to 40#), a double-seater (18′6″, 65#), a high-performance ocean tourer (19′, 40#), and a stable, roomy type (17′, 42#)—showing top and side views, listing specifications and optional equipment, and quoting descriptions from the designer. Kayak construction features a vacuum-bagged high-performance laminate, vinylester resin, aircraft glass, roving, and unidirectional reinforcements. Another sheet describes 2 parafoil models which can be used for canoe or kayak sailing. The price sheet additionally lists 5 whitewater kayaks including one for children, and high, medium, and low volume models in standard, super, or standard/super constructions, kayak kits for 7 models, and a variety of accessories (spray skirts, cockpit covers, flotation bags, pads, paddles, life vests, deck access ports, paddle brackets, bulkheads, hatches, car rack brackets, a compass, fishing rod holder, and sea sock). Customer height, weight, and length of legs are taken into consideration with each order. Touring kayak rentals are available on a daily and weekend basis.

FOLBOT CORPORATION
P.O. Box 70877
Stark Industrial Park
Charleston, South Carolina 29405

Catalog, 76 pages; Order form; Form letter with vinyl and hypalon fabric swatches. $2.

This "Fabulous FOLBOT Magazine" is packed with color photos of folbots in a multitude of contexts, testimonials from satisfied customers, and descriptions of the craft, their wood-frame constructions, designs, and their many uses. The catalog also provides a sample floor plan and list of camping cargo, a boat selection guide, advice on boating and navigating, suggestions and guides for trips, and personal experience stories regarding trips and boat construction. Eleven models of rigid "portable" finished folbots are offered, 10 of which are available also in prefab kit form, and 5 of which may come finished as folding boats; these boats are covered with vinyl or hypalon-coated fabrics. Lengths vary from 10′ to 17′6″ for singles, and from 13′6″ to 19′6″ for doubles/triples. These models

generally take after kayaks, but one, a two-seater, broadly square-sterned with a planing hull, is suitable for an outboard. Other models may be rigged for sail. A 12′6″ single or 16′ double kayak, a wider 16′ "cayat" with sailing and trimaran options, and 14′ and 15′ square-sterned sailboats are available in finished or kit form, three kinds of completion kits being offered (basic, finishing, plywood/ longitudinal); these boats feature fiberglassed or painted plywood exteriors. In addition to these boats, a fold-flat dinghy in three lengths (8′, 10′, 12′), books, and a variety of accessories and equipment (paddles, seat pads, floor cloth, spray cover, flotation and storage bags, protective vests and helmets, yoke, carriage, car-top carrier, lashes, travel marina, motor crossbar, outboard motor) are offered.

GREAT CANADIAN
45 Water Street
Worcester, Massachusetts 01604
(617) 755-5237

Brochure, 4 pages; Price list. Free.

The brochure presents brief information about the shallow V-hull design and materials in which Great Canadian canoes are available, showing photos of only a few boats and paddles. Specifications are listed for the full range of boats: 3 fiberglass canoes with keels (13′ to 16′), 3 fiberglass canoes without keels (16′ to 17′), 2 fiberglass canoes with keels and square sterns (15′6″ and 17′), one Royalex canoe without keel (16′), 3 aluminum canoes with keels (13′ to 17′), 6 cedar strip and PVC-coated canvas canoes (15′ to 18′) with keel options, 4 fiberglass kayaks (11′6″ to 16′), and several fiberglass lapstrake boats (2 hp 8′ tri-hull dory; 3 hp 11′6″ Andrea dory; 15 hp 13′ Lord Nelson, 20 hp 14′ and 25 hp 16′ Nantucket dories). All fiberglass is hand-laid-up. The numerous accessories available are briefly described on the price list: Indian-made maple, spruce, spruce-birch, and spruce-red cedar paddles, aluminum/ABS paddles, solid spruce or maple oars, a sail rig, rudder and tiller, side motor mounts, oarlocks, thwarts, carrying yokes, car-top carriers, spray skirts, life vests, canoe seats and back rests, waterproof bags, tie-downs, canoe wax, river guides and a few other items. Of special note are the Indian-made birch bark canoe models and moose calls. Any canoe parts broken under normal use or wear will be replaced free for the life of the canoe.

HARMONY PADDLES
Route 8, Box 50B
Easley, South Carolina 29640
(803) 855-3968

Pamphlet, 8 pages; Order form and price list. Free.

Harmony furnishes descriptions and photographs of its whitewater-tested line of canoe and kayak paddles in this pamphlet. Paddles are available in fiberglass, graphite, or fiberglass (shaft) and graphite (blade) combined. Kayak paddles can come with flat or spooned blades; spooned varieties have right-hand control, left-hand control, non-feathered, and take-apart options. Lengths range from 200 cm to 220 cm in two-centimeter intervals for kayak paddles, and for canoe paddles, from 52″ to 66″ in two-inch increments. Canoe costs vary according to materials. Perception, Inc., also sells the paddles.

HAUTHAWAY KAYAKS
640 Boston Post Road
Weston, Massachusetts 02193
(617) 894-1027

Brochure, 6 pages; Form letter; Price list. Free.

As Hauthaway claims, his "catalog" is hopelessly out of date: Hauthaway currently builds 6 kinds of whitewater kayaks (10′6″ to 13′, 24# to 31#), and 5 kinds of decked solo canoes (10′6″ to 12′, 19½# to 35#), but only 4 of these boats are described and pictured (top- and side-views included). Still, the catalog, together with the update, gives a good idea of Hauthaway's boats and the variety of double-bladed and T-grip paddles (fir shafts, fiberglass blades), spray and cockpit covers available. Foot braces, portaging straps, back rests, preserver cushions, and sprit sails for the canoes are also sold. These boats "are made of a hand laminate of all fiberglass cloth in semi-flexible polyester resin"; whitewater kayaks include a layer of polypropylene cloth for extra strength. Upon request, Hauthaway may furnish offprints of articles regarding his boats and kayaking which have appeared in *Down River* (July 1977), *Field and Stream* (March 1973), *The Mariner's Catalog, National Fisherman* (March 1971, June 1975, January 1979) and *Small Boat Journal* (April 1980).

ILIAD INC
199 Weymouth Street
Rockland, Massachusetts 02370
(617) 878-3404

Pamphlet, 4 pages; Price list. Free.

Though brief, this pamphlet goes into some detail describing the construction of Iliad canoe and kayak paddles, listing specifications and offering advice on choosing shaft length and blade size (photos are included, as are descriptions and photos of waterproof storage bags). Blades of fiberglass are moulded onto shafts of aluminum tubing bonded to exterior vinyl tubing; the paddles float. Both canoe and kayak paddles come with flat or spooned blade options. Take-apart kayak paddles are available. Iliad will manufacture paddles to individual specifications at a slight extra cost. The firm will also replace paddle blades and grips.

INDIAN BRAND CANOES
Rivers and Gilman Moulded Products, Inc.
P.O. Box 408
Hampden, Maine 04444
(207) 862-3600

Catalog, 16 pages. Free.

Plugging itself as Maine's oldest manufacturer of fiberglass canoes and the world's oldest builder of Royalex canoes, Rivers and Gilman gives its opinions regarding canoe materials, keels, paddles, and the size motors and sails that can be used with Indian Brand canoes. Specifications, color photos, and descriptions are presented for 6 kinds of hand-laid, woven fiberglass canoes (13′ to 18′, 61# to 90#)—one with a square stern—and one kind of Royalex canoe (17′, 82#). Each canoe is fitted with vinyl outside gunwales and replaceable vinyl bang plates. Rivers and Gilman offers a patented birch bark hull design in addition to solid colors. An outboard motor bracket, yoke shoulder pads, car-top carriers, and hardwood paddles are also available.

IRIS BOAT WORKS
Jim Hanna
Marshfield, Maine 04654
(207) 255-4216

Informational sheet. Free.

Jim Hanna builds to order a 20′, 150# "Grand Laker" transom-sterned canvas- or fiberglass-covered canoe of cedar planks and ribs with brass fasteners, a mahogany deck and transom, and ash rails, thwarts, stems, and keel. He usually sends inquirers a personal letter including current prices, construction time, and answers to specific questions along with his hand-made "handbill" which furnishes two color photos of the boat and briefly lists its specifications and construction materials.

ISLAND FALLS CANOE
North Branch Woodworking
RFD 3, Box 76
Dover-Foxcroft, Maine 04426
(207) 564-7612

Various informational sheets. Free.

Island Falls canoes are built on authentic E. M. White forms, planked with the finest white cedar, covered with no. 10 cotton duck canvas, and put together with brass and bronze marine fastenings. Sheets explain the "E. M. White Tradition," list specifications, and provide photos and descriptions of 5 canoes, a 14-footer (60#), two 16-footers (standard, 65#; featherweight, 52#), and two guide canoes (18′, 85#; 20′, 95#). A keel or half-ribs may be fitted to the bottom on request. Most canoes are built to special order; the Island Falls staff likes to work as closely as possible with the customer during production of a canoe. Canvas filler and Stelmak's *Building the Maine Guide Canoe* are also available for the do-it-yourselfers.

KLEPPER AMERICA FOLDING BOATS, KAYAKS, INFLATABLES
Hans Klepper Corporation
35 Union Square West
New York, New York 10003
(212) 243-3428

Brochure, 6 pages; Order form; Various promotional brochures and instruction sheets. Free.

Klepper's mail-order brochure includes no illustrations and only the barest descriptions of the items offered. Fifteen-foot single and 17′ double folding kayaks (50# and 70#) are available in "complete for paddling packages" which include a generous number of accessories in addition to basic parts. Sailing equipment is available for both kayaks, in package form for the double. Some, but not all, accessories are included with Klepper's hand-made fiberglass rigid kayaks, a single or double sport/touring type (14′, 16′; 40#, 68#), and 2 slalom-shaped whitewater varieties (13′3″, 40#). Klepper also sells a number of

Hauthaway Kayaks   Greenland kayak.

Hauthaway Kayaks   Rob Roy canoe.

double-bladed paddles, spray covers, rudder assemblies and other sailing and outboard accessories, protective clothing and flotation/storage bags, a car-top carrier and boat cart, repair and service kits, many instruction and travel books, and miscellaneous boating comforts and conveniences.

Additional color brochures provide photographs and round out descriptions of the folding kayaks. Color photographs and descriptive material regarding accessories and other products are available upon request. Also furnished on request are a list of reading materials for planning a folding kayak expedition, a "Cruising in the Klepper" reprint from *Small Boat Journal* (March 1980), a bumper sticker, and instruction sheets, "Hints for New Kayakers," "Sailing Pointers for Kayakers," "Next Time Pack Your Kayak," "List of Articles in Magazines," and many others covering parts, assembly, and repair of specific kayak models.

LEAVITT QUALITY CRAFT
RFD 1 Newburgh Box 1549
Hampden, Maine 04444
(207) 234-2341
Brochure, 4 pages; Price and specification sheet. Free.
Jim Leavitt aims to construct the finest cedar canoe with the best materials available: hand-selected native white cedar for planking, ribs, and one-piece outside and inside gunwales; a combination of hardwoods for the decks; ash or oak for the frames in hand-caned seats; brass and bronze hardware with brass or aluminum stembands; and a highest quality fiberglass coating. Three models are offered: a slightly round-bottomed 18′6″ family canoe

(80#), a stable flat-bottomed 16′ canoe (65#), and an 11′6″ canoe similar to a guide boat (45#). Hand-caned or folding seats, motor mounts, carrying yokes, special order paddles, custom full or partial canvas canoe covers, and additional canoe materials are also available. Since Leavitt's inventory is somewhat limited, he advises ordering well in advance.

A. C. MACKENZIE RIVER COMPANY
Department A, P.O. Box 9301
Richmond Heights, Missouri 63117
(314) 781-7221
Catalog, 10 pages; Order form. Free.
The "Sylvester-Pole"—a three-pound, twelve-foot canoe pole made of lightweight aircraft aluminum—is the focus of this booklet, which contains a series of short articles promoting poling, and comparing aluminum vs. wooden poles and poles vs. paddles. Among its specified virtues, poling apparently makes upstream trips easier, hence round-trips, thus eliminating car shuttles. Mackenzie River Co. sells the floatable poles, a canoe-poling book, and provides poling exploration trips and instructional clinics.

MAD RIVER CANOE
P.O. Box 610, Mad River Green
Waitsfield, Vermont 05673
(802) 496-3127
Catalog, 12 pages; Order form; Price lists. Free.
Best known for its versatile expedition canoes, and first to construct canoes of Kevlar, Mad River currently builds its special shallow V-bottom hulls in fiberglass, Royalex, and Kevlar. The catalog offers information on the construction and design of Mad River canoes; a guide for choosing canoe material; color photographs, specifications, and descriptions of 11 canoes (mostly expedition types, some specialty), 3 new specialized models (flat water, whitewater, the Kruger tripping canoe), and a new rowing rig; and a comparison chart of handling characteristics for 14 canoes. Canoe models vary from 13′ to 18′6″, and weigh from 42# to 78# for fiberglass, Royalex, and Kevlar. Descriptions and photographs are provided for some of the many accessories; available, notably, are spare parts and repair materials, and miniature canoes, in addition to paddles, car-top carriers and portage yokes, storage/flotation bags, chairs, sailing and rowing rigs, and motor mounts. Write for information on receiving monthly journals regarding Verlen Kruger and Steve Landick's "ultimate canoe challenge"—28,000 mile journey.

MARINER KAYAKS
1005 E. Spruce
Seattle, Washington 98122
(206) 622-7215; 322-1658
Two brochures, 8 pages and 4 pages; Price list; Various informational sheets. Free. Mariner User's Manual, 25 pages. $1.
The Mariner brochure and an additional informational sheet on the "Escape" give very detailed technical information regarding these "ultimate" sea cruising kayaks, furnishing photos and test results, and explaining

the speed, paddling ease, tracking, maneuverability, seaworthiness, safety, comfort and convenience of the boats in terms of their special designs. The illustrated "Mariner Self Rescue" excerpt from the User's Manual thoroughly discusses methods and "back ups" for righting the capsized kayak and getting out of the water and into the boat as quickly as possible; the techniques might be adaptable to other kayaks. Including an expanded version of the self-rescue exerpt, the Mariner User's Manual fully describes, with illustrations, Mariner features (integral rudders and T-grip handles) and options/accessories (rear and bow hatches and bulkheads for gear stowage; adjustable sliding seats; spray skirts, bow and stern painters, rear deck and seat back storage and grab lines, paddle pockets, pumps, U-bolts; chart holders, deck pockets, fishing rod holders). The Mariner and Escape (18'5", 16'6"; 40# to 50#, 35# to 45#) are built of woven and unidirectional fiberglass laminated with tough vinylester by vacuum-bag process. An additional outside seam on the Escape, extra reinforcements for strength and rigidity, and custom layups (super heavy duty, or ultralight with Kevlar and graphite) are possible. Option and accessory packages are available at a savings.

KEVIN MARTIN
RFD 1, Box 441
Epping, New Hampshire 03042
Informational sheets (5). Free.
Kevin Martin is just getting started building wooden Rushton canoes and Adirondack guide boats, trying to revive the skill and craftsmanship required to build traditional boats to suit the individual and his specific locale. The sheets briefly describe the evolution of these boat designs, show their plans, and furnish fairly elaborate information (listing some options) of Martin's construction methods and materials (information is sketchy on the kinds of woods used in the guide boats, however). Martin offers the canoes in 9' to 17' lengths, and the guide boats in 13' to 18' lengths, and he will also custom build canoes to the customer's plans or will find plans to suit. For smoothskin and lapstrake models of the guide boat, prices include hand-caned seats, a pair of oars, two sets of oarlocks, a paddle, and a carrying yoke. The price for a lapstrake solo version of the canoe includes hand-caned seats, two paddles, a painter's ring, and a carrying yoke.

MENTHA WOODEN BOAT COMPANY
Route 2, 23rd Street
Gobles, Michigan 49055
(616) 628-2568/679-4706
Brochure, 4 pages. Free.
Mentha aims for exceptional quality in building boats slowly, one at a time, using the finest cedar, oak, ash, and mahogany, and brass and copper fastenings. The brochure gives only sketchy descriptions of the firm's offerings: lapstrake canoes in 12' and 15' solo, double blade, and 17' tandem models; an 18' strip canoe and asymmetrical 14' solo and 16' models (complete or in kit form); a lapstrake or strip 9'6" Lawley tender (sail package available); a 12' rowboat in traditional or W.E.S.T. system strip construction; a duckboat with several design options;

Great Canadian.

and laminated paddles, foam bulkheads, car-top carriers, and yokes. The company also offers boat repair and restoration services.

MITCHELL PADDLES, INC.
Canaan, New Hampshire 03741
(603) 523-7004
Paddle pamphlet, 6 pages; Accessories pamphlet, 6 pages; Price list. Free.
Mitchell paddles—shafts, blades, and tips—come in a variety of wood laminates depending on purpose—slalom competition, expedition, rough water racing as well as milder exertions. The 4 kinds of kayak paddles pictured can be made in any length (Junior paddle up to 190 cm), in either right or left control; all have curved and spooned blades with metal or wood tips (wood only for the Junior). The 2 types of canoe paddles are approximately 64" long; the slalom variety can come with either wood or metal tip. After meticulous hand-finishing, each paddle is completed with three coats of polyurethane. Including prices for two models of pyranha slalom kayaks and the variety of paddles available through Mitchell, the accessories pamphlet describes and illustrates a Mitchell paddling jacket and wool hat, Harishok life and spray decks, and an Ace helmet.

MOHAWK CANOES
P.O. Box 668
963 N. Highway 427
Longwood, Florida 32750
(305) 834-3233
Three leaflets, 2 pages each; Brochure, 4 pages. Free.
Mohawk furnishes photographs, specifications, and brief descriptions of its 8 canoes on one leaflet: a recreational family canoe in fiberglass or Royalex (16' or 17'4", 62#, 65# or 75#), a fiberglass child's canoe (10'6", 30#), 2 short sports/recreational fiberglass canoes (14', 45# or 60#), a square-sterned fiberglass canoe which takes a motor up to 3 hp (16', 85#), a whitewater canoe of Royalex (16', 75#), and a fast fiberglass canoe for the performance-oriented paddler (18', 58#). Fiberglass canoes feature heat-treated gunwales, polyurethane foam flotation, hull reinforcements of hand-laid woven roving, glass-covered end-grain balsa wood ribs, and a five-year guarantee on seat pans. A second leaflet elaborates exclusively on the recreational family canoe, while the third goes into greater detail

regarding Royalex and the two models offered in it. The brochure offers quite a bit of advice on the selection of paddles as well as canoes (which are covered in terms of length, hull design, and material), and makes suggestions regarding transporting and entering a canoe in addition to paddling one. Paddles and motor mounts are also available. By the time this synopsis is published, Mohawk promises to have a new assortment of brochures ready.

MORLEY CEDAR CANOES
P.O. Box 147
Swan Lake, Montana 59911
(406) 886-2242
Pamphlet, 6 pages; Price sheet. Free.

Offering nice but small color photos of most of Morley's models, the pamphlet addresses questions commonly asked by customers before they order—queries about cost, quality, maintenance, custom canoes, sail rigs, paddles, and ordering. The price sheet lists the firm's range of standard designs, briefly describing the performance, standard equipment and options of each model and providing specifications in chart form. All models are built of the highest grade western red cedar with laminated white oak stems, seat frames and thwarts, fastened with silicon bronze and brass screws, lined with a layer of 6 oz. fiberglass cloth, and sheathed in two layers of 7½ oz. fiberglass cloth. Available are a Guide canoe (15' to 18'; 55# to 85#), a square-sterned camping and fishing canoe (16', 105#) that can take an outboard, a "Personal" fishing/hunting/exploring canoe (13', 50#), a solo touring canoe (14', 40#), and a touring kayak (16', 35#). A 17' Whitehall and an 18' rowing dory, as well as custom designs or types are also available upon request. A mast-step and thwart can be built into a canoe, and a complete lateen sail kit may be purchased which includes leeboards, a kick-up rudder, hollow spars of sitka spruce, and a 40 square-foot dacron sail. The firm also manufactures canoe and kayak paddles with shafts of Sitka spruce encased in laminated oak, and blades of western red cedar and Sitka spruce reinforced with clear fiberglass. A Northwest Coast Indian design may be hand-painted on the length of the canoe, or a Northeastern Fur Trade Fiddlehead design of spliced spruce applied to the bow and stern.

NATURAL DESIGNS
4849 West Marginal Way S.W.
Seattle, Washington 98106
(206) 935-3998; 525-0109
Booklet, 15 pages. Free.

Stressing handling techniques, Dan Ruuska waxes eloquent describing the performance of his kayaks in terms of their design, construction, and in comparison to other kinds of kayaks. Ruuska concentrates on utmost craftsmanship, structural integrity, and safety in creating responsive designs that feel secure and are easy to paddle skillfully. His "Outrage" series consists of 5 "playing whitewater" and 2 racing kayaks (11'2" to 13'2", 30# to 34½#); he offers a lone "Polaris" model for ocean touring (17', 40#). Presently vacuum-bagged, but possibly hand-laminated in the future as in the past, the boats are composed of woven roving of polyester and glass fabrics with some nylon, vinylester resin, and NO gelcoat; S-glass is optional. All boats feature adjustable seat locations and heights, padded semi-rigid seat straps, and precision fiberglass outside seams; Outrage boats have full-length high-strength foam walls for entrapment protection. Flotation bags are occasionally in stock. Ruuska will lend advice regarding accessories and the best buys. Photos are planned for subsequent editions of the booklet.

NIMBUS PADDLES LTD.
2330 Tyner Street, Unit 6
Port Coquitlam, B.C. V3C 2Z1
Canada
(604) 941-8138
Catalog, 24 pages; Order form. Free.

This catalog provides generous photographs and good descriptions of canoe and kayak paddles, and a large assortment of kayaks and accessories (flotation and storage bags, spray skirts and sea socks, protective clothing, foot rest, rescue bag throwlines, hatches, paddle tips, take-apart paddle ferrules, car-top carriers, and some kayaking and building books). Also available are boat builder's supplies, kayaking classes, and ocean kayak rentals. Nimbus sells British "New Wave" kayak paddles, an inexpensive take-apart wooden kayak paddle, and another inexpensive kayak paddle with an aluminum shaft and indestructible polypropylene blade, in addition to canoe and kayak paddles composed of a variety of wood laminates, tipped with metal or urethane, and coated with Kevlar for whitewater or reinforced with fiberglass for touring. Nimbus offers 4 whitewater, 2 racing, 2 touring, and 2 surfing kayaks, 3 decked canoes, and one river playboat (2.45 to 5.18 meters, 20# to 42#) in finished or kit form. A special boat building program is available where the customer can build a Nimbus kayak at the factory with staff help and expertise. Kayaks are vacuum-bagged, of vinylester construction, and the customer may choose among several combinations of fibers. Five kinds of Perception kayaks may also be obtained.

NOAH COMPANY
Route 3, Box 193B
Bryson City, North Carolina 28713
(704) 488-3862
Catalog, 8 pages; Order form and price list. Free. "How To Begin and Continue in Whitewater" brochure, 16 pages. $1.

This catalog packs descriptions of Noah fiberglass kayaks, racing canoes, and materials with safety tips, discussions of the firm's capabilities, and advice regarding kayak and canoe materials, constructions, design and selection. Available in kit or finished form are 6 kinds of cruising kayaks (12' to 13'2", 21# to 23#), one which will do as a racing boat (13'2", 19#), a child's boat (11'6", 17#), 3 racing kayaks (13'2", 17# to 18#), a decked double canoe (15', 28#), and 5 single canoes (12'2" to 13'2", 19# to 23#). Racing, cruising-expedition, and play-expedition constructions are possible. Seamed kits with additional options (grab loops, gloves, seats, knee braces, T-shirts, and construction materials) are available. The firm also sells fabrics, tapes, and resins for advanced FRP composites. A brochure of papers regarding chemically-activated polyester, presented at various meetings by Noah chief Vladimir Vanha, may be purchased for $1. The 16-page brochure, "How to Begin and Continue in Whitewater," expands upon topics presented in the free catalog.

NORTHWEST RIVER SUPPLIES

430 W. 3rd
P.O. Box 9186
Moscow, Idaho 83843
(208) 882-2383

Catalog, 32 pages; Order form; Sales insert. Free.

Testing most products before listing them, Northwest River Supplies "is dedicated to providing quality whitewater equipment and related products at reasonable prices." Including large color photos of many of the inflatables and whitewater accessories for canoeing, kayaking, or any kind of river boating, the catalog presents discussions and comparisons of the various brands (including Northwest River Supplies' own), and descriptions of approximately 800 individual goods offered. Available are Achilles, Avon, Campways, HBIE, and UPISCO rafts; Sevylor, Sea Eagle, Semperit, and Campways inflatables; raft frames, oars, paddles, pumps and blowers, hardware, oarlocks, stands, stoppers, adhesives, thinners, cleaners, boat and rescue bags, and other inflatable accessories. Also listed are waterproof and other gear bags; kayaking and canoeing paddles, flotation bags, spray skirts, protective clothing and accessories; Yakima and Quik-N-Easy car-top carriers; camping equipment and supplies; wetsuits and life jackets; canoeing, kayaking, and rafting books and river guides. "Don't hesitate to ask questions when selecting equipment from NRS." Seasonal flyers introduce new offerings and announce sales and closeouts.

NU-LIFE MARINE CORPORATION

P.O. Box 4013
Clearwater, Florida 33518
(813) 535-3576; 531-2844

Informational sheet; Form letter. Free.

Leavitt Quality Craft.

Mentha Wooden Boat Company.

Nu-Life manufactures 30, 40 and 55 square-foot sail rigs for canoes. The sheet provides illustrations of each size rig and lists specifications and features. Leeboards, rudder, tiller and thwarts are solid mahogany coated with marine varnish; the sail is dacron; mast and boom aluminum; and fasteners and fittings, all supplied, are stainless steel, solid brass, or aluminum. Easily assembled and taken apart, the hand-made rig includes a boom vang which works in combination with the main sheet. All rigs meet or exceed Class A, B, or C standards of the A.C.A.

OAT CANOE COMPANY

Jeff Hanna
RFD 1, Box 4100
Mt. Vernon, Maine 04352
(207) 293-2694

Literature unavailable. Products, services, and terms described in letter upon request.

Preferring to stay small and work on a custom basis, Jeff Hanna restores and recanvases canoes, and builds an 18' wood and canvas canoe (85#) for whitewater and wilderness travel. The boat can carry two people and plenty of gear, stay dry in Class 3 whitewater, be easily maneuvered, and cruise well on flatwater. Ribs and planking are fashioned from northern white cedar; stems, rails, thwarts, yoke and caned seats from ash; deck plates from a colorful hardwood. Canvas is no. 10 cotton duck and fastenings and hardware are brass, bronze, or copper. All wood is saturated and brought to a satin finish with a penetrating oil that sets up and will not absorb dirt or darken. Canvas stretched around the hull is filled with latex base filler and finished with marine enamel after the edges have received extra preservative. Upon request, Hanna may loan color photographs of his canoes along with a four-page write-up of his canoe and his reasons for its design. This information will appear in Bob Speltz's fourth volume of *The Real Runabouts.* Hanna rents storage space and "sells just about anything needed for building and repair."

OLD TOWN CANOE COMPANY
Old Town, Maine 04468
(207) 827-5513

Catalog, 12 pages; Order form and price list; Informational sheets (2); Comparison chart. Free.

Old Town manufacturers a large variety of canoes and some kayaks, makes available a multitude of canoe parts and repair supplies, and sells a good lot of canoe and kayak paddles, covers and spray skirts, flotation bags, PFDs and protective clothing, car-top carriers, carrying yokes, motor mounts, rowing fixtures, and other accessories and miscellanies. Unfortunately only 16 (less than half) of the boats are pictured and given specifications in the glossy color catalog—additional, more technical information on specific models, constructions and accessories should be requested. Old Town makes 7 whitewater, all-around canoes (12′ to 18′, 30# to 85#), a dinghy and a Rangeley in Oltonar (Royalex); 2 high-performance canoes—one in 16′ and 17′ lengths and a 15′6″ solo model—with wood or vinyl rails in fiberglass or Kevlar; a family/lake fishing canoe in 14′ and 16′ lengths and a 17′7″ rowing shell, in fiberglass; an unassembled all-purpose "Oltonar Royalite" canoe in two lengths; a dinghy, Rangeley, and 4 kinds of canoe (15′ to 20′, 72# to 104#); 2 touring and 2 slalom kayaks (13′3″ to 14′3″; 31# to 34#) with varying layup options; and a wooden cedar stripper canoe kit. The two sheets furnish good illustrations and go into some depth giving instructions for rigging an Old Town canoe for sailing and fitting it with mast, seat/steps, and aluminum or wooden rudder.

OUTDOOR SPORTS
P.O. Box 1213
Tuscaloosa, Alabama 35401

Catalog, 20 pages; Order form. Free.

Growing out of author George C. Shelton's efforts to locate quality canoe-building plans, Outdoor Sports makes available fine building plans for 9 models of touring and family kayaks (including two folding and one all-wood), 8 models of touring and whitewater kayaks, 6 models of racing kayaks, a square-sterned or double-ended canoe, a pirogue, 2 models of outboard fishing skiffs, and 3 varieties of small sailing craft (including a dinghy) with several rigging and outfitting options. Shelton peppers the catalog liberally with down-home advice about boats and boatbuilding, describing the construction and structural details and specifications of each model, usually including a photo and occasionally information regarding evolution of the boat's design. (Shelton selected the plans for these models based on ease of construction and quality of the final product, and he stresses that the plans are designed for the first-time builder who is familiar with basic hand tools.) Books regarding canoeing, kayaking, boatbuilding, and outdoor survival are also available.

PACIFIC WATER SPORTS
16205 Pacific Highway South
Seattle, Washington 98188
(206) 246-9385

Folder, 2 pages; Informational sheets (4); Form letter; Price list. Free.

Pacific Water Sports boasts the largest selection of canoes in the Pacific Northwest, stocking 35 models (including aluminum, cedar strip, fiberglass, Kevlar, and Royalex types) and 9 manufacturers (Beaver, Blue Hole, Graham Corporation, Mad River, Michi-Craft, Mohawk, Sawyer, Wenonah, and Pacific Water Sports). Also available are a fiberglass Graham rowing shell, 2 Northwest Whitewater and 4 Perception kayaks, a child's kayak, and 4 Pacific Water Sports kayaks in complete or kit form. Canoes are available from kits to completed models. Of the four sheets enclosed in the folder which describes Pacific Water Sports' operation, one offers advice on selecting a canoe on the basis of materials, hull shape and internal layout; two others discuss cruising and double kayaks with respect to the performance and design of Pacific Water Sports' own models; and the final sheet, now out of date, describes a seakayaking photo contest. Pacific Water Sports offers river and pool training and classroom instruction; sells fiberglass supplies, molds, kits, and a complete line of the best equipment; gives complete directions for kits; and upon request, sends frank advice and more specific information on boats or accessories stocked.

PELICAN BOATWORKS
P.O. Box 343
Sullivan's Island, South Carolina 29482
(803) 883-3941/3135

Booklet, 8 pages. Free.

This booklet provides good large illustrations, and explains the design, performance, comfort and safety of the one 14′ kayak, the "Halfmoon Explorer," that Pelican builds. The boat can store large amounts of gear and can be used in whitewater, swamps, flatwater, surf, windy lakes, and heavy seas. A "convex-trapezoidal cross-section" is the basis of its design. The kayak is vacuum-bagged using E-glass and CAP cloths, a vinylester resin blend, and high-strength epoxy resin for seams; custom layups are available using a variety of carbon fibers, S-glass, Kevlar, and epoxy resin.

PERCEPTION
P.O. Box 686
Liberty, South Carolina 29657
(803) 859-7518; 855-3981

Catalog, 16 pages; Informational sheets (2); Pamphlets; Order form. Free.

Provided with gorgeous color photos of Perception boats in action (some of which—the photos—are available as custom-mounted prints) the catalog briefly explains Perception's boating and building philosophy, describes and lists the specifications for 3 kayaks and 4 canoes, and pictures and describes the accessories available. The price list replicates the catalog's photos of the accessories: Harmony paddles; Perception helmets, life vests, and paddling jackets; spray skirts, canoe seats, flotation bags, foam pillars, knee braces and pads; storage and safety throw bags; car-top carriers; and a variety of comforts, conveniences, and safety items. The 7 kayaks and the one racing canoe are "roto-molded out of durable, cross-linked polyethylene" (12′1″ to 13′2″, 35# to 42#); the 4 canoe models are offered in Royalex (13′6″ to 16′, 48# to 75#).

One of the sheets describes, lists specifications, and provides photographs of a new Vagabond-Cruiser kayak-canoe of linear plastic construction (13'2", 42#). The other sheet pictures and describes features of a new sculptured seat platform (for a canoe) which doubles as a water-tight storage compartment. One pamphlet lists where in the United States and Canada one can learn to kayak; another describes five river awareness groups and provides membership forms for them.

PHOENIX PRODUCTS, INC.
U.S. Route 421
Tyner, Kentucky 40486
(606) 364-5141
Brochure, 10 pages; Informational sheets (3); Price sheet. Free.
Phoenix's brochure discusses the criteria for selecting a kayak (design, strength, weight, features, cosmetics, safety), provides specifications and design and performance information for 7 of its fiberglass and nylon-reinforced plastic kayaks, and presents good descriptions and photos of Phoenix fiberglass and Phoenix/Azzali wooden paddles, Phoenix flotation (canoe and kayak) and waterproof storage bags, spray skirts, cockpit covers, paddle jackets and pants, helmets and life vests. Pictured with striking photos are two slalom racing designs (13'1½", 27#), a downriver racing design (14'9", 29#), a racing/recreational whitewater kayak with various seat and color options (13'2", 28#), a large-volume recreational whitewater model (13'9", 33#), a long-distance tripping kayak (14'9", 33#), and a two-person family/touring/exploring kayak (16'7", 60#). Two additional sheets depict and describe 2 more kayaks, one an extremely durable model (13'1½", 37#) made of "a proprietary tri-polymer composite," and the other, the firm's most popular whitewater playboat (13'1½", 39#). A third sheet promotes Phoenix's kayak kits, available for any of its models, consisting of instructions, finished deck, hull, cockpit/seat assembly, and the materials to put them together. Foot braces, foam walls and seats, various replacement parts and repair items, and Robco waterproof storage bags are also available.

RAINBOW BOATWORKS
P.O. Box 159
Newport, Vermont 05855
(802) 766-2601
Brochure, 4 pages; Price list. Free.
Rainbow's full line includes a high-volume hunting-fishing-family outing canoe in 3 lengths (13', 15', 17'), a 16' Royalex heavy or quiet water canoe, a 16' solo flatwater canoe and a whitewater version, a 16' class IV whitewater canoe, a 13' medium-volume recreational kayak, and an 8' pram designed to be a tender. Except for the Royalex canoe, all hulls are hand-laid-up in a polyester-resin system; most of the canoes are also available in Kevlar. Except for the kayak, the boats are finished with Vermont white ash rails, cane seats, wooden end decks, and carrying yoke are standard. The pram, complete with foam flotation, motor board, brass oarlocks and horns, and a brass tow ring on the bow, can take a maximum of 2 hp. The brochure lists the basic specifications and provides

brief but full descriptions of the design and performance of each model; some photos are furnished.

SAWYER CANOE
P.O. Box 435
234 South State
Oscoda, Michigan 48750
(517) 739-9181
Brochure in poster format; Price sheet. Free. Pamphlets on individual canoes free upon request.
Sawyer builds solo, competition, fast cruising, wilderness/whitewater, and family/fishing/gunning canoes. Twelve models are offered in fiberglass or Kevlar (16'6" to 24'; 40# to 82# for fiberglass; 29# to 58# light, 29# to 68# standard Kevlar), a multipurpose canoe in Royalex (17', 72#), and economical "Oscoda line" canoes (2 family recreation, 2 fishing, hunting, trapping) in fiberglass only (13' to 18', 68# to 83#). The brochure details the firm's history, philosophy, and canoe building techniques, and provides solid descriptions, including specifications and photos, of its canoes. The price sheet charts all canoe models, furnishing specifications as well as prices, and lists the accessories available through Sawyer: Sawyer, Kruger Perma, Carlisle, and Featherbrand canoe paddles and Kruger and Sports Equipment kayak paddles; Quik-N-Easy and Yakima car-top carriers and parts; spray skirt, motor mount, portage yoke, foot braces, self bailer, seats, end caps, preservers, and apparel; and a full range of repair and replacement parts and materials. The back side of the price sheet presents glossary illustrations of a solo "Loon (Kaynoe)" and a cross-section of the Royalex canoe. Free for the asking are a pamphlet written by Molley Stark on women's solo canoeing, and individual pamphlets by Marketing Director Harry Roberts discussing in a chatty manner canoe aerobics and the design and performance of specific models (i.e., Canadian, Charger, Cruiser, DY Special, Loon, etc.).

SEA EAGLE
Division Harrison-Hoge Industries, Inc.
104 Arlington Avenue
St. James, New York 11780
(516) 724-8900
Two brochures, 8 pages each; Three sales brochures, 4 pages each; Form letter; Price sheet. Free.
One brochure covers the Explorer Series, and another the Heavyweight Series of Sea Eagle "special formula PVC" inflatables. Amply illustrated with color photographs and embellished with excerpts of letters from satisfied customers, they list specifications for all models and describe the construction, materials, and designs of the boats. In the Heavyweight Series, Sea Eagle offers 2 pack boats (6'8", 8'3"; 15#, 19#), 3 canoes (9'8" to 12'5", 21# to 34#), and 4 motor boats (8'8" to 11', 24# to 40#), one of which comes with floorboards (12', 81#). Three canoes (9'6" to 12'5", 28# to 40#), a broader yacht tender with floorboards (9', 43#), and 2 motor sports boats (11'5", 12'6"; 92#, 130#) are available in the Explorer Series. A briefer summer sale color brochure covers Sea Eagle's "fun floats," and another Sea Eagle's standards (orange and blue): 3 pack boats (5'8" to 7'4", 8# to 14#), 3 sport canoes

Morely Cedar Canoes   All canoes are made of the highest grade western red cedar from this company.

(9′8″ to 12′6″, 21# to 30#), and 2 motor boats with floorboards (8′8″, 12′; 20#, 81#). A third two-tone brochure and the form letter promote the new sailing inflatables, offering three sail rig options at introductory sale prices. Life jackets, floorboards, pumps, seats, paddles, oars, storage bags, motor mounts, and repair materials, are also available; some of these items are pictured and described throughout the brochures. A request to be put on the mailing list will ensure receipt of sales literature.

SEDA PRODUCTS
P.O. Box 997
Chula Vista, California 92012
(714) 425-3222

Watercraft catalog, 8 pages; Accessory catalog, 12 pages; Form letter; Price list; Christmas catalog, 24 pages. Free.

The canoe and kayak catalog provides photos, discusses the design and performance, and lists the standard equipment of only the most popular Seda boats—3 general purpose, 4 racing, and one surfing kayak (9′6″ to 16′, 19# to 35#), and 4 touring and 3 decked whitewater canoes (13′2″ to 18′6″, 21# to 75#). Two pages in the accessory catalog give specifications for these boats and list the kinds of constructions available; the price list provides similar information for all models. Except for 3 canoes offered in Royalex, Seda's complete line is available in two to four constructions: standard (fiberglass with isophthalic resin), competition or lightweight (Kevlar, fiberglass, and vinylester resin), heavy duty (Kevlar, S-glass, fiberglass, and vinylester), and Sedaflex (Kevlar, graphite, and epoxy resin). The accessory catalog furnishes photos and good descriptions of Seda's canoe and kayak paddles with graphite shaft and Kevlar blade(s) or with epoxy pole-vaulting shaft and epoxy or polyester blades, wetsuits, a variety of paddling apparel and safety equipment, spray skirts, cockpit covers, flotation and waterproof gear bags, car-top carriers, and repair materials and kits. A dealer list should be requested.

SHAW & TENNEY, INC.
P.O. Box 213
20 Water Street
Orono, Maine 04473
(207) 866-4867

Brochure in poster format; Order form and price list. Free.

This "poster" is a work of art itself, presenting descriptions of the firm's offerings along with an illustrated oar-length formula and photographs of oars and paddles under construction and displayed in their customary settings. Paddles and oars, the mainstay of the company, are traditional handcrafted designs, mostly fashioned of a single piece of wood—ash, maple, or spruce. Available are 4 types of solid wood canoe paddles: one laminated variety, and a solid wooden double-bladed canoe paddle; 2 flat-bladed and 2 spoon-bladed oars in solid wood or laminates, and a solid two-piece option. The accompanying price list conveniently charts the paddles and oars according to length, material, and price. The firm will also make "everything from sculling oars to steering paddles... replications, duplications or prototypes at surprisingly reasonable prices" to customer specifications. In addition Shaw and Tenney manufactures and sells canoe seats, thwarts, and yokes; paddle and canoe trophies and wall plaques; fraternity paddles; a 1930s boathook of ash with manganese bronze hook; oar leathers, copper tips for oar blades, and manganese bronze rowing hardware made specially for the company by Wilcox-Crittenden. A small selection of related books is also offered on the price list.

SILVER CREEK CANOE AND KAYAK PADDLES
Silvermine Road Box 5
Bryson City, North Carolina 28713
(704) 488-9542

Pamphlet, 4 pages. Free.

Silver Creek "offers a complete line of canoe and kayak paddles incorporating well thought out laminate systems and careful blade and shaft shaping." Custom hardwood edgings, shaft shaping, and extra-durable epoxy finishes are available. Featured in the pamphlet is a "Cruiser" model for kayaking (198 to 214 cm) or canoeing (54″ to 64″), with oval-grip shafts of ash and yellow pine, blades of basswood/willow/birch, and tips of 28 gauge stainless steel or hickory with fiberglass roving inlay. The kayak paddle, curved with dihedral power surface, foil on nonpower surface, measures 8″ by 17″; the canoe paddle, with dihedral shaped reversible surfaces, measures 8″ by 19″. Finished with polyurethane, the blades are veneered with epoxy-impregnated 2 oz. fiberglass cloth; complete epoxy-impregnation and dynell sleeves are available. Also shown but not described are flatwater, whitewater, competition, and custom canoe paddles, and a standard T-grip with custom layup. These paddles and a heavy duty model are available on special order; further details may be requested.

TRAILCRAFT
P.O. Box 392
Concordia, Kansas 66901
(913) 243-2435

Brochure, 4 pages. Order form. Free.

Manufacturing wood and canvas canoe kits from 1962-1977, Trailcraft now offers step-by-step pictured instructions and patterns for making the "famous 16 Trailblazer" in wood and canvas. These plans and plans for a 16′ two-seater wood and canvas kayak, cost $5 each. Canoe paddle-making instructions at $2 are free with canoe or kayak plans. In addition the rather inexplicit brochure lists and minimally pictures sale-priced cane canoe seats, poly-webbed seats, bow and stern handles, and bang strips available. Trailcraft also sells a large number of books under the following headings: Wilderness Ventures, Trips and Trails, Food and Cooking, Hunting, Fishing, Nature, Archery, Guns, Treasure Hunting, Backpacking, and Outdoor Skills.

VENTURES
P.O. Box 3306
Simi Valley, California 93063
(805) 527-5649
Informational sheet; Order form and price sheet. Free.
Front face oars, the mechanism, and a fixed seat rowing rig for canoes are the only products offered by Ventures. The sheet promotes the idea, provides photographs, and briefly explains the materials, operation and installation of the contraptions. Paddles and handles are manufactured from varnished select laminated hardwood and bonded to an aluminum oar reversing mechanism which oscillates on nylon bushings using no gears. Oar supports, furnished with all units, are bolted to boat gunwales or, for canoes, to fixed seat rowing rigs. The oars fold out of the way when not in use.

VOYAGEUR'S, LTD.
P.O. Box 409
Gardner, Kansas 66030
(913) 764-7755
Catalog, 8 pages; Supplement, 8 pages; Price list. Free.
Since 1967, Voyageur's has specialized in manufacturing waterproof bags for canoeing and kayaking which feature patented air/watertight sliding closures and woven plastic over bags for durability. Available are polyethylene "camp paks" and polypropylene over bags of various sizes for different uses, vinyl flotation-gear and split flotation or storage bags (for decked canoes as well as kayaks and open canoes), nylon ultra-light flotation bags and "float totes," vinyl camera bags and waterproof pouches. Also offered are helmets and life vests, a paddling jacket and gloves, knee pads, a portage harness, tie-down bumper hooks, canoe and bag carriers, boat tape and repair kits, throw, floating, climbing, and tent pole ropes, sportsfishing rods, reels, and line, eyeglass guards, and some camping basics. An illustration and good description are furnished for each item.

WABASH VALLEY CANOES
616 Lafayette Avenue
Crawfordsville, Indiana 47933
(317) 364-1141
Price list; Form letter. Free.
Wabash Valley is offering several new canoes and kayaks, including a Pro cruiser (18′6″) and an ICF marathon cruiser (21′4″) in Kevlar, 3 K-1 Olympic flatwater kayaks, 2 performance-oriented whitewater racers, and several recreational canoes from short solos to full-size trippers. The price sheet furnishes specifications and construction

details for 2 C-1 cruisers (16′, 17′), 4 C-2 cruisers (18′6″ to 24′) besides the Pro and ICF, 2 Olympic C-1s, 2 Olympic K-1s, and 3 recreational canoes (16′ to 18′6″). The boats are available in fiberglass and/or Kevlar with composite, foam, or honeycomb cores, and aluminum, wood, or deluxe hardwood trims. Information on custom options must be requested.

WE-NO-NAH CANOES
P.O. Box 247
Winona, Minnesota 55987
(507) 454-5430
Catalog, 16 pages; Informational sheet; Canoe and accessory price list. Free.

This catalog discusses the evolution of the firm and Jensen canoe and paddle designs and offers advice on choosing a hull material and on using sliding seats and flotation; it also explains the materials and constructions of the canoes, and provides descriptions of most models including good top- and side-views, some specifications and some photographs. The canoe retail price sheet lists all models, indicates the features of each according to the materials and construction techniques in which it may be built, and gives additional explanations regarding some of the features and options. Hand-built in fiberglass or Kevlar, in a variety of stiffenings (PVC core, center-rib, cross rib, extra fiberglass) for whitewater and flatwater, racing and recreation, are 4 models of marathon canoes (18′6″ to 21′4″, 35# to 63#), 2 solo canoes (16′, 17′; 27# to 49#), 3 whitewater models (18′ to 18′6″, 47# to 73#), 3 touring canoes (14′ to 17′, 30# to 69#), and 2 all-purpose types (17′ and 18′; 36# to 65#). A separate sheet describes We-no-nah's 2 models of performance- designed Royalex canoe with optional all-wood trim (16′, 65# to 70#). Given scant attention in the catalog, the accessories available are Cadorette, New York Elbo, and Minnesota Elbo paddles; canoe seats and foot braces; sliding seats, kits and parts; yokes and We-no-nah yokes and car-top carriers; flotation, dry, camera, paddle, tote, and ski bags; ethafoam; and a host of repair parts and materials. A dealer list is available for each region in the United States.

WEST SIDE BOAT SHOP
P.O. Box 157
Station B
Buffalo, New York 14207
(716) 877-3305
Catalog, 9 pages; Informational sheet; Price sheet. Free.
This small boat manufacturing shop builds fiberglass and Kevlar kayaks, fully outfitted and ready to paddle, to customer's specifications (including laminating the customer's name into the boat). The catalog and inserts provide a photograph and list some specifications and features for each model: one British-designed Olympic class flatwater kayak in fiberglass only (17′2″, 26#), 2 marathon racing kayaks (14′9″, 14# to 22#), 2 slalom-type river-running playboats (13′2″, 24# to 32#), one low-volume slalom racing design from Austria (13′2″, 18# to 24#), one seagoing expedition kayak designed by Derek Hutchison (15′5″, 35# to 40#), 2 wildwater downriver boats (14′9″, 21# to 26#) one of which is designed by

Gerhard Peinhaupt of Austria, and one Super Tourist touring kayak designed by Roland Pagnoulle (14'9", 32# to 38#). Listed options and accessories (Mitchell, Norse, and Carlisle paddles; Voyageur and Perception flotation bags; Extrasport paddle and life jackets; Perception spray skirts, paddle jackets, helmets, safety throwline, storage bags; Quik-N-Easy and Yakima car-top carriers) are priced upon request. West Side also carries Coleman canoes and skanoes and all models of We-no-nah canoes. "Don't hesitate to discuss your needs and specifications."

"WET DREAMS"... CANOEING, KAYAKING, RIVER RAFTING & ROWING!
P.O. Box 2229
Van Nuys, California 91404
(213) 997-7577

Catalog, 28 pages; Order form. Free.
A business based on providing personalized service and keeping prices low, "Wet Dreams"... offers "a comprehensive line of boats, equipment and supplies of the highest quality." Short on illustrations and photographs, the catalog, of over 300 items, generally furnishes reasonable descriptions, but sometimes only lists items: Nona and Perception kayaks and canoes, Shane Wave Skis and paddles, Avon and Camp-Ways inflatables and accessories, Don Hill McKenzie River dories in three stages of completion, and Martin trainer plans; Canham rafting frames; Harmony, Mohawk, and Nona canoe and kayak paddles; Camp-Ways river rafting paddles and Carlisle river rafting oars and assemblies; waterproof bags, boxes, and cases; Voyageur's flotation bags; Wilderness wetsuits and accessories; name-brand PFDs, helmets, Res-Q-Ropes, spray skirts, knee pads, and paddling apparel; Yakima and Quik-N-Easy car-top carriers, kits, and parts; maintenance and repair items; Richmoor freeze-dried food; books, gifts and novelties. The catalog also lists recommended newsletters and magazines, and favored organizations which serve to protect, preserve, and promote river sports. Kayak, canoe, and accessory rentals are available for southern California patrons.

WHITE BROTHERS
Division of Kayko Industries Ltd.
P.O. Box 845
Niagara Falls, New York 14302
(416) 262-4644

Brochure, 4 pages; Order form and price list. Free.
This company offers only one whitewater kayak (13', 40#), a leakproof, unsinkable, one-piece seamless construction of high-impact polyethylene, with a frame-free interior. The brochure furnishes several product photos but not enough description of the kayak. It offers a nylon spray skirt, adjustable aluminum foot braces, and adjustable kayak racks. A kayak paddle (7') and a canoe paddle (4½' or 5'), both with Royalex blades and aluminum shafts, are also offered and minimally described on the order form.

WHITE CANOE COMPANY, INC.
P.O. Box 423
82 N. Brunswick Street
Old Town, Maine 04463
(207) 827-7950

Catalog, 8 pages; Price list. Free.
The designs of this oldest canoe company in America date back to 1889 when E. M. White patterned his original canoe after a birch bark canoe of the local Indians. All present-day White canoes except for a 17' Royalex wilderness model are built of hand-laid-up fiberglass using the highest quality fabrics, reinforcing materials, and flexible resins. Pictured in color and briefly described are the Royalex canoe, a wooden-ribbed canoe with brass end caps (14' and 16'), an economy lightweight recreational canoe (16'), 3 models with fiberglass-reinforced ribs and optional balsa floors (14', 16', 17') with ABS end caps, vinyl gunwales, and cane seats, and 3 balsa-sandwich canoes (14' to 20') with spruce and mahogany gunwales, brass end caps, and cane seats; specifications are listed for each length canoe. Also shown are a folding slat chair of ash, ash Beavertail-design paddles, a motor mount, a foam block carrier, a T-shirt and hat, and a fiberglass outrigger with foam flotation, ash crosspieces, and a 45 square-foot sail.

WILLIS ENTERPRISES, INC.
Melvin Willis
Curtis Road, RFD 3, Box 114A
Freeport, Maine 04032
(207) 865-3830

Two brochures, 4 pages each; Various leaflets and informational sheets; Price sheet. Free. Two brochures, 4 pages each. $1.
One color brochure depicts the 17' Micmac epoxy-saturated wood-strip/fiberglass canoe, details its construction and characteristics, offers advice regarding the use of canoes, and explains the building contract. Additional sheets furnish some of the description presented in the brochure, explain kit options, contents, and payment schedules, and give a précis of kit instructions ($5) which are meant to supplement Hazen's *The Stripper's Guide to Canoe-Building* and Gilpatrick's *Building a Strip Canoe.* The other color brochure describes the features and characteristics of the 18" "Seaward Lucket" half-model, available complete or in kit form, built after the 18' tabloid cruiser "Picaroon," for which background information is also given; an insert includes elaborate ordering information involving numerous color, mount, and other options; the plainer brochures and additional sheets replicate some of this information. A companion sheet to all brochures lists the brochures, kit instruction books, half-models, and canoe kits available. Literature is mailed primarily to inquirers and only intermittently to people on the mailing list, in the latter case, presumably in the form of special offers on off-season orders. A small catalog is in the works to replace the current handful of sheets and brochures.

See also, under:

Small Open Boats
Country Ways
Devlin
Duck Trap
Freedom
Mystic
North Shore
Old Wharf
Payson
RKL
Rice Creek
Tender Craft
Wilce

Specialty Craft
Sheehan

Yachts
Glen-L

Tools
Woodcraft

Seats, Bedding...Lighting
C Cushions (knee pads)

Nautical and Outdoor Clothing
Bauer
McKenzie
Recreational Equipment

General Catalogs
Airborne
Austad's
Bart's
Cal
Chartroom
Defender
E & B

Fore and Aft Marine
Goldberg's
M & E
M.M.O.S.
Manhattan
Marine Center
National Marine
Overton's
Port Supply
Sears
Stone Harbor
Turner's
Warehouse

Books
Hearst
Woodenboat

Rowing Shells, Whitehalls, Other Pulling Boats, and Accessories

B & S CORPORATION
Harrison C. Sylvester
Bessey Ridge Road
Albion, Maine 04910
(207) 437-9245
Frederick R. Brown
18 Forbes Street
Westboro, Massachusetts 01581
(617) 366-7834

Two leaflets, 2 pages each. Free.
B & S manufactures hand-laid-up fiberglass Whitehalls in 10', 12', and 16' lengths, with styrofoam flotation, bronze hardware, and varnished mahogany seats and gunwales. The 10-footer at approximately 100 pounds can be car-topped; it offers two rowing positions and can be fitted with a sprit sail. The 12-footer (155#), molded from an original wooden Whitehall, features two rowing positions, and is available with gaff or sprit sail rigs. The 16-footer (200#) offers three rowing positions and can be fitted with sprit or gaff main and jib rigs. Sails are of dacron, spars of spruce. The two sheets provide photos of each model with and without sail rigs, and list features, specifications and construction information briefly. Trailers, oars, leathers and buttons, gunnel guards, and covers are available but neither described nor priced.

CONCORD YACHT COMPANY
P.O. Box 424
Sudbury, Massachusetts 01776
(617) 443-3691

Various informational sheets; Order form and price list. Free.
These sheets briefly describe, picture, and tout the virtues and uses of a 21' "Clipper" class pulling boat and "Dolphin" sea skiffs in 17' and 19'5" lengths for singles or doubles, respectively, which Concord manufactures in hand-laid-up fiberglass with foam flotation. Good for recreational rowing and one-design pulling boat racing, the Clipper, with 3 rowing stations, may be rowed as a single or double. The standard model comes with varnished ash seats and trim, while a second model has narrow fiberglass decks and seats instead; this second model may be fitted for racing with outriggers, 2 pair Piantedosi 9'9" sculls, and 2 sliding instead of 3 fixed seats. The standard model is also available in kit form and its price includes the standard rowing equipment package: 2 pair 8" Shaw and Tenney spoon blade oars, sewn leathers, walnut spoon blade tips, and 2 pair polished bronze offset pattern oarlocks. The Dolphin, designed to be used with 9'9" racing sculls, is fully decked and has a self-bailing cockpit, making it one of the safest rowing boats available. Good for camping, cruising, and training for competitive racing, the boat is easily car-topped and offers plenty of storage space. Available in kit form.

FREYA BOAT WORKS
909 Third Street
Anacortes, Washington 98221
(206) 293-6143

Pamphlet, 5 pages; Inserts (2); Informational sheets (4). Free.
Freya Boat Works is a custom boat building and repair business whose capabilities include planking and structural work, spars, rigging, refinishing and restoring, interiors, and surveying. One sheet briefly describes the kind of work that David Jackson, the shop's founder and builder, has done using indigenous and exotic woods with copper and brass fastenings—a variety of traditional rowing and sailing craft including a St. Lawrence River skiff, a Herreshoff sloop, a Barnegat Bay sneakbox, and a

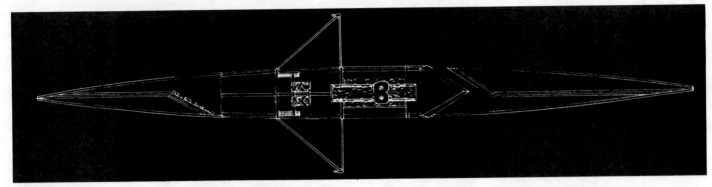

Little River Marine Company Combining speed, safety, and economy, the Dolphin sea skiff is light and one of the safest rowing boats available.

Norwegian fiord boat. Construction drawings, lines, and offsets for a Jackson-modified Piscataqua River wherry are available; two of the remaining sheets provide small scale copies of the drawings and the third, a copy of an article published in *Shavings* (Summer 1981), describes the modifications Jackson made in the traditional wherry build. The pamphlet and inserts, while perhaps nicer in format than the sheets, only briefly list the firm's services, present illustrations/photos and descriptions of three recent projects, and advertise the future availability of a 46' pilot schooner for charter.

LIGHTHALL MARINE
Homer H. Lighthall, Jr.
105 Bronson Street
Santa Cruz, California 95062
(408) 425-8155

Informational sheets (2); Form letter; Price list. Free.

As the form letter briefly explains, Lighthall builds a variety of custom, hand-laid-up fiberglass, self-bailing pulling boats with watertight and ample storage compartments, and transoms that accommodate small outboards. A second sheet shows photographs and lists specifications for 2 boats, "the versatile ocean adventure GIG" (13'5", 110#) for family fun and serious rowing, and "the complete fitness machine," the Lighthall 18 (17'9", 185#). The price sheet offers another photo of the Lighthall 18 and lists its specifications and hull packages available. The bare hull for a Lighthall can hold one or two rowers, and the hull for a 22'9" Lighthall can hold up to three rowing stations. Outriggers, mahogany rowing stations with adjustable footrests, and Schoenbrod sliding seats cost extra. A variety of Gull and Piantedosi oars and accessories are also available.

LITTLE RIVER MARINE COMPANY
P.O. Box 12722
Gainesville, Florida 32604
(904) 378-5025

Informational sheets (2); Order form and price list. Free. Brochure and handbooks available upon request.

Offering photos and striking side- and top-views, these sheets efficiently describe three "River Shell" models. All 24' long and 22" wide, the single shell (50#) has a 7½' cockpit with space for light gear and an extra passenger, and the double (65#) and longboat (55#) have 11' and 11½' cockpits, respectively, and can be operated by one or two rowers, with a special conversion option; the longboat can carry approximately 400 pounds of passenger and gear for serious long distance camping trips. Featuring positive flotation and an inverted keel fore and aft, the shells are custom built to order and are handcrafted of hand-laid fiberglass with stainless steel and aluminum hardware and rigging, and hardwood interiors, ribs, and splashrails. Rigging, oars, and foot assemblies are fully adjustable. Available but undescribed are sculls of spruce or aluminum, rigging assemblies, canvas covers, passenger seats, car racks, and T-shirts.

MARINE SERVICES
John Aydelotte
265 W. Cornet Bay Road
Oak Harbor, Washington 98277
(206) 675-7900/8896

Informational sheets (2). Free.

Marine Services builds a 13½' Whitehall of fiberglass and fine woods with brass and bronze hardware and the customer's choice of wood trim and hull color. One sheet briefly explains the history and design of the Whitehall, provides a nice side-view illustration, and indicates that the boat can be powered with suncharged batteries, a jib with or without spritsail, and by one or two persons with oars. The bare hull can be purchased separately; options include centerboard trunk, flotation, and seat rails. An additional sheet advertises the firm's landing craft for hire which is also available outfitted as a floating shop.

MARTIN MARINE COMPANY
P.O. Box 251
Goodwin Road
Kittery Point, Maine 03905
(207) 439-1507

Brochure, 4 pages; Informational sheets (2); Order form and price list. Free.

Martin's brochure furnishes color photos and brief descriptions of the firm's patented sliding seat rowing assembly, 2 Alden ocean shells, an ocean shell-racing scull Trainer, a rowing-sailing "Appledore Pod," and a fuel efficient cruiser designed to carry or tow other Martin boats. Specifications are presented for all boats, additional literature must be requested for the cruiser. Single and double shells (16', 18'; 40#, 68#), the Trainer (20'6", 40#), and the pods (16', 19'; 110#, 150#) are constructed of fiberglass with foam flotation; the 16' pod is available in epoxy-saturated wood. The pods, which incorporate the sliding seat for more conventional rowing or sailing, can be equipped with portable sail rigs, upping the price of both the 16-footer and 19-footer. An additional sheet expounds the virtues of the 19' pod, fully listing its features and offering photos and a side-view illustration. Another sheet introduces a sliding-seat, plywood Kittery skiff (15'8", 40#) available only as an easy-to-assemble kit, whose contents are fully listed. Complete plans and instructions for building the Trainer in fiberglass C-flex or in wood are offered for $30 which is refunded upon receipt of a photo of the customer's completed boat. The order form lists the "Oarmaster" rowing assembly, Douglas oars, a full range of parts, and miscellaneous items such as bailer kits, car racks, coamings, nylon covers, rub rails, T-shirts, and two booklets, "How to Row," and "Recreation and Amusement." The main brochure indicates where to write for information regarding membership in the Alden Ocean Shell Association.

ROWING CRAFTERS
Gordon Nash
520 Waldo Point
Sausalito, California 94965
(415) 332-3577
Catalog, 16 pages. Free.
Selling used as well as Martin, Laser, and Small Craft rowing boats, Rowing Crafters also hand-builds fiberglass duplicates, with hand-done wood trim, of original boats: a 13' Chamberlain dory, a 16' Swampscott dory, a 14' New York Whitehall, a 22' Viking Whitehall, a 14' Catalina skiff, and a 22' California wherry. Built off molds made from the hulls of existing boats, these duplicates weigh the same as their originals. The catalog offers photos, specifications, and discussions of each model sold, giving more elaborate treatment to and better photos of the firm's own products. Also included are a promotional bit on rowing, diagrams illustrating sliding seat measurements and showing the basic rowing stroke with a sliding seat, a map of the shop's location, a brief background of the shop's practicing oarsman (Gordon Nash), a brief schedule of rowing regattas around the United States (mostly in California), and a list of used boats available and their prices. A monthly leaflet, "Recreational Rower," and updated used boat lists are available. The shop also sells Douglas F. Collar Imported, and Piantedosi oars; Lister Brothers and Anderson spoons; sleeves, buttons, hand-grips, sliding seat systems and parts, and custom-designed sail rigs, none of which is described or priced in the catalog. Boat hull and kit prices are quoted on request.

Martin Marine Company   Appledore 16, fiberglass version, with sail.

SMALL CRAFT, INC.
387 N. Main Street
P.O. Box 1021
Norwich, Connecticut 06360
(203) 886-5549
Brochure, 4 pages; Informational sheets (2). Free.
Presenting photos and brief descriptions, the brochure covers the 13'2" and 17'2" Mystic Seaport Boston Whitehalls that Small Craft reproduces in fiberglass with ash rails, mahogany seats, and foam-filled tank flotation. These boats are available in a bare-hull form, ready to trim, or complete for rowing or sailing. The additional sheets advertise with photos and limited descriptions Small Craft's 18'6" "Warning!" single scull, presumably of fiberglass, and the 18'6" multi-use recreational single open rowing boat, "Encounter," built of fiberglass with spruce-capped rails, mahogany breasthooks, and stainless steel rigging. A "tub top" carrier pictured is also available.

THAYER & COMPANY
2106 Atlee Road
Mechanicsville, Virginia 23111
(804) 746-0674
Newsletter-catalog, The Tholepin (*monthly but comes out irregularly*); *Informational sheet. $2 per year.*
Jim Thayer fills *The Tholepin* with personal experience stories of boat trips taken and shows attended, interspersing his commentary with boating advice, boating book reviews, recipes, and news of his business, his boats'

performances, and future boat trips and meets. The last sheet of this tome lists and explains the 4 Whitehalls Thayer makes in fiberglass with Honduras mahogany trim and bronze fastenings. The sailing Whitehalls, the "Lil' Pickle" and the "Fourteen Footer," are available decked or undecked, plain or fancy, in various stages of completion. Two open rowing Whitehalls, the "Livery" and the "Express" can also be procured in various stages of completion and fanciness. Further information on kits, which offer savings of 60% of the finished boat price, may be requested. The informational sheet insert provides some illustrations of the boats and expands upon their descriptions.

UNITED STATES ROWING ASSOCIATION
#4 Boathouse Row
Philadelphia, Pennsylvania 19130
(215) 769-2068
Guide to Equipment, 23 pages. Free to member organizations and
the rowing community.

This handy guide furnishes a list of 88 businesses which manufacture or supply all manner of rowing equipment and accessories from recreational and competitive shells, sweep and sculling oars, rowing machines, conversions and parts, to stop watches and megaphones, books and journals, rowing apparel and shoes, medals, emblems, trophies, jewelry, posters and calendars. A companion "Product List" charts the kinds of equipment the companies supply. Also included is a short list of manufacturer's discounts offered to member organizations.

Small Craft, Inc.   Buoyant enough for gear and passengers, the elegant, well-balanced Essex Class Dinghy, is sleek enough to run smoothly through water when rowing or being towed.

See also, under:

Canoes	**Small Open Boats**	Rice Creek
Canoe Magazine	Apprenticeshop	Wilce
Easy Rider	Cannell	**Sports and Commercial Boats**
Morley	Country Ways	North End
Old Town	Duck Trap	
Pacific Water Sports	Freedom	
"Wet Dreams"	Mystic	

Small Open Boats—Sail, Row, Power

THE APPRENTICESHOP
Maine Maritime Museum
375 Front Street
Bath, Maine 04530
Pamphlet, 6 pages. Free. Brochure, 6 pages; Update sheet. $1.
Current Apprenticeshop publications are briefly described and illustrated in the pamphlet: boat plans, in one to seven sheet sets that include lines, offsets, and construction details; half-model templates; posters of traditional boats; a boat list; and books on half-modelling, Norse boatbuilding, and the evolution of the Apprenticeshop. Plans are presently available for a Delaware ducker, a North Shore dory, a Washington County peapod, a small

Whitehall, a small clinker-built peapod, the Durgin livery boat, and the Mary Baker Eddy boat; half-model templates for a Tancook Whaler and a Key West smackee. The brochure offers historical and descriptive data, large, rich photographs, and good side-view illustrations of some of the small traditional craft built at the shop: a 16' surfboat, a 15'3" Washington County peapod, a 22' Muscongus Bay sloop, a 25' Crotch Island pinky, and a 19' Oselver. An inserted sheet lists the 23 kinds of boats built at the shop, including their lengths (11'3" to 36'8"), and if pertinent, their constructions, shapes, and sail rigs; not all models are currently for sale.

AQUA-TERRA ENTERPRISES, INC.
Captain George Henry Jennings
RFD 1, Box 459, Northport
Belfast, Maine 04915
(207) 338-3705

Leaflet, 2 pages; Illustration; Reprint from National Fisherman (March 1978). Free.

Captain George Henry Jennings offers a 22' fiberglass, trailerable "Inheritance Class Cutter" (a cutter-rigged sloop with 307 square-foot sail area) as a basic hull with detailed construction plans for the home-builder or as a finished boat trimmed with white ash and mahogany. The leaflet furnishes specifications, base prices, a general description, and large photos of the cutter. The side-view illustration and the reprint provide additional, very helpful details. Captain Jennings advises prospective customers to make arrangements to visit Northport and "test drive" the boat.

THE BACK 'N FORTH COMPANY
43 East 22nd Street
New York, New York 10010
(212) 673-1027

Informational sheets (2). Free.

The Back 'N Forth Company builds a plywood dinghy in three lengths (6'10", 8', and 9'10") with an optional sprit sail rig. Very simply and straightforwardly, the literature provides side- and top-view illustrations, specifications, construction and design details, and explanations of plan/pattern, kit, and complete model packages available. Fall and winter schedules may be requested for designer Redjeb Jordania's seminars on wooden boatbuilding technique, at South Street Seaport Museum in New York City, and on his weekend workshops at New York City's YWCA, where participants build their own dinghies.

BEACHCOMBER BOAT BUILDING
P.O. Box 206
4800 S.E. Anchor Avenue
Port Salerno, Florida 33492
(305) 283-0200; 546-5692

Pamphlet, 4 pages; Various informational sheets; Reprints (3); Form letter; Order form. Free.

Available from Beachcomber are an 18'4" adaptation of a New England dory, a 14'11" car-toppable bateau, and an 8' or 8'11" dinghy, all built of hand-laminated fiberglass with foam flotation, hardwood trim, and bronze, brass, or stainless steel hardware. Wood grain is molded into the dory's hull and bulkheads and a lapstrake design into the dinghy's hull. The dory can be procured in various stages of construction with sprit or sloop sail rigs, and an inboard motor well; containing three stowage areas, it may be converted into a comfortable overnighter. Both bateau and dinghy may be outfitted with outboards, and come in rowing, conversion, and sailing models. Various covers, cushions, seats, and oars are available from the firm, and prices are quoted on request. The sheets and pamphlet offer photos or illustrations of each boat and discuss each model's features. Accompanying reprints expand upon the characteristics of the boats, while the respective price sheets indicate the boat packages and options available.

The Apprenticeshop   Workshop view of a recently completed 14' Washington County Peapod. *Photo:* Halsted.

BETSIE BAY BOATWORKS
Number 10 Tenth Street
Frankfort, Michigan 49635
(616) 352-9361

Various informational sheets. Free.

A custom boat shop catering to the classic boat enthusiast, Betsie Bay Boatworks offers custom built wooden boats up to 20 feet, boat restoration and repair, boat building supplies for the wooden boatbuilder, and marine supplies. According to the first sheet, boats are constructed of the highest quality marine grade materials available: white cedar, tamarack or five-ply mahogany marine plywood, white ash or white oak for frames, silicon bronze and copper fastenings, and a choice of finishes. Boats for sailing feature weighted centerboards and sprit sail rigs with vertically-cut, tan-bark colored Dacron sails, one set of reef points, steam-bent wooden mast rings, and solid spruce spars. Specifications, photos, and information regarding the design, construction, and performance of 2 row/sailboats are provided on two of the sheets—a double-ended, V-bottomed lapstrake Lake Michigan surf boat in 16', 18', and 20' lengths, and a flat-bottomed Manitou skiff of combined traditional and contemporary construction in 7', 9', 13', 15', 17', and 20' lengths. Also described are the contents and construction of a 13' Manitou skiff kit. Another sheet, complete with illustration and brief description, offers a Watervale punt kit ideal for children. The final sheet lists boat and kit prices and provides brief information regarding the boat lumber, fastenings, and marine supplies available; the Skookum Fastenings catalog, current lumber prices, further information regarding marine supplies, and quotes for other boat plans and proposals must be specifically requested.

WILLIAM B. CANNELL BOATBUILDING COMPANY INC.
American Boat House
Atlantic Avenue
P.O. Box 911
Camden, Maine 04843
(207) 236-4188/8500

Informational sheets (8). Free.

Providing backgrounds of three of the firm's members, the front sheet explains that Cannell Boatbuilding is "dedicated to the building, restoration, and brokerage of traditional and classic wooden boats, and to the renewal of the standards of quality in workmanship and aesthetics which produced such boats." "We do patternmaking and build quite a few spars," says Bill Cannell in the personal cover letter, adding, "Soon we will be East Coast representatives for Davey and Co. of London. They manufacture a line of traditional marine hardware including many items no longer available in the U.S." Each of the remaining seven sheets is devoted to one of the classic boats the shop produces—a 17' centerboard knockabout, the Murray Peterson 7'9" yacht tender, the 14'9" Whitehall, a 7'9½" Herreshoff pram, a 17' flat-bottomed double-ender, and an 18' double-ended pulling boat. Each sheet offers good photos and a brief, often historical description of the boat, and lists specifications including the kinds of woods, fastenings, and finishes used. The staff will gladly offer assistance and expertise in discussing problems and ideas regarding new, custom boats or the old classics.

CAPE COD SHIPBUILDING COMPANY
P.O. Box 152
Wareham, Massachusetts 02571
(617) 295-3550

Catalog, 8 pages; Price sheet. Free.

Founded at the turn of the century and operated by the present management since 1939, Cape Cod Shipbuilding Company discontinued wood boat construction around 1949 and currently offers a variety of open and decked sailboats for racing or family daysailing from 9 to 30 feet, in fiberglass, with aluminum spars. Company policy is to build quality boats, to maintain service on parts for boats previously built, and to employ the country's foremost naval architects to design new models. The company purchased exclusive rights in 1947 to manufacture several Herreshoff one-designs, including the "Bull's Eye" (15'8½"), the "Goldeneye" (18'3"), and the "H-12" (15'8½"), which are described in the firm's "Small Boat Catalogue." In addition to 2 dinghies (9'1½" and 11'6"), designs by Sidney Herreshoff, Philip Rhodes, and Sparkman and Stephens are featured: a 15' Mercury sloop, a 16' "Gemini" planing hull with twin boards, a "Rhodes 18", a 30' "Shields," and the 20' "Gauntlet." Except for 3 boats illustrated and briefly treated on the back page, entries in the catalog furnish for each model a photo, a side-view illustration, a good description, and lists of standard and sailing equipment and specifications. The price sheet indicates the cost of standard equipment for each boat.

CHARLES W. CARTER
P.O. Box 226
Sylvan Avenue
Miller Place, New York 11764
(516) 473-0309

Various informational sheets; Photograph of boat; Reprint. Free.
Set of detailed color photographs. $6 (includes postage and handling).

Claiming that he loves sailboats and likes to build beautiful strong wooden ones, Carter uses W.E.S.T. system materials (epoxy-saturated red cedar veneer) exclusively in putting together his 8' Norwegian sailing prams, designed by Frank Davis for the Gougeon Brothers. Carter provides inquirers with a photo of the boat; a reprint from *Woodenboat* furnishing a description, specifications, a side-view illustration, and lines and offsets for the boat; and a sheet elaborating the boat's construction and materials and explaining prices and ordering instructions. At additional cost, options available are a gold sail, bronze oarlocks and towing eyes, a centerboard cap for towing, and a polyurethane finish.

COUNTRY WAYS, INC.
15235 Minnetonka Boulevard
Minnetonka, Minnesota 55343
(612) 474-1142

Catalog, 30 pages; Various inserts; Order form. Free.

Offering kits for a variety of items including snowshoes, snowshoe furniture, skiing equipment, outdoor wear and gear, knives, bird decoys, and musical instruments, Country Ways also supplies boat kits designed by Jack Holt and Ken Littledyke. Containing all hardware, pre-cut and pre-shaped mahogany plywood panels, easy-to-understand step-by-step instructions, and for sailing boats, mast, boom, rigging, and sails, kits are available for an 8' pram with sail kit option, 8' and 11' sailing dinghies, a 13' catamaran, a 13' "Streaker", 11½' and 13' Brooks Lake

Beachcomber Boat Building   Available from this company are its hand-laminated fiberglass adaptation of a New England dory and a car-toppable bateau.

Boats, a 15′ New England skiff, 16′ and 17′ canoes, 16′ to 19′ kayaks, and in kit, finished, or completely finished form, an 8′ rowing dinghy and a 16′ rowing shell. Kits may also be obtained for rowing sculls, canoe and kayak paddles, spray skirts and flotation bags, canoe seat lacings, a canoe yoke, car rack, sailboat wheels, launching trolley, and a scale model of the 17′ canoe. Nice color photos, specifications, and brief descriptions are provided for each kit in the nine pages of the catalog devoted to the boat. Additional brochures offer more photos, drawings, specifications, and full descriptions of features and assembly procedures for the rowing shell and the rowing dinghy. Also available are books about canoes, sailboats, boat building, canoe-tripping, and sailing.

SAMUEL S. DEVLIN
Boatbuilding and Design
2431 Gravelly Beach Loop NW
Olympia, Washington 98502
(206) 866-0164
Catalog, 48 pages; Informational sheets (2). $5.

Devlin's catalog presents, in one of the nicest portfolio formats to be found, fifteen designs suitable for amateur construction using the W.E.S.T. system and sewn-seam construction. According to Devlin, boats built according to these designs and methods are strong and seaworthy, they are intended to be attractive, affordable, and well-suited for their uses, and their rigs are simple to use. Study plans ($5), plans, and in some cases kits, bare hulls, and complete boats are available for an 8′ rowing/sailing dinghy, 12′ mid-sized rowing/sailing boat, 12′ version of an old duck hunting skiff, 15′ decked cruising canoe, 13′ and 15′ sneakboxes, 15′ utility skiff, 16′ barge, 19′ sailing dory, a number of open and cruising sailboats from 15′ to 26′, 16′ cruising and harbor tugs, and 25′, 26′, and 30′ motorsailers. Each boat receives a page of description (specifications and mostly design and performance information) followed by one or two pages of pleasant illustrations showing profile/sail plan and interior layout. One page illustrates the sewn-seam construction method. Additional sheets list prices for some of the firm's more popular boats, smaller rowing/sailing boats, and larger sailing and motor sailing boats.

JACK DILLON
66 Richland Road
Greenwich, Connecticut 06830
(203) 531-7559
Form letter. Free.

An initial inquiry nets a form letter from Dillon which details the design and performance features of his 12′ shallow-draft, easily portable, "Gunkholer" dinghy design with sliding gunter rig. The cost of additional information is also given: $30 including postage for a complete set of plans (3 sheets detailed plans, 3 pages instructions, 3-page bill of materials), or $3 for study plans (photo of boat and sheet of illustrations showing top, side, and rear views). Plans but no study plans are also available for an easily towed, rowed, or "hoisted-aboard" 6′ dinghy that anyone can build with a minimum of tools in less than 24 hours; descriptive literature and a photo will be sent upon

request, possibly at a price. The "Dink A Day" and apparently the Gunkholer can be built of marine plywood. Dillon is currently working on a sailing version of the dink, and in the future promises a catalog of various boat gadgets including navigational devices and windvanes that anyone can make.

DOUGHDISH INC.
William G. Harding
Marion, Massachusetts 02738
(617) 784-0334
Brochure, 4 pages; Form letter; Price list. Free.

A small version of a substantial yacht, the Doughdish is a reproduction of the original (1914) wooden Herreshoff 12½-footer (15′10″ LOA) in foam sandwich fiberglass construction with teak trim and foam flotation. Ideal for learning to sail, H-class racing, or casual daysailing, the boat can be sailed, rowed, or motor-powered by one to six people of all ages. The cover letter proclaims the boat's outstanding attributes, while the brochure provides numerous large photos, side- and top-view illustrations, and detailed lists of specifications, features, optional equipment and standard colors, and, further, covers the history, construction, materials, and design of the boat. The Doughdish with main sail and jib are standard equipment but the recommended varnish finish, cradle, spinnaker and gear add another thousand to the price. A variety of covers, trailers, outboard mounts, nameboards and a few other accessories are available too.

DUCK TRAP WOODWORKING
Walter J. Simmons
P.O. Box 88
RFD 2, Cannan Road
Lincolnville Beach, Maine 04849
(207) 789-5363
Catalog, 36 pages; Order form. Free.

The largest portion of Duck Trap's business is building custom boats to any stage of completion, generally in cedar over oak lapstrake construction, with mahogany trim and bronze and copper fastenings. More information is available on request for most of the boat types built, illustrations of which are included in the building plan section of the catalog. Plans for each type, drawn by Duck Trap head Walter J. Simmons, permit the construction of one boat only, and include besides the usual lines and offsets, construction details, sail plan, and complete listings of the fastenings and hardware required, giving exact sizes and types for each portion of the particular boat. Briefly describing the original models and Duck Trap's versions of each type, the catalog lists a 19′3″ Newfoundland trap skiff, a 16′ Matinicus double-ender, a 13′ to 16′ Lincolnville salmon wherry (J.R. Griffen model), a 10′7″ Rhodes wherry, a 10½′ yacht tender, a 12½′ Great Island rowboat, 13′ to 17′ lapstrake canoes, a 9′ dory skiff, a 9½′ lobsterman's skiff, a 7′10″ lumberyard punt, and a 9′7″ Maine skiff. Specialized plans are available for oars, a Matinicus double-ender deck plan, and a combined sail plan for lapstrake canoes.

The catalog also provides extensive reviews of most of the other products the firm sells: Maine cedar planking,

Cap's oil finish, Rule heavy duty marine sealant, mast hoops, copper roves, burrs and rivets, bronze holdfast nails, silicon bronze carriage bolts and flat head wood screws, a range of bronze hardware, a bronze anchor, various tools (rove iron, holding iron, folding rule, lap clamps, clamp handle, bevel, bronze rivetting hammer, 24" bandsaw, Wetzler clamps), and books by Simmons on lapstrake boatbuilding and on building specific boats. Also listed and described are the workshops held throughout the year on building a specific type of boat.

DUCKLING BOATS

Peter Niemann
P.O. Box 12386
Seattle, Washington 98111
(206) 329-8303

Informational sheets (4); Price list. Free.

This firm offers 7', 8', 9', and 10' Norwegian-type lapstrake prams in rowing or sailing versions, a 10' Lawton lapstrake tender, and a 15'6" skiff, all in epoxy/marine-plywood construction. Sailing versions of boats include the mast, sprit, boom, dagger board, rudder, sprit sail, and sheet. Boats can be built to individual specifications including custom finishes, rigs, and accoutrements such as lockers, bailers, and fenders. Each sheet provides a photo of one of the boats (excluding the 8' and 10' prams), its specifications, and a bit of design, construction, and performance information.

FLORIDA BAY BOAT COMPANY

270 Northwest 73rd Street
Miami, Florida 33150
(305) 754-9022

Brochure, 4 pages; Reprint; Price list. Free.

In scrapbook format, the brochure provides lots of photos of a family's weekend outing with Florida Bay's "Marsh Hen," a shallow-draft, cat-rigged, 17' double-ender, built

Florida Bay Boat Company   The Mud Hen, while big enough to haul a gang of kids to the beach, is small enough for one person to launch and will comfortably hold three couples.

of hand-laid fiberglass with teak trim and foam flotation. The boat converts to a roomy weekender with its built-in icebox, stowage space, and optional canvas dodger. The whole rig, boat and trailer, weighs less than 1000 pounds. The brochure also lists specifications, standard and optional equipment, and furnishes side- and top-view illustrations and a discussion of the boat's features. The boat includes sail rig and outboard bracket. A trailer, bimini top, cushions, ground tackle, oars and other accessories are listed as options. Kit boats and unlisted options are available on request. A reprint from *Cruising World* (November 1981) printed on the backside of the price sheet elaborates further on the Marsh Hen's characteristics and explains her design as an evolution from small, working watercraft of the Chesapeake.

Jack Dillion   The 12' shallow-draft, portable, "Gunkholer" dinghy with sliding gunter rig.

THE FLYING DUTCHMAN

International Flying Dutchman
Class Association, United States
Peter Wells
P.O. Box 152
Rindge, New Hampshire 03461

Pamphlet, 6 pages. Free.

Showing photos of the boat and crew in action, this pamphlet describes the characteristics and performance of the 20' racing class Flying Dutchman, its design concept and construction, and the class organization. Becoming the first trapeze boat in the Olympic Games with its selection in 1960, the boat is rigged with main sail, Genoa, spinnaker, and she is raced with two people. Lightweight and shallow in draft, she is easily beached and launched anywhere, car-topped or trailered, she can hold up to six people. Owners may choose a builder, or if experienced, build the boat at home. While the shape of the hull, the underwater profile of the centerboard and rudder, and the sail plan must be strictly controlled by measurement, the cockpit size, layout, and running and standing rigging have broader guidelines, allowing the owner a certain amount of license. The majority of boats have been constructed of wood or fiberglass, and most spars are aluminum.

FREEDOM BOAT WORKS

Anthony R. Bries and Richard J. Heinzen
Route 1, Box 12
North Freedom, Wisconsin 53951
(608) 356-5861

Catalog, 12 pages; Addenda (4); Price list; Color photos of specific models added to mailing per request. Free.

A custom boat shop that only builds and repairs traditional wooden boats, Freedom Boat Works constructs all of its boats of Northern white cedar on white oak frames, fastening them with bronze and copper or brass, and finishing them with a variety of hardwoods. Boats listed in the catalog are built on a routine basis by customer order only, but construction of other traditionally-built types up to 18' will be considered. Good size lines and offsets or construction plans are provided in the catalog and on the four inserted sheets for Rushton-based 17'7" lapstrake touring and 12'8" lapstrake solo cruising canoes, a Rangeley-type double-ended pulling boat (14'4"), Culler-designed flat-bottomed sailing skiff in two lengths (13'6", 15'8"), a 16'2" Piscataqua River wherry, and an 11' dinghy for rowing or sailing. Also given for each model, excluding the wherry and dinghy which appear on the inserts, are specifications and a discussion of the boat's design origins, form, construction, use, and performance. A dory skiff for outboard motor or rowing (14'9") and a rib-plank wilderness-tripping canvas-covered canoe (17'3") appear only on the price list. Inquiries regarding oars and paddles are welcome.

DANNY T. GREENE

Colebrook Road
Little Compton, Rhode Island 02837

Reprint from Cruising World (July 1980). Free.

Greene details in this article the design evolution, construction, and performance of his 9'4" "Two Bits" dinghy for rowing and sailing, built with double-chined plywood hull, composed of two nesting sections (60# stern section and 48# bow section), and fitted with leeboards and modified lateen rig. Greene emphasizes the boat's ease of construction, section and rig assembly, and propulsion with oar or sail. Claiming the boat can be put together with three sheets of exterior plywood for about $200, he offers plans and building instructions for the boat at $30. The reprint also provides specifications, side-, top-view and cross-section illustrations, and a photo of the boat.

H & H SAILCRAFT

Division of Dynamic Plastics, Inc.
8207 State Route 121
New Paris, Ohio 45347
(513) 437-7261/7055

Informational sheets (6); Price list. Free.

H & H Sailcraft offers a number of racing one-designs in foam fiberglass construction: the 20' Flying Dutchman, the 14' Rhodes Bantam, the 13' Flying Junior in competition or seat models, the 8' Optimist in dinghy or pram models, and the 16' Contender with two cockpit layouts for end-boom or mid-boom sheeting. Sails and trailers are available for all models but the Optimist, and each boat can be purchased in a complete kit or in kit parts (deck, hull

shell, double-bottomed hull, or hull and deck). Replacement parts may also be obtained. Each sheet provides photos, specifications, a brief description of the design and construction, and often a list of standard equipment and options for one of the boats.

Freedom Boat Works   A 14' Rangeley rowboat.

HALCYON BOAT CORPORATION

1155 Mueller Avenue
Melbourne, Florida 32935
(305) 254-6063

Various informational sheets; Reprint; Price list. Free.

Halcyon builds in fiberglass with teak trim 7' and 9' rowing or sailing dinghies with foam flotation, and a 12' cat- or sloop-rigged daysailer. The sheets provide color photos and specifications for each boat while the price sheet lists the features (usually the types of materials used for boat and sail parts) included in the base price for each model, and presents the options (conversion models, sail rigs, teak seats, lifting rings, bilge drain, butterfly sail, 6'6" Sitka spruce oars with copper tips, leathers and buttons) available at extra cost. Mentioning that the 9' model is based on a Thames River pilot boat—a lapstrake cockle with heart-shaped transom—the reprint from *Small Boat Journal* (October 1980) traces a 90-mile voyage of the Halcyon boat across the Gulf Stream.

INTERNATIONAL DRAGON

American International Dragon Association
302 Lakeside Avenue South
Seattle, Washington 98144

Informational sheets (3); Reprint; Price and membership registration sheet. Free.

The International Dragon, a three-man racing sailboat of traditional Scandinavian design and the world's most widely sailed one-design displacement keelboat, may be sailed single-handedly and makes a pleasant daysailer. Built of wood or fiberglass, rigged with aluminum or wood spars, 285 square-foot main and genoa, and 155 square-foot spinnaker, the boat weighs 3,740 pounds and measures 29'2" in length. One sheet discusses the racing class and membership in it ($20 per year), and explains the design, performance, and construction of the boat. The official building plans include rules and measurement forms and cost $30. Lists of boats for sale can usually be furnished upon request. With side-view illustration and photos, a second sheet shows the foredeck and cockpit arrangement of a modern Dragon; a third sheet, simply a Xerox photo of a Dragon on the water. Sir Gordon Smith discusses fifty years of technical development within the Dragon class in the accompanying article.

ISLAND CREEK BOAT SERVICES
George Surgent, Designer and Builder
Box 151, Williams Wharf Road
St. Leonard, Maryland 20685
(301) 586-1893

Informational sheets (2); Price sheet. Free.

Based on the South Jersey Beach Skiff, Surgent's "Island Creek 18'" is sold in kit form including plans and full-size patterns, or complete with fiberglass hull, integral flotation tanks, full sprit main and jib sail rig, and wooden deck, interior, rudder, tiller, and hollow mast. On one side, the sheet shows a photo of the boat, and on the other, nice side-, top-, stern-, and bow-view illustrations plus specifications and a list of the materials used for various parts of the boat. A rowing kit, outboard motor (6 hp) bracket, sails, and trailer may also be purchased. Detailed information regarding kits, ordering and shipping should be requested. The firm also offers repair, construction, and design services for fiberglass and wood.

LIBERTY YACHT CORPORATION
Route 2, Box 548
Leland, North Carolina 28451
(919) 371-3999

Pamphlet, 3 pages. Free.

Available in kit form from bare hull to finished rowing or sailing model, Liberty's 8½' dinghy, "Patriot 8," is fabricated of hand-laminated fiberglass with mahogany trim and bronze or stainless steel hardware. Sliding-lug rigged with 33 square-foot sail, the boat can be launched and rigged in minutes. She also will take a 1.9 hp outboard. The boat is easily car-topped or stowed on cabin top or deck. The pamphlet provides several photos of the boat, a small side-view illustration, specifications, and a brief explanation of the boat's features and performance. Liberty also builds a 28' yacht for which literature is available—see *Yachts and Cruisers,* page 49.

MARINE CONCEPTS
14520 60th Street North
Clearwater, Florida 33520
(813) 535-4521

Information sheet; Form letter; Order form and price list. Free.

Adapted from the Herreshoff 18' Carpenter hull, the Sea

Pearl 21 (21') is promoted as an affordable camper/cruiser, easy to sail alone, and capable of comfortably carrying eight people or four to five with camping gear. Lightweight and shallow in draft, the boat can be easily beached and trailered with a compact car; it can take a 3 to 4.5 hp outboard, and it can be rigged in less than ten minutes. The hull and deck are reinforced with a balsa core and hand-laid woven roving; fittings are stainless steel, bronze, or black acetal resin; all wood, but the mast and tiller handle is teak. The sheet furnishes color photos of the boat and parts, a side-view illustration, specifications, and elaborates on the boat's features—self-bailing cockpit, lee boards, free-standing rigging, kick-up rudder, tonneau cover, auxiliary power, and hull design. The order form lists standard equipment and suggested retail prices for the basic boat and several options (convertible top, berth cushion, tilt trailer, motor brackets, teak rowing seat/table); the back of the sheet offers explanations and side-view illustrations of both lug and wishbone rigs fitted to the boat. The form letter fully discusses the evolution of the boat's design and provides a list of dealers and a questionnaire to help prospective buyers determine the suitability of the boat.

MYSTIC SEAPORT MUSEUM
Attn: Boat Lines
Curatorial Department
Mystic, Connecticut 06355
(203) 536-2631

List, 6 pages; Order form. Free.

The museum makes available 121 sets of boat plans, 99 of which represent craft in the museum's collection. A variety of offerings appears in each of the list's categories: canoes (12' to 22'), dory/flat bottom boats (10' to 35'), kayaks and dugouts (15' to 31'), yacht tenders (9' to 16'), Whitehalls and other transom-sterned pulling boats (11' to 25'), St. Lawrence River skiffs (15' to 20'), hunting and angling boats (10' to 15'), round-bottomed work boats (11' to 46'), catboats (12' to 21'), yachts (14' to 26'), surfboats (25'), whaleboats (28'), power boats (15' to 57'), large vessels (111' to 244'), and miscellaneous (oars and sail rigs). The list indicates whether a given set of plans includes a lines plan, offset table, construction plan, and/or sail plan, and additionally, whether the boat is recommended for amateur builders. Plans range in price from $3.50 to $25. Several boats are also listed for which plans are in progress. The museum's *Watercraft Catalog,* by Maynard Bray, can also be obtained from the museum ($18 paper, $25 cloth); it describes 220 craft in the collection and contains sample plans of 25 boats.

THE NEST 14 COMPANY
Ramon Alan
242 Grove Street
Lexington, Massachusetts 02173

Information sheet; Price list. Free.

The "Nest 14," a 14' traditional wooden sloop, breaks down into five nesting sections constructed of waterproof veneer panels. Each section, the heaviest weighing 42 pounds, has its own flotation, and all connections are above the waterline. Nested, the sections take up 3' × 4' of space and fit on top of a compact car. The boat can be rowed or sailed with 60 foot main and/or working jib or genoa. The informational sheet offers side-view and interior illustrations, photos of the full and nested boat, and a brief description of its features. The reverse side of the sheet describes *The Nest 14* book, showing its table of contents and some illustrations from the book. In addition to the book and the completed boat, a sail rig, sails and several kits (basic plywood, factory-cut plywood hull, hardware) are available. The book—172 pages with 41 photos and 70 pages of completely dimensioned drawings—covers the history and development of the boat and explains how to build the hull, spars, sails and hardware. Those who buy this book and register a hull number will receive a planned series of notes that record observations and experiences of people who have built the boat according to the book.

NORTH SHORE YACHTS
P.O. Box 78, Anderson Road
North Sebago, Maine 04029
(207) 787-3880
Brochure, 14 pages; Promotional sheets (2); Price sheet. Free.
Photos and lists of standard features and sailing equipment accompany brief descriptions of North Shore's fiberglass tenders (8′, 10′, 12′, 15′) molded from a wooden hull of traditional design, and its 8′ dinghies; both types are available with hardwood trim and bronze hardware or with fiberglass seats, aluminum spars, vinyl rubrails, and cheaper hardware. Standing lug and gunter rigs are also discussed. Sketchily described and pictured are North Shore's 16′ and 18′ canoes built in fiberglass cloth, mat and woven roving or balsa-sandwich constructions, with ash and rawhide seats and either solid mahogany gunwales and decks or the cheaper vinyl gunwale extrusions. An 8½′ canoe in the lighter, cheaper build is also available and 8½′ and 16′ canoes can be built with keels. Also presented are plans to build fiberglass versions of Mystic's "Noman's Land Boat," and McKie Roth's 22′ Friendship sloop, for which side-view illustrations and some data are furnished; according to the price sheet, a 15′ utility/fishing skiff and a sailboard will soon be available.

The brochure also features advice on canoe paddle length, descriptions of Cadorette paddles, and reprints of manufacturers' literature regarding Minnesota Bent paddles, Isotope and Chesire catamarans, British Seagull "forty-featherweight" and "Cruise 'N Carry" outboards, and Awlgrip finishes. Pettit paints, Deks Olje, Shaw and Tenney oars and paddles, Shorelander trailers, and Stearns life vests may also be purchased. North Shore also offers fiberglass and Awlgrip refinishing, complete fiberglass repair, antique boat restoration, and help for the amateur boat builder. Enclosed updates announce, with descriptions and illustrations, the availability of a 9′ open or decked "Wind's Will" class sailboat, and from the Small Craft Center (P.O. Box 81, Route 114), an 18′ trailerable racer-weekender sailboat.

OLD WHARF DORY COMPANY
Box W
Old Chequesset Neck Road
Wellfleet, Massachusetts 02667
(617) 349-2383

Information sheets (7). $1.
Working alone, Walter Baron builds to order mostly traditional designs and their derivatives, using marine plywood or a combination of plywood and traditional construction, and sheathing the hulls with epoxy resin and polypropylene cloth for a durable, abrasion-resistant finish. Specializing in beach boats and shallow draft cruisers, mostly dories and sharpies, he has built boats from an 8′ pram to a 25′ sharpie. One sheet describes Baron's business in general; another provides an illustration and specifications for a 20′ Elver canoe-yawl with overnight accommodations; three others furnish line drawings, detailed construction data, prices and options, and a lengthy testimonial regarding the design and performance of Baron's 17′ Swampscott dory; and two more sheets include a description by William Short of the San Francisco Pelican and Baron's explanation of his versions of the boat and its sister Great Pelican. Baron easily makes custom changes in stock plans, builds bare hulls for the owner to finish, and finishes fiberglass hulls for work or pleasure boats such as the Sisu 22. He provides estimates for a nominal fee.

PAN PACIFIC YACHTS, LTD.
5732 Rhea Avenue
Tarzana, California 91356
(213) 881-2873
Two brochures, 4 pages each; Informational sheet; Order form and price list. Free.
Providing several photos, top- and side-view drawings, and ample lists of specifications, features, and standard equipment, the bulk of this literature covers the "Dolphin Nesting Dinghy," available in 8′8″ × 3′6″, 8′8″ × 4′1″, and 9′6″ × 4′4″ sizes for rowing, sailing, or powering with a 2 hp outboard. Constructed of hand-laid-up foam-sandwich fiberglass with foam flotation, the dinghy nests in itself to half its normal length, each section weighing half the total (90#, 100#, 135#). The hardware of stainless steel, naval bronze, anodized aluminum, or marine grade plastics, is covered by a unique total replacement policy, should the oarlocks, bolts, grommets, blocks, and such wear out, fail, or be lost. With one of the brochures, Pan Pacific also offers an 80 hp 30′6″ fiberglass trawler-yacht with teak interior and forward and side decks, and stainless or bronze hardware, that can be used for pleasure or for commercial fishing.

HAROLD H. PAYSON & COMPANY
Pleasant Beach Road
South Thomaston, Maine 04858
(207) 594-7587
Instant Boat study packet, 19 pages; Dory study packet, 13 pages; Order forms. $3 per packet.
Philip G. Bolger, designer, and H. H. Payson, builder, teamed up to produce tested "instant boats" which, built in plywood, usually take less than forty-eight hours to complete. Study sheets at 50¢ per sheet, plans, and patterns for some, are available for a 12′ kayak, 16′ sailboard, 6′ and 8′ row/sail/power punts, 10½′ pointy rowing skiff, 12′ double-ended flat-bottomed sailboat, 14′ sailboat with free-sailing sailboard sail, 16′ double-ended

daysailer and a bow-steering version, 15½' sailing crab skiff and a 20' model, and a 31' light open Gloucester schooner which folds in half. A photo, and nice, large scale drawings showing several views and details are provided for each boat; some boats receive greater descriptions including reprinted articles from *National Fisherman* and *Small Boat Journal.* An estimate of the time and skill required to build each boat, and sometimes a list of materials needed, are also furnished. Completed kayaks and schooners, dacron sails for some craft, a book on instant boat/plywood boatbuilding, and instant boat T-shirts may be purchased.

Payson also provides plans and study sheets for over 40 dories and take-offs, mostly of traditional design, for rowing, sailing, or power, with or without cuddy cabins. The boats range from 14' to 45' and include Cape Ann sailing and Gloucester Gull rowing dories, Carolina and Texas dory/skiffs, Grand Banks and St. Pierre dories, Texas dory/bateaux, runabout types, "Sampan Expresses," "Surfmasters," and more. Most but not all boats are represented with side-view illustrations or photos; some of the traditional dories receive some description and larger or more illustrations and photos. Also available is Payson's construction manual for the Gloucester Light dory ($7.50).

PENGUIN CLASS DINGHY
International Penguin Class
Dinghy Association
Leonard E. Penso
122 Hesketh Street
Chevy Chase, Maryland 20815
Reprints (4). Free.

Two standard 4' × 12' sheets of waterproof plywood provide all the planking for the 11'5" Penguin (4'8" beam, 140#, 72 sq. ft. sail area). Easily launched and car-topped, the two-person racer can hold up to three adults or four youngsters. The home builder may purchase a set of plans (including lines and offsets, a construction plan, a set of paper frame templates, and a detailed set of instructions and specifications) from Leonard Penso; more than one boat may be built from the plans on payment of a number tax. Purchase of the plans or a number entitles the recipient to membership in the dinghy association for the balance of the year in which the purchase is made. Active membership in the class is bestowed upon approval and measurement of the completed boat. In lieu of a concise pamphlet, the articles offer photos, a side-view illustration, and specifications for the boat; information regarding the performance of the boat; and histories and descriptions of the boat design and the racing class organization. Additionally, recommended professional builders are listed for people who prefer not to build their own Penguins.

PORTA-BOTE INTERNATIONAL
P.O. Box 2287
Menlo Park, California 94025
(800) 227-8882; (415) 961-5334; 325-9919
(AK, CA, HI) Collect
Brochure, 4 pages; Informational sheets (3); Order form. Free.
The collapsible, unsinkable Porta-Bote is composed of

tough, puncture-proof "nearly indestructible" polypropylene, and fitted with time-proven hinges. Available in 8', 10', and 12' lengths, the boat can be rowed, sailed, or powered. New olive drab versions for duck hunting, guaranteed for ten years, are available (39# to 59#). Porta-bote sail kits, 7.5 hp gas engines, motor mounts, rowing equipment, and other accessories may also be purchased. The brochure shows photos and specifications and provides testimonials and considerable technical information regarding the boat. Additional sheets furnish a favorable review of the boat, comparisons with boats of other materials, description of the new line of camouflage duck hunting models, and full specifications for the engine offered. The boats and accessories may be obtained in some areas from dealers.

MICHAEL PORTER, BOATBUILDER
Chebeague Island, Maine 04017
(207) 846-3145
Pamphlet, 8 pages, Price list. $1.
This pamphlet provides photos of some of Porter's work: a sailing skiff, outboard skiff, and semi-dory in various stages of completion; an 18' Friendship sloop; and lobsterboat repair work. The majority of space in the pamphlet is devoted to discussion of the 17' Swampscott or "Friendship" dory built of pine lapstrakes on oak frames, fastened with galvanized boat nails and screws and copper clench nails in the laps. A large photo is provided, as are specifications and a list of materials of which the various boat parts are constructed. The price sheet lists other stock boats, besides the Swampscott, another fore and aft plank bottomed "semi-dory" designed by John Gardner for use with outboards (14', 16', 20'), and 3 kinds of cross-plank bottomed skiffs—an 11½' rowing punt or flatiron skiff, an

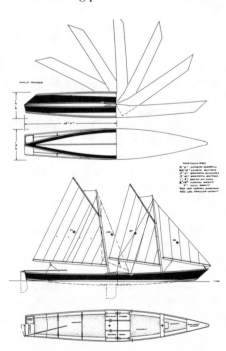

Harold H. Payson & Company   This Gloucester Schooner is actually two 15'6" skiffs secured end to end. Extremely fast, two people are needed to sail her, but the schooner will carry many more.

outboard skiff (14', 16', 18'), and a Culler-designed sailing skiff (13½). Ash and spruce oars as well as custom equipment, fixtures, or features are available. Custom built boats up to about 40' will be possible upon completion of the firm's new shop.

R.K.L. BOATWORKS
Mt. Desert, Maine 04660
(207) 244-5997

Catalog, 12 pages; Order form and price list. Free.
R.K.L. boats, built using the W.E.S.T. system, and made to last for years with minimum maintenance, were selected for easy handling, seaworthiness, and maximum performance. Prefaced with an explanation of R.K.L. boat construction and beautifully illustrated with color and black and white photos of most of the boats, and with line drawings of some of the boats, R.K.L.'s catalog lists ample specifications for most boats and gives a little design history along with information regarding each boat's performance and features. Available are a Rangeley in two lengths (14', 17', 85#, 140#), a Herreshoff-based pram tender and an Abeking and Rasmussen-based tender (both 8', 58#), a Lawley tender (11', 85#), a Herreshoff-based Columbia tender (11½', 85#), a touring canoe in two lengths (15', 17'), and a tandem flatwater canoe (18'). Sailing conversions may be purchased for the pram and Columbia tenders; a variety of options including Shaw and Tenney oars are listed on the price sheet along with detailed shipping information. Custom orders are invited. Literature outlining repair and finish maintenance accompanies each boat; further repair advice and materials are offered for customers outside the easy pick-up and delivery area.

RICE CREEK BOAT WORKS
Lew Miller, Proprietor
9715 Jackson Street N.E.
Blaine, Minnesota 55434
(612) 780-3349 after 6 p.m.,
all day Saturday or Sunday

Brochure, 4 pages; Order form; Update sheet. Free.
Lew Miller offers plans and kits for five of his designs: a Stripper canoe (14'4", 17', 18'), a 14' pram, a 17' pulling boat, a 14' fisherman's skiff, and a 12'6" board sailer. Except for the board sailer, the boats are to be built of red cedar strips with epoxy-fiberglass sheathing; they are also available as semi-complete hulls or as fully complete custom boats. Each boat is minimally described in the literature—additional information and a color photo is available for each boat for $1. All plans include full-size templates, a materials list, and a source-list for materials. Each kit description briefly lists the materials included. The loose sheet explains Miller's solo canoe design and announces the availability of assembled, pre-woven caned canoe seats in the customer's choice of wood.

ROOSTER SAILBOAT CLASS
Rooster Boat Company
111 Willard Avenue
Wakefield, Rhode Island 02879

Information sheet; Form letter; Price and order sheet. Free.

As the form letter explains, plans for the one-design racer/day-sailer, 9'7" Rooster (46" beam, 65# hull, 95# fully rigged, 37 sq. ft. sail area) cost $10 and they include eleven pages of drawings, a bill of materials, a set of building instructions, and specifications. The number of boats built from the plans is not restricted, provided they are not fabricated for sale. Construction time runs from 50 to 75 hours. The sheet (copy of an article) provides photos, a side-view illustration, specifications, and brief information regarding the design, performance, and operation of the craft.

SAN FRANCISCO PELICAN CLASS
William H. Short
21 Terry Circle
Novato, California 94947

Brochure, 4 pages; Information sheet; Reprint. Free.
A sailing-dory-pram with standing lug rig carrying 105 square feet of sail, the 12'2½" San Francisco Pelican, a center-boarder, combines the lines of a Banks fishing dory with an Oriental sampan bow. She can be sailed comfortably with a crew of one to four, but will safely hold more. A complete set of building plans for the boat, to be constructed of marine plywood, costs $22 and includes 3 pages of detailed drawings with full views of all joinery work, an alternate design for a kick-up rudder, and a 48-page illustrated book, *Building the San Francisco Pelican*, which in turn details every step of construction and includes sailing and handling information and full racing specifications. On request, information will be provided on partially-complete or ready-for-painting kits and completely finished Pelicans from franchised builders. Designer Short also offers plans for a larger 16' "Great Pelican", with or without cuddy cabin or raised deck cruising cabin; plans for an 18' "Great Pelican Yangtze"; and for each of the 3 boats, plans for safe Chinese lug-rig sails with five full-length battens and sheet lets. With few photos, the brochure amply describes the basic Pelican—construction, design, performance, specifications—and lug and cat or sloop rigs, while the sheet discusses the Great Pelican, comparing it with the smaller model. Short's development of the design is covered in the copy of an article from the *San Rafael Independent Journal* (June 12, 1980).

SMITH'S BOAT SHOP
Don R. Smith
764 Samish Island Road
Bow, Washington 98232
(206) 766-6883/6231

San Francisco Pelican brochure, 4 pages; Price sheets (2). Free.
A builder of San Francisco Pelicans, Smith's Boat Shop furnishes the same brochure that William Short does, and sells Short's complete building plans for $20 plus postage. An accompanying price sheet for Smith's Pelican shows a side-view illustration of the boat, lists the materials with which the boat is constructed (⅜" marine fir plywood for the bottom, ¼" marine fir plywood for the sides, Douglas fir, Sitka spruce, bronze nails, brass screws, Woolsey paints and sealers, Weldwood glue), lists a number of options available (various construction details on completed boats,

sail and cockpit covers, sails, stainless hardware kits, tilt-bed trailers), and describes the kinds of Pelican packages available. Another sheet offers similar information and options for an "El Toro" 7'11" sailing pram, built with materials similar to the Pelican's and available complete or assembled and ready for painting.

E. D. STOKES ASSOCIATES
4408 Perkins Avenue
Cleveland, Ohio 44103
(216) 431-5333
Brochure, 4 pages; Update sheet; Reprint; Price sheet. Free.
With side-view illustrations and large photos, the brochure briefly describes the construction, performance, and features of Stokes' "Coho" (13'6", 95#), a replica of a boat created to fish trout on New York's Finger Lakes in the 1920s, and "Conny" (9'3", 85#), a replica of a tender to the Consolidated Express Cruiser, circa 1930. Both boats are composed of hand-laid-up fiberglass with a white gel coat, positive flotation, mahogany or oak wood parts, stainless steel fastenings, and epoxy-resin-coated joinery. Built with two rowing stations, they are equipped with 7' spruce oars, leathers, buttons, and manganese bronze horns, and the Conny can be rigged for sail for an additional price. The reprint offers fuller information on the construction of these boats, and the price sheet lists a variety of construction options. The update sheet introduces, without photos or illustrations, 2 new boats, 8'2" versions of the Conny: the "Caddie" is an economical version of the "Cowrie," which, in turn, offers the same fancy construction details and fittings as the Conny. The firm will also build to order exact scale models from designers' lines, completing them to any degree of detail, from a simple sheer-line half-model to a full model completely rigged and detailed down to the instrumentation. The price depends on the project; call or write for a quotation. Custom work such as the manufacture of winch handle pockets and helmsman's seats, is also available, primarily on a local basis.

SWANSON BAGGINS & COMPANY
Mark Swanson and Abe Baggin
1000 E. Main St.
Medford, Oregon 97501
Informational sheets (2); Letter. $1.
This firm builds no stock boats, but will adapt a specific boat type to the customer's unique requirements. As Mark Swanson says in his personal letter, he predominantly pursues authentic Norwegian small boats, 2 of which are pictured and described in the accompanying literature. The Scandinavian pram is shell-built of nine to eleven strakes in 8' to 20' lengths from cedar, spruce, fir, hackmatack, copper and bronze. Built of oak, cedar, spruce, hackmatack, copper and bronze, the open Norwegian double-ender comes in 14' to 30' lengths. Both boats can be finished with the traditional linseed oil and pine tar or the contemporary Deks Olje bright finish; both can come equipped with or without sailing rigs and traditionally-shaped oars. Inquiries are welcomed regarding other boat types such as the three-strake Oselver

and five-strake Strandebarmer from western coastal Norway, Bindals and Elveboats of far northern Norway, or any small traditional or contemporary North American wooden boat. Repairs, restorations, custom oar and spar (hollow and solid) work, marlinspike and rigging services, are also available.

TANGENT DEVELOPMENT COMPANY
J. G. Merritt, President
1715 Harlequin Run
Austin, Texas 78758
(512) 837-9170
Study package, 7 pages; Drawing and photo. $2.
With designs in the works for a 16' garvey hull for sail, oar, or power, and a 26' sailing dory with overnight accommodations, the folks at Tangent Development intend to offer study packages and plans for a group of boats that require low skills to build and a minimum investment in materials. Currently, a study package and plans are available for an 11'2" "dory-dinghy" for rowing or sailing, which can be built from "lumberyard materials." The study package includes a two-page cover letter describing the boat and explaining the firm's design philosophy, a four-page bill of materials, a one-page list of necessary tools, a large drawing of the boat's general arrangement and sail plan, and a color photo of the boat. If ordered within 30 days of receiving the study package, the building plans will cost $2 less than the usual $15. They include, in addition to the study package materials: lines and construction plan drawings; full-size frame, stern, and transom patterns; full-size detail sheets for cleats, rudder pintle and gudgeons, and oarlock sockets; a source-list of materials; a set of building instructions; and, when available, a U.S. Coast Guard bulletin, CG-466, "Safety Standards for Backyard Boat Builders."

THE TENDER CRAFT BOATSHOP
67 Mowat Avenue, Suite 031
Toronto, Ontario M6K 3E3
Canada
(416) 531-2941
Catalog, 8 pages; Informational sheets (9). Free.
Tender Craft offers quite an array of small boats, accessories, books, Mystic Seaport and other plans, boat and sail kits, building supplies, fasteners, and brass fittings and hardware. Since 1921, the firm has turned out Western red cedar planked canoes (16') and cedar strip tenders (10'9"), double-ended rowing/sailing skiffs (16'), and runabouts (14' to 18'). Vee-stern and flat wide transom canoes for motors and heavy loads are available; all canoes feature white cedar ribs, solid white oak gunwales and keels, copper clench nails, and clear fiberglassed exteriors. Skiffs, tenders, and runabouts come with copper fastenings and white oak ribs, keels, and stringers; tenders and runabouts contain some mahogany; skiffs and runabouts are finished with marine spar varnish; the tenders are finished with clear fiberglass which is optional on the skiffs. Also offered are an 8' V-bottom rowing/sailing pram in kit form or complete with fiberglass cloth/resin-epoxy paint and varnish finish, and an 8' L. F. Herreshoff pram/tender with clear or

painted finish and sail option; both boats are composed of various hardwoods and brass and copper fastenings. And also available complete or in kit form are a 14'7" mahogany and canvas touring-whitewater kayak with brass fastenings and hardware and a plywood child's canoe (8').

A photo, some specifications, a description of components, and a list of options are provided for each boat. Some of the numerous options available include sail kit packages and parts for various boats, handcrafted hardwood paddles and oars, bronze oarlocks and sockets, leathers and buttons, a folding anchor, various canoe seats, carriers, electric motors, and a multitude of equipment and fittings for the runabouts. Also described and pictured is a plywood canoe kit (16'); a Hazen strip canoe kit is also offered. Fasteners available include brass and copper clench nails, silicon bronze nails with ringed threads, Robertson brass wood screws, naval bronze bolts, brass flat washers, and galvanized screws. Building materials include marine mahogany plywood, complete pre-cut and patterned hardwood and cedar parts for canoes and other boats, canvas and fiberglass covering materials, numerous finishes and sealers, adhesives, caulking materials, and some related tools. Additional literature and information is available on many items.

STEPHEN WILCE BOATS
P.O. Box 962
Winters, California 95694
(916) 795-4816

Catalog, 10 pages. Price list. $1.

Stephen Wilce devotes two pages of his catalog to the discussion of the features common to all of his boats, in particular, his unique thermoplastic sheet, double-hull construction which makes them quiet, well-insulated, and easy to repair, and gives them great flotation and self-bailing capabilities, excellent strength and durability, ultra light weight, and a uniform fine finish. The wood parts are fir, mahogany, or mahogany marine plywood; the finish, Deks Olje. His sail rigs feature unstayed, rotating wooden masts of Douglas fir, if solid, or of laminated woods, if hollow. Since his tooling costs are low with this construction method, Wilce will build any custom design as long as he feels comfortable with it. Remaining pages of the catalog provide nice side- and top-view illustrations and discuss the design origins, features, and performance of Wilce's 5 stock boats: a 12' pack canoe (24#) with optional sail rig or rowing package, an 8' pram (36#) and a 12' "flatty" skiff (70#) with leeboard bermuda or sprit sail rigs, a 16' sharpie (85# to 135#), a 20' clipper yawlboat (190#), and a 21' fast gig (a 90# high performance rowing boat). "Ruggedized" versions of these models are available.

WINDMILL CLASS ASSOCIATION
P.O. Box 183
Hartland, Wisconsin 53029

Pamphlet, 6 pages; Informational sheets (2). Free.

The 15½' Windmill is a light displacement, two-person, non-spinnaker, non-trapeze, high-performance one-design racing sloop. Designed for the home builder by Clark Mills of Clearwater, Florida, the boat is also available

as a professionally manufactured fiberglass boat. Complete plans for wood or fiberglass construction, and a free information package which includes more boat information, prices, and a list of class members in the customer's region, may be obtained from the organization. The pamphlet presents photos, specifications, a profile illustration, and pertinent information regarding performance, construction, membership, and the availability of new or used boats. Two accompanying sheets describe the hull and deck construction and standard equipment, furnishing prices for options and accessories as well, for complete new Windmills manufactured and sold exclusively by McLaughlin Boat Works, 6111 Dayton Boulevard, Hixson, Tennessee 37343; (615) 842-4894.

Y-FLYER
Gregory W. Kleffner
American Y-Flyer Yacht Racing Association
12241 Rain Hollow Drive
Maryland Heights, Missouri 63043
(314) 576-6364

Variety of promotional literature. Free.

Building plans for the 18' two-crew Y-Flyer may be obtained only from this association, costing members $20, and non-members $35, which covers an associate membership. Included in the literature that Kleffner may send are a membership/order form, a 6-page pamphlet from the U.S. Yacht Racing Union about one-designs, a 4-page brochure offering photos of the "versatile flat V-bottomed centerboarder with willowy rig" and reprinting excerpts from articles regarding sailing the boat, a 12-page edition of the latest Y-Flyer newsletter which furnishes specifications for the boat and lists used boats for sale and manufacturers of complete boats and sails/covers, and finally, a price list from one Y-Flyer manufacturer and a pamphlet from another. L. E. Lundquist and Company (Route 2, Box 60 DD, Ninety Six, South Carolina 29666; (803) 277-1874) offers fiberglass Y-Flyers in traditional or liner models, in race-equipped, day-sailer, or bare hull versions; a variety of equipment and sails, and a trailer are also available. In its pamphlet, Turner Marine (R.R. 1, Neoga, Illinois 62447; (217) 895-3395) lists no prices but provides photos of the boat and descriptions of its performance, design and fiberglass construction.

Stephen Wilce Boats   Diver's model of a 16' Sharpie, 92 lbs.

See also, under:

Canoes
Apple Line
Folbot
Great Canadian
Mentha
Old Town
Outdoor Sports
Rainbow
"Wet Dreams"

Rowing Shells
B & S
Freya
Lighthall
Marine Services
Martin
Rowing Crafters
Small Craft
Thayer

Specialty Craft
Pederson
Popular Mechanics

Sports and Commercial Boats
Hankins
Hill
Lavro
Lucander
New River
Nexus
North End
Payne & Franklin
Texas

Yachts
Benford
Brewer
Clark Craft
Glen-L
HMS
Heritage
Luger
North Carolina
Roth
Schooner

Multihulls
Fast Boats
Marples

Materials and Supplies
Dean
Gougeon

Nautical and Outdoor Clothing
Afterguard

General Catalog
Cabela's
Chartroom
E & B
Fore and Aft Marine
Goldberg's
International Sailing
M & E
Port Supply
Sears
Turner's

Books
Hearst
Woodenboat

Specialty Craft

Hovercraft

ALASKA HOVERCRAFT INC.
1120 East 1st Avenue
Anchorage, Alaska 99501
(907) 277-5686

Pamphlet, 6 pages; Form letter. Free.

The "Maverick," a 12'9", 450# hovercraft with fiberglass foam composite body, is the focus of this pamphlet, which furnishes photos of the "air cushion vehicle," explains the boat's utility for year-round recreation and numerous difficult terrains without damage to the environment, and lists the boat's features and specifications in some detail. As the form letter explains, the firm also designs and builds custom hovercraft including larger, commercial-grade vessels and a stock 5.5 ton "Contender;" a 2.5 ton hovercraft and other classes are currently in the works. Heretofore working mainly within the State of Alaska, the firm now hopes to expand and introduce its hovercraft to other areas where a high-speed, multi-terrain amphibious vehicle might be useful.

NEOTERIC-USA-INCORPORATED
Fort Harrison Industrial Park
Terre Haute, Indiana 47804
(812) 466-2303

Informational sheets (2) on "Lemere" model. Free. "Nova II" information pack, 25 pages; Order form. $8. Overseas $11.

Neoteric makes available two models of multi-terrain, multi-season hovercraft of fiberglass and PVC foam composite construction—an 11'6", 428# "Lemere," and a 14', 750# "Neova II." The Lemere, for which specifications and photos appear on the sheet, is offered fully assembled, a single-axle flat-top trailer is extra. The Neova II can be purchased fully assembled or incomplete in several kit forms: the economy kit, the standard kit, and the super kit, which includes both engine and trailer. Plans for the Neova II may also be obtained for building the vessel of plywood, mild steel, and plastics. The "Neova II Information Pack" provides photos and a side-view illustration of the vessel, explains the hovercraft principle, lists a variety of hovercraft organizations, and describes the company, the craft, its features, specifications, performance, and options, including the plan pack, the three kits, and the six modules (pictured) of which kits are composed. A two-page "Neova II kit catalog-7," to be used with the plan pack, details the parts (and prices) that make up each kit module and indicates packing and crating charges and terms of payment; prices are summarized on an additional sheet.

See also, under **Performance Powerboats:** Popular Mechanics

Ice Boats

INTERNATIONAL DN ICE YACHT RACING ASSOCIATION
Peter Johns
260 East Wood Street
Decatur, Illinois 62523
(217) 424-1290

Year Book, 64 pages. $4.

Listing by-laws and the constitution, current and past officers, members, clubs, and championships, the year book also provides several pages of official specifications including elaborate construction details and diminutive official plans for the DN ice boat. Ads throughout the book indicate several ice boat builders, sail makers, clubs, and hardware manufacturers/suppliers. Official full-scale plans for the boat may be obtained for $2.

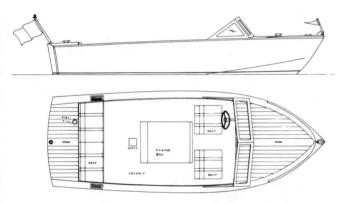

Norman Pederson   Interior and side-view of the Norseman, a vee bottom, inboard runabout.

WILLIAM B. SARNS COMPANY
Ice Boat Hardware — Machine Work
38101 Huron Point Drive
Mount Clemens, Michigan 48045
(313) 463-4269/468-3531

Price list. Free.

This company makes all the hardware, runners, and rigging required for the DN ice boat, selling complete hardware kits, separate items, a variety of runners, a runner sharpener fixture, and plans for the ice boat. No catalog or pictures are available; the price list indicates the material(s) of which each piece of hardware is made in addition to the price for each item.

DAN SHEEHAN
Cal-Tek Engineering
29 Pemberton Road
Cochituate, Massachusetts 01778
(617) 653-0355

Informational sheet. Free.

On one side of the sheet, Sheehan presents his new high-performance five-meter "International Challenger" ice boat, a second-generation fiberglass (sandwich-core) design with elliptically-shaped fuselage and Sarns hardware. He offers, in photocopy, an illustration of the boat, lists of features and specifications, an explanation of

the materials of which the boat rigging is made, and discussions of the performance, construction, light weight, high strength, aerodynamics, and relatively low cost of the boat. Both completed boats and completed fuselage kits for DN owners are available. Described and pictured on the other side of the sheet are two fiberglass canoes (with foam flotation) based on traditional Native American models—an Ojibway "solo sport" canoe (13′1½″, 40#) and a large-volume "Long Nose" wilderness-tripping/flatwater-racing canoe (17′, 70#). The designs, constructions, and performance of these boats are briefly explained and their specifications given.

See also, under **Materials and Supplies:** Gougeon

Performance Powerboats — Racers, Runabouts, Water Ski Boats

AMERICAN SKIER BOAT CORPORATION
14015 N.W. 19th Avenue
Opa Locka, Florida 33054
(305) 945-1776/685-8321

Brochure, 4 pages; Informational sheet; Performance reports (3); Price list. Free.

American Skier manufactures in hand-laminated fiberglass 3 models of water-skiing/performance boats, loaded with standard features: the 18′ "American Skier" tournament boat, the 20′7″ "Volante" pleasure runabout or waterskiing performance boat (both competition model and regular), and the 20′7″ Barefoot Skier. The brochure offers color photos, specifications, descriptions of standard equipment, and a list of accessories and options for the Volante, while the single sheet does the same for the American Skier. A performance report from *Powerboat* or *Lakeland Cruising* covers each boat, discussing features and performance data at length. The price sheet covers the accessories, Volante, and Barefoot Skier, but omits the American Skier while listing the Volante competition model, not mentioned elsewhere.

CLARK CRAFT BOAT COMPANY
16 Aqua Lane
Tonawanda, New York 14150

Powerboat catalog, 48 pages; Order form. $1.

This catalog provides photos and/or illustrations, specifications in most cases, and an inconsistent lot of information regarding the performance, design, features, and available kits/plans for 19 runabout/cruisette/ sports and utility/water ski boats (12′ to 22′6″), 9 high performance speed/ski boats, some with tunnel hulls (11′ to 19′), 12 hydroplanes (8′ to 17′), 21 cabin cruisers (19′ to 53′), 2 trawler-yachts (29′ to 37′), and 6 houseboats (18′ to 40′), some of which are trailerable. Plans and patterns are available for most designs, hull or complete boat kits for the smaller boats in each category, frame sets for small- to medium-size boats, and study prints and mold frame sets for the larger boats. Kit boats generally are to be constructed of marine plywood, and the larger boats for which only plans, patterns, and study prints and sometimes mold frame sets are available, are designed for wood, fiberglass, ferrocement, steel or aluminum. Prices and thorough descriptions are not given for some of the designs. As in the sailboat catalog, special sale prices are offered on some plan sets.

ELIMINATOR BOATS

Ron Ossenberg
1010 N. Grove Street
Anaheim, California 92806
(714) 630-7150

Brochure, 8 pages; Price list, 6 pages. Free.

Listing specifications, features, and options, and furnishing color photos for each model, Eliminator's brochure covers 13 racing and water skiing boats ranging in length from 18′ to 30′ and including bubble deck and tunnel hull designs, hot performers, day-cruiser party boats, and one offshore boat with underdeck cabin space. While available through dealers, these boats may be purchased directly from Eliminator. Prices vary and depend on the kind of engine installed in the boat.

HAL KELLY'S TESTED PLANS

P.O. Box 1767
Fort Pierce, Florida 33450
(305) 464-1526

Catalog, 16 pages.; Price list. 60¢

The largest purveyor of outboard racing plans in the world, selling them for over twenty-five years, Kelly provides plans for 9 racers, including pleasure and Class A, B, C, D, and Junior runabouts (9′ to 15′) and Class A, B, C, and D hydroplanes (9′ to 11′). All of the plans contain full-size rib drawings and the boats are to be built from exterior and marine-grade plywood. The catalog explains the plans, provides photos of successful boats built according to the plans, and furnishes a list and photo of the tools required. Each boat for which there are plans receives at least one photo, top/side-view illustrations, a good description of its characteristics and the contents of the plans package, a list of specifications, and estimates of the time and cost involved in building the boat. Kelly also sells propellers and offers advice regarding their selection; enclose a stamped, self-addressed envelope when writing for such information.

NORMAN PEDERSON

5817-43rd Avenue N.E.
Seattle, Washington 98105

Brochure, 6 pages; Price sheet. Free.

Norman Pederson offers large size plans, showing all standard views, for 8′ and 11′ open sail boats, a 14′ outboard runabout, and an 18′ outboard cruiser with accommodations forward for two, all of which may be constructed of sheet plywood, and for 18′ and 22′ inboard runabouts, a 32′ inboard cruiser with accommodations for two, and a 28′ gaff-rigged sloop for offshore cruising with berths for four, which boats must be put together with more conventional planking. The inboards are designed for up to 140 hp, the outboard cruiser for up to 150 hp,

and the outboard runabout will take 10 to 60 hp. The brochure gives specifications and nice side- and some top-view illustrations, which include interior layouts, for the boats.

PERFORMANCE PLANS

Morley S. Smith
712 N. Pine Street
Mt. Prospect, Illinois 60056

Catalog; 28 pages; Order form and price list. $3.

This catalog begins with a lengthy discussion of the evolution of hydroplane hulls, from catamarans and deep Vs to the competition and pleasure tunnel designs and stepped hulls. A general explanation of the plans offered and the construction of the boats in marine plywood follows. Plans, some with patterns, are available for 12 hydroplanes (9′6″ to 22′), most with tunnel hulls, some with stepped hulls. Specifications, large illustrations of top- and side-views and a cross-section, and solid information regarding performance, design, and construction, are provided for each boat. Requests for further information about given models, inquiries regarding building problems, and comments and suggestions are welcome. The firm conducts extensive research and model testing, and does custom design work from time to time.

POPULAR MECHANICS

Plans Library
P.O. Box 1014
Radio City Station
New York, New York 10101
(800) 351-1363; (915) 643-2517

Informational sheets (3). Free.

Popular Mechanics' "Plans and Ideas Catalog" sells for $1 and includes plans for a variety of boats as well as workbenches, tool chests, and power tools (drill presses, cutoff saws, boring machines, milling tables) which might appeal to the home boatbuilder. Two of the sheets sent promote the catalog and present sample offerings including the workshop equipment. The third sheet shows the two pages from the catalog which very briefly describe and minimally illustrate the boats for which there are plans—an 8′ row/sail/power dinghy, an 11′ fiberglass-planked sailboat, 12′ buckboard, 2 "scuba tows," a 10′ hydroplane, 14′ air-cushion vehicle, 13′ and 14′ runabouts, 16′ V-hull "sports sled," 17′ cabin cruiser with plans for a trailer, and a 25′ trailerable houseboat. In some cases plans include full-size patterns.

See also, under:

Canoes
   Clark Craft

Small Open Boats
   Mystic
   Payson
   Tender Craft

Sports and
Commercial Boats
   Texas

Yachts
   Glen-L
   Luger

Fasteners
   Kisly

General Catalogs
   Overton's

Books
   Hearst

Pontoon Boats

ROTOCAST FLOTATION PRODUCTS
Pontoon Boat Department
P.O. Box 1059
Brownwood, Texas 76801
Brochure, 4 pages; Informational sheets (6); Form letter; Order form. Free.

This firm offers 17', 20', and 24' Dura-Float pontoon boats in easy-to-assemble kits. Modular pontoon sections, rotationally-molded from high density polyethylene plastic and filled with closed cell urethane foam are bolted to a galvanized frame. The brochure shows photos, side/top-view and cross-sectional illustrations, presents features of the three models in chart form, and briefly describes kit contents and assembly. The additional sheets furnish photos, illustrations, specifications, technical data, and lists of features for Dura-Float modular pontoons.

Sailboards/Windsurfers and Accessories

MATLACK WINDSURFING
711 W. 17th Street, G-6
Costa Mesa, California 92627
(714) 642-1400
Catalog, 12 pages; Order form and price sheet. Free.

Providing large illustrations and lists of features for each item included, this catalog makes available a select group of recommended windsurfing paraphernalia: daggerboards, cleats, mast extensions, footstraps and inserts, harness grips and lines; safety harnesses, carryall bags, jackets, pullovers, T-shirts, and long johns; car-top carriers, a kite, an anemometer, a marine watch, a marine camera, and a windsurfing manual. Featured are Matlack's harness, incorporating added lower back support with quality workmanship, and a host of custom sails, "Matlack Marginals," and "Santa Barbara Surf Sails"—"Marginals," "Cabrillo Cut," "Blast Reachers," "HAR Blades," "Trophy Series"—available in dacron, and some in varieties of mylar.

WINDSURFING U.S.A.
186 Forbes Road
Braintree, Massachusetts 02184
(617) 848-9658
Catalog, 20 pages; Order form. $1.

Including only tested products of the highest quality and best value, this catalog provides color photos and brief descriptions of a wide variety of windsurfing equipment and accessories. Available in numerous models and brands are harnesses, harness hooks and webbing, line and rope, joints and fittings, mast extensions, footstraps and inserts, daggerboards, skegs, sails, and sail mast bags and duffles; special windsurfing clothing (wetsuits, shoes, gloves, shirts, trunks), casual beachwear and dressy sailing garb

Windsurfing U.S.A.   One of many windsurfer sails available from this east coast company.

(sweaters, pile jackets, pullovers, T-shirts, shorts, trousers); car-toppers and board walkers; manuals, posters, and gift items with windsurfing or marine motifs. A separate price list may be obtained for Windsurfer brand sailboards, components and accessories. Because the firm operates several stores, desired items not pictured in the catalog may be available upon request.

Sports and Commercial Fishing Boats, Workboats, Utility Skiffs

AMERICAN COMMERCIAL MARINE, INC.
19320 - 63rd Avenue N.E.
Arlington, Washington 98223
(206) 659-2414/6333

Informational sheets (5). Free.

American Commercial Marine builds a variety of commercial fishing boats, including bowpickers, gill-netters, and combination vessels, with hulls of one-piece molded fiberglass construction, and houses, if desired, of molded balsa-core construction. Backed with side-view illustrations of 24', 28', and 32' models, one sheet lists specifications for a bowpicker and gives prices for hulls in various stages of completion, different engine options, steering/control, electrical, and hydraulic systems, deck hardware, some fishing apparatus, and a finished cabin interior. A 32' gillnetter receives the greatest coverage including two pages of side/top-view illustrations, a price sheet detailing engine and equipment options and their costs, and another sheet briefly but fully describing the features of the boat (from hull and house construction to engine, fuel, steering, electrical, and hydraulic systems, interiors, and deck hardware), offering the hulls in several stages of completion. Similar but less information is provided for 40' and 46' combination vessels, both of which are available in several stages. Quotes are given on kits, other equipment, and partially complete boats.

GEORGE CALKINS
P.O. Box 222
Nordland, Washington 98358
(206) 385-3649

Brochure, 10 pages; Form letter. $2.

Designer and originator of the double-ended "Bartender," a combined dory and planing hull, Calkins offers plans for 19', 22', 26', and 29' versions of the boat. Plans include a materials list, easy-to-follow step-by-step instructions, profile and deck arrangements, lines and offsets, construction details and jib plans. The plans, calling for sturdy construction of AA grade marine plywood over plenty of ribs, must be lofted full size in order to build a Bartender. His brochure discusses the history, design, and performance of the boat and provides, for each length, photos, specifications, and large side- and top-view illustrations that include interior layouts. The open 19' Bartender is designed for day fishing with an outboard (30-60 hp). The 22' outboard (60-100 hp)/inboard (70-200 hp) model, great for weekend fishing, will accommodate a head, galley, and two bunks. The 26' and 29' offshore fishing, inboard models (120-280 hp and 170-300 hp respectively) call for more elaborate accommodations.

CAPE FEAR SKIFFS
Bill Burnett
205 Apache Trail
Wilmington, North Carolina 28403
(919) 799-8099

Informational sheets (4). Free. Set of color photos (6). $3.

Combining the best features of two proven coastal Carolina designs, the "Carolina dory/skiff" and the "Outer Banks fishing skiff," the beamy 16'8" Cape Fear skiff is constructed of hand-laid-up fiberglass with semi-V hull and aft inboard motor well. The boat is available in economy or standard models, which differ according to interior finish, and it can take outboards up to 70 hp. Since the boat is built for commercial use, foam flotation is optional. The sheets variously provide specifications, fairly detailed design and construction information, numerous photocopies of photos of the skiff, and several top-view illustrations indicating possible interior layouts with side or center console, optional aft seat, or raised casting platform. A bimini top and galvanized trailer figure in the list of options; a supplementary list of options (such as windshields, special seats, Evinrude outboards, a forward cuddy cabin) appears on the back side of a copy of an article from *National Fishermen* (July 1982) which describes the skiff's capabilities. Custom combinations of interior features are possible.

CHESAPEAKE WORK BOAT COMPANY
Division of Glass Marine, Inc.
P.O. Box 261, Route 3
Hayes, Virginia 23072
(804) 642-2800/2860

Brochure, 4 pages; Informational sheets (6); Price list. Free.

This company fabricates commercial workboats in 36', 42', and 44' lengths for a variety of uses including research, sports and charter fishing, and many kinds of commercial fishing. The boats are available in bay-working or slightly larger offshore versions; they may be custom built and fitted out; and they may be procured as bare hulls, hulls with fiberglass deck and cabin, or as completed boats. The brochure provides numerous photos of the boats and lists the principle dimensions, engine-power options, standard and optional equipment, and describes the hull, deck, and cabin. Additional sheets in sets of two furnish for each length boat, specifications, side/top-view illustrations, house profiles, and construction data regarding its hull, girder system, decks, cabin, and standard outfit package. Quotes will be given upon request for other options and equipment desired.

CLIPPER CRAFT MANUFACTURING CO., INC.
James E. Staley
6507 N. Monteith Avenue
Portland, Oregon 97203
(503) 286-3013

Brochure, 4 pages; Reprint; Price sheet. Free.

An all-purpose boat that can cruise in any waters, take a minimum of maintenance and storage costs, and that can be trailered, the Clipper Craft dory is available in 20' open, and 23' and 26' open or cabin models, in any stage of completion from the bare hull to partially complete and finished boats. The lightweight, semi-V-bottom hull is sided with mahogany-surfaced marine-grade fir plywood lapstrakes separated by high-resin fir strips; the ⅝ medium density overlay ply bottom is battened with four one-foot wide ⅝ ply stringers; and the glued seams use stainless steel screws. The brochure briefly explains the performance, construction, and design of the boat, offers photos, and provides side-view illustrations, specifications, and lists of features for 8 versions of the boat, most with cuddy cabins that sleep two. The reprint of an article from *National Fisherman* (1971) explains at length the evolution of the Clipper Craft dory and details its performance and construction. All models can be set up to accept inboards or outboards; maximum horsepowers range from 85 to 175 depending on the boat.

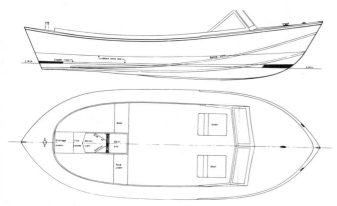

George Calkins   Interior and side-view of the Bartender, a combined dory and planning hull.

DUSKY MARINE, INC.
110 N. Bryan Road
Dania, Florida 33004
(305) 945-9564; 922-8890

Two brochures; Informational sheets (5); Form letter; Price sheet. Free.

Short on descriptions of performance, design, and construction, each sheet/brochure covers one of Dusky's seven sports fishing boats, furnishing many photos and lists of specifications, standard equipment, and features. Built to order of hand-laid fiberglass with foam flotation, stainless steel screws, vinyl gunwales, and fancy consoles, windshields, rails, seats and other fixtures, the models range from a 16'6″ open outboard and 20'3″ and 23'3″ open outboards or inboards, to 22'6″ and 25'6″ inboard/outboards and 25'11″ and 26' inboards with numerous deluxe options such as cuddy cabins and fishing towers. The price schedule indicates the cost of models depending on outboards, inboards, and stern drives chosen; it also provides an extensive list of available electrical equipment, accessories, teak fixtures, seatings, covers, and tops.

FLYE POINT MARINE
P.O. Box 13
Brooklin, Maine 04616
(207) 359-2007

Brochure packet, 28 leaves. Free.

Patterned on the tradition of the lobster boat style but offering larger work areas, these work boats in 20', 25',

and 31' lengths, feature one-piece, hand-laid-up fiberglass hulls, and can be delivered in any stage of completion from bare hull and deck, kit, partially complete boat, to "turn-key." A brochure is devoted to each length boat, providing many large poster-quality side/top-view illustrations, luscious photos, specifications, some design and performance information, and lists of equipment and options available for the basic fishing boat, the complete model, and the kit. The 25' and 31' boats are available also as cruisers, and their features and options are also listed. Each boat is built with the cooperation of the owner.

AL GROVER'S MARINE BASE, INC.
195 Woodcleft Avenue
Freeport, New York 11520
(516) 378-0510

Informational sheets (10); Price lists (2). Free.

In business for twenty-five years, Grovers are very proud of their diesel-powered "Groverbuilts," evolved from the Verity skiff and reproduced in fiberglass with foam flotation, teak trim, and bronze screws, bolts, shaft, skeg, rudder, prop, and through-hull fittings below the waterline. Offered generally in 26' and 28' lengths (with 4 or 6 cylinder Lehman diesels), a 24-footer was recently designed for the U.S. Coast Guard. Three of the sheets include photos of the boat along with general descriptions including the design's evolution and Grover's design orientation. Five sheets elaborate the specifications and construction details of the 26-footer, while the price sheet lists standard and optional equipment for both lengths.

Al Grover's Marine Base, Inc.   Evolved from the Verity skiff, the Groverbuilt is built of fiberglass with foam flotation and teak trim.

CHARLES HANKINS
Box 7, Highway No. 35
Lavallette, New Jersey 08735
(201) 793-7443

Brochure, 4 pages; Information sheet. Free.

Offering photos, specifications, and some construction detail, the sheet presents the Hankins Sea Bright dory surf boat available in 16′ and 18′ lengths as a rowing or power surf boat or a sprit-rigged sailing sea skiff. All models are constructed of white cedar (lapstrakes and transom) and white oak (gunwales, caps, and natural-growth crook stem and stern posts), with two pair of rowlocks and copper-riveted, bronze, and brass fastenings. Sailing models are equipped with centerboard, rudder, Sitka spruce spars, and dacron sails. The 16′ power boat takes up to 10 hp and the 18′ model up to 20 hp; the propeller is protected. Also showing photos, but more elaborate specifications and construction detail, and listing standard equipment, the brochure covers Hankins' Jersey sea skiffs, built in traditional lapstrake fashion with emphasis on detail work, for rugged offshore fishing or cruising. Open models are availabe in 22′, 24′, 26′, and 28′ lengths; standard cabin sea skiffs with roomy cabin, two bunks, and enclosed head, are offered in 22′, 24′, and 26′ lengths, but custom boats from 22′ to 40′, single or twin screw, laid out for two to six persons, can be constructed.

Munson Manufacturing, Inc. A general use vessel, one of Bill Munson's many diesel powered aluminum skiffs.

DON HILL RIVER BOATS
Dwight L. Bastian
P.O. Box CC
1075 Clearwater Lane
Springfield, Oregon 97477
(503) 726-8951; 746-7499

Pamphlet, 4 pages; Order form. Free. Price lists (4); Announcements of special sales upon request. Free.

Showing photos of a completed boat and boat and frame kits, the pamphlet describes briefly the contents of the plans and assembly manual packages and the two kinds of kits available for a 14′ or 16′ standard McKenzie River drift boat, or a 16′ high-sided version. Boat kits include instructions and all of the parts and materials necessary to complete a wooden boat; assembly requires no special abilities or hand tools, about forty hours of work, and a one-car garage is sufficient work space. Frame kits include a

set of plans, an assembly manual, a bow stem, transom, and a complete set of assembled ribs. The complete price list specifies numerous wood boat parts, finishes and repair products, standard wood boat hardware, and wood boat accessories available in addition to assembled unfinished wood boats (from 10′ pram and 12′ drift boat to 20′ Litton Grand Canyon and 22′ sports dories), custom finishes, and aluminum drift boats (14′ to 16′) and sleds (16′ to 22′). No specifications other than length, and partial if any construction details indicating the materials of which boat parts are made, are provided in any of the literature; the "Wet Dreams" catalog offers some of the missing information.

HULLS UNLIMITED-EAST INC.
Deltaville, Virginia 23043
(804) 776-9711

Catalog, 6 pages; Price sheet. Free.

Offering low freeboard for bay operation or up to 12″ additional freeboard for offshore work, this firm builds quality fiberglass workboats in any stage of completion, from bare hull to fully outfitted boat. The catalog provides photos, specifications, and construction and performance details for the 26′ "Deltaville garvey," and the 32′, 38′, and 42′ "Deltaville Deadrise." Several optional house configurations and outboard, out-drive, inboard, gas or diesel power options are available for the garvey, hand-laid-up in twelve to sixteen alternate layers of mat and roving. The larger boats feature a molded one-piece fiberglass hull reinforced with a balsa core and composed of thirteen to fifteen layers of cloth; decks are built of fiberglass-covered plywood. Completion options and optional equipment are specified on the price sheet. Quotes are given upon request for other options available. Engine locations, fuel capacity, and tankage can be varied along with the style of cabin and accommodations.

KACHEMAK WELDING AND FABRICATION
Cliff Calkins
P.O. Box 2020
Homer, Alaska 99603
(907) 235-8748

No literature available.

Calkins has built over 60 custom aluminum boats in the past five years, mostly commercial salmon boats ranging from 15′ set net skiffs to complete 34′ seiners, but also 26′ to 28′ pleasure boats. All boats are one of a kind, built to the customer's specifications, and to desired stages of completion. The customer decides on the engine, hydraulics, electronics, and other equipment to be used. Custom rigging, davits, tanks, and anything that can be built of metal and used on a boat are also available. Since all work is custom, Calkins furnishes no literature nor price lists and all boats are built on a firm bid basis. Letters and phone calls are welcome.

LAVRO INC.
16311 - 177th Avenue S.E.
Monroe, Washington 98272
(206) 794-5525

Catalog, 16 pages; Informational sheets (2); Price list. Free.

New River Boat Company, Inc.   The Sea Gypsy is a traditional displacement boat and is available as an open workboat, gaff-rigged sloop, or full cabin cruiser.

Lavro's drift boats and trawler-dories are constructed of layers of hand-laminated 24 oz. woven roving; the drift boats feature rolled edges, a uniflex bottom which gives upon impact, and up to nineteen layers of roving in high-wearing areas. The catalog lists specifications and standard equipment and amply describes the design, construction, and performance of each model, providing numerous photos of the boats, their optional and standard equipment, and many of their standard and optional features (rails, seats, covers, tops, windshields, steering). The 3 models of 20'10" trawler-dory (trawler stern, dory bow)—basic, sportsfisher with motor well, and elaborate sea dory with removable cabin—can each handle up to 100 hp. Drift boats can tolerate up to 10 hp each and include a 16'3" outfitters dory with adjustable seats, a 17'10" drift boat with optional motor well and cabin, and 13'11" and 16'3" models available in versions arranged for fly fishing. The two sheet inserts offer photos, specifications, brief descriptions, and lists of options and accessories for a 16'3" whitewater touring dory with three independent watertight storage compartments and 14' and 16' economy drift boats. The price sheet lists an extensive array of options and accessories (including 8' to 10' ash, spruce, or aluminum oars), repair kits and replacement parts for the dories and drift boats.

NILS LUCANDER MARINE AND INDUSTRIAL DESIGN

"Speed At Sea Designs"
5307 N. Pearl Street
Tacoma, Washington 98407
(206) 752-4205

Various informational sheets. Free.

Nils Lucander offers study sheets and building plans for over 100 stock designs ranging in length from 14' to 80' and including commercial fishing vessels from dories and trollers to trawlers and seiners; sailing-fishing boats such as albacore clippers; other specialized workboats like barges, tugs, patrol boats, and oil-rig mud boats; and trawler yachts, cruisers, motor boats, and other pleasure boats such as sailboats, motorsailers, party fishing boats, and sightseer cruisers. Two sheets redundantly list boats, according to

length, for which there are plans, furnishing each with a short description, the year designed, the length, beam, depth, draft, and type of material in which the boat was first built. Not all of the designs available are listed, including an 8' rowing/sailing dory-dinghy. Two accompanying sheets, ad samples, show small side-view illustrations for some of the boats. Lucander has individual brochures showing drawings/photos and supplying performance and design information for most of his designs; he may furnish brochures for specific boats upon request. His "complete data portfolio," which includes copies of his articles and technical papers, may be obtained for $25. Lucander operates his design service in part with marine architect/engineer Dave Dowhos from whom some plans are available; write him at 222 Crescent Avenue, Thunder Bay, Ontario, Canada.

MUNSON MANUFACTURING, INC.

P.O. Box 611
178 West Dayton
Edmonds, Washington 98020
(206) 776-8222

Catalog, 39 pages. Free.

Munson Manufacturing is constantly involved in making heavy-duty, all-aluminum boats available in traditional and accepted designs. Presented in the catalog, each with several pages of large photos and description including specifications, the design concept, and the boat's features, power requirements, and options are: 7 utility skiffs of traditional design (14' to 21'), 2 with transom motor mount and wood cross seats, 2 (with outboard well) which can be outfitted for rowing, hauling, or "sporting;" and 3 (with outboard well) in which the operator may work from the bow; 5 models of seasleds (18' to 26'), versatile seaworthy and rugged hulls with several bottom options, small outboard or inboard/outboard power requirements, and a house option for the 24' and 26' boats; 3 models of super seasleds, large versatile inboard/outboard hulls, with aft house and a variety of interior layouts, in 30' and 32' lengths with flat or dished bottoms; a versatile mid-size inboard/outboard heavy-water boat with house and trunk cabin for commercial use or pleasure in 24', 26', and 28' lengths; and a 15' "seatractor," a small, lightweight, tough, and maneuverable diesel-powered "workhorse skiff." Also included in the catalog are photos of boats in use, cross-section illustrations of bottom configurations, a reprint regarding Munson boats, and a personal experience story from the president of the firm, Bill Munson. "If your community or area requires a certain style of boat not currently available in welded aluminum, then contact us [Munson] for any of your design requirements."

NEW RIVER BOAT COMPANY, INC.

2007 S.W. 11th Street
Fort Lauderdale, Florida 33312
(305) 523-8220

Brochure, 7 pages; Price sheets (2). Free.

Similar in design to the New England trap-skiff, New River's "Sea Gypsy" is a traditional 23' displacement boat, both seaworthy and fuel efficient, constructed in fiberglass with internal stringers and a heavy bronze rudder and skeg. The boat will accept up to 20 hp and it is available as an open workboat, workboat with cuddy cabin, center console launch, gaff-rigged sloop, or full cabin cruiser. Hulls may also be purchased in various stages of completion. The brochure offers many large color photos of the boat mostly as an open workboat; profile illustrations of the other models, specifications, and some description are also given. One price sheet lists the various models, standard equipment, and engine options, while the second sheet lists prices for the partially complete hulls, engine assemblies, and a complete sailing kit.

JARVIS NEWMAN, MARINE BROKER
P.O. Box 1147
Main Street
Southwest Harbor, Maine 04679
(207) 244-5400

Four sets of informational sheets, 3 to 5 pages each. Free.
Newman builds and sells hand-laid-up fiberglass lobster boats, either completed or in kit form, in 32', 36', 38', and 46' sizes. The 38' and 46' boats were designed by Lowell and Spaulding, and the 38' model can be outfitted as a pleasure boat. Each set of sheets offers photos, side/top-view illustrations, specifications, and prices for one of the boats. Current price lists are available for the variety of used commercial fishboats which Newman sells; ranging from 21' to 65', they include lobster boats, musselers, scallopers, draggers, gillnetters, seiners, and combination boats.

NEXUS MARINE CONSTRUCTION
3816 Railway Avenue
Everett, Washington 98201
(206) 252-8330

Informational sheet. Free.
These long-time custom builders have fished Bristol Bay and construct 3 kinds of strong and durable skiffs of epoxy glue, marine plywood, appropriate hardwoods, and vertical grain Douglas fir. The Alaskan skiff and Alaskan power garvey are available in 22' set net or 28' cargo lengths, and the Carolina dory/skiff in 14'9" end skiff and 20' utility lengths. Side- and top-view illustrations of the Alaskan boats, a photo of the Carolina boat, specifications, and some construction information are provided on one side of the sheet; the other side shows a glossary illustration of a skiff cross-section, supplies additional specifications and construction details, and indicates the standard features and options available that allow a customer to tailor a skiff to the strength and durability desired.

NORTH END MARINE AND FIBERGLASS ENGINEERING, INC.
P.O. Box 342
Rockland, Maine 04841
(207) 594-8821

Two brochures, 14 pages in all; Informational sheets (4). Free.
Showing nice clear photos and generally listing only the barest information (specifications and standard

equipment/features) one brochure and the sheets individually present North End's fiberglass lobster tanks and the firm's stock boats built in fiberglass with foam flotation. Available are an 11'9" sailing dinghy complete with sails and rig; a more fully described and illustrated 28' dory complete with sailing equipment in daysailer or cuddy cabin models, or built with an outboard well; and a commercial fishing dory in a 28' cabin model or in 25', 28', or 35' seining models with optional outboard well. Another brochure, well-embellished with photos, briefly explains the firm's specialization in the design and building of plugs and molds for manufacturing sail and power boats, internal glass units, and headliners; provided is a list of recent projects including sailboards, rowing shells, and power and sailboats from 18' to 59'. Literature is also furnished for three recent projects, 18', 21', and 23' "Pointers," Pointer Corporation's open outboard fishing/utility boats with optional dodgers; the 23' boat is also designed for inboard power, and a cuddy cabin model is available. It is not clear whether the Pointers may be purchased from North End; for more information, contact Bill Legge, Pointer Corporation, Box 443, Yarmouth, Maine 04096; (207) 829-5248.

WILLIAM H. S. OEHRLE
2 Elwood Street
Acushnet, Maine 02743

List of boat plans; Letter. Free.
Mr. Oehrle, who has been around boats since he began walking, was a commercial fisherman for over twenty-five years, and has been designing boats and writing about them since 1934, now, in his retirement, offers plans for a variety of commercial fishing boats, including lobster boats, draggers, and combination boats from 26' to 57', mostly to be built of steel, but some of wood. Completely new designs, drawn to the customer's specifications, take him about a month. He cautions that his plans are not works of art. His list of boats indicates the length, construction material, and horsepower for each boat, and supplies additional information such as the person(s) for whom the boat was originally designed, or publications which feature the boat.

PAYNE & FRANKLIN, INC.
Aluminum Small Craft—Sail and Power
31 Hazard Avenue
North Kingstown, Rhode Island 02852
(401) 295-5149

Brochure, 11 pages; Informational sheets (3); Price sheet. Free.
Specializing in welded aluminum hulls and providing boats in any degree of completion from the bare hull on up, Payne and Franklin have designed and built a wide variety of boats ranging from 8' prams to 34' passenger launches, and additionally, a variety of aluminum structures such as simple brackets, radar support towers, control consoles, fuel tanks, mast-boom assemblies, and harvesting/sorting equipment for quahog divers. The sheets describe the firm's capabilities, and showing photos, list specifications and features of two stock boats: an 8' aluminum dinghy (85#) with two rowing positions, optional sailing kit, and outboard power capability up to 2

hp; and a heavy duty aluminum skiff with foam flotation in 14′, 15′10″, 17′6″, and 19′6″ lengths—the 19′6″ boat is also available in extra heavy duty aluminum, capable of handling up to 40 hp. The brochure describes at length the firm's passenger launches, modified garvey hulls approved by the U.S. Coast Guard. Some photos, specifications, and side- and top-view illustrations delineating interior layouts are provided for 22′ 10-passenger, 22′6″ 14-passenger, and 26′8″ 26-passenger inboard diesel launches (50 hp), a 32′3″ 34-passenger twin outboard model (85 hp), and a 44′ 49- passenger twin inboard diesel model (200 hp).

RICHARD S. PULSIFER
RFD 3—Mere Point Road
Brunswick, Maine 04011
(207) 725-5457/2243
Pamphlet, 6 pages; Reprints (2); Informational sheet. Free.
Powered by a 16 hp diesel inboard, Pulsifer's 22′ Hampton is built of white pine strip-planks with steam-bent oak frames and cedar floorboards, fastened with silicon bronze and copper. Pulsifer sometimes uses timber from the family wood lot. The completed boat includes all controls, instrumentation, and automatic bilge pump. The pamplet offers mostly photographs and a very general description of Pulsifer's Hampton and its inspiration, Charlie Gomes' Hamptons. The accompanying sheet goes into greater depth regarding the design evolution, construction, specifications, and standard features of the boat. A four-page article from *Small Boat Journal* (November 1979) and a two-page article from *Commercial Fisheries News* (February 1981), copies of which were provided with the other literature, go into still greater detail regarding the Hampton design, its strip-plank construction technique, and Pulsifer's contribution.

RAWSON, INC.
P.O. Box 83
9001 - 151st Avenue N.E.
Redmond, Washington 98052
(206) 885-4455
Brochure, 8 pages, Informational sheets (11); Two sets of sheets, 6 and 8 pages. Free.

In production for the last twenty-three years, Rawson boats are semi-custom fiberglass craft offered in kits from bare hulls to the complete boat. The brochure provides specifications, photos including interior shots, some profile and accommodation plans, and some design and performance information for a 32′ Bristol Bay gillnetter, 2 combination versions, and 34′ and 38′ Monk-designed seiner/gillnetters. Additional sheets present a diesel performance report for the 34-footer, offer profile and arrangement plans for each length boat, and list base boat prices, engine, machinery, and electronics options; one price sheet indicates the availability of 15′ and 18′ open set net skiffs, and a 24′ drift skiff in open and two cabin models, but no illustrations are provided. Sheet sets offer specifications, photos including interior shots, profile and accommodation plans, full description of features and components for a 30′6″ cruising yacht and a family

cruising liveaboard version; these boats may be obtained as bare hulls or as "Basic Builders" with additional option packages available.

SISU BOAT, INC.
Industrial Park
Dover, New Hampshire 03820
(603) 749-4452
Main brochure, 6 pages; Three additional brochures, 4 pages each. Free.
Designed by Royal Lowell, Sisu's 22′, 26′, and 30′ boats, available in various stages of completion, are strongly built of hand-laid fiberglass with balsa core, and they can be used for commercial or sport fishing, cruising, or as research vessels, yard boats, yacht tenders, skin diver boats, or island commuters. The smaller boat can be completed with forward cabin, rigid canopy, or folding top, and it will take inboard or outboard gas or diesel power. The two larger boats feature diesel inboards and forward cabins. The brochure provides photos, dimensions, and general descriptions of features and options for each boat. Individual brochures for each boat furnish a contract form, a statement of terms, fuller specifications, and an extensive list of color, cabin, deck, commercial fishing gear, and basic boat component options, most of which are priced. A Business Reply postcard is enclosed for the customer to complete when interested in more information.

TED'S RADONCRAFT, INC.
Point Hudson
Port Townsend, Washington 98368
(206) 385-2377/0581
Brochure, 4 pages. Free.
Designed and first built in Santa Barbara, California, for abalone-diving, the Radon boat is currently in use from California to Alaska for commercial fishing, sports, pleasure, and harbor patrol. Built in 15′ to 36′ lengths of indestructible multi-course fiberglass construction, Radoncraft are made to carry heavy loads at high speeds safely in any ocean condition. The boats are fitted out to

Payne & Franklin, Inc.   This roomy heavy gauge marine aluminum dinghy stands up to beaching on rocks, gravel, or shells. Gunwale fendering all around.

customer specifications. The brochure provides a general explanation of the basic boat and standard features, a side-view illustration of the hull, and photos of several sizes fitted out for trolling, gillnetting, and bowpicking. Some features such as engine and house type for some of these standard models, and optional equipment, are also listed. Demonstration rides are recommended.

TEXAS DORY-BOAT PLANS

Captain Jim Orrell
P.O. Box 720
Galveston, Texas 77553-0720

Informational sheets (4); Reprint; Order form. Free.

Captain Jim Orrell offers 51 plans for "gas-saver dory skiffs" such as bateaux, the Barnegat Bay sneak box, Cape Ann and Gloucester sailing dories, Carolina and Oregon dory/skiffs, Grand Banks and St. Pierre dories, Nahant surf and Sea Bright dories, sharpies, and more; some specifications and performance data are presented for 10 of the boats. Also available are 13 plans of John L. Hacker designs for runabouts, hydroplanes, and motor cruisers from 14' to 36', taking speeds up to 60 knots. The blue on white blueprints in new standard format of 17" × 22" on 70-pound paper are exact reproductions of original plans. Most of the designs specify marine-grade plywood for construction. For $15 an illustrated 200-page portfolio may also be obtained, which includes study sheets for 70 plans, and photos and performance data for completed boats. In addition to listing the plans available, the sheets show some photos of completed boats, offer excerpts of letters from customers regarding the construction and performance of two Carolina dory/skiffs, and present similar information for an Oregon dory/skiff, including a reprint from *National Fisherman* (January 1978) giving a good description of the boat modified for longlining.

F. L. TRIPP & SONS, INC.

Westport Point, Massachusetts 02791
(617) 636-4058

Catalog, 15 pages. Order form and price sheet. Free.

Offering numerous large photos, a side- and top-view illustration, and specifications, this generous catalog details the performance, layout, construction, features, and

standard equipment of a 22'2" open or cabin, inboard or outboard "Compleat Angler," and an 18'3" open outboard version, both of one-piece fiberglass construction with mat roving, polyester resin, heavy-duty plastic-covered marine fir plywood stringers, vinyl rubrails, bare-wood oiled teak trim, and bronze/chromed-bronze and stainless steel hardware. Designed for one-man bass, blues, and moderate offshore fishing, the larger boat can sleep two, and will take up to 200 hp. The smaller boat, designed for "sports fishing and other water pleasure," handles 40 to 85 hp and its shallow draft permits beaching and simple trailer loading. The price sheet lists much optional equipment and gives base costs for each model.

JOHN M. WILLIAMS COMPANY, INC.

Hall Quarry
Mt. Desert, Maine 04660
(207) 244-7854

Two brochures, poster format. Price sheet. Free.

These poster-type brochures furnish specifications, good photos, and large profile and interior layout drawings for a 45' gillnetter and a 36' commercial fishboat with several cabin options. Both boats are available as bare hulls or in any stage of completion. This literature provides only the barest information, obscurely indicating that the boats are built of fiberglass. The price sheet for the larger boat lists some construction details and options.

R. K. WILMES, BOATBUILDER

P.O. Box 192-Warner Road
East Haddam, Connecticut 06423
(203) 873-1051

No literature available.

Operating only a small shop, Wilmes builds and repairs wooden sail and power boats up to 40' in length. With the exception of a 17' stock launch, all boats are custom built to order only. The launches, also built to order, can be modified to a certain extent to suit the customer; the choice of gas or diesel engine governs the price of the boat. For description and pictures of the boat, Wilmes refers customers to the front cover of *Small Boat Journal* (October-November 1982) and an article appearing inside.

See also, under:

Canoes
  "Wet Dreams"
Small Open Boats
  Devlin
  Mystic
  North Shore
  Pan Pacific
  Payson
  Porter
  Rice Creek

Yachts
  Benford
  Crosby
  Dickerson
  Fibersteel
  Glen-L
  Hankinson
  Holland
  Legnos
  Liberty

  Luger
  Nordic Tugs
  Outer Reef
  Sprague
  Wittholz
Tools
  Morty
Books
  Hearst
  Woodenboat

Yachts and Cruisers—Power or Sail

Ted Brewer Yacht Designs, Ltd.   The Grand Banks 28.

A & T MARINE SERVICES, INC.
P.O. Box 1423
Tacoma, Washington 98401
(206) 584-8563

Brochure, 4 pages; Various informational sheets; Reprint. $2 (for handling).

This firm makes available Whisstock's of England 30' multi-chine W.E.S.T. system sailing cruiser, the NAJA, as a finished boat or as a kit offered in three stages of completion. Each kit includes "absolutely everything… down to the last nail and screw," and is designed to be assembled by nonprofessionals in less time than any other comparable kit. The brochure furnishes photos, top- and side-view illustrations, specifications, and information regarding the boat's design, performance, construction, and features. A reprint from *Sailing* (February 1982) provides similar information. One accompanying sheet set lists six pages of detailed specifications for kit and complete boat components; the other set presents prices, illustrations, a sample of an instruction sheet, and three pages of specifications and prices for optional equipment. A & T can reserve shop space for NAJA builders in Tacoma; temporary building shelters are also available. The firm has a network of subassemblers and dealers throughout North America who can offer building sites or who will construct the boat to any stage of completion.

JAY R. BENFORD
P.O. Box 399
Friday Harbor, Washington 98250
(206) 378-4244

Brochure, 2 pages; Form letter; Reprint; Order form. Free.
Benford's brochure, usually printed in the *Tiller,* lists almost 100 of his over 200 designs for which there are study plans or stock plans. Designs represent comfortable boats, many of wood and many of traditional design, from 8' and 11' sailing dinghies to a 131' ketch, and in addition include canoe yawls, catamarans, cat boats, skiffs, utility boats, dories, sloops, cutters, schooners, cruisers, motorsailers, trawler-yachts, and houseboats. The list indicates the material(s) of which each boat is to be built. Yacht design posters are also available for $5 a set and on the back contain additional information on study and stock plans. The brochure also provides a sample plan, testimonials from satisfied clientele and professionals, and information regarding plans, posters, Benford's pricing philosophy, and his construction cost estimates. A reprint from *Friday Harbor Journal* (October 4, 1978) presents a biographical sketch of Benford and discusses his designs. Benford also operates a marine brokerage, selling boats of his design and bartering gear, equipment, supplies, or other useful items. Inquiries regarding unlisted designs, used boats, or barter are welcome.

FRED P. BINGHAM
Yacht Design and Construction
249 Montana Way
Los Osos, California 93402
(805) 772-1623

Design catalog sheet. $1.50. Information packages on specific boats. $2.

Bingham offers study prints, plans, and in some cases, templates or paper patterns for 5 yachts: a 20' sloop, "Flicka," a 24' cruising cutter, "Allegra," and a 30' schooner or cutter, "Typee," to be built in C-Flex, a 28' yacht, "Victoria," for plywood construction, and a 29' steel cutter, "Isabella." The Allegra can also be built in wood, and complete, partially complete, or kit Allegras and kit Isabellas may be available on both coasts. The Design Catalog Sheet furnishes a profile, specifications, and construction information for the 5 boats. The information package for each boat offers specifications, more and larger illustrations including interior layouts and cross-sections, and discussion of the boat's design, performance, construction, accommodations, and plans. The Allegra package contains a reprint from *Cruising World* (May 1982) and a report from Bingham on progress made in licensing builders for the boat.

BLUE WATER BOATS, INC.
Jerry Husted
P.O. Box 625
Woodinville, Washington 98072
(206) 481-1303

Brochure, 8 pages; Pamphlet, 13 pages; Price sheet. Free.
Based on the classic lines of Colin Archer's Redningskoite, the "Ingrid 38," a 38' heavy-displacement, double-ended, fiberglass, heavy-weather, ocean-sailing ketch, is available from Blue Water part by part, or in several semi-complete packages. The brochure furnishes some photos, a side-view illustration, top-view illustrations of six representative interior layouts, and specifications for the boat, sails, and component parts. Also provided are

lengthy explanations of the boat's sailing characteristics, the firm's building philosophy, cost estimates and purchasing suggestions, and a list of recommended readings. The price sheet briefly lists the contents of each completion package. Study plans, a cutter rig sail plan, a catalog of Ingrid components ($1), and an "Interiors Sketch Book" ($5) are also available. The pamphlet, "Fiberglass Strength for Ocean Sailboats," reviews lamination methods used in the boating industry; other free information regarding boat strength is available.

TED BREWER YACHT DESIGNS, LTD.
217 Edith Point Road
Anacortes, Washington 98221
(206) 293-2282

Data sheet sets for each boat design, 3 pages each. Send large stamped self-addressed envelope. Book, 144 pages. $4.

Written in conjunction with designer Robert E. Wallstrom, Ted Brewer's *Cruising Designs* (New York: Seven Seas Press, 1976) presents chapters on cruising auxiliary hull design trends, layout, performance, power plants, and design selection. Specifications, side- and top-view illustrations, and at least a half page of design, construction, and performance information are also provided for each of 31 cruising auxiliary designs ranging from a 20' sloop and 21' Cape Cod catboat to a 56' schooner and 61' ketch—and 8 powerboat designs—from 18' and 20' outboard to 37' offshore cruisers; photos of a few of the boats are included. Hoping to inspire boats that are a pleasure to own, Brewer sells study plans and complete plans for these stock designs and new ones as they are completed. Upon request, Brewer will send 3-page data sheet sets for a specific model, and these include much the same information as is given in the book—a page of specifications and description, a page with an illustration of the boat's profile, and a page with top- and side-view illustrations showing interior layouts.

GEORGE BUEHLER
Yacht Design and Construction
P.O. Box 10279
Bainbridge Island, Washington 98110
(206) 783-8183

Catalog, 96 pages. $6.50.

Buehler designs mostly double-ended cruising sailboats of wood and steel for the home-builder, specializing in boats with a heavy-duty rather than a traditional look, and emphasizing simplicity of construction and a low price. His catalog presents advice on hull materials, building costs, and construction time; information on sailboat types, designs, performance, sail plans, and powerboats; and a description of his custom design service, his study plans, and his plans packages which include a 250-page construction manual. The catalog also furnishes specifications, construction and design information, and several side- and top-view illustrations, some showing interior layouts and structural members, for each of 26 stock designs which represent boats from 20' to 67', including a sloop, 8 schooners, 7 cutters, 2 cutter-ketches, a

ketch, yawl, yawl workboat, Block Island cowhorn turned cruising sailboat, a sailing barge, 2 cruising powerboats, and a motorsailer.

CHERUBINI BOAT COMPANY, INC.
P.O. Box 8
Roebling, New Jersey 08554
222 Wood Street
Burlington, New Jersey 08016
(609) 499-2200; 386-3342

Poster-brochure, 12 leaves; Informational sheet; Price list. Free.

Boatbuilders for three generations, the Cherubinis currently offer their hand-laid-up fiberglass yachts (with epoxy-saturated and fiberglass-sheathed wooden beams, bulkheads, decks, bulwarks, cabin sides, and bowsprit) in three stages of completion—a minimum structural package, a "ready for water, motoraway" package, and a fully rigged package, less the interior. Opening out to a full size print of a 44' Cherubini complete with specifications, the brochure, on the reverse side, provides photos of the boat and interior, a sail plan, an accommodation plan, various hull profiles, and details regarding the construction of the hull, deck, cabin, hardware, and mechanical and electrical systems. An additional sheet furnishes specifications, side/top-view illustrations, and design information for the firm's 48' staysail schooner. The price list specifies the three unfinished model packages available.

CLARK CRAFT BOAT COMPANY
16 Aqua Lane
Tonawanda, New York 14150-7787

Catalog, 56 pages; Order form. $1.

Clark Craft's sailboat catalog offers plans and patterns for over 50 sailboats, more than half of which are larger boats (18' to 70') with accommodations—yachts, Cross cruising trimarans—most of which are Bruce Roberts designs. Study prints, frame sets (completely assembled solid mahogany), or mold frame sets (cut but not assembled) are available for most of these boats, from the 14' to 21' trailer sailers on up. Frame sets are also available for 15'6" one-designs, 10' and 14' catamarans, an 18' Cross trimaran, and the 12' trailer sailer. Complete boat kits containing all parts minus hardware and optional accessories, may be obtained for most smaller boats—8' and 10' sailing dinghies, 12' sailboards, a 12' car-toppable sailboat, Snipe and Windmill one-designs, and a 14' catamaran. Various sail, spar, rigging, hardware, fiberglass, and paint kits may be purchased along with boat or frame kits for some of the smaller boats. A good number of the smaller boats are to be built of marine plywood, while larger boats call for fiberglass, foam-fiberglass, strip-plank, steel, or ferrocement constructions. The catalog furnishes general explanations of plan and pattern sets, frame sets and boat kits, and for each boat provides specifications, photos and/or illustrations, lists of kit/set contents, and usually some information regarding the performance, features, and design of the boat. Special prices are offered on some plan sets.

CLARK CUSTOM BOATS

3665 Hancock Street
San Diego, California 92110
(714) 297-2795

Brochure, 7 pages; Price lists. Free.

Offered in several stages of completion from bare hull to completely finished boat, Clark's "Clark 31" is a 30'2" hand-laminated fiberglass version of Francis Herreshoff's H-28 design, longer by means of a counter transom, wider on deck, deeper in section, with a taller more powerful rig and a higher ballast ratio to support it. The bulwarks are made of teak-capped mahogany, the bowsprit of Sitka spruce, boomkin of ash, hatches of teak, interior all of wood, and all hardware is bronze. The brochure furnishes specifications, construction details, an accommodation plan, and a profile illustration. The price sheets list the numerous completion packages and their contents.

CROSBY YACHT YARD, INC.

72 Crosby Circle
Osterville, Massachusetts 02655
(617) 428-6958

Brochure, 6 pages; Form letter; Price list. Free.

Crosby's newest offering is a 21' or 26' pleasure tug which, built of hand-laid-up fiberglass with heavy longitudinal stringers and heavy duty bronze skeg, can be built not only as a pleasure cruiser, but as a working tug, trawler, or open launch. Some standard models are available, but most work is custom. Partially completed tugs, hulls, and components may also be purchased. The price sheet outlines the various components available. The brochure furnishes numerous photos of versions of the boat and some interiors, offers profile and accommodation plans and specifications, and explains the design, construction, and power features of the boat. Established in 1850 and responsible for the Crosby catboat design, the firm also builds the 29' "Hawk," 30' "Canyon Runner," 32' "Wasque," 24' "Wianna Senior" one-design knockabout, and any hull to custom specifications and any degree of completion. Inquiries are welcome and quotes for custom work are given upon request.

CUSTOM STEEL HULLS

Ron Barnes
P.O. Box 1951
St. Augustine, Florida 32084
(904) 824-6643

Informational sheets (4). Free.

Operating a small, low-overhead business for maximum productivity and minimum aggravation, Ron Barnes and associates build bare steel hulls with steel decks, rudder, rudder post, engine bed and shaft log installed, for stock cruising sailboat designs. Steel house sides or tops are included with some of the models, and engine installations are possible, but generally the client is responsible for the interior finish work. The literature Barnes sends includes long discussions of steel yacht design and steel as a building material, plus designer Tom Colvin's comments on the performance of certain designs and on the use of auxiliary power for cruising yachts. Profile and interior layout illustrations, specifications, and some design information

are furnished for 4 Colvin designs—the 37' "Radian," 42' "Gazelle," and 51' "Pipistrelle" or "Memory." The firm has also built Weston Farmer's "Tahiti Ketch" and Philip Bolger's "Solution 48" in steel. Yard visits are welcome, but weekend tours must be arranged in advance.

Cherubini Boat Company, Inc.

DICKERSON BOATBUILDERS

R.D. 2, Box 92
Trappe, Maryland 21673
(301) 822-8556

Portfolio, includes two brochures, 6 and 8 pages; Price sheet. Free.

Specializing in 100% American-built traditional cruising ketches since 1946, and building workboats for Chesapeake Bay watermen for two generations, Dickerson provides brochures for a Hazen-designed 37' family cruising yacht with fiberglass-cored hull and decks, and a Kaufman-designed 50' fiberglass world class yacht. Each brochure offers a page of design criteria written by the designer, elaborate lists of specifications and standard equipment, and several side- and top-view illustrations. Photos are shown mostly on the portfolio jacket which also contains a brief explanation of the customer's involvement in the construction of a boat. The price sheet lists the base price for the 37' boat and specifies numerous options available. The boats are not available in kit form. Arrangements may be made to inspect the facilities and yachts under construction. Information packages are also available on Dickerson's charter service for cruising the Chesapeake aboard these boats.

EASTSAIL YACHTS

3 Rochester Neck Road
Rochester, New Hampshire 03867

Brochure, 5 pages. Free.

Built by Rumery's Boat Yard in Biddeford, Maine, and designed by Eliot Spalding, the "Eastsail 25" is a 25' rugged, tabloid world cruising cutter of traditional lines, carrying a full keel and full headroom, and designed for single handling. The hull is constructed of Airex-core sandwich fiberglass with stringers and bonded bulkheads; the cabin interior is finished in native and teak woods. The boat can be custom built to any requirements and components may be purchased at any stage of completion. The brochure provides specifications, illustrations showing sail plan and interior layouts, and brief descriptions of the boat's concept, design, designer, and performance, and the make-up of various components. One page furnishes some information regarding Rumery's, showing its location.

Crosby Yacht Yard, Inc.   The 24′ Crosby Stripper has a fiberglass hull with non-skid decks, teak trim, and molded protective keel and skeg.

EDEY & DUFF
Peter Duff, President
Harbor Road
Mattapoisett, Massachusetts 02739
(617) 758-2743

Booklet, 20 pages; Three brochures, 6 pages each; Poster-brochure. (There may be a charge.)

Edey and Duff sell directly to the customer, offering only in finished form a Bolger-designed 21′5″ open rowing-sailing cruiser, "Dovekie" (with Airex foam sandwich fiberglass hull, deck, bow and stern thwarts, stowage bins and rudder), a Crocker-designed 23′4″ fast cruising diesel auxiliary sloop, "Stone Horse" (with Airex PVC foam sandwich fiberglass hull and deck and teak or mahogany exterior trim), and reproductions of the Herreshoff-designed "Doughdish." Wishbones, discussed thoroughly in one brochure, are available for the sloop. The poster-brochure provides side/top-view and cross-sectional illustrations and many photos of the Dovekie, and furnishes specifications and much description of the boat's features, construction, performance, and design, most of which is excerpted from Bolger's *The Folding Schooner and Other Adventures in Boat Design,* available from the firm. A companion brochure provides a testimonial, a reprint from *Cruising World,* more photos and illustrations, and lists of standard equipment and options. A similar price list is provided for the Stone Horse along with a 20-page booklet which offers, in addition to specifications, many photos, and nice side/top-view illustrations, lengthy discussions of small cruising and racing boat characteristics and the Stone

Horse's size, accommodations, hull, cockpit, rigging, construction and materials, reefing methods, and auxiliary engine power. Visits are encouraged, but arrangements should be made in advance. Phone calls instead of letters are suggested for discussing questions; evening calls are fine. A Stone Horse is available for charter to experienced sailors.

FIBERSTEEL CORPORATION
Louis L. Watson, Jr.
1708 Ferndale Circle
West Sacramento, California 95691
(916) 371-4874

Brochure, 4 pages; Price sheet. Free.

Fibersteel makes available a 55′ sailing yacht, "Valeo," in a patented monolithic molded steel laminate ferrocement construction, which has been fitted out as a schooner, ketch, motor yacht, and fishing trawler. Structurally complete, sea ready, and fully complete versions are available. The brochure supplies specifications, photos, construction information, and success stories of disaster-stricken boats. The price sheet shows top/side-view illustrations, lists features, and specifies the equipment and structural members included in the various boat outfits.

FLAT POINT BOAT COMPANY, INC.
1112 N.E. 177th
Portland, Oregon 97230

Brochure, 4 pages; Reprint; Cruise report. Free.

Flat Point Boat Company markets "The Dipper," a fuel-efficient, 16′ trailerable, two-person, cruising tug with sailing capabilities, designed by Samuel Devlin and built of wood using the W.E.S.T. system. The reprint from *Nor'Westing* (March 1982), shows a profile and gives a description of the boat. Flat Point's brochure lists specifications, presents performance data, and describes the boat's features with the use of numerous photos of the boat and its interior. The boat is designed to take a 10 hp outboard. The cruising report shows that the boat used 13 gallons of fuel going 123 miles in 25 hours travel time spread over 6 days.

GLEN-L MARINE DESIGNS
P.O. Box 756
9152 Rosecrans
Bellflower, California 90706
(213) 630-6258

Catalog, 146 pages; Brochure, 24 pages; Order forms and price lists. $2.

This catalog begins with thirteen pages explaining Glen-L's plans and patterns; frame, fastening, hardware, rigging, spar, and fiberglass-covering kits; several boatbuilding books; and plywood/wood, fiberglass, and steel constructions. Remaining pages furnish specifications, good illustrations, some photos, and good descriptions for almost 200 boats, including paddleboards, sailboards, canoes and kayaks, sailing dinghies, small sailboats and sloops, overnight and cabin sloops, cruising sailboats and motorsailers, small rowboats, John boats and duck boats, rowing and power dories, drift boats, utility boats, runabouts, hydroplanes, racers, ski and sports/bass boats, power cats, houseboats and modules, mini-cruisers, cabin cruisers, cruising yachts, and power workboats. Accompanying price lists indicate graphically and clearly what kinds of plan packages or kits are available for each boat. Trailer plans are also available with the purchase of a construction guide. The boatbuilding supplies brochure offers a variety of boatbuilding books, marine glues, and fiberglass materials, resins, planking, foam, and tools; fastenings, fittings, hardware, and aluminum spars; steering systems and powerboat fins, all fairly well described and often illustrated or photographed. The firm has been in business for thirty years.

Edey & Duff   The Stone Horse, a fast cruising diesel auxiliary sloop. *Photo:* Norman Fortier.

HMS MARINE, INC.
904 W. Hyde Park Boulevard
Inglewood, California 90302
(213) 674-4540
Brochure, 4 pages; Price sheet. Free.

A responsive, but not a quick boat, the 15′ trailerable West Wight Potter, a cabin sloop described as "a pocket cruiser for the first-time builder," is constructed in hand-laid-up fiberglass with foam flotation and molded from an English-built wooden original. She is offered complete with sails, rigging and quite a bit of equipment; the price sheet lists standard features and optional accessories and on the back furnishes a profile illustration, photo, specifications, and performance, design, and construction information. The accompanying brochure, a reprint from *Trailer Boats Magazine* (March 1979), provides more photos, many of the interior, and a favorable report of a test run with one of the boats. The firm also sells

"Docsteps," hand-laid-up fiberglass boarding steps in two-, three- and four-step models with integral storage compartments and optional handrails.

KEN HANKINSON, NAVAL ARCHITECT
P.O. Box 2551
La Habra, California 90631
(213) 947-6862
Catalog, 34 pages; Order form and price sheet. $2.

Hankinson, in business since 1961, prefaces his catalog with a discussion of steel, plywood/wood, and fiberglass construction materials and methods. Good descriptions, specifications, nice illustrations and some photos are provided for 3 power dories (22′ to 27′), 7 workboats (21′ to 42′), 4 cabin cruisers (24′ to 38′), 8 trawler-yachts (24′ to 49′), and 17 sailing yachts (19′ to 49′), most of which are also represented in Glen-L's catalog. Hankinson only offers plans/patterns, and for some of his boats, study prints. Boat trailer plans including a construction manual are available as well as several "how to" books. A plans purchase includes, free upon request, consultation, power and propeller recommendations, a lumber supplies listing, and boatbuilder references. Questions regarding designs listed in the catalog, custom modifications, or custom designs, are welcome.

Glen-L Marine Designs   The Vee Gull 20, with it's full walkaround deck, is an ideal boat for the serious fisherman.

JACK A. HELMS COMPANY, INC.
P.O. Drawer A
Highway 60 West
Irmo, South Carolina 29063
(803) 781-5133
Two brochures, 4 pages each; Informational sheets (4); Price sheet. Free.

Noted for its quality craftsmanship, this firm offers 24′, 27′, and new 32′ sailing yachts designed by Stuart Windley and built with one-piece hand-laid-up fiberglass hulls and integral molded sheer knuckle for longitudinal strength. One brochure describes the "Helms 24" and the other the "Helms 27," furnishing construction information, full lists of specifications and standard features, a photo, and sail, inboard profile, and accommodation plans. Similar but less information is provided on two sheets for the 32′ model. Prices for many options on the 24′ and 27′ boats are listed on the price sheets. A testimonial letter and reprint praise the boats, the business, and the owner. Customers are referred to dealers or owner-representatives where available, but direct sales are possible in more areas than not.

HERITAGE BOAT COMPANY
1331 Country Club Road
Hood River, Oregon 97031
(503) 386-1526

Five brochures; Informational sheet. Free.

Heritage Boat Company offers repair and restoration services in addition to building sailboats. The literature covers a range of boats including a sailing "El Toro," a 20' cruising Cape Cod catboat and 22' knockabout, both Benford designs, a Martin-based Redline 24, and 26' and 30' Yankee auxiliary cruisers. Except for the El Toro which is built of marine plywood, these boats are constructed in hand-laid-up fiberglass with a glass-to-resin ratio between 40% and 48%. The El Toro, described only with a price sheet, lists standard features and options. Two fancy brochures describe the Benford boats, furnishing numerous sail plan, profile, and interior layout drawings along with specifications and information regarding obtaining the boats in semi-complete stages; a price list for the catboat indicates the completion packages, their components, and study plans available. While the brochure on the Redline 24 provides a profile, a pricing summary, and several pages of kit specifications and options, the boat is apparently available only through dealers. Various top/side-view illustrations and descriptions of the contents of the various completion packages are included in the sheet sets for each Yankee model. The customer's participation is a must in determining how these boats will be finished. A business reply form is available for requesting additional information or periodic mailings from the firm.

HOLLAND MARINE DESIGN
J. P. Hartog
3510 Geary Boulevard
San Francisco, California 94118
(415) 387-3110

Booklet, 18 pages; Inserts (9). There may be a price.

Presenting only a small selection of Hartog's stock designs, the booklet provides specifications, sail plans, profiles, and sometimes views of the interior layout and cross-section, for a variety of boats which have been constructed in wood, steel, or ferrocement by amateur builders. Complete building plans, including hydrostatic and stability curves plus standard conditions of loading for most commercial designs, are available ($40 to $350 postpaid) for sailing sloops, ketches, and cutters (21' to 62'), 26' sports fishing boats, and a number of commercial fishboats (26' to 100') including gillnetters, combination types, trawlers, crabber-packers, and motorsailing albacore boats. Plans are available for other designs as well as custom designs, and all requests for further information will be promptly and gladly answered.

LEGNOS BOAT BUILDING COMPANY, INC.
973 North Road, Route 117
Groton, Connecticut 06340

Three brochures; Price lists. Free.

These brochures offer photos, some in color, side- and top-view illustrations, specifications, and design, performance, and construction data for three fiberglass boats, a 20' cat- or sloop-rigged yacht, a 30' cutter, and a 35' sports or commercial fishing boat. The price sheets list standard and extra equipment for each boat. Its hull built with an Airex or Klegecell PVC core, and braced with plywood bulkheads and laminated hull and engine stringers, the fiberglass fishing boat can be built to any stage of completion and outfitted or varied to the customer's specifications. Large enough to permit a generous working area, this fuel-efficient boat will take a 130 to 300 hp diesel. This boat can be delivered for an additional charge. A 15' catboat is also available. Shop visits are welcome weekdays from 8 P.M. to 4:30 P.M.; Saturday appointments must be arranged. Price quotes are made in accordance with the customer's specifications.

LETCHER OFFSHORE DESIGN
P.O. Box 104
Southwest Harbor, Maine 04679
(207) 244-7347

Informational sheets (5); Reprints (4). Free.

Letcher sells stock plans ($250 to $295) including full-size patterns for his "Aleutka" long-distance cruiser design in 25' and 29' lengths, double-ended, twin-keeled cutters to be built with a "batten-mold" method. The design, performance, building technique, and the use of oars only as auxiliary power are elaborated in reprints of Letcher's contributions to *Cruising World,* the *Mariner's Catalog,* and *National Fisherman.* This literature, of course, provides

Glen-L Marine Designs   Deck and arrangement plan for the Lodestar on this and the following page.

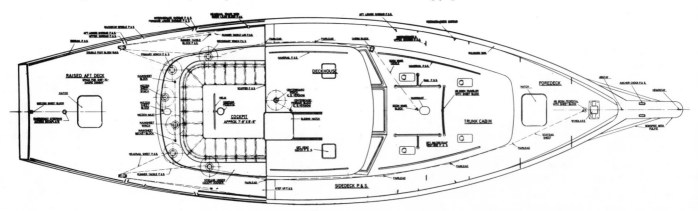

photos and some side/top-view illustrations of the 25-footer; the sheet announcing the availablity of plans for the boats furnishes specifications as well as sail, accommodation, and deck plans, and lists of features and package contents.

Letcher also offers a computer lofting service for naval architects and boatbuilders, defining computer lofting as "a full-sized body plan produced on a computer-controlled x-y plotter from a mathematical representation of the three-dimensional shape of a hull, embodied in a computer program... in effect it fairs the plan and profile views internally...," and explaining in five pages the kinds of fairline lofting or fitting procedures available, their use to marine architects and builders, and pricing and negotiating practices. Another sheet, his "Software Catalog," indicates prices for several design programs; a one-page brochure is available for each program, free with self-addressed stamped envelope. Letcher also sells his books on celestial navigation and on self-steering. Aleutka 25 hull/deck kits are available from P & M Worldwide.

LIBERTY YACHT CORPORATION
Route 2, Box 548
Leland, North Carolina 28451
(919) 371-3999
Brochure, 4 pages; Price sheet. Free. Study blueprints. $6.
Offering a safe working platform in all conditions, with ample backup power in a 15 horsepower diesel, Liberty's "Pied Piper 28" cruising yacht (27′9″) easily holds 6 to 7 knots in breezes. The firm's brochure provides specifications, top- and side-view illustrations (top includes interior layout), several photos mostly of the interior, construction and performance details, and lists of the completed boat's exterior equipment and hardware, engine and electrical parts, rudder and centerboard features, and interior appliances, furnishings, and layout. Several kit options are also explained: bare hull, fiberglass parts, custom sailaway, and power option. The price sheet lists numerous options available, ranging from electronics and interior furnishings to sails and rigging for the completed boat, and from rough-cut parts to sails for kits. Liberty's 8′6″ dinghy, discussed in *Small Open Boats,* page 26, is available at a reduced price with the purchase of a complete Pied Piper 28.

LOOMIS YACHTS
Lyon Loomis
P.O. Box 575
South Dartmouth, Massachusetts 02748
(617) 999-3200
Brochure, 4 pages; Form letter; Price sheets (2). Free.
Available from Loomis Yachts is the C. W. Paine design, "Sarah 32," a 34′3″ double-ended world class cruiser of moderate displacement, with hull and deck solidly constructed of hand-laid-up fiberglass and interior finished in hardwoods. Two owner-completion packages are also offered—a basic package consisting of the hull and deck with ballast and rudder installed, and a sailaway package which includes a roughed-in interior, the engine, sails, spars, rigging, and a variety of deck hardware and exterior teak trim and accessories. The brochure provides specifications, profile, sail and accommodation plans, and information regarding the boat's design, performance, and construction. The price sheets detail the contents of the completion packages as well as options and sailing equipment for the completed boat. Custom modifications are standard procedure; each "Sarah" is unique.

LUGER INDUSTRIES, INC.
3800 West Highway 13
Burnsville, Minnesota 55337
(612) 890-3000
Catalog, 48 pages; Order form. $1.
Luger Industries, in business for thirty years, offers all-fiberglass, trailerable boats in kit form requiring only final assembly and finishing touches that anyone can do; basic or "interior included" kits are available for boats over 16′. The boats—8′ International Optimist, 14′ Olympic-type competition sailboat, 11′ and 12′ car-toppable sailboats, 15′ all-purpose outboards, 15′ and 16′ high performance runabouts, 16′ weekender sloop, 16′, 21′, 26′, and 27′ sailing cruiser-racers, 30′ sloop/ketch, 30′ motorsailer, and 26′ sportsfisher with pilothouse option — receive extensive coverage including numerous illustrations, color photographs, and lists of specifications and optional equipment. Trailers partially or fully assembled, sails and rigging, rails, pulpits, deck hardware, windshields, running and interior lights, cabin windows,

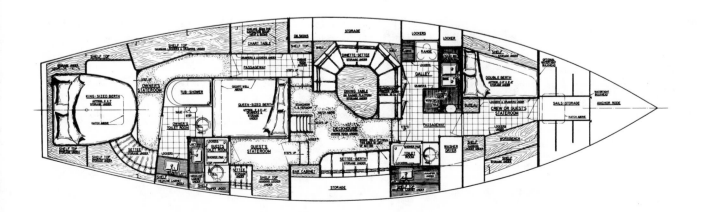

galley and head equipment, steering systems, motor mounts, and convertible tops are among the items available for specific models at additional cost.

MARSHALL MARINE CORPORATION
P.O. Box P-266
South Dartmouth, Massachusetts 02748
(617) 994-0414

Brochure, 6 pages; Informational sheets (4). Free.

Marshall Marine offers three catboat designs, based on exhaustive research and study of famous catboats, and built with one-piece fiberglass hull and deck. One sheet offers photos, a profile illustration, and specifications for a 15′6″ Sandpiper model with aluminum spars and varnished oak trim; a trailer, outboard motor, and outboard bracket are available. More information is provided for the 18′2″ "Sanderling" class catboat

Luger Industries, Inc.   Offerings include: 1) the Tradewinds 26, has full cruising accommodations for five, 2) the Voyager 30, 3) the Seabreeze 16.

including—besides photos and a sail plan—an accommodation plan, lists of standard and optional equipment, and description of the boat's design, features, and performance; the boat sleeps two and is built with foam flotation. Larger photos, including some interior shots, and two sail plans are furnished along with accommodation plans, specifications, and lists of optional and standard features in the brochure for the 22′2″ cat which can sleep four and be sloop- or cat-rigged.

MOONEY MARINE, INC.
Route 33, P.O. Box 280
Deltaville, Virginia 23043
(804) 776-6392

Brochure, 8 pages; Reprints (4). Free.

Mooney Marine, a leading builder of quality steel cruising yachts, offers the Wittholz-designed "Departure 35," a 35′ full-keel, moderate-displacement, steel cruising cutter which may be ketch-rigged. The boat is available in owner-completion packages from the completed hull to a sailaway/motoraway package. Interiors for completed boats are built on a semi-custom basis, and the literature shows two arrangements. In addition to providing sail, profile, and accommodation plans, the literature offers specifications, information regarding the boat's design, performance, and construction details, and five pages justifying steel as a building material. Reprints from *Cruising World* (June 1982), *Sail* (May 1982), and *Sailing* (July 1982) show photos of the boat and round out its description.

NORDIC TUGS
P.O. Box 314
Woodinville, Washington 98072
Boatyard: (206) 481-5502

Pamphlet, 8 pages; Price sheets (2); Plan sheets (2); Color photo sheet. Free.

Built by the same crew that builds Blue Water Boats' Ingrid 38, the 26′4″ fiberglass Nordic tug is a roomy, fuel-efficient, semi-displacement boat available in workboat, sports, and cruiser models. The boat is available complete or in parts, outlined on one price sheet; any engine from 36 to 100 hp may be chosen. The pamphlet and other price sheet together provide profile and accommodation plans, specifications, and lists of standard features for each model, along with general information regarding the boat's features and options. Large profile and accommodation plans for each model and color photos of two boats are pictured on the additional sheets. A form is included for requesting a set of color prints of the tug's interior and complete specifications ($5), and information about an air-fare policy to visit the plant and ride a tug; one can also ask to be put on the mailing list and kept informed about special offers.

NORTH CAROLINA STEEL BOAT COMPANY
Gavin Frost
Route 1, Box 400
Bayboro, North Carolina 28515
(919) 745-5272

A "fistful of miscellaneous bumf"—Informational sheets (13). Free.

Offering "twenty to sixty feet of rugged fireproof hull," these custom builders like to build to a known designer or to their own plans. A 10-page prospectus devotes four pages to "some thoughts on steel," a page to the company's executives, and remaining pages to descriptions and costs of several stock hulls ranging from a Roberts 40' "Spray" and Colvin's 42' "Gazelle" to the firm's 57' yachts; other stock hulls include a 26' dory, 29' racing sharpie, 2 Herreshoff sharpies (34' and 47') and 2 cruising ketches (32' and 34'). Completed versions of at least the 57' yacht and a 50' Gazelle are available, and color photos, various illustrations, specifications, lists of features, and a personal story about rebuilding a Gazelle are provided on additional sheets. Estimates are supplied free on these standard vessels. Yvonne Frost's subsidiary, Woven Wings, produces fabric cruising sails for the firm as well as other customers, typically at $4 per square foot.

OUTER REEF MARINE
P.O. Box 1865
Bradenton, Florida 33506
(813) 722-8963

Brochure, 4 pages; Informational sheets (6); Price list. Free. Scale drawings. $3.

Outer Reef builds and sells 26' and 32' hand-laid-up fiberglass, stable, hard-chine, fuel-efficient trawlers in yacht or workboat versions in any stage of completion, from bare hull to completed boat. The brochure shows the 26' yacht (69 hp) in color photos and accommodations plan, also listing specifications, features, and standard equipment. A companion sheet offers a profile and accommodation plan for the work boat. The two 32' versions (80 hp) also receive a page each of profile and accommodation plans and a page of specifications and features. A price list details the costs of the 32' boats' components. Purchase of a kit boat includes shop drawings and prints. Customers are invited to visit the shop on a regular basis to watch their boats being built. Since all vessels are custom-built, each boat may be modified to the owner's specifications; such features as flying bridges, aft cabin enclosures, and extended houses are possible.

P & M WORLDWIDE INC.
P.O. Box 10281
Costa Mesa, California 92627
(714) 548-6617

Informational sheets, (3). Free.

Trying to minimize the many indirect costs of boatbuilding, this company offers fiberglass parts kits including the hull and deck and "basic builder's units" with ballast, bulkheads, and deck installed for the "Aleutka 26," "Westsail 32," "Cruising 36," "Westsail 39," and "Columbia 50." These boats are also available in more complete stages, but subcontractors finish them beyond the basic builder's unit stage; quotations must be given for completed boats after detailed discussion with prospective buyers. P & M's sheets show very small sail and accommodation plans for each boat, detail the firm's building and selling philosophy, and list kits/units available and their basic contents. More specific information must be requested at a price: further information regarding a specific boat costs $2, while a sail plan and interior blue print costs $5. The firm also operates

a parts service "whereby major items (masts, rigging, engines, etc.) are provided at O.E.M. cost plus 10%."

C. W. PAINE YACHT DESIGN, INC.
P.O. Box 763
Camden, Maine 04843
(207) 372-8147

Brochure, 8 pages. $3.50.

Paine sells study plans and fully detailed construction plans for his stock designs, refers customers to several boatbuilders who offer his boats completely or partially finished, and also works with customers to create custom designs. His brochure provides small photos, profile-accommodation plans, and design and performance information for thirteen production designs ranging from a 23' Down East schooner, 24' catboat, and popular 26' double-ended "Frances" to 30' long-distance, 32' luxury, 36' high-performance offshore, and 42' bluewater cruisers; plans and kits are available for only some of these boats. Additional information explains Paine's stock, production, and custom designs in general, and briefly presents Paine's design experience and philosophy.

Nordic Tugs   Cruiser tug model.

BRUCE ROBERTS
35 Belleview Drive
Severna Park, Maryland 21146
(301) 544-4311

Catalog, 120 pages; Seasonal sales literature; Order form and price sheet. Free.

Embellished with testimonials from owners and color photos of owner-built Roberts' boats, this catalog provides specifications, profile and accommodation plans, and some description of over forty Roberts' designs, mostly sailing yachts from 19' to 64' including the "Spray" series (21' to 40'), and some sportsfisher/ cruiser/ trawler-yachts, including the Waverunner series (20' to 56'). Building plans are available for all of the boats, and for only some of the boats there are study plans, steel hull and deck kits and fiberglass hull materials packages. Each plan set includes all versions of the design, all of its sail plans, information regarding all construction methods for the material in which the boat is to be built, and design sheets showing how to make tools, fittings, a self-steering vane, mast, dinghy, and trailer (for trailerable boats). Technical advice is offered free at all times with a plans purchase, and custom designs are available. Sixteen pages of the catalog are devoted to describing a variety of building materials, methods, and tools. Boatbuilding books, navigation equipment, interior and exterior hardware and appliances, sails, standard rigging kits, mast kits, and deck hardware kits may also be obtained. Specials are offered from time to time on plans, kits, full boats, and various equipment.

Bruce Roberts   Interior and side-view of the Roberts Power Sailer - 369.

RODGERS YACHT & DESIGN, INC.
4501 Ulmerton Road
Clearwater, Florida 33520
(813) 577-2662
Four informational sheet sets, 3 to 5 pages each. Free.

Sold complete, with various comforts and racing equipment costing extra, Rodgers' stock hand-laminated fiberglass yachts include a 24′ trailerable centerboard cruiser/club racer, a 26′ racing "cruising machine," a champion 33′ racer with custom-specified rig-type and deck layout, and a related 33′ racer/cruiser. The 33′ boats receive the greatest coverage in the literature: in addition to the specifications, illustrations of the profile and interior arrangements, and description of the boat's performance, features of each boat's hull, deck, mast and rigging, engine, controls, electrical system, and cabin are provided; additional features are indicated for the cruiser's galley and racing package option. Specifications, illustrations, some performance information, but no construction information, are given for the 24′ and 26′ yachts; lists of standard and optional equipment (including a trailer) and racing package components are listed for the 24′ boat. These boats are sold factory-direct, but they may be available through dealers in some areas.

McKIE W. ROTH, JR., ASSOCIATES
P.O. Box 50
Bath, Maine 04530
Informational sheet. Free.

Possessing twenty-five years of wooden boatbuilding experience, Roth currently offers complete plans for 22′, 25′, and 29′ Friendship sloops to be built with cedar or mahogany planking. The descriptive sheet provides small photos, a variety of plans and drawings, and some description of the "typical" Friendship sloop along with dimensions and construction specifications for the 22′ model. A folio of study plans for twenty wooden boat designs, power and sail, ranging from 10′ to 40′ is forthcoming.

RYDER CUSTOM YACHTS
47 Gooding Avenue
Bristol, Rhode Island 02809
(401) 253-8554
Portfolio, 23 pages; Price lists. Free.

The largest and most experienced builder of semi-completed fiberglass yachts in North America, Ryder offers, in three completion packages, a 22′6″ Alberg design, the 24′ Brewer "Quickstep," 28′ and 34′ Luders yachts, and 30′, 34′6″, 35′, and 43′ Gillmer designs. The basic brochure explains Ryder's completion program and packages and the designs available, furnishing some photos. Enclosed sheets provide specifications and sail, profile, and accommodation plans for each boat. A pamphlet included for each design lists the contents of each completion package as well as options.

SANFORD BOAT COMPANY, INC.
Lower Pleasant Street
Nantucket, Massachusetts 02554
(617) 228-4108
Brochure in poster format; Two booklets, 8 and 17 pages; Various informational sheets; Reprint. Free.

The mass of literature regarding the 26′ Alerion, designed by N. G. Herreshoff to be his personal sailboat, and offered complete by Sanford in composite keel construction (cold-molded mahogany and cedar with "metallic keel centerline structure") provides many large, handsome photos, profiles, and line drawings of the boat along with a full discussion of specifications and lengthy explanations of the boat's origin, design, reproduction, construction, and rig. Another lump of literature describes at length composite keel construction and attacks fiberglass construction, with the aid of illustrations, photos, and charts comparing various building materials. The remaining sheets feature Sanford's 44′ "Shadow Class" and 51′ "Magic Class" sailing cruisers, offering profile and accommodation plans, specifications, and descriptions of features.

SCHOONER CREEK BOAT WORKS
Steven Rander
6740 N.E. 42nd
Portland, Oregon 97218
(503) 287-2800
Catalog, 10 pages; W.E.S.T. systems brochure, 16 pages; Various informational sheets; Price sheet. Free.

One of the largest Oregon builders of high-quality custom yachts, Schooner Creek handles both cruising and high performance orders up to 60 feet, using W.E.S.T. system products and techniques, and offering repair work in wood and fiberglass. Stock designs available include 6½' and 12' sailing dinghies, an 18' canoe yawl, William Garden's 24' daysailer/ weekender, a 24' Friendship sloop, and a 42' ocean racing sloop. Side-view illustrations and brief lists of features and standard equipment are provided for the 3 small boats; a photo and specifications are given for the Garden boat along with lengthier information about the boat's design, performance, and construction; specifications, sail plan, inboard profile, accommodation plan, and some design and construction information are furnished for the 2 sloops. The firm acts as Northwest distributor of W.E.S.T. system products and will furnish the full range of official literature including the product catalog and study sheets for boats for which there are plans. Skookum fasteners are also available.

SHANNON BOAT COMPANY, INC.

P.O. Box 388
19 Broad Common Road
Bristol, Rhode Island 02809
(401) 253-2441

Three brochures, 13 to 18 pages each; Reprints (2). Free.

Building only a limited number of semi-custom cruising yachts each year, Shannon currently offers in completed form a 28' cutter, 38' cutter or ketch, 38' pilot cutter, and 50' ketch, with one-piece hand-laid-up fiberglass hulls. Each length boat is well covered in one of the brochures with plenty of photos (including interior shots), sail plan, drawings of several interior layouts, detailed lists of specifications, features, and standard equipment, and considerable discussion of the boat's construction, hull design, interior and deck layouts, and rig; reprints from *Yachting* (June 1980) and *Sail* (January 1982) furnish more information, photos, and illustrations. Building standards for the Shannon 28—which was conceived as a rugged bluewater cruising vessel, practical in price and size — exceed specifications found on many 40' production sailboats. The boat can easily be handled by one person, and the cockpit will seat six adults comfortably and sleep two. Visits to the shop to examine the building process are encouraged. A 4-page quarterly newsletter *The Shannon Scroll* is available, offering news of Shannon boats, their owners and builders, and announcing used boats for sale.

SOUTH COAST MARINE

788 W. 16th Street
Costa Mesa, California 92627
(714) 646-5445

Three informational sheet sets, 2 pages each. Free.

South Coast Marine offers kits of custom-complete "Westsail 32s" and "Westsail 39s," supplied with "basic builder's units" (hulls, decks, and fiberglass parts) from P & M Worldwide. South Coast's literature lists two pages of deck and interior features and standard mechanical, electrical, plumbing, navigation, and safety equipment for each completed yacht. As indicated in the third set of sheets, the firm sells a number of interior and exterior

fixtures such as teak dorade boxes, boom gallow parts, laminated wood davits, teak light covers, doors and drawers, in standard and custom sizes, developed as a result of the builders' custom woodworking experiences. Custom woodworking and complete marine services are also offered and references are available for custom work.

SCOTT B. SPRAGUE

P.O. Box 10635
Bainbridge Island, Washington 98110
(206) 842-5003

Design booklet, 30 pages. $7.50.

Sprague makes available builder's plans, whose price includes consultation during construction, and study plans which are full-size blueprints, for a number of stock designs including a 24' plywood or planked tug and utility boat, 30' motorsailer, 34' fishing and inland cruising vessel, 35' trawler-style inland cruiser, 21' schooner, 35' V-bottomed traditional sailboat (plywood, plank, or steel), 29' foam- fiberglass cutter, a 33' wood-strip plank cutter, 37' and 39' steel cutters, 38' steel junk, and a 42' modern cruising cutter. His design booklet provides sheets of sail/ profile and accommodation plans for most of these boats, accompanied with sheets giving design, performance, and some construction details for the tug, motorsailer, cutters, and junk. Preliminary drawings are also enclosed for a 30' daysailer, 29' and 35' cruising yachts, 40' schooner, 44' inland cruiser, and a 49' motor vessel. Sprague is willing to modify stock designs to individual requirements and he will work with customers to create custom designs.

Sanford Boat Company, Inc.   The 26' Alerion with composite keel construction (cold-molded mahogany and cedar with metallic keel).

SUNWARD YACHT CORPORATION

8118 Market Street
Wilmington, North Carolina 28405
(919) 686-7532

Brochure, 6 pages; Color photo. Free.

Producing only 2 custom boats a year, Sunward Yachts offers only a 48' heavy-displacement, full-keel cruising ketch, a Sparkman and Stephens design, constructed in hand-laid fiberglass. Custom partially-completed versions are available. The brochure furnishes specifications, photos including interior shots, double-spreader-rig sail plan, plans for two interior layouts, performance characteristics, and a detailed list of features, standard equipment, and construction details.

WESTLAWN ASSOCIATES
Montville, New Jersey 07045
Brochure, 10 pages. $1.

Originally prepared fifty years ago and based on a Dutch type used for centuries on the turbulent North Sea, Westlawn's Grey Dawn ocean-going auxiliary designs are available in plans for 16' and 22' roughwater and 29' and 37' long-distance versions with various rigs. Specifications and sail and accommodation plans are provided for each model along with brief information regarding the design and accommodations. A general introductory statement explains the evolution and characteristics of the design, likening it to a Down East/Gloucester dory without its snappy roll.

WINDJAMMER YACHTS
P.O. Box 5782
Huntington Beach, California 92646
(714) 556-8920
Brochure, 4 pages; Form letter. Free.

Windjammer currently offers a one-piece, hand-laid-up fiberglass hull, a molded, one-piece, hand-laid-up fiberglass flush deck, and a fiberglass rudder for a 34' classic Colin Archer cruising yacht design which combines maximum seaworthiness with comfort and spaciousness below decks. The hull purchase includes blueprints, drawings, and free consultation, and all major hardware components are available to assemblers at a discount. The brochure furnishes specifications, some description, and numerous illustrations, including profiles and interior layouts. Inquiries and plant visits are welcome; there are openings for "Windjammer 34" representatives.

CHARLES W. WITTHOLZ, NAVAL ARCHITECT
100 Williamsburg Drive
Silver Spring, Maryland 20901
(301) 593-7711
Catboat design booklet, 13 pages. $2. "Wittholz Designed, Chesapeake Built" catalog, 14 pages. $2. "Motor Yachts" catalog, 28 pages. $4.

Specializing in small craft design, this firm offers a variety of plans for the professional and amateur builder for construction of sailboats, powerboats, workboats and fishing boats. The catboat booklet, introduced with a discussion of the catboat's evolution and characteristics, and concluded with reports from owners, provides specifications, some photos, sail plans, inboard profiles, accommodation plans, and construction and design information for 9 catboats ranging from 14' to 29' and including plywood, fiberglass, round-bottomed, and sloop-rigged versions; plans are sold for the construction of one boat only. The "Wittholz Designed" catalog furnishes specifications, plans, and descriptions of numerous designs that have been built by independent boat builders on the Chesapeake, traditionally of wood planking, but also with more recent materials; designs shown include sloops, ketches, sailing, diesel, cabin, and fishing cruisers, trawler yachts, cruising tugs, river tour and party boats, and a diesel houseboat, with lengths ranging from 16' to 58' (although a 230' steel bark is in the works)—prices are available upon request for these designs. The motor yacht booklet lists some of the builders with whom Wittholz has worked, offers some advice about motor yachts and their construction, and presents the usual specifications, illustrations, photos, and descriptions of 22 boats from 32' to 66', including a variety of cruisers and cruising tugs, motorsailers and trawler yachts, trawlers and sports fishing boats.

WORLDCRUISER YACHT COMPANY
1300 Logan Avenue
Costa Mesa, California 92626
(714) 549-9331
Four brochures, 4 pages each; Informational sheets (4); Reprint. Free.

Using the fiberglass hulls and decks available for production designs, Worldcruiser offers the customer a custom yacht at production prices by allowing customers to work closely with the engineering staff and construction crew in designing and finishing the rest of the boat, and in selecting the materials and equipment for it. The customer may choose from over fifty stock designs, ranging from 20' to 55', which are available to Worldcruiser, or Worldcruiser can arrange to purchase the parts for other stock designs. Worldcruiser will finish a boat to any stage of completion and offers a variety of trouble-free completion kits (basic boat, rough interior, handyman, and sailaway) for builders of varying skills. A design decision kit is also available for $10 to help the customer design an interior layout. One brochure explains at length the Worldcruiser building scheme, while another, coupled with a reprint from *Pacific Skipper,* describes in full the various kits. The remaining two brochures are packed with information regarding the firm's own 44' and 50' schooner designs. Plans for over 100 of president Bud Taplin's designs also may be obtained for nominal fees. Price estimates on completed or kit boats will be sent if the customer specifies the exact boat and price range desired.

YACHT CONSTRUCTORS, INC.
7030 N.E. 42nd Avenue
Portland, Oregon 97218
(503) 287-5794
Brochure, 6 pages; Price sheets (4). Free.

Beginning in 1954 as one of the earliest manufacturers of fiberglass sailboat hulls, Yacht Constructors builds 23', 27', 29', 36', and 42' cruisers and racers with carefully hand-laid-up fiberglass hulls, tops, floor timbers and bulkheads, paneling the visible interiors of most boats with marine mahogany plywood. The boats are available in kit form, or as completely finished boats. The brochure explains the firm's construction techniques and provides some photos, side/top-view illustrations, specifications, and some design and performance information for each model. The price sheets list features and much optional equipment for the basic 23' and 27' boats, specifying the numerous kits available for all of the models.

See also, under:

Canoes
Apple Line
Rowing Shells
Freya
Martin
Small Open Boats
Aqua-Terra
Cape Cod

Devlin
Mystic
Pan Pacific
Specialty Craft
Clark Craft
Pederson
Popular Mechanics

Sports and Commercial Boats
Lucander
North End
Rawson
Multihulls
Callahan
Books
Hearst
Woodenboat

Multihulls—Catamarans and Trimarans

Multihulls   Before the decision was made to restrict this catalog to U.S. companies, several foreign firms responded favorably. Crowther Multihulls (P.O. Box 35, Turramurra, New South Wales 2074, Australia) sent a brochure with illustrations and descriptions of some catamarans and trimarans, and also a listing of forty-two designs for which study plans and plans are available; the multihulls range from 18′ to 71′, and include daysailers, ocean cruisers and racers, and commercial vessels. Ian Farrier (P.O. Box 128, East Brisbane, Queensland 4169, Australia) sent a twenty-page booklet explaining his four designs (19′ to 33′), for which study plans are available. He also enclosed a sample of the *Trailerti* newsletter and a form for joining the club. Derek Kelsall (Sandwich Marina, Sandwich, Kent, England CT13 9LY) sent a sheaf of sixteen sheets depicting numerous catamaran and trimaran designs (20′ to 80′); study sheets, plans, mouldings, hulls, and complete boats may be purchased. Malcolm Tennant (Multihull Data, 45a Forest Hill Road, Henderson, Auckland 8, New Zealand) sent a forty-eight page booklet of his catamaran and trimaran designs (20′ to 49′). This catalog is available at $6.50 (airmail). Richard Woods Designs (Foss Quay, Millbrook-Torpoint, Cornwall PL 10 1EN, United Kingdom), sent thirteen informational sheets showing catamaran and trimaran designs (4.3m to 18.3m); plans and study plans are available. Presumably most of this literature, like Tennant's, may be obtained for a fee.

BINARY BOAT SYSTEMS, INC.
Terry Roy Johnson and Carolyn Orr
Wharram Catamaran Plans
P.O. Box 22342
Fort Lauderdale, Florida 33335
(305) 581-7860

Brochure in poster format; Order form and price sheet. $6.50 (includes postage and handling).

Offering top views and other interesting drawings and photos of the boats, the poster lists specifications and provides information regarding Wharram's business, his design principles, the Classic and PAHI designs and their constructions, and the kinds of sail rigs to be used with the boats. The eleven classic "Polynesian Catamaran" designs, to be constructed in plywood, range from 12′ and 14′ car-toppers and a trailerable 16-footer to cruisers and racers of 23′ to 51′. The two trailerable (20′ and 26′) and two ocean cruising (31′ and 42′) PAHI designs are to be built with a maximum of quick-growing renewable softwoods. Johnson and Orr keep in stock a ready supply of Wharram's study plans and full sets of building plans; Wharram's technical papers and books are also available.

STEVEN CALLAHAN
Movement Sailing Vessels
Box 277, RFD 2
Ellsworth, Maine 04605
(207) 667-8516

Informational sheets (2). Free. Skiff-catamaran informational package, 7 pages; Sloop package, 12 pages. $5 each.

Responding to all inquiries and divulging costs with a hand-written personal letter, Steve Callahan offers a plans package for a 20′ skiff-catamaran, "Mr. Toad," to be built using the W.E.S.T. system; a semi-custom completed 21′ or 22′ "Solo" competition sloop in FRP or W.E.S.T. construction; and plans for the sloops only for the experienced home-builder. The free informational sheets describe the design and construction of "Mr. Toad," an inexpensive, easily-built, well-performing lake or ocean cruiser, and one of five winners in the 1978 Cruising World design competition; contents and prices of the study package and plans package are also given. The study package provides two sheets of "reduced sail plan and accommodation and deck layout half tones," a sketch of trailer and "demounting" ideas, a "strongback sketch," a detailed list of rigging, spars, associated fittings, and their prices, and two pages furnishing design criteria, specifications, and construction, performance, cruising, and trailering information. The sloop's study package contains four pages of illustrations, two pages of cost and labor estimates for producing the boat, a page listing options, a page reporting the results of a shakedown cruise, and four pages presenting specifications and information regarding the boat's design, performance, construction, accommodations, and safety.

CROSS TRIMARANS

Norman A. Cross
4326 Ashton
San Diego, California 92110
(619) 276-0910

Catalog #7, 20 pages; Brochure, 8 pages; Order form and price sheet. $6.

Thirteen of seventeen designs, from 18′ daysailer to 52′ ocean racer, are treated in this catalog with lists of specifications, small photos of most of the boats, and medium-size illustrations of each boat's cross-section, side, top, and front views. Study plans and plans are available for all of the boats, and full-size patterns for most of them; all of the boats can be constructed in marine and exterior plywood using normal workshop tools. The catalog also furnishes small photos of some interiors and boats under construction, presents the designer's credentials, and covers design features, performance, and construction of the boats. The brochure offers discussions of particular design features (solid wing decks, shallow draft and flush decks), estimates of building costs and hours, and news of and from builders of Cross trimarans.

FAST BOATS, INC.

P.O. Box 248
Glasco, New York 12432
(914) 336-6582

Informational sheets (3). $1.

The Newick-designed 37′ "Trice III" trimaran, a very fast ocean passagemaker or easy 100-mile weekender, is available from Fast Boats in hand-laid-up unidirectional Orcon S-glass and Airex foam sandwich construction. The boat may be purchased subassembled and try-fitted, or completed as an economy cruiser, Grand Prix cruiser/racer, shorthand racer, or crewed racer. One sheet provides a profile, layout, cross-section, and specifications for the boat, descriptions of the design concept, construction, gear, fittings, and sloop rig, and brief descriptions of the 5 models. The additional sheets picture and briefly explain a new fastback option. Not yet shown nor described is a 7½′ fiberglass foam-core sailing dinghy.

EDWARD B. HORSTMAN

Tri-Star Trimarans
P.O. Box 286
Venice, California 90291
(213) 396-6154

Brochure in poster format; Informational sheets (10). Free. Catalog, 46 pages. $6.

Horstman's trimarans include more than twenty-six designs, from 5 trailerable models between 18′ and 31′ to a luxurious 80′ giant, to be built with foam fiberglass sandwich construction. The plans, leased to the builder for the time required to construct a boat, come with full-size frame patterns, except for the largest boats. Study plans, several books on trimaran construction and sailing, and an 18′ trimaran kit are also available. Offering specifications, some photos and description, and illustrations of most boats from the side, top and front, the catalog presents Horstman's design philosophy, details boat features, construction techniques and materials, the basics of trimaran sailing, and furnishes tales of Horstman-trimaran voyages. The poster contains synopses of much of the information presented in the catalog, including specifications and smaller versions of the top- and side-view illustrations for most models. Additional sheets also duplicate some of the catalog and comprise seven pages of commentary from Horstman regarding daggerboards and other design specifics, eight pages of testimonials, observations, and personal experience stories from trimaran enthusiasts and owners, and an updated price sheet giving a detailed summary of boat specifications and construction information.

HOULTON BOAT COMPANY

P.O. Box 966
Oldsmar, Florida 33557
(813) 855-3435

Informational sheets (2). Free.

Houlton Boat Company sells the 20′ Tornado racing catamaran, completely finished in W.E.S.T. system molded cedar veneers plus installed sail rig, partially completed, or in kit form. The kit boat differs from the completed boat only in hull materials, and all materials, provided un-cut, must be prepared according to the blueprints and offset drawings; also supplied is the one unusual tool, a Gougeon Scarffer for cutting the necessary plywood joining angle. Building time is estimated at 300 to 400 hours. Without any illustrations or photos, one sheet explains the kit and sail rig contents and the kit boat's construction method, and the other sheet describes the construction of the completed boat, its features, and the contents of the sail rig package.

JOHN R. MARPLES MULTIHULL DESIGNS

4530 Firmont Drive, S.E.
Port Orchard, Washington 98366
(206) 871-5634

Design portfolio: Poster; Two brochures, 14 pages each; Two technical papers, 14 pages; Price sheet and owner's agreement form. $5.

John Marples and co-designer Jim Brown offer plans and a multitude of literature regarding three lines of multihull designs. The Constant Camber series, described in a 14-page brochure showing illustrations and some specifications, and designed to be built of cold-molded panels cut to desired shapes, includes an 8′ dinghy, 26′ folding multihull cruiser, 30′ and 32′ high performance trimarans in daysailer or cabin models, and 37′ and 44′ fast live-aboard cruising trimarans. The poster covers the "Searunner" line of cruising trimarans (25′, 31′, 34′, 37′, 40′), to be constructed of plywood and sheathed in fiberglass, showing illustrations of interior layouts, listing specifications, and giving construction information and advice on the selection of a cruising multihull. The 14-page sheaf on "Seaclipper" economy sailing cruisers (28′, 34′, 38′, 41′), which also involve plywood-fiberglass construction, provides specifications, illustrations, photos, and a sample plan sheet. Also included in the portfolio are Marples' technical papers, the 3-page "Notes on Making

Your Own Metal Parts," and the 11-page "Backyard (or Basement) Vacuum Bagging (Or, Bag It in the Backyard)," which contains photos and illustrations. Also available are 12-pages of particulars on the Constant Camber building method, a 29-page booklet of standard details for the Seaclipper and Constant Camber trimarans, a construction manual for Seaclippers and Constant Cambers, another for Searunners, and two multihull cruising manuals.

MYERS CATAMARANS INTERNATIONAL
1701 Bronco Lane
Vienna, Virginia 22180
(703) 938-5909

Design portfolio, 32 pages (11" × 17"); Price list. $10.

Myers' portfolio presents lengthy technical discussions, embellished with graphs, drawings, and photos, of multihull shapes and their effects, structures and sail plans, and safety considerations such as stability. Some photos and description and several large format drawings showing structural details and sail plans are provided for 28', 36', 43', 46', and 58' catamarans. A 39' catamaran is discussed at length and a related paper, "Ocean Racing Multihull Design Considerations," is available for $4. Another technical paper on sailing theory and ocean racing yachts ($4), plans for the catamarans described and a 33' racer/cruiser and 44' racer not described, custom designs, consulting services, and sail safe automatic sheet releases are available.

RICHARD C. NEWICK
R.F.D.
Vineyard Haven, Massachusetts 02568
(617) 693-9603

Design portfolio, 12 sheets; Reprints (3); Informational sheets (2). $10.

Newick's fourteen stock high performance multihull designs range from the 23' Tremolino to a 60' trimaran. His portfolio includes study plans for 11 of the boats — 9 trimarans and 2 proas. Several of the designs are available with Gougeon Brothers wing mast rigs. Newick leaves more detailed discussion of particular boats to an article from *Sail*

(May 1977) which tells of a Newick trimaran winning the 1976 OSTAR, and to reprints from *Multihulls* (July/August 1978) and *Cruising World* (January 1978), a copy of the two sheets from Tremolino Boat Company, which describe the Tremolino in depth. (See Tremolino Boat Company, page 64.)

OCEANSPACE DESIGN
Andrew M. West, President
19327 Northampton Drive
Saratoga, California 95070
(408) 252-7445

Catalog, 14 pages. $3.

Andrew M. West, designer of the "Flying Cat" series of catamarans and founder of the International Flying Cat Club, designed the original Flying Cat as a family boat for sailing on San Francisco Bay. He currently offers plans for two 17'6" flying cats, a 22'6" version, and a $1/10$ scale model of one of the 17'6" boats; the boats can be constructed of marine plywood. The catalog provides photos, specifications, and good-size side- and top-view illustrations of the boats for which plans are available; cost estimates of materials and fairly detailed descriptions of each boat's design, performance, and construction, are also furnished. To be available soon are plans for a flying cat with hydrofoil, plans for a scale model of it, and plans for a scale model of the 22'6" cat. Future works include plans for smaller and larger flying cats, sail boat jet drives, monohull sail boats, jet boats, and flying boats.

SEPARATE REALITY INC.
Michael Spiegel
199 Palm Avenue
Miami Beach, Florida 33139
(305) 531-4835

Booklet, 12 pages. $3.

Determined to build a stable and secure ocean-going

Steven Callahan   Side-view and accommodation and deck layout of the 20' skiff-catamaran, Mr. Toad.

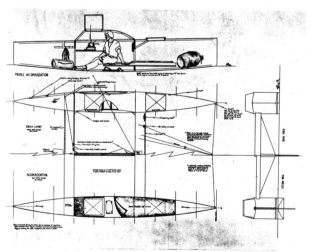

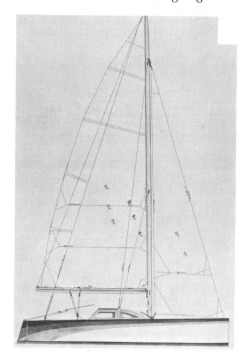

multihull, Michael Spiegel developed the patented rotated step-vee hull shape, which he describes in great technical detail with charts and illustrations in this booklet. The first trimaran built in this design, the "Quark 32," was constructed in Airex foam sandwich with 6061-T6 aluminum-arced I beams. Large illustrations of interior layouts and side views are furnished for 34' and 38' versions which are available in production models to be built preferably in the Miami Beach area; builders in other locales will be considered. Spiegel and associates will design any size or type of multihull using the patented rotated step-vee hull shape; they also welcome questions and new ideas or applications for their design which will promote the renascence of sailing "as an alternative means of economic or personal life style."

SHARK

John and Linda Rogers
72 Maiden Lane
Canandaigua, New York 14424
(716) 394-6853

Informational sheets (5); Price list; Color photo. Free.
Recently recognized by the American Shark Association as official builders, the Rogerses are encouraging the renascence of the Shark one-design racing class by producing all-wood W.E.S.T. system 20' Shark catamarans with laminated cedar hulls and five-ply mahogany decks and trampolines. Hoping soon to publish a brochure, the Rogerses currently send two sheets of membership information and three sheets of Shark description listing features and specifications and providing design, performance, and construction data. The Rogerses produce new boats on a custom order basis, they rebuild and redeck existing boats, replace parts, and refer customers to used boats for sale. Tom Fowler (Class Secretary, 2 Meadowlark Road, Ithaca, New York 14850) may be contacted regarding membership ($15 per year) which includes receipt of the newsletter, *The Shark's Tale,* which comes out three or four times a year, plus information on boat care, regattas, and used boats for sale.

TREMOLINO BOAT COMPANY

P.O. Box 4
Excelsior, Minnesota 55331
(612) 448-6855

Reprints (2); Newsletter; Testimonials; Purchase and sales agreement. Free.
Furnishing the same literature regarding the 23' Tremolino trimaran as Newick sends, except for one more testimonial letter and the purchase and sales agreement, Tremolino Boat Company offers a conversion parts kit to complete the home-built boat, using a standard Hobie 16. Including testimonials and news of Tremolino owners, the literature provides photos, illustrations, and specifications for the boat, lists options, depicts improvements and new options, and lists the contents of the conversion package. The plans, available from Newick, specify ¼" ply and W.E.S.T. system construction.

CHRIS WHITE

Box 801
Mathews, Virginia 23109

Information package, 21 pages. $5.
Chris White furnishes plans packages for his stock designs: 15' and 30' Malibu outrigger types, a 20' trimaran daysailer, and 42' and 54' cruising trimarans. The 15' and 20' boats, designed for Constant Camber mold-wood/epoxy construction, can be easily dismantled for cartopping. The 42' design calls for W.E.S.T. system construction, while a vacuum-bag, Constant Camber mold construction is to be used for the 54' boat. Sheets in White's information package provide specifications, illustrations, lists of features, and estimates of the cost of materials and the number of hours of labor for all but the 30' "Fish Truck" boat, for which only an illustration and specifications are given. Sheets describing the cruising trimarans contain additional design and performance information, and the special design package for the 54' boat, which includes drawings for a Constant Camber mold with matched platen vacuum bag, is detailed in several pages. A 5-page reprint from *Multihulls* (November/December 1980) explains White's version of the Constant Camber construction method. White also offers a "preliminary custom design study" which includes general display drawings of the profile, sail plan, accommodation plan, rough calculation of displacement, sail area, and tankage, and estimates of costs and labor required, according to the customer's specifications. Complete custom designs are available at 5% of the construction costs.

See also, under:

Canoes	Yachts	General Catalogs
Apple Line	Benford	Golden Fleece
Folbot	Clark Craft	Murray's
Small Open Boats	**Sails and Canvas Goods**	**Books**
North Shore	Mare Company	Hearst
	Sailrite	Multihulls

Houseboats

HOLIDAY MANSION

Division of Mohawk, Inc.
2328 Hein Road
Airport Industrial Complex
Salina, Kansas 67401
(913) 827-9681

Brochure, 6 pages; Data sheets (4); Price list. Free.

Holiday Mansion offers one-piece molded, reinforced fiberglass houseboats, "Barracudas," in 35′ and 36′ lengths with several interior arrangements available which will sleep eight to ten people. The brochure furnishes specifications, a list of standard equipment, top-view illustrations showing interior layouts, and many color photos and drawings most of which are interior shots. The accompanying data sheet lists options, Barracuda prices according to engine(s) chosen, presents construction details and photos of the boat under construction, reprints a testimonial letter from a very satisfied customer, and prints excerpts of articles giving flattering test run results and information about powerboat hulls. More literature is available upon request.

LAZY-DAYS MANUFACTURING COMPANY, INC.

6000 Holiday Road
Buford, Georgia 30518
(404) 945-7517/4345

Brochure, 8 pages; Optional equipment booklet, 8 pages; Price list. Free.

Lazy-Days' 14′6″ wide, all-aluminum cruising houseboats come in several one-level or split-level models, ranging from 50′ to 62′ with various power options. The hull design features twin bow sections that taper to a flat bottom aft, giving a soft ride with excellent stability, exceptional maneuverability, and using minimum power. The smaller Sportsman models, designed for use on lakes, rivers, and inland waters, have a high bow option for a drier ride and increased front deck space. The largest houseboats are designed for extended cruising in moderately heavy seas. The 50′ Sportsman has a 200 hp Volvo twin inboard engines with outboard stern drive, and the 62′ Motor Yacht a 310 hp inboard twin Detroit diesels with V-drive. The brochure lists specifications and standard features, and provides floor plans and large color photos or drawings of most models.

SKIPPERLINER HOUSEBOAT

3222 Commerce Street
LaCrosse, Wisconsin 54601
(608) 781-1200

Brochure, 6 pages; Price list. Free.

Constructed of heavy-duty 10-gauge steel with numerous channel ribs, SkipperLiner's 14′ wide hulls can take substantial abuse. With modified V-bow and three 4-inch keels, each houseboat glides smoothly and runs true. The one-level Fantasy Island series features 35′, 39′, 40′, and 44′ models with 12′ wide cabins, while the Commander series comes in 42′, 47′, 52′, 57′, and custom lengths, with numerous deluxe floor plan options. The brochure provides color photos of a variety of houseboats, lists standard features of all models, and briefly describes the two lines of houseboats. The Fantasy Island series price sheet shows floor plans for the four models and lists specifications, standard features and equipment, options and accessories; the boats come with a 120 hp MerCruiser sterndrive. Standard equipment, options and accessories, and prices depending on engines chosen are listed on the Commander series price sheet.

See also, under:

Specialty Craft	**Yachts**
Clark Craft	Benford
Popular Mechanics	Glen-L
	Wittholz
	Books
	Hearst

Holiday Manison   Alternative arrangement plans for the Aft Cabin Barracuda.

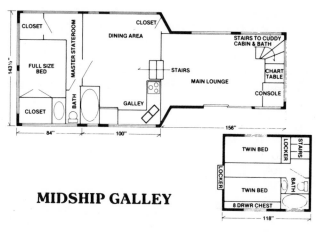

MIDSHIP GALLEY

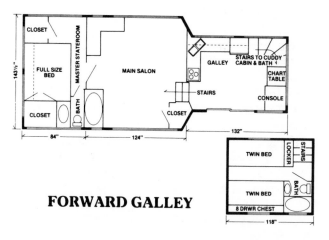

FORWARD GALLEY

Half-Models, Scale Models, and Others

THE DOCKYARD INC.

Mike de Lesseps
P.O. Box 74
South Freeport, Maine 04078
(207) 865-3465

Catalog, 10 pages; Price list. Free.

The Dockyard offers semi-scale working models of a knockabout, sandbagger, and two versions of an English Channel cutter (8½" to 23"); custom working models and scale half-models are also available. Beautiful photos, good descriptions, and specifications are provided for the stock working models which, hand-carved of solid wood and painted, feature Dacron sails, brass fittings, and properly turned, tapered, stained, and varnished hardwood spars. Also furnished are a glossary of sailing terms, full operating instructions, and information regarding the general construction and maintenance of the craft. Half-models are explained; they can be built from the customer's own boat or from one of the historic vessels in the firm's files; each model is mounted on a mahogany plaque with brass nameplate. Spare parts, listed at length on the price list, may be obtained.

JOHN GARDNER

R.F.D.
Penobscot, Maine 04476
(207) 326-8829

Form letter. Free.

Building ship models all his life, Gardner has made the pursuit his livelihood since 1974. Experienced with all types of watercraft including passenger steamboats, the American Cup defender, "Ranger," nineteenth-century lumber and cargo schooners, and private yachts, he can make any model to the desired scale. He provides a firm price estimate (which includes both model and mounting plaque) after studying pertinent information regarding a specific model. Payment in thirds begins upon signing a contract. Shop visits may be arranged and references are available on request. All work is done on commission and details of your order can be worked out by phone or mail, if a shop visit is not possible.

ROLAND E. RICHARDS

Custom Nautical Carvings
1622 Wilmette Avenue
Wilmette, Illinois 60091
(312) 251-9291

Pamphlet, 2 pages. Free.

Richards hand-carves and finishes each half-model to

The Dockyard Inc. Hand-carved of solid wood, this working model of an English Channel cutter features Dacron sails and brass fittings.

specifications, generally fashioning the hull and sails from clear pine, painting the sails with satin white enamel, and the hull with gloss or semi-gloss enamels. Fine details such as handrails and pulpits are not included. His pamphlet offers color photos of his work, and presents sample prices for a variety of half-model types: "traditional style" (16" and 20"), "hull and deck structures" (including cabin, cockpit coaming, hatches, stub mast, and no cockpit (12", 16", 20"), and "complete with sails" (12" and 14"). The standard mounting board is finished redwood; Honduras and Philippine mahogany board and engraved brass or trophy plates are available at extra cost.

ALAN WELLS

P.O. Box 6115
Charlotte, North Carolina 28207
(704) 372-2658

Pamphlet, 4 pages; Order form. Free.

Wells hand-carves each model to order from pine and mahogany, as accurately to scale as possible, finishing it with hand-rubbed oil or a high satin lacquer. Each is mounted on a redwood or mahogany plaque complete with a brass nameplate that can be engraved. Most models measure 5" × 16" and the plaque 9" × 24"; custom miniatures with sails, lacquer finish, and 10" × 12" plaque, larger models up to 4', custom painting, engraving, and mountings, as well as sailing trophies, are also available. The pamphlet shows photos of some of Wells' work, briefly explains half-models in general and the composition of Wells' offerings, and furnishes a detailed order form.

See also, under:

Canoes	**Multihulls**	**General Catalogs**
Great Canadian	Oceanspace	Commodore
Willis	**Gifts**	Goldberg's
Small Open Boats	Mystic	**Books**
Apprenticeshop	Preston	Woodenboat
Country Ways		
Stokes		

2. MATERIALS, SUPPLIES, AND TOOLS FOR BOAT CONSTRUCTION, MAINTENANCE, AND REPAIR

Fasteners
Trim
Tools
Knives
Drafting Equipment
Lofting Instruments

Small Craft, Inc.   The Warning, a fast and stable recreation shell, is an uncomplicated, patient, and forgiving boat for beginners, but offers the speed necessary for experienced oarsmen.

Materials and Supplies

AIRCRAFT SPRUCE & SPECIALTY COMPANY
P.O. Box 424
201 W. Truslow Avenue
Fullerton, California 92632
(714) 870-7551

Catalog, 278 pages. $4.

Primarily a distributor of aircraft supplies of all types, specializing in aircraft materials and components for the home-builder, this firm also furnishes supplies such as epoxies, fiberglass cloth, foams, spruce wood, plywood, and Aerolite wood glue to boatbuilders. Recognized as the most comprehensive catalog in the industry in providing reference information in addition to a wide selection of products, the catalog contains solid descriptions (including illustrations) of the products offered, informative introductions to several of the major sections, and a detailed index, boring chart, and several conversion tables. The catalog breaks down into the following well-marked sections: Composite Materials (cloth, resins, foams, tools, safety equipment), Wood Products (spruce, plywood, glass), Metals and Plastics (tubing, sheets, bars, fabricated parts), Hardware (bolts, nuts, washers, fittings, fasteners, nails, screws, rivets, rivnuts), Airframe Parts (plastics, rubber goods, fuel supplies, control system components, bearings, tie rods, throttles and controls, propellers), Landing Gear, Engine Accessories, Engines and Engine Parts, Covering Supplies (fabric, tapes, grommets, inspection rings, dynel, foam, epoxy resin, dopes, thinners, finishes, chemical products, registration stencils, placards, decals), Instruments, Electrical and Radio (lights, wire, terminals, batteries, radios, antennas), Tools, and Pilot Supplies, Books, and Ultralights.

*AMERICAN ACOUSTICAL PRODUCTS
9 Cochituate Street
Natick, Massachusetts 01760
(617) 237-4223; 655-0870

Brochure, 4 pages. Free.

Dense, flexible, rot- and mildew-resistant, properly non-combustible or self-extinguishing, easily installed, and made to withstand extremes of heat and cold, the varieties of "hushcloth" reduce noise levels in boats. Fiberglass/lead and foam types are for use in lining engine and generator compartments. A foam variety with perforated vinyl facings in a variety of rich colors is for use in cabin interiors. Floor mats and underlinings keep noise below deck. The brochure provides photos, some specifications, descriptions, and application information for these products.

AMERICAN KLEGECELL CORPORATION
204 North Dooley Street
Grapevine, Texas 76051
(817) 481-3547

Data packet (brochures, technical bulletins, price lists, foam samples), 38 pages. Free (to amateur and professional boatbuilders).

American Klegecell manufactures rigid and flexible P.V.C. foam in plain and contoured sheets. Several densities may be purchased in any thickness from 3 mm to 3″ and in three contour styles — 1½″ or ¾″ squares with or without scrim backing, or 1½″ squares cut half-through on both sides. Plain sheets may also be obtained with a pressure-sensitive backing. Klegecell P.V. core kits and a marine composites seminar textbook are also available. The literature enclosed provides extensive information regarding the physical properties of Klegecell, including the results of tests and comparisons (cost/weight, flexural and mechanical properties) with related materials. Lists of builders and lists and photos of boats using Klegecell are furnished along with foam-type recommendations for specific boat sizes.

BOULTER PLYWOOD CORPORATION
24 Broadway
Somerville, Massachusetts 01245
(617) 666-1340

Catalog, 7 pages. Free.

Boulter Plywood specializes in fine marine and hardwood plywoods manufactured in the finest mills to specifications higher than industry and government grading regulations require. The firm has also offered precision plywood cutting (¹/₁₆″ tolerance) services for over thirty years. In addition to the numerous varieties of hardwood and marine plywoods, a full line of hardwood lumber, some hardwood veneers, several softwood plywoods and modern composites are listed. The composition of each type of plywood is briefly described. Prices are given per sheet as well as per square foot for pieces cut to size. Quantity discounts are available. Samples of all products will be mailed upon request. "Telephone quotations are cheerfully rendered on all our products including the cost of cutting and shipping upon request."

CHEM-TECH, INC.
4669 Lander Road
Chagrin Falls, Ohio 44022
(216) 248-0770

Manual, 32 pages; Price list; Order form. $2.50.

As outlined on the price list, Chem-Tech sells kits of its T-88 structural adhesive, L-26 sheathing resin, and F-9 surfacing compound, as well as versatex polypropylene fabric, thickening powder, gloves, and, advertised in the last few pages of the manual, skin cleanser, cream, applicators, a pour-easy pail rack, and Trailex aluminum trailers. The manual reprints several articles describing and comparing Chem-Tech adhesives and sheathing materials and provides results of experimental tests regarding the peeling properties and the impact-, tear-, and abrasion-resistance of composites incorporating the materials. Instructions for preparing surfaces and applying sheathing are also given. Prices and additional literature for the trailers must be requested. Quantity discounts are available.

W. A. CLARK AND ASSOCIATES
Susan Clark
Sugarloaf Star Route
Boulder, Colorado 80302
(303) 444-1890

Catalog, 11 pages. Free.

Intended primarily for the whitewater boatbuilder, and listing all reinforcements and some ancillary materials needed to build high-strength whitewater boats, sailboats, surfboards, and skateboards, this catalog is also useful to others who fabricate advanced or impact-resistant composites. To help with the selection of reinforcement, considerable technical data are informally presented regarding laminate design, the Kevlar 49 and S-Glass fabrics available, resins, and the quantities of resins and reinforcements to use. In addition to the variety of Kevlar and S-glass cloths listed, polyester veil, bag molding supplies, glass microspheres, high-aspect-ratio mica flakes, and Walbridge, Rock, and Myers' *Boat Builder's Manual*, may be purchased.

DALY'S WOOD FINISHING PRODUCTS
1121 N. 36th Street
Seattle, Washington 98103
(206) 633-4204

Brochure, 4 pages; Various informational sheets; Price list and order form. Free.

Daly's specialty for over thirty years has been custom stain-matching. In addition the firm carries a complete line of quality woodfinishing materials including exterior stain, interior finishes, stains, treatments, wood filler, a special line of Danish tung oils, finish and stain removers, bleaches, cleaners, wire brushes and an iron bark scraper. Most of these products are depicted and briefly described in the brochure, and detailed specifications are provided on three additional sheets for the specifically marine products—Seafin teak oil, Ship 'N' Shore sealer, and Seafin one-part teak cleaner. An additional sheet shows and explains several woodfinishing guides and numerous supplies and equipment such as brushes, sponges, sandpaper, steel wool, and more. Daly's will develop custom products to solve specific problems.

THE DEAN COMPANY
Olympic Manufacturing Company Division
P.O. Box 426
Gresham, Oregon 97030
(503) 665-2161

Price lists (2). Free.

The Dean Company makes available a number of veneers for cold molding including 1/8″, 1/16″ and 1/20″ Western red cedar, 1/8″ red meranti, 1/8″ Douglas fir, 1/6″, 1/8″, and 1/20″ Sitka spruce, 1/10″ Burma teak and 1/8″ Port Orford cedar. The price list furnishes brief information regarding each veneer's grade and the widths and lengths available. The firm also sells a pram package containing 200 square feet of 1/8″ Western red cedar veneer. Standard Gougeon Brothers W.E.S.T. system publications, plans, and a product evaluation kit, listed on the second price sheet, may also be obtained.

DUNBAR MARINE SPECIALTIES
P.O. Box 531
East Longmeadow, Massachusetts 01028
(413) 734-4231

Catalog, 8 pages. Free.

Five pages of the catalog list the products available and their prices. A number of fiberglass materials and tools may be purchased: chrome-treated cloth, chopped-strand mat, woven roving, fab-mat, and glass tape priced by the yard and the roll; polyester resin with catalyst, hardener, acetone, pigments, thixotropic powder, styrene, polyester super putty, and commercial talc; aluminum rollers, plastic gloves, resin brushes, sanding discs and paper. Resorcinol two-part glue is also available. A full line of Gloucester "Sea Jacket" marine paints and related products is offered at 40% to 50% below list price. Fastenings illustrated and priced according to size and quantity include cut copper tacks, brass escutcheon pins, nickel-plated brass oval head slotted wood screws and finish washers, silicon bronze flat head slotted wood screws and ring-barbed boat nails, 303 stainless steel smooth rod, and 18-8 stainless steel full threaded rod, self-tapping screws, slotted machine screws, hex head cap screws, full-finished hex nuts, flat washers, and split lock washers. An additional two pages explain types of fiberglass fabrics and fillers and provide instructions and hints for hand-laying fiberglass materials.

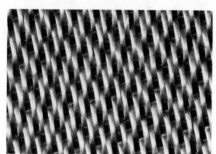

W.A. Clark and Associates   This S-glass fabric is a 4-harness satin or crow's foot weave. It is about 70% stronger than the same weight fabric in E-glass.

FLOUNDER BAY BOAT LUMBER
Bob and Erica Pickett
3rd and "O" Streets
Anacortes, Washington 98221
(206) 293-2369

Price lists (4). Free. Three brochures. 25¢ each.

Serving the boating industry nationwide for over a decade, Flounder Bay offers custom milling and the finest quality western softwoods and specialty hardwoods for building boats. The softwoods listed and priced according to stock include Douglas fir, Sitka spruce, Western red cedar, and Alaska yellow cedar; Port Orford cedar may also be obtained. Apitong, ash, balau, iroko, iron bark, kapur, locust, dark red mahogany, honduras mahogany, bending oak, white oak, and teak plus fifteen specialty and less common varieties are listed among the hardwoods available. Exterior teak and mahogany, marine fir, and Bruynzeel plywoods and blocks of lignum vitae may also be purchased. Ripping, planing, resawing, and shaping services are available and custom cuts such as strip, canoe, or light skiff plankings can be prepared to specifications. Other products offered are Skookum Fastenings' copper rivets, roves, clench and edge nails, Fuller bits and cutters, Savage Forge hand-made carving and woodworking tools, a fairly complete line of fiberglass supplies, cold cure epoxies, square drive bronze screws, Z Spar paints and finishes, Dolfinite compounds, 3M sealants, and other glues, nails, and preservatives. The price list provides brief and helpful descriptive information for each major product category, while an additional 4-page "Guide to Hardwoods for Northwest Boatbuilding" covers at length the properties of apitong, ash, balau, iron bark, iroko, kapur, Philippine and Honduras mahoganies, red and white oaks, teak, and yew. How-to brochures, "Air-Drying Lumber" and "Steam Bending," each two pages, may also be purchased.

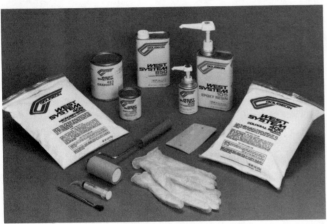

Gougeon Brothers, Inc.   W.E.S.T. system products, popular in boat repair, hold a special place in this firm's list of offerings.

GOUGEON BROTHERS, INC.
706 Martin Street
P.O. Box X908
Bay City, Michigan 48707
(517) 684-7286

Catalog, 8 pages; Price list. Free. Various promotional materials available upon request.

Gougeon Brothers' products may be obtained directly, or through dealers and distributors nationwide, for which regional lists are available. Standard literature includes the catalog, which pictures and describes the epoxies, fillers, metering dispensers, application tools, cleaning products, publications, and plans available; a 6-page color brochure which explains the method; a 4-page brochure which discusses boat repair using W.E.S.T. system products; a sheet which explains the preference for wood; and a sheet which advertises *The Gougeon Brothers on Boat Construction*. Another 4-page brochure, furnished by one distributor, presents profile and interior layout plans, specifications, and brief descriptions of 8′ and 10′ sailing prams, an 18′ cruising sloop, and a 19′ sailing dory for which there are plans; plans may also be procured for a DN iceboat. Other dealers and distributors may send their own lists and descriptions of the products. The 30-page *W.E.S.T. System Technical Manual* ($2), complete with many photos and

illustrations, "describes the theories and techniques of forming a composite engineering material by using wood and W.E.S.T. system brand resins."

The third edition of the illustrated 316-page *The Gougeon Brothers on Boat Construction* ($20), edited by Kay Harley, will soon be available upon demand. It "covers as many details of boat construction as possible" with the aim of providing a useful boatbuilding guide for professional as well as first-time builders. There are chapters on estimating costs and labor, on using and buying wood, lofting and making frames and molds, on laminating hulls in a variety of methods, constructing interiors, decks, and plywood hulls, and on installing hardware.

*JOTUN-BALTIMORE COPPER PAINT COMPANY
840 Key Highway
Baltimore, Maryland 21230
(301) 539-0045

Technical data manual, 66 pages; Booklet, 16 pages; Brochure, 10 pages. Free.

The technical data manual provides color and comparison charts for Jotun-Baltimore's Regatta/Seaproof line of marine coatings, including numerous antifouling paints, spar varnishes, epoxy coatings, net dips and preservatives, pot and buoy paints. A description of each type of paint and directions for preparing the surface and applying the paint are also given. The booklet, a guide to boat "paintenance," briefly describes the variety of paints and gives suggestions regarding the use of paint in general, on specific materials, and for particular purposes. The brochure, designed to be a handy, quick reference to boat protection for boat owners, once again gives very brief descriptions of the kinds of paint available, discusses safety measures and preventive maintenance, and lists a synopsis of morse code, code flag, and letter code signals.

KRISTAL KRAFT, INC.
P.O. Box 787
1507 - 17th Street East
Palmetto, Florida 33561
(813) 722-3206

Two brochures, 4 pages each; Various informational sheets; Price list and order form. Free.

In business since 1946, Kristal Kraft offers a broad range of plastics and fiberglass materials. A color brochure briefly describes each product available: fiberglass cloth, tape, mat and woven roving; foam for flotation, insulation, or reinforcement; several polyester resins, hardener, solvents, thinners, cleaners, repair compounds and kits; epoxy resin, glue, repair kits and compounds, metal base coatings and resin, and styrofoam coatings; color pastes, polyurethane clear varnish, and a wood aid for rotten wood. A second brochure goes into greater detail on the use and application of the firm's polyester and epoxy resins. A data bulletin listing the features and proclaiming the virtues of each product may be obtained upon request; some bulletins furnish information regarding application and indicate the quantities in which the item is available.

*MARINE DEVELOPMENT AND RESEARCH CORPORATION
116 Church Street
Freeport, New York 11520
(516) 546-1162
Catalog, 8 pages; Order form. Free.
Marine Development puts out an annual power and sail catalog mainly for its dealers and distributors, but it can be used as a reference tool for the retail customer. A number of products are available including fuel treatments, fuel-saving additives containing no methanol or alcohol; antifouling paint for depth finder transducers, chrome/brass/ stainless/clear plastic cleansers, cleansers and coatings for vinyl, aluminum, and wood, rust removers, deckshoe renewal kits, mildew and humidity treatments, marine deodorizers and toilet chemicals, waterproof urethane-coated nylon covers for a variety of electronics and boat equipment, decorative and repair tapes, and "fibergrip" nylon fasteners. Each product is briefly described and pictured in its customary container.

MORGAN'S MARINE SUPPLY
600 Petaluma Boulevard North
Petaluma, California 94952
(707) 763-5111
Catalog, 6 pages. Free.
Morgan's Marine is a marine supply and discount house that specializes in epoxies, paints, and coatings for wood, fiberglass, ferrocement, and other construction materials. Available at very competitive prices are epoxies, curing agents, sealers, adhesives, fillers, and repair putty; epoxy primers and tank primers, top-coats, non-skid coating, and paint remover; a coating for aluminum; aliphatic linear and elastomeric polyurethane coatings; polysulfide rubber caulking, polyurethane flotation foam, and Ara-Bol deck coating and lagging adhesive; anti-fouling bottom paints, plastic and vinyl paints, enamel paints, varnish, and solvents; fiberglass cloth, woven roving, mat, continuous strand roving, and carbon/graphite cloth and fiber; and polyester laminating resin. The characteristics of most of these products are briefly described in the catalog, but additional information may be requested, especially for items not fully explained or listed.

OZARK FIBERGLASS PRODUCTS
Box 900
Highway 65 N.
Branson, Missouri 65616
(417) 334-4381
Catalog, 15 pages. $1. Fiberglass repair manual, 46 pages. $5.
This catalog provides brief descriptions and pictures of the many items available from the firm including (mostly Lan-O-Sheen brand) gelcoat, epoxy and fiberglass repair kits, resins, hardener, acetone, fiberglass mat and cloth, coloring agents, filler powder, repair putties, primer, waxes and polishing/rubbing compounds, boat cleaners and applicators, Interlux brushable polythane, antifouling paints, thinners, primer, and non-skid compound, Mira-Plate epoxy paint and Mar-Hyde vinyl paint, sandpaper, brushes, tools, mask, respirators, masking tape,

and a Preval paint sprayer. Some manufacturers' promotional literature is reprinted and free color charts on epoxy and polythane paints are available; not all prices fall below the manufacturer's suggested list prices. Also furnished are guides for estimating average paint requirements and for ordering coloring agents for gelcoats. Also available for $5 is *Does Your Fiberglass Boat Need Repaired?* (sic), a guide to fiberglass repair with chapters on removing scratches and scuff marks from gel coats; repairing nicks, deep scratches, cracks, and broken fiberglass; refinishing the boat, removing algae, "anti-fouling" the hull, and keeping the boat surface in good condition.

PARTNERSHIPS LIMITED INC.
P.O. Box 6503
Lawrenceville, New Jersey 08648
Catalog, 11 pages; Price list and order form. Free.
The objective of this firm is to stock a complete line of composites and accessories including carbon, graphite, aramid, S-glass, and polyester fibers, polystyrene and polyurethane foams, aluminum honeycomb, resins, moulding accessories, tools, and manuals. The catalog furnishes detailed technical data sheets on the properties, forms, and uses of carbon/graphite fibers, Kevlar, foam and honeycomb core materials, glass fiber, and epoxy resigns. Pictures show the weaves of carbon and Kevlar cloths. One sheet reviews *Moldless Composite Homebuilt Sandwich Aircraft Construction,* an informative guide to the "inside out" method of building foam and fiberglass aircraft components; a companion introductory materials practice kit is available. New products apparently are introduced monthly and ads and product releases announcing them may be available from time to time.

*PERMALITE PLASTICS CORPORATION
1537 Monrovia Avenue
Newport Beach, California 92663
(714) 548-1137
Two brochures, 4 pages each; Informational sheets (2); Price list. Free.
Presenting specifications, packaging and application information, one brochure covers Permalite's anti-corrosive, acid-resistant, anti-abrasive epoxy coatings available clear or in custom or fifteen stock colors, in pint, quart, gallon, five gallon, and fifty-five gallon kits. The other brochure gives short descriptions and some specifications for the full line of marine coatings (water-proofing, antifouling, polyurethane, thinner), epoxy putties, and marine specialties (compound for frayed rope ends, and fiberglass, plastic pipe, and multipurpose epoxy adhesives); coverage tables for these products are printed on an additional sheet. Another sheet charts available solvent cements and recommended usages.

QUALITY WOODS LTD.
P.O. Box 205
Lake Hiawatha, New Jersey 07034
(201) 927-0742
Price sheets (2); Order form. Free.
This company makes available Thai teak veneer, teak

plywood, surfaced, kiln-dried teak lumber, teak handrails in a variety of lengths, a teak magazine rack, glass holder, and tissue holder. Illustrations are furnished for the teak fixtures, and prices are listed for all items according to the quantity ordered. Teak plugs are also available. Quantity discounts are available.

SAV-COTE CHEMICAL LABS, INC.
P.O. Box 770
1094 Route 9
Lakewood, New Jersey 08701
(800) 631-2164; (201) 364-4700

Catalog, 8 pages; Two brochures, 4 pages each; Product sheets (2); Color and application charts; Price list and order form. Free.

Sav-Cote stakes its reputation on its flexible "liquid plastic" coating and antifouling paints which can be used on wood, canvas, metal, aluminum, fiberglass, and plastic. The catalog promotes the coatings (available in a variety of colors presented on a color chart), listing their characteristics and uses and providing testimonials. The catalog describes, in addition, caulk, putties, sealers, fillers, deck coatings, varnishes, stains, styrofoam and antifouling primers among others, retarders, metal cleansers, paint removers, reinforcement cloth and bedding compound, and brushes that are available from the firm. Additional brochures describe and promote Sav-Cote's Diamond Seal all-purpose one-part epoxy coating and "Sav-Cloth" Dynel fabrics. Additional sheets advertise vinyl antifouling paint with no copper for outdrives, a clear plastic coating, a silicone liquid preserver/ waterproofer, and a new fiberglass refinishing kit. A second chart recommends application systems for the various paints.

SEASYN DISTRIBUTING COMPANY
229 Tewksbury
Point Richmond, California 94801
(415) 236-4242

Booklet, 22 pages; Price sheet and order form. Free.

Seasyn manufactures and markets "System Three," a third-generation epoxy resin system designed specifically for the uneasily controlled conditions that face the backyard home boatbuilder. The booklet explains the development of the system, describes the characteristics of the system and its components, and discusses the system's uses as protective coating for bare wood, as laminating resin, as structural adhesive, and as filleting material. Safety, handling, and storage are also treated, and selected recipes and quantity estimates are given. The epoxy resin, hardeners, fillers, application tools, unidirectional reinforcing fabrics (S-glass, carbon, Kevlar), and woven fiberglass cloth available are all listed and priced on the price sheet.

SEEMANN FIBERGLASS, INC.
P.O. Box 13704
3520 Pine Street
New Orleans, Louisiana 70185
(504) 482-1179

Catalog, 18 pages; Various reprints; Form letter; Order form and price sheet. Free.

Working in fiberglass over ten years, and developing

C-Flex fiberglass planking, Seemann is directly involved in all aspects of boat construction and can offer customers a great deal of technical advice and assistance. The firm now carries a full line of resin and glass supplies including C-Flex (CF-65 and CF-39), fiberglass cloth and woven roving, chopped strand and woven mat, milled fibers, microspheres, polyester, vinylester, chemically-resistant resins and others, pigments and gelcoats, acetone, foam-glass, and some carbon, Kevlar, S-glass and E-glass cloths or tapes. All of the tools needed for fiberglass work are also available including electric and power pneumatic tools, brushes and rollers, drum racks and wrenches, staple guns, squeegees, sandpaper and discs, and more. The catalog provides brief descriptions of the items and furnishes some photos of tools and weaves. An explanation of resin terms and physical properties of C-Flex are also given. An 8-page reprint from *The Amateur Boat Builder* explains with photos the procedure for using C-Flex planking; a 3-page reprint from *Lakeland Boating* (February 1977) presents a condensed version of the procedure along with numerous photos of boats built using C-Flex; and a 2-page reprint from *National Fisherman* (March 1981) follows the process of building a 72' Lucander shrimper with C-Flex. Quantity discounts are available.

SHREWSBURY FARMS
Dr. James B. Shrewsbury
P.O. Box 150
505 South Jefferson Street
Princeton, Kentucky 42445
(502) 365-6119

Informational sheets (2). Free.

Dr. Shrewsbury, who sailed on the Wawona in 1937, ships genuinely high-grade, sap-free, air-dried white oak in limited amounts, selectively cut to order from his property, for quality wooden boatbuilding. The "Notes On Boat Lumber" he sends explains his offerings and philosophy and the inadequacies of lumber for boatbuilding which is graded according to National Hardwood Lumber Association rules and marketed in bulk board foot quantities of random lengths and widths. John Gardner covers Shrewsbury's unique and refreshing approach to hardwood supply in *National Fisherman* (October 1981).

SMITH AND COMPANY
Industrial and Marine Synthetic Resins and Specialties
5100 Channel Avenue
Richmond, California 94804
(415) 237-5986/6824

Informational sheets (8). Free.

This company offers free consulting services regarding the proper application of its high-performance adhesives and coatings—common to the aerospace industry but not well known in the commercial market place—to the maintenance and repair of wood, steel, aluminum, fiberglass, and ferrocement hulls. Available from the firm and described at length on the data sheets are polysulfide adhesives and coatings, epoxy adhesives and laminating resins, cold mold laminating epoxy, 150 series epoxy paints, clear penetrating epoxy sealer, hard vinyl copper and tin antifouling paints, and urethane foam. Ferrocement hull coating instructions are provided as well as brief descriptions of some new fairing and tropical hardwood epoxies and two books, the 42-page *How To Fix Your Wooden Boat* especially with the use of modern adhesives and paints, and the 45-page *How To Finish Your Ferrocement Hull*. The books are $5 each, deductible from the first $50 purchase; another manual, *How To Make Silicone Rubber Molds*, may also be available. Primers, solvents, thinners, void filling epoxy, polyurethane linear paint, and urethane non-skid decking, solvent-free fish hold liner, and flexible roofing paints, listed on the price sheet, may also be procured.

SOUNDOWN INC.

Richard S. Cleary
34A Gregory Street
Marblehead, Massachusetts 01945
(617) 631-6453/1353

Five pamphlets, 24 pages in all; Informational sheets (12); Price list. Free.

Specializing in marine noise control, Soundown manufactures acoustical insulation used within engine spaces, foam-backed headliner and hull-liner materials, acoustical carpet underlayments, hot exhaust wrappings, custom generator enclosures and outboard motor kits. Additionally, recommendations will be given for tested products not available from the firm. A generous amount of literature on the techniques and materials that can be used to minimize the noise present in any vessel may also be had. There are sheets on understanding noise and the effects of noise, and on soundproofing commercial vessels with insulating their machinery areas; more sheets describe white-facing vapor barrier and lead composite insulation, comparing the physical properties of composite, foam, fiberglass, and lead insulations, polyester film facing, and ultrasorb underlayments. Pamphlets cover soundproofing sailboats and engine boxes, and measuring and ordering acoustical insulation for both power and sail boats; other pamphlets describe the materials, measuring procedures, and installation of exhaust wrap and outboard motor kits. "Noise Questionnaires" regarding power or sail boats are available for the customer to fill out and submit to the company for advice. Samples of the materials may be obtained. Quantity discounts are offered.

TORIN INC.

125 Sheridan Terrace
Ridgewood, New Jersey 07450
(201) 445-2088

Two brochures, 10 pages in all; Two pamphlets, 15 pages in all, Various informational sheets; Form letter; Order form and price lists. Free.

Torin stocks Airex rigid and soft foams, Mor-Bond fairing compound and fiberglass adhesives, Somvyl expanded PVC foam ceiling and wall-covering, and Termanto rigid expanded PVC-based panels for use as insulation, structural stiffening, and sandwich structure. The brochures and pamphlets contain some description but mostly photos and illustrations of the Airex, Somvyl, and

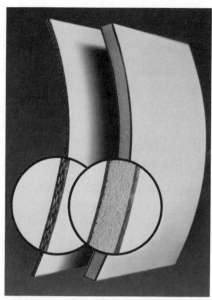

Torin Inc. Airex®/Fiberglass Sandwich Construction. The total hull thickness for a 40' boat is approximately 1-1 ⅛" compared to about ⅜" for conventional single skin fiberglass construction.

Termanto materials and their uses; a chart is provided outlining the mechanical and physical properties of the various Termanto types. Price list/data sheets cover Airex flotation boat cushion foam and the Somvyl material, and additional sheets list Somvyl's features and describe in detail the properties and application of Mor-Bond products. An order form lists sample packages and additional in-depth literature describing mostly Airex fiberglass sandwich construction, female mold applications, and general design information. Quantity discounts on the materials are available.

*TRAVACO LABORATORIES, INC.

345 Eastern Avenue
Chelsea, Massachusetts 02150
(617) 884-7740

Catalog, 16 pages; Brochure, 4 pages; Order form. Free.

Travaco offers at list prices a host of maintenance, repair, and restoration materials including Marine-Tex epoxy-based putty and liquid repair kits, epoxy waterproof sealers, teak cleaner and sealer, rust remover, silicone grease, marine varnish, epoxy caulking compound, windshield cleaner and de-fogger, bilge cleaner, bilge and head deodorants, and protective hand cream. Each product is pictured and its characteristics and uses promoted in the catalog. The additional brochure pretty much repeats the products and information presented in the catalog. Lists of dealers in the customer's locale are available.

TUGON CHEMICAL CORPORATION

P.O. Box 31
Cross River, New York 10518
(203) 762-3953

Catalog, 4 pages; Brochure, 4 pages; Informational sheet; Order form. Free.

Tugon makes available a variety of marine epoxy

adhesives and coatings—non-skid decking, sealant, glue, filler, primer, resin, caulking, and rotten wood aid. Each product is pictured and its characteristics promoted in the catalog. An additional sheet provides answers to common questions about the non-skid decking, and the brochure explains the uses and application of the rotten wood aid. Customers are encouraged to call or write regarding questions, particular problems or circumstances.

WICKS AIRCRAFT SUPPLY

410 Pine Street
Highland, Illinois 62249
(618) 654-7447

Catalog, 184 pages, Order form. $3.

Catering mainly to the home-builder and restorer of aircraft, Wicks supplies some materials that may be of interest to boatbuilders. The items offered, rarely pictured and minimally described, are: marine-grade mahogany and fir plywoods, aircraft-grade mahogany and birch plywoods, aircraft-grade spruce, wood glues and sealers, a variety of aircraft foams, epoxy forming, filling, and laminating materials, fiberglass cloth, tapes, and skinning materials, tools for fiberglass construction, swaging tools and a variety of aircraft tools, countersinks and drills, steel and aluminum tubing, rod and other stock, plastic tubing, aluminum, steel, and plastic/nylon fittings, aircraft fasteners (very few of brass or corrosion resistant materials), electrical terminals and parts, control cable, thimbles, copper nicopress oval sleeves, turnbuckles and parts, aircraft wheels, tires, brakes, engine hardware and instruments, aircraft coverings, coatings, paints, chemicals, and supplies, lighting systems, and aircraft kits. A table of contents and detailed index are included.

YUKON LUMBER COMPANY

520 West 22nd Street
Norfolk, Virginia 23517
(804) 625-7131

Informational sheets (3). Free.

This company sells random widths and lengths of alder, ash, basswood, birch, bubinga, aromatic red cedar, cherry, cocobola, Honduras/Philippine mahogany, birdseye maple, hard maple, soft maple, red oak, white oak, padauk, pecan/hickory, clear white pine, poplar, purpleheart, rosewood, Sitka spruce, teak, American walnut, wenge, and zebrawood. Air-dried white oak not cut in boards and sugar pine shelving are also available. Most stock is rough cut, but planing and ripping services are available. Upon request, quotes will be given on milled lumber. The sheets list the woods available, priced according to thickness and quantity, and furnish a good explanation of the "board foot" measure and how to calculate it and the amount of wood to order. Quantity discounts are available.

See also, under:

Canoes
　Clark Craft

Small Open Boats
　Duck Trap
　North Shore
　Tender Craft

Fasteners
　Jamestown

Tools
　Harra
　Wade
　Wooden Boat Shop
　Woodworker's Store
　Woodworker's Supply
　Zimmerman

Engines
　Marine Drive

Sailing Hardware
　Freeman
　H & L

Docks
　Vandermeer

Seats, Bedding…Lighting
　Wind and Sea

Nautical and Outdoor Clothing
　Afterguard

General Catalogs
　Cal
　Commodore
　Defender
　E & B
　Fore and Aft Marine
　Goldberg's
　Golden Fleece
　M & E
　M.M.O.S.
　Manhattan
　Marine Center
　Murray's
　National Marine
　Nautical Boatique
　Overton's
　Port Supply
　Sears
　Stone Harbor
　Voyager
　Warehouse

Fasteners

BERCO FASTENERS COMPANY

P.O. Box 343
Randallstown, Maryland 21133

Order form for desired literature. Free.

Rather than sending a complete catalog of available fasteners, Berco furnishes a form for ordering individual catalog pages on specific items. Each page supplies illustrations of the point and head type of the individual fastener, and lists prices according to size and quantity ordered. Fasteners offered are 18-8 stainless steel, 316 stainless steel, brass, silicon bronze, or hot galvanized steel nuts, bolts, screws, and washers; handy-packs of 18-8 stainless steel wood screws and sheet metal screws, and handy-packs of silicon bronze wood screws. Also available are stainless steel hardware for power boats and sailboats, stainless steel sailboat rigging hardware, sailboat winches, chrome-plated hardware and hot galvanized steel hardware for boats, and nylon and dacron rope for boats. Customers can ask to be put on the mailing list to receive catalogs.

BRYCE FASTENER COMPANY

2924 Western Avenue
Seattle, Washington 98121
(206) 622-7440

Catalog, 25 pages. Free.

This catalog consists of net price lists and illustrations of available fasteners, priced according to size. The quantities in which fasteners are priced and must be ordered are not specified, however. Fasteners listed are brass machine screws, wood screws, nuts, and washers; chrome-plated brass machine screws and wood screws; silicon bronze wood screws, hex head cap screws, nuts and washers, carriage bolts, and lag screws; stainless steal sheet metal screws, hex head cap screws, nuts and washers, machine screws, carriage bolts, lag screws, cotter pins, and wood screws; and hot-dip galvanized hex head bolts, nuts and washers, carriage bolts, slotted flat head screws, and lag screws. Apparently nylon fasteners are also available and an additional sheet presents in chart form the fasteners in stock; items not in stock may be procured. Power bits, hand drivers, and Fuller counterbores, countersinks, drills, plug cutters, and stop collars may also be obtained.

CHESAPEAKE MARINE FASTENERS
2118 Forest Drive
Annapolis, Maryland 21401
(301) 266-8973; 841-5263
Catalog, 30 pages. $2.
Chesapeake's catalog lists most available fasteners, priced according to size and usually per 100, but not illustrated. Offered are type 18-8 stainless steel hex machine screw nuts and finished nuts, finished jam nuts, flat, fender, and SAE washers, lockwashers, countersink finishing washers, hex head cap screws, carriage bolts, hex head lag screws, socket head cap and socket set screws, square head set screws, thumb screws, slotted machine screws, slotted sheet metal screws, slotted wood screws, cotter pins, U-bolts, and forged shoulder nut eye bolts. Also listed are T420 stainless tension pins, and soft annealed stainless wire; silicon bronze machine screw nuts, hex finished nuts, lock and flat washers, flat head machine screws, oval head strut bolts, carriage bolts, lag screws, hex head cap screws, and flat head wood screws; brass cap nuts, hex nuts, machine screw nuts, wing nuts, flat and finishing washers, machine screws, escutcheon pins, brads, and wood screws; nylon insert lock nuts, cap and wing nuts; aluminum back up washers and copper tacks; plain rod in 18-8 stainless steel or silicon bronze, and threaded rod in stainless, brass, or silicon bronze; blind rivets in aluminum or stainless; and ring-barb boat nails in silicon bronze or 316 stainless steel. The firm can also supply galvanized wood screws and bolts, chrome-plated brass screws, common copper nails, grade 8 cap screws, metric fasteners, brass pipe fittings, Kitz ball valves, electric terminals, nylon clamps and ties, Magna driver bits, twist drills, Black and Decker industrial tools, Ryobi power tools, and soft sanding pads. Non-standard fasteners are available.

JAMESTOWN DISTRIBUTORS
P.O. Box 348
22 Narragansett Avenue
Jamestown, Rhode Island 02835
(401) 423-2520
Fastener catalog, 26 pages; Mini-catalog, 2 pages; Product list and order form. Free.
A wholesale retail distributor of boatbuilding and marine supplies, Jamestown Distributors was established in 1977 as a supplier of stainless steel screws to local boatbuilders. As the product list discloses, stainless steel, silicon bronze, brass, galvanized and zinc/plain fasteners, nails, galvanized, brass and rigging hardware, electrical components, tapes, bungs, rope, caulking cartridges, fiberglass products, paints, solvents and related accessories,

sandpaper, tools, ladders, gloves, safety items, and a host of other items are now available from the firm. The mini-catalog furnishes prices for some copper and silicon bronze nails, stainless steel nuts, washers, and some screws, flat-head wood screws, caulk, a variety of fiberglass supplies, sandpaper, discs, drill bits, and belts. The larger catalog lists the tremendous variety of fasteners, the sizes in which they are available, and their prices; only a few other supplies are included. Upon request, pricing information and descriptions of all supplies appearing on the product list will be sent at no charge.

KISLY MANUFACTURING COMPANY, INC.
18 Pearce Avenue
Manasquan, New Jersey 08738
(201) 223-8850
Informational sheets (2); Order form. Free.
Providing a tough life-time waterproof bond and requiring no plugs, Kisly's wooden, epoxy-sealed "K" trunnels can be used to plank, refasten, or restore any wooden boat, and can be applied to plywood, particle board, sandwich-type fiberglass constructions, teak decks, trim, frames, cabin soles, cabinets, tables, hatches, and coamings. One sheet explains the installation and uses of the trunnels, while the other furnishes prices for standard size locust, mahogany, white oak, and teak trunnels. W.E.S.T. system one-to-five part epoxy sets and monoject syringes are also available. Trunnels can be custom manufactured of any wood desired. A sample kit consisting of 25 K trunnels, drill, bore, and syringe is available. The firm is also noted for its custom boat work including a recent 19' speed boat entirely fastened with trunnels.

S & B MARINE PRODUCTS
P.O. Box 6727
Laguna Niguel, California 92677
(714) 956-3760
Catalog, 42 pages; Order form. Free.
Presented on sheets color-coded according to material, and priced per piece and per 100 according to size, the available fastenings include 18-8 stainless steel nuts, washers, cotter pins, hex head cap screws, socket head cap screws, buttonhead socket screws, flathead socket screws, cup point socket set screws, square head set screws, carriage bolts, lags, machine screws, wood screws, sheet metal screws, and threaded rod; 316 stainless steel hex nuts, flat washers, split lockwashers, threaded rod, and hex head cap screws; forged non-magnetic 316 stainless shackles and 304 stainless eye bolts; silicon bronze nuts, washers, threaded rod, hex head cap screws, carriage bolts, lag screws, socket head cap screws, round and flat head slotted machine screws, boat and wire nails, and slotted flat head wood screws; and hot-dip galvanized carriage bolts with nuts, lag bolts, wood screws, flat washers and split lockwashers. Gesipa aluminum and stainless steel blind rivets and a complete line of riveting tools, teak and mahogany wood plugs, and "Vibra-tite" locking fluid are also available. A chart enumerates the weights per hundred of the various fasteners. Quotes will be given for larger quantities or items not listed.

SKOOKUM FASTENINGS

805 Sixth Street
Anacortes, Washington 98221
(206) 293-7469

Catalog, 12 pages; Order form. Free.

For six years partners Martin Langeland and Diana Siegfried have been making copper rivets, roves, and clench nails to help wooden boatbuilders make craft which, in Chinook jargon, are "mamook delate" (made right). They offer their catalog as much as an educational tool for understanding fastenings, as a product list. In addition to the sizes and prices for copper rivets, roves, clench nails, finish nails, panel nails, no-skid deck nails, and wire nails for copper solar collectors, illustrations and often long descriptions of the fastenings, their recommended uses, installation procedures, and some technical data are given. A riveting hammer, rove set, and clenching bar are available and custom nails can be fabricated. Offered for a limited time only is "Tales from the Nailery," a paper expounding the 5,000 year history of the nail, emphasizing its maritime use.

TREMONT NAIL COMPANY

8 Elm Street
P.O. Box 111
Wareham, Massachusetts 02571
(617) 295-0038

Catalog, 16 pages; Two pamphlets, 6 pages each; Price lists and order forms (5). Free.

Tremont's "Catalogue of General Merchandise" presents pictures and brief descriptions of its "Country Store" stock. Four pages cover O. Mustad and Son's line of 100% hard-drawn copper square boat nails and dished roves, and the firm's hardened steel cut masonry nails (including some for boats), old-fashioned cut nails, and special decorative nails. Also treated in the rest of the catalog are a company history, colonial hardware, hand-wrought iron hinges and fixtures, decorative wall plates, bathroom accessories, hooks and hangers, kitchen gadgets, unfinished wooden items, and a small selection of country living books. One pamphlet and the additional sheets repeat the catalog pages, describing and offering the copper boat nails and roves, old-fashioned cut nails, wrought-head nails, and cut nails in special and old-fashioned patterns. Another pamphlet presents some specialty items including nail jewelry and a collector's set of nails.

See also, under:

Small Open Boats	Tool Works
Tender Craft	Woodcraft
Materials and Supplies	Woodworker's Store
Aircraft	Woodworker's Supply
Dunbar	**Sailing Hardware**
Flounder	Tops-In-Quality
Marine Development	**General Catalogs**
Wicks	Airborne
Tools	Commodore
Fisher	Defender
Shopsmith	Fore and Aft Marine

General Catalogs *(continued)*

Goldberg's	National Marine
M & E	Port Supply
Manhattan	Stone Harbor
Marine Center	Warehouse

Trim

TRIM-LOK, INCORPORATED

7220 Compton Boulevard
Paramount, California 90723
(213) 531-0231

Catalog, 4 pages; Price list. Free.

Trim-Lok's brochure furnishes photos and minimal descriptions of available trim types, and charts their styles, sizes, colors, textures or finishes, and clip materials. Regular trims consist of flexible PVC 80 to 85 Durometer with steel or aluminum clips, and they come in a variety of textures, black, white, or tan. Flexible "trim-seal" is available in black fine-pebble finish, chrome, or teak, with nitrite vinyl foam or neoprene bulbs. Simulated rubber, and other chrome or teak trims with steel or aluminum clips may also be procured. One page illustrates several practical applications of the trim.

WEFCO RUBBER MANUFACTURING CORPORATION

1655 Euclid Street
Santa Monica, California 90404
(213) 393-0303/0304

Catalog, 40 pages; General manufacturers' literature. Free.

Wefco is the largest manufacturer in the U.S.A. of replacement boat gunwales and boat bumpers for all existing boats regardless of age or model. The "no bounce" material used is Butyl rubber, which stands high heat, sunlight, and cold weather without powdering and cracking. Standard colors are white or black, but other colors are available in quantities of 150 pounds or more, upon request. The extrusions are fabricated in desired lengths; over 1,100 types and styles are offered. Customers are asked to submit a ¼" to ½" sample piece or a suitably dimensioned sketch of the damaged or worn gunwale. Custom parts can be made at a nominal charge for the die or mold. Brief descriptions of the firm's dock bumpers (50 types and sizes, 10' lengths, white or black), "H" window rubber, "U" trim rubber (50 sizes, black and white), windshield and hatch rubber, and dock wheels are similarly provided, as well as a few pages picturing gunwale/extrusion cross-sections and giving prices. A more complete set of cross-section illustrations is apparently available; some help may be needed to understand the order in which the cross-sections are pictured and the extrusions listed. Most of this catalog's pages are devoted to pictures and prices of the antique auto trims in which the firm specializes.

See also, under:

Sailing Hardware
Beckson
Sailing Specialties
General Catalogs
Defender
M & E
National Marine

The Wooden Boat Shop.

Tools, Knives, Drafting, Layout, and Lofting Instruments

ADJUSTABLE CLAMP COMPANY
417 North Ashland Avenue
Chicago, Illinois 60622
(312) 666-0640

Catalog, 8 pages; Brochure, 4 pages; Informational sheets (3); Price lists (8); Order form. Free.

Offering the most extensive line of clamps available, this literature is the same used by wholesale distributors in their purchasing files. Featuring "Jorgensen" and "Pony" brands, the catalog provides illustrations and descriptions of hand and press screws, band, spring, edge, steel/wood bar, hinged, "C", and hold down clamps, clamp swivels, fixtures, and accessories. Suggestions for the selection, use, and care of the clamps are also furnished. The accompanying brochure explains with illustrations how to make a mitre clamp and veneer press frames with the use of Jorgensen hand or press screws; additional illustrations show proper applications of a variety of clamps. A number of corner and splicing clamps, butt and square gages, a drill sharpening attachment, and a "kerf-kutter," are depicted and explained on the loose sheets. The price list helpfully contains a picture of each item placed next to the appropriate chart of stock and code numbers, sizes, quantities, and prices.

BENNER-NAWMAN, INC.
Corporate Headquarters
3070 Bay Vista Court (Al)
Benicia, California 94510
(800) 528-5502; (707) 746-0500;
Arizona: (602) 684-2813

Informational sheet; Press release. Free.

Available directly from Benner-Nawman is an 18″ long "UP-B99" hand tool for cutting wire mesh and stainless steel stranded cable up to ¼″ in diameter. Ideal for use on overhead guywire and support cable, this safe tool "incorporates a compound leverage action to cut the cable material." The replaceable cutting blades are drop-forged from a specially-made high-grade tool steel. The sheet shows a large color photo of the tool and lists its features; the press release pretty much replicates the information. Call for more information.

CONOVER WOODCRAFT SPECIALTIES, INC.
18125 Madison Road
Parkman, Ohio 44080
(216) 548-3481

Catalog, 32 pages. $1.

Pleasant in format, the Conover catalog provides ample photos or illustrations, specifications, and good descriptions and discussions of a variety of woodworking tools and machinery; a number of woodworking books are also covered. Among the hand tools and accessories offered are some first-quality, low-priced used hand tools, some of Western origin, from China (four-fold rulers, chisel sets, plane irons, iron spokeshave); some Michael Dunbar-inspired reproductions of antique tools (spokeshave, scorp, spoon bits, panel raising plane); Conover's thread boxes and accessories, complete or in kit form, palm planes, blind nailers, scraper planes, wood bits, auger bit, drill collar set, bit brace, "Metalspy," abrasive belt cleaner, Grobbet checkering files and Arkansas whetstones. Among the machines available, many of which are almost entirely composed of highest quality cast iron parts, are sanders, a woodcutting band saw, cabinet maker's saw, industrial joiners, industrial surface planers, industrial shapers, drill press, planer/knife sharpener, and a dust collector; some Hitachi stationary machinery is also represented. Detailed instruction manuals for these machines may be purchased. Occasional mailings announce seasonal sales, closeouts, and used machinery for sale. A 6-page brochure inserted in the catalog describes and offers summer woodworking workshops. Customers are encouraged to visit the retail showroom to see the manufacturing facilities, the complete line of woodworking machinery, an extensive offering of antique tools, and other unique items not covered in the catalog.

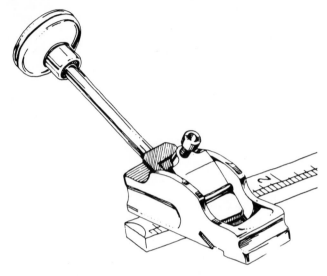

Conover Woodcraft Specialties, Inc. The cast brass body of the Conover Palm Plane is only 2¼" long, is beautifully polished and fitted with a warranted steel iron. Here illustrated at full size.

DINGO CUTLERY COMPANY
4509 N.W. 23rd Avenue, #9
Gainesville, Florida 32606
(800) 874-8499; (904) 376-2220
Catalog, 24 pages. $2.50.
Made to exacting specifications by dedicated craftsmen from premium quality materials, Dingo's mostly imported cutlery is sold at wholesale prices. Briefly described and shown in vivid color photos are a rigging knife, fish filleting knife, professional diving knife, hemostats, and flytying scissors along with knives for hunting, skinning, throwing, collecting, camping, cooking, and other mostly outdoor, survival activities. Commemorative knives, an axe and a rock pick are also available.

THE FINE TOOL SHOPS, INC.
20-28 Backus Avenue
Danbury, Connecticut 06810
(800) 243-1037; (203) 797-0183
Japanese tool catalog, 12 pages. Free. Catalog, 132 pages;
Introductory brochure; Form letter; Order form. $5.
Equipped with a general index, this deluxe catalog provides color photos and good descriptions of almost 1,800 fine quality mostly woodworking tools made in England, Germany, Switzerland, Japan, and the U.S.A. Available in a great variety of models are palm planes, spokeshaves, scrapers, veneering tools, wooden-bodied

planes, metal-bodied planes, rasps, files, sharpening stones, saws, drawknives and woodturning tools, hand drills and bits, carving chisels, gouges, templates and accessories, clamping devices, measuring and marking tools, screwdrivers, mallets, hammers, pliers, jigs, woodthreading kits, brushes, miniature tool sets including one for sportsfishers, a sail repair and sewing kit, and some specialty craft tools. Also offered are small power tools, large power planers and joiners, safety equipment and clothing, workbenches and tool chests, woodworking books, a full line of Swiss Army knives, some Solingen cutlery, and a few miscellaneous camping items. The Japanese tool catalog illustrates in color and describes chisel and gouge sets, heavy-duty carving tools, planes, sharpening devices, and saws. Some gardening tools are introduced in a color brochure. Expert advice regarding woodcarving, woodworking, and antique tools among other topics may be obtained. Free tools, a free one-year subscription to the *Woodworkers Journal,* and discounts on purchases upon buying over $100 or $500 worth of the firm's products, are promised to regular customers.

FISHER POWER EQUIPMENT COMPANY
Route 53
Hanover, Massachusetts 02339
(617) 826-2522
Brochure, 4 pages; Informational sheets (5). Free.
Specializing in pneumatic production tools for wood or wire assembly and construction, Fisher stocks a complete parts inventory and a great variety of pneumatic fasteners, available for immediate shipment either for purchase or evaluation. The brochure furnishes illustrations or photos, and lists some features of staple guns, nail guns, carton closing guns, wire cutters, stainless steel pliers, hog ring tools, Aerosmith bulk nail hammers, some fasteners, air compressors and some accessories. Additional sheets provide more photos, brief information, and prices for many of these tools, hog rings, pneumatic power scissors, a hand-held nailer, and a wire bender. Questions regarding production problems are welcome and complete repair services are offered.

FROG TOOL COMPANY, LTD.
700 W. Jackson Boulevard
Chicago, Illinois 60606
(312) 648-1270
Catalog, 100 pages; Order form. $2.50 (one-time fee for first
catalog).
Frog Tool Company offers a full range of first-rate hand woodworking tools made in the U.S.A., Europe, and Japan. Complete with a fairly detailed index, the catalog provides photos, specifications, and good descriptions for the many available models of drills, taps and dies for wood, other wood-boring equipment, dowelling tools, measuring tools, scrapers, saws, saw blades, clamps, vises, sanding equipment and finishing materials, hammers, screwdrivers, wooden and metal planes, spokeshaves, veneering tools, Japanese tools, chisels, gouges, Italian hand-made rifflers, rasps and files, carving knives, sets, and accessories, mallets, handles, woodturning lathes, sharpening stones and equipment, caning supplies,

Dingo Cutlery Company   Survival Blades and Filleting Knife. The filleting knife (left) floats and has a detachable stripping spoon in the handle top.

specialized hobby tools and accessories, workbenches, tool chests, canvas tool bags, and safety equipment. A Foredom power tool, Leigh Flex grinder, and numerous books on building boats, furniture, musical instruments, toys, and birds/decoys, on wood, tools, woodworking technique, carpentry, carving, finishing, and repairing, blacksmithing, log cabin tools, guns, knives, and old ways are also covered. Tips on sharpening tools are furnished. A free brochure (36B) is available for the firm's large power equipment (tilting arbor saw, band saw, scroll saw, jointer, and sander).

GILLOM MANUFACTURING INC.
1700 Scherer Parkway
St. Charles, Missouri 63301
(314) 724-1812

Four brochures; Reprint; Price lists and order form. Free.

Founded over forty years ago, this company offers a line of 7 basic power tools in kit form; the customer builds the plywood and wood frame and obtains the machined mechanical parts from Gillom. Embellished with reprints of articles describing several kits and their assemblies, the literature furnishes illustrations/photos, specifications, and considerable description for 12″ and 18″ bandsaws, a 9″ tilt/table saw, 10″ tilt/arbor saw, a circular saw table, 12″ lathe-drill press, a wood shaper, and a 6″ belt sander. Various plan and kit packages are available and the parts are priced, pictured, and listed individually. Chrome-plated circular saw blades and Dado saw sets may be purchased too. Some description of the kits in general is also provided.

HANDCRAFTED SAILORS' AND RIGGERS' KNIVES
J. R. Allen
2458 Jacoby Creek Road
Bayside, California 95524
(707) 822-4123

Informational sheet. Free.

Aiming to provide a custom-made, high-quality, affordable knife, Allen offers one specifically designed for rigging work and "all those other jobs around a boat, both delicate and rugged." A sheath knife eight inches long and weighing six to seven ounces, it is composed of a high-carbon, high-chromium stainless tool steel, with brass guard, fabric-reinforced phenolic resin handle, and a

full-grain leather pouch-sheath. Wooden handles of zebra, black locust, black walnut, or teak are also available; quotes will be given for special designs and other materials. At $100, the knife may be returned for a full refund if the customer is not pleased. Allen's literature explains the composition and design of this knife, and his reasons for incorporating them.

JOHN HARRA WOOD AND SUPPLY COMPANY
511 West 25th Street
New York, New York 10001
(212) 741-0290

Catalog, 90 pages; Order form and price list. $3.

Proven dependability, durability, efficiency, and good design are the criteria for including the products featured in this catalog, which are used in the firm's cabinetmaking shop and woodworking school. Sections in the catalog cover American and imported hardwoods, plywood, and specialty lumber; a few woodworking books, Makita power tools, Powermatic machinery, Greenlee woodcrafting tools, sawblades, bits and custom-made router shape bits and shaper accessories, hammers, clamps, measuring instruments, finishing products, safety equipment, sandpaper and abrasives, and Festo specialty woodworking machines. The catalog and many of the sections are prefaced with detailed indexes and introductions to the tools or materials described. Each tool and piece of machinery is illustrated and well-described, and a general discussion of hardwoods is presented. Shop visits are welcome.

HOOVER TOOL WORKS, INC.
Jack L. Hoover, Jr.
P.O. Box 91
125 Beech Avenue
Tiverton, Rhode Island 02878
(401) 624-6476/2239

Brochure, 6 pages. $1 to be put on mailing list.

Good size photos and minimal descriptions are provided for a fruitwood-rosewood hand router with brass adjusting knob, handmade brass and rosewood 4″ and 8″ squares, 10″ T-bevel, and 12″ mitre square, a rosewood spokeshave, 20″ ash bow saw with brass tension rod and knob also in kit form, and a leather apron. Gift certificates are available.

IRON HORSE ANTIQUES, INC.

RD#2
Poultney, Vermont 05764
(802) 287-4050

Brochure, 6 pages. Free.

Many books on tools, and reprints of old tool catalogs, available from Iron Horse, are listed in the brochure. Also provided is a brief description of the firm's catalog-newsletter, *The Fine Tool Journal,* which comes out ten times a year and costs $10 per year or $15 for two years: "Each issue is packed with information on hand tools: antique, obsolete and contemporary. Auction Reviews, many tools for sale, feature articles, 'Whatsit' column, news, and more will be found in each issue." Subscribers receive a 10% discount on the firm's books.

Handcrafted Sailors' and Riggers' Knives   Custom-made knives, by Jack Allan, especially designed for the sailor and rigger.

LEICHTUNG, INC.

4944 Commerce Parkway
Cleveland, Ohio 44128
(800) 321-6840; (216) 831-6191

Catalog, 66 pages; Order form. Free.

Leichtung offers a broad, manageable selection of tools and related handy household and tool shop items. The catalog provides small color photos and good descriptions of Bausch and Lomb magnifiers, a boxwood rule, a caliper rule, pantograph and router, a miter gauge, mitering tool, Japanese and other cabinet-making saws, scrapers, shave hooks, a Japanese planer/shaper/carver, chisels and gouges, rifflers and files, Greenlee lathe tools, carving sets, no-bounce and other hammers, nail pulls and claws, screwdrivers, self-locking wrenches, snips, glass cutters,

scorers, and doweling equipment. Also available are Makita power drills, finishing sanders, and miter saws, Forstner and German-made woodbits, plug cutters, counterbores and drill accessories, abrasives, a work bench, bench duster, electrical multi-outlets and cord caddies, a hand truck, web clamp, mini-hoist, a weather station kit, parts and equipment for home projects, and a woodburner set. Some gardening tools, kitchen and hearth equipment, a few finishes, rust removers, a few other shop chemicals, and some books are also listed.

METRIC MACHINERY COMPANY

Route 2, Box 391
Advance, North Carolina 27006
(919) 998-4051

Hitachi power tool catalog, 38 pages; Price sheet. Free.

To afford retooling, the manager of this wood sign manufacturing business became a distributor for Hitachi power tools, and he willingly passes on the prices, service, and advice that only a professional woodworker can provide. His price list indicates substantial cuts in list prices for a number of circular and mitre saws, routers and planers, drills and sanders. Hitachi's catalog offers color photos and diagrams, and lists specifications and grinders, sanders, saws, planers, routers and trimmers; some precautions regarding the use of these tools are furnished.

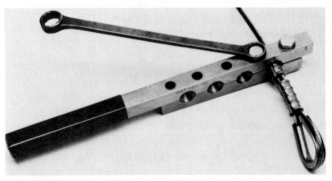

S & F Tool Company   Swage-It tool No. 3 for nicopress copper oval sleeves only. Swaging pressure is applied by using a wrench to tighten bolts.

MORTY THE KNIFE MAN

P.O. Box 7
Little Neck, New York 11363
(516) 546-1495

Two Catalogs, 16 pages and 30 pages; Price list and order form. $2.

Morty the Knife Man offers a marvelous, large assortment of fine quality knives and working tools, at 25% to 50% below retail prices, for the commercial fisherman, seafood processor, sportsfisherman, chef or cook. Beautifully photographed in both catalogs, and briefly described as well in the larger version, are numerous shellfish knives; filleting, gutting, ripping, cutting, heading, splitting, steaking, processing, cleaning, and trimming knives; rigging, netting, mending, rope- and twine-cutting knives; folding and pocket knives; fish and sailor shears, fish scalers, bait stringers, fish maul/mallet, awls and picks, crab tongs, fish box hooks, boat scrapers, a caulking iron, wire cutters, a marlin spike, chipping hammer, needles, a sewing palm, mesh gloves and aprons; knife sharpeners; a chart divider and chart/map/paper shears; and many cook's and chef's knives. These knives, many from Brazil, England, France, Germany, and Sweden, represent some of the most illustrious knife manufacturers in the world. Advice regarding knife sharpening and fish handling is also included in the catalog. The firm also sells a custom-outfitted fiberglass Chincoteague Dead Rise Scow in 18′ and 20′ models, manufactured by Arvidson's Glass Boat Works in Virginia; a brochure showing and describing the boat is available.

S & F TOOL COMPANY
P.O. Box 1546
1245 Logan Avenue
Costa Mesa, California 92626
(714) 546-8073

Brochure, 4 pages. Informational sheet. Free.

S & F Tool offers 3 precision-made steel nicopress tools—two for copper oval sleeves of variable sizes, and one for nicopress $1/16''$ oval or stop copper sleeves—cable cutters and hard wire cutters made of aircraft quality steel "heat treated to a file hard surface with a tough core for long life of cutting edges." All of these tools are cadmium-plated with a gold iradite finish for maximum rust protection; the cutters "incorporate a unique handle design with thick 'T' shaped vinyl handle grips, for maximum comfort." Also pictured and described in the brochure are several items that S & F distributes: H. K. Porter shear-type cable cutters and hard and non-alloy chain cutters, zinc-plated copper oval sleeves, regular and heavy duty stainless steel thimbles for marine use, and, listed on the additional sheet, nicopress stop and special stop sleeves of plain copper, oil-free or hard-white-vinyl-covered type 302 stainless steel cable for marine use, and lubricated galvanized aircraft cable, preformed and manufactured in the U.S.A. Stop sleeve instructions are printed on the reverse side of the additional sheet; an instruction sheet is included in the purchase of each nicopress tool.

SHOPSMITH INC.
750 Center Drive
Vandalia, Ohio 45377
(513) 898-6070; Ohio: (800) 762-7555
Continental U.S.A.: (800) 543-7586

Brochures on specific items. Free. Catalog, 48 pages; Order form. $1.

This "Better Woodworking Catalog and Guide" is broken down into the following sections: layout and measuring tools (including French curves and other drafting equipment), sawing tools, drilling tools, turning tools, portable tools and accessories, carving tools, sanding tools, scraping tools, clamping tools, screwdrivers and hammers (including some fasteners), specialty tools (including brass weather instruments), sharpening tools, picture framing supplies, project components, project plans and books, special tool values, safety equipment, Shopsmith Mark V, stationary power tools, routing tools and accessories,

overarm pin router, Shopmate dust collection system, and workshop aids. Tips on the selection and use of the pertinent items precede most sections, and each item receives a color photo and good description. Additional brochures, mostly in color, provide further information about the 12″ thickness power planer, the router arm, the Mark V multipurpose machine, its numerous accessory packages, and special purpose stationary tools in general (for which a free information kit is available).

BUD STEERE ANTIQUE TOOLS
110 Glenwood Drive
North Kingstown, Rhode Island 02852
(401) 884-5049

Five tool catalogs per year, 24 pages each. Available in lots of 2 and 3. $7 and $10. Left-over lists. $3.

Each catalog offers for sale the latest of around 350 used or antique tools that Bud and Vera Steere have found. Arranged according to "lot" or tool type (sort of), each tool is shown in a photo adjacent to a good description of the tool's condition and most outstanding features. The tools available include wood-bodied, metal-bodied, and Stanley planes, Stanley pre-laterals, beech slide arm plows, rip, turning, and specialty saws, drills and push drills, axes and adzes, hammers, slicks, chisels and sets, knives and cutters, braces, wrenches, calipers, rules, squares, levels, miscellaneous items such as routers, wood scribes, clapboard markers, a blacksmith's axle gauge, a variety of hooks including a grappling hook, loggers' calks, and early machines such as a drill press, boring machines, shaper, jig saw, and wood turning lathes. Tools not sold from past catalogs are listed at reduced prices. Some tool registers and reprints of catalogs, briefly described, may also be obtained.

SUB ENTERPRISES, INC.
1368 W. 11th Street
Long Beach, California 90813
(213) 432-6622

Two brochures, 7 pages in all; Informational sheets (14); Price list. Free.

Sub Enterprises offers several models of hydraulically-operated underwater hull scrubbers, powered by diesel or gas engines. One brochure and four sheets provide prices, photos, and detailed lists of features and specifications for the larger "Brush Sub" systems, their engines, hydraulic systems, hoses and reels, brush units and brushes, and accessories (the Brush Sub unit alone costs $29,000 and the most deluxe assembly costs $99,000). Three more sheets furnish prices, photos, and lists of components for the smaller sea scrubber units; another sheet lists accessories for these systems. Four sheets offer photos, prices, detailed lists of specifications and features, and recommendations for use and selection for the "Hydro Brushes" available; and two other sheets picture and describe oil-free low-pressure compressors. Another brochure presents a resume of responses to the most asked questions about starting a hull cleaning operation using this equipment. Demonstrations of sea scrubber equipment and ocean training sessions can be arranged at the factory for potential buyers, upon request.

THE TOOL WORKS
111 8th Avenue, Room 715
New York, New York 10011
(212) 242-5815

Catalog, 55 pages. $2.

Founded ten years ago with the idea of providing
hard-to-find or discontinued tools by mail, the firm has
grown to offer solid ranges of woodworking and carpentry
supplies and select lines of the most necessary and desired
tools at substantial discounts. Reproducing much
manufacturers' literature, and organized according to
manufacturer, the catalog furnishes illustrations,
descriptions, and advice regarding "Jorgensen" and "Pony"
clamps, Columbian woodworker and machinist vises,
Hargrave tools, Wetzler clamps, Stanley tools, General
measuring devices, Disston saws, Greenlee bits, drills and
plug cutters, Garland mallets and hammers, and Kennedy
tool chests and boxes. Also featured and well-discussed are a
Chinese multi-purpose vise, one of the largest selections of
Norton sandpapers, numerous rasps and files, solid brass
and bronze vintage hardware (mostly hinges and key
escutcheons), quite a range of wood screws, other fasteners,
and escutcheon pins, in brass, silicon bronze, stainless steel,
zinc-plated steel, or copper. Not all available items are
represented in the catalog, so shop visits and inquiries are
encouraged.

GARRETT WADE
161 Avenue of the Americas
New York, New York 10013
(800) 221-2942; (212) 807-1757; (NY, AK, HI)

Introductory catalog, 16 pages; Order form. Free. Catalog, 244
pages; Price list and order form. $3.

Intended equally as a source of valuable information as a
presentation of tools for sale, Garrett Wade's "Master
Catalog" provides large, lovely, mostly color photos, and
considerable discussion and description of over 2,500
products representing almost every type of woodworking
tool ranging from basics such as saws, chisels, hammers,
screwdrivers, and carving tools, to specialties like
combination moulding planes, froes, European
workbenches, and Japanese water stones. Some tools are
made by familiar manufacturers like Stanley, Greenlee, and
Starrett, while other come from important but less known
European firms such as George Ott, Rabine Austerman,
and Record Ridgway. Many of the most specialized tools are
made by small family businesses, and some tools have been
designed and fabricated specially for Garrett Wade.

The introductory catalog provides a detailed list of
tools available in the Master Catalog and presents a selection
of the firm's offerings. Equipped with a detailed table of
contents, the Master Catalog is organized into sections on
accessories, books, carving and sculptors' tools, chisels and
knives, clamping tools, drilling tools, files/rasps/rifflers,
finishing supplies, Inca power tools, Japanese tools,
marking tools, planes, plans, saws, scraping tools,
screwdrivers and awls, sharpeners, turning tools, and
workbenches. Each section is prefaced with a detailed, often
illustrated, general discussion of the pertinent items. There
are no boat plans or boatbuilding books among those
offered. Wood screws, French curve templates, adzes and

bow saws are available. A large retail showroom is located at
the above address.

WATERLINES INCORPORATED
Burge Whiteside
P.O. Box 1534
Southold, New York 11971
(516) 765-1960

Catalog, 22 pages; Price list; Order form. Free.

"This catalog contains a comprehensive selection of the
instruments and materials generally used in laying down
the lines of small craft and aircraft, whether drawn for
full-size or scale-model construction." Described and
pictured are spline weights and splines, Linex Copenhagen
ship curves (42 of them and discounts for orders of 18 or
more), French and other curves, protracters, divider and
compasses, straightedges and rulers, scales, planimeters,
triangles (square and inking edge), templates, tracing
vellums, Mars-Lumigraph pencils and leads, a leadholder,
pointers and sharpeners, pens, ink, opaquing, cleaners,
erasers, tick-strip tape, vinyl boardcover, reducing glass,
drafting accessories, and some navigational instruments.
"Each item listed has met high professional standards for
quality and for suitability to small craft and aircraft design
work, and each is fairly described and priced." Plans are in
progress for supplying heavier and lighter splines, drafting
film and the instruments and ink to be used with it. If a
demand can be shown for specialized instruments that are
no longer produced, certain companies may be pressed to
supply them once again. Interested persons should write to
the Waterlines staff, indicating the instruments they would
like to acquire.

WETZLER CLAMP COMPANY, INC.
43-15 11th Street
Long Island City, New York 11101
(212) 784-2874

Catalog, 12 pages; Price list. Free.

Wetzler's catalog presents pictures, detailed specifications,
recommended uses, and some description of its numerous
clamps and related tools, offered in a variety of sizes: band,
regular and heavy-duty bar, cross, deep throat, drill press,
piling, spring, universal, and welders' clamps, quick action
clamps with wood or wing nut handles, clampettes, pipe
clamp fixtures, welders' clamping frames, regular and
glue-shield hand screws, press screws, veneer press frames
and sectional glueing presses. Repair and replacement parts
are available for all clamps and a separate price list for them
may be requested. Small production runs of spindles and
tapped matching pieces, and special sizes of certain clamps
or parts, can be supplied to the customer's requirements.

WILKE MACHINERY COMPANY
1519 Mount Rose Avenue
York, Pennsylvania 17403
(717) 846-2800; 843-4924

Catalog (quarterly), 40 pages. Free.

Representing only a portion of the firm's products, this
catalog provides photos and lists of features and
specifications for a host of stationary metal and

woodworking machinery of various makes. The woodworking machines featured, many of which contain heavy-duty cast-iron parts, include lathes, sanders, grinders, vertical bandsaws, shapers, table saws, planers, jointers, a hollow chisel mortiser, power mitre box, lathe chisels, woodworkers' vises and gauges. The Fowler line of professional machinist's tools, as well as metal lathes, drill presses and tapping machines, milling and drilling machines, bandsaws, cutters, grinders, milling and drill press vises, are available for metal work. Any machine in the catalog may be leased, and a form is provided for making such arrangements. The catalog comes with an index.

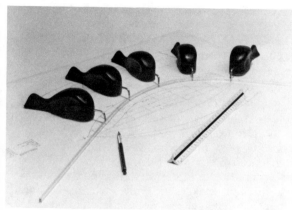

Waterlines Incorporated   Dolphin spline weights.

WILLIAMS AND HUSSEY MACHINE CORPORATION

Division of O. K. Tool Company
W & H Molder-Planers
Milford, New Hampshire 03055
(800) 258-1380; (603) 673-3446

Brochure, 4 pages; Price sheet; Form letter. Free.

Manufacturered for over twenty-seven years with heavy cast-iron bases and heads, steel upright tubes, and only the highest quality materials throughout, the W & H molder-planer is available in hand-feed and power-feed models. The brochure furnishes photos, specifications, lists of features, and descriptions of the machine, while the price sheet offers, on the back, illustrations of standard patterns for which knives may be procured (there are up to 1,000 patterns available). David Rego (Cabinetmaker-Master Carpenter, 49 Downing Street, Fall River, Massachusetts 02723) also sells these machines and a dowel-hole drilling machine; he sends much the same literature, plus a reprint from *Popular Mechanics* that claims the molder-planer is "a veritable planing mill" that can "convert waste and rough-sawn material into dressed lumber free of wave and chatter marks." The parent company occasionally offers special sales of machine and accessory packages.

WOODBUTCHER TOOLS

Shelter Institute Building
38 Center Street
Bath, Maine 04530
(207) 442-7939

Catalog, 28 pages; Price list and order form. Free.
An affiliate of the original school for energy-efficient and

cost-conscious housebuilding, Woodbutcher Tools opened in 1979 to offer durable, necessary, versatile and specialized, high quality tools from around the world, at reasonable prices. Illustrated handsomely by Diane Schelble, graduate of Shelter Institute's building course, the catalog provides good descriptions and large pictures of a comprehensible selection of hand tools including measuring and marking devices, sharpeners and stones, drilling tools, saws and Japanese saws, a drawknife, scrapers and rasps, metal-bodied planes including palm planes, spokeshaves, chisels, carving knives, hammers, mallets, nail pullers, pry bars, clamps, handscrews, tool carriers, safety gear and some wood harvesting tools. New stock is being added continuously.

WOODCRAFT SUPPLY CORPORATION

41 Atlantic Avenue
P.O. Box 4000
Woburn, Massachusetts 01888
(800) 225-1153; (800) 842-1234 (MA);
(617) 935-5860

Tool catalog, 116 pages; Projects catalog, 42 pages; Order forms. Free.

Offering over 3,500 carefully screened and selected products, this catalog touts the widest selection of quality woodworking tools and supplies available in the U.S.A. The Table of Contents reflects sections on books (none on boats), boring tools, Bosch power tools, carving tools, chisels and gouges, clamps, files, finishes, furniture plans and hardware, glues, hammers, hardware (brass hinges and wood screws), Japanese tools, layout and measuring tools, planes, sanding equipment, saws, scrapers, screwdrivers, sharpening tools, spokeshaves, turning tools, veneering tools, vises, woodthreading kits, workbenches and accessories, musical instrument making and log building tools, a Myford lathe, and safety equipment. Each item receives a photo, usually in color, and a good, sometimes lengthy description. General informative introductions preface most sections. The Projects Catalog offers only a canoe paddle kit, a couple of canoe-building books, and some novelty decoy and scrimshaw kits, that might be of interest to boatbuilders; a range of home workshop tools is also featured. Sessions featuring professional woodworkers on specific topics (John Gardner on boatbuilding, for instance) are held during the year at the retail store.

Woodbutcher Tools   The Rabbet Plane—the cutter can be positioned for bullnose cutting and for normal rabbeting.

Williams and Hussey Machine Corporation   The W & H molder-planer is available in hand-feed and power-feed models.

WOODEN BOAT FOUNDATION

Point Hudson Marina
Port Townsend, Washington 98368
(206) 385-3628

Informational lists (6). $1.

In addition to sponsoring an annual wooden boat festival and wooden boat builders' symposium every September, offering workshops throughout the year, and publishing a quarterly newsletter to members of the Wooden Boat Society, the Wooden Boat Foundation occasionally furnishes helpful information such as "A Listing of Sources for Marine Tools and Hardware," which was available at the 1982 festival. Over 100 addresses of companies that offer catalogs are listed, approximately half of which are reviewed in this book. The list may be available from the Foundation upon request. The several kinds of membership in the society offer a free year's subscription to the newsletter, discounts on books and other articles, access to a lending library of over 400 marine titles, wooden boatbuilding instruction, wooden boat referral and information services, and a free listing of the member's boat and gear in the society's anti-crime registry. The more deluxe memberships grant admission to the annual festival, discounts on symposiums and other programs, or complete "free" access to all foundation events.

THE WOODEN BOAT SHOP

1007 N.E. Boat Street
Seattle, Washington 98105
(206) 634-3600

Catalog, 28 pages; Price list and order form. Free.

Although new boats are occasionally built in the back rooms, the Wooden Boat Shop, founded in 1977, is basically a store specializing in traditional marine goods, offering a fairly extensive line of hardware for boats of all sizes, and stocking a good selection of woodworking hand tools and books. Equipped with a brief index, the catalog provides great photos and knowledgeable, helpful, often lengthy discussion of a representative lot of the store's goods, including books, lofting and laying down tools, chisels, gouges, planes, drawknives and spokeshaves, diamond whetstones, saws, bits, augers, plug cutters and

removers, sturdy canvas tool bags, Mustad rivets and roves, Skookum fasteners, some adhesives and cold molding supplies, caulk and sealants, finishes and surfacing tools, rigging supplies, marlinspike books and supplies, bronze deck hardware and rowing hardware, manila bow fenders, and crawdad traps. The catalog does not cover all of the items available, especially not all of the deck hardware, so inquiries about specific items not shown are welcome. Once on the mailing list, customers will receive occasional newsletters which indicate upcoming catalog changes; while the catalog is directed to the non-local buyer, the newsletter is available to local customers as well.

WOODLINE THE JAPAN WOODWORKER

1731 Clement Avenue
Alameda, California 94501
(415) 521-1810

Catalog, 52 pages; Order form. $1.50.

Specializing in Japanese woodworking tools, this firm obtains its tools from small merchants, usually with no English-speaking personnel, who in turn traditionally specialize in tools from the very best master toolmakers. Woodline accepts tools only after determining the identity and reputation of the maker, and conveys this information in its catalog. New items such as tools for left-hand use, additional chisel and gouge sizes, and Aogami (blue steel) tools, are included in this catalog along with carpenter's hatchets and adzes, wood-bodied planes, saws, saw rasps, hammers, woodworking as well as chef's knives, chisels, gouges, and woodcarving tools, scissors, water stones, gauges and layout tools, clamps and woodworker's accessories, some Hitachi, Inca and other power tools, and books. A photo and good description is provided for each item; general discussions of specific brands or kinds of tools may be found throughout the catalog; and "tools as art" are treated in a special section.

THE WOODWORKERS' STORE

21801 Industrial Boulevard
Rogers, Minnesota 55374
(612) 428-4101

Catalog, 114 pages; Order form. $1.

Featuring many woodworking books, furniture plans, picture frames and framing tools, furniture/door/window hardware and supplies, special wood mouldings and trims, carving tools and supplies, and kits for boxes, clocks, game boards, and coffee grinders, this catalog offers products mostly for the hobbyist. Boatbuilders might take interest in some of the other items listed, however: hardwood lumber (birch, cherry, mahogany, maple, oak, walnut), flexible veneers and veneer assortments, veneering and laminating tools, power sanders and abrasives, scrapers, saws, gauges, drills, clamps, sharpening stones, wood finishes and repair kits, finishing supplies, adhesives, and brass wood screws. Most of the products are shown in color photos or illustrations, and brief descriptions are provided. Some instructions are furnished for veneering, caning, wood finishing, and installing various hardware. The catalog includes a detailed index.

WOODWORKER'S SUPPLY, INC.
5604 Alameda N.E.
Albuquerque, New Mexico 87113
(800) 228-2028, ext. 340; (505) 821-0500
Catalog, 32 pages; Order form. $2.

The leading distributor of woodworking tools, machinery, and supplies in New Mexico and southern Colorado, catering mainly to the professional and advanced amateur, this firm services what it sells in the catalog. Emphasizing the power tools available, the catalog begins with carbide saw blades and router bits, shaper cutters, rotary cutting tools, other power tools and accessories. Following sections cover, in order, clamps, some fasteners and fastening tools, adhesives and finishers, abrasives, Japanese tools, marking and layout tools, carving sets and knives, European carving tools, sharpening devices, scraping and shaving tools, chisels, handsaws, turning tools, shop equipment, wooden specialties (plugs, pins, buttons, veneers), cabinet hardware, and books (no boats). Each item receives a brief description and a small photo; some items, mostly the power tools, are covered more fully.

ZIMMERMAN PACKING AND MANUFACTURING, INC.
2768 Highland Avenue
Cincinnati, Ohio 45212
(513) 731-1767
Catalog, 59 pages; Brochure. Free.

Available alike to distributors and retail customers, this catalog contains literature and price lists depicting and describing several gasket cutters, punches, punch sets, hammers, replacement parts, and accessories such as cutting boards and pads, extension arms, pins and blades; gasket materials (neoprene sheet, Buna N sheet, pure gum floating stock, red sheet, EPR sheet, FDA sheet, viton, silicone, plant fiber, compressed asbestos, and teflon sheets); compression packings (Kevlar, teflons, graphite or carbon filament, asbestos and graphite, regular flax braids; asbestos handhole and manhole gaskets; teflon sealant tape), and flexible packing hooks. The composition of each gasket and compression packing material is given along with recommended uses. The technical publication "Non-Metallic Gasket and Sheet Packing Handbook" takes up sixteen pages of the catalog to assist in the selection, proper installation, and maintenance of the materials for a wide range of applications. The additional brochure presents a synopsis of the gasket cutting tools and materials.

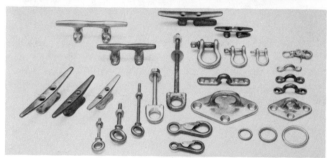

The Wooden Boat Shop   The shop interior and a sampling of some of the fairly extensive line of traditional and hard-to-find boat gear found in this unique shop.

See also, under:

Specialty Craft
Popular Mechanics

Yachts
Letcher

Materials and Supplies
Aircraft
Flounder
Wicks

Fasteners
Bryce

Chesapeake
Jamestown

Sailing Hardware
Marlin
Nashmarine
Tops-In-Quality

General Catalogs
Airborne
Austad's
Cabela's

Defender
E & B
Goldberg's
Golden Fleece
M & E
Manhattan
Murray's
Nautical Boatique
Pastime
Transmar

3. EQUIPMENT FOR BOATING AND SAILING

Nathaniel S. Wilson, Sailmaker   The 400-ton Iron Barque Elissa, owned by the Galveston Historical Foundation, sports 12,000 sq. ft. of sail made by this firm.

Engines, Transmissions, Drive Systems, Trim Planes, Bilge and Oil Pumps

ADVANCED MARINE TECHNOLOGY
P.O. Box 131
Stratford, Connecticut 06497
(203) 378-5362

Booklet, 13 pages; Informational sheets (4). Free.

Advanced Marine's booklet, *Hi-Performance Boat Information,* to be read with all owner's manuals associated with the specific boat and power package, describes and illustrates various powerboat bottom shapes and propellor types, provides a propellor selection chart and speed and safety tips, and explains boat bottom blueprinting procedures, weight distribution, proper motor height on the transom, and the uses for trim tabs and vertical hydraulic engine lifts for outboards. More detailed information including how to find special parts and hardware may be obtained upon submission of $1, the question, and a stamped self-addressed envelope to Department Q at the above address; for detailed answers, include a phone number. A "Propellor Almanac" (three sheets) lists, according to power-weight ratios, proper propellor sizes and materials for the more popular outboard/stern drive/high performance/racing engines. The only item offered for sale, a vertical hydraulic "Speed Lift" for outboards, pictured and described on one sheet, can be obtained from local dealers or, if no dealer, from G & M Enterprises, Inc., 117 E. Locust, El Dorado, Arkansas 71730; (501) 863-0212.

AQUABUG INTERNATIONAL, INC.
100 Merrick Road
Rockville Centre, New York 11570
(516) 536-8217

Catalog, 8 pages; Reprint. Free.

Color photos, specifications, and considerable promotional description are provided for Aquabug's 3 two-cycle one-cylinder "AquaMatic Drive" outboards which easily and safely slip from neutral to low to high by throttle alone (1.2, 1.75, 3 hp; 13#, 19#, 24#), standard and automatic

bicycle engines (1 hp; 11#, 13.2#), and portable generators (19#) for charging batteries, running DC camp accessories, radios, fans, AC and DC lights, ham and CB radios, bilge pumps, and portable refrigerators. Some spare parts are available and a shrouded bicycle engine will soon be on the market. A reprint from *Popular Mechanics* explains how to motorize a bicycle.

BEACON PLASTIC AND METAL PRODUCTS, INC.
50 Park Avenue
New York, New York 10016
(212) 679-4180

Manufacturer's literature, 4 pages. Free.

Beacon sells direct only 2 Solé Diesel marine engines imported from Spain, the improved "Mini 3" one-cylinder (12 hp), and the "Mini 18" two-cylinder (18 hp). Both are equipped with special suspension, thermostat, alternator, starter, wet exhaust, fuel pump, spin-off replaceable fuel filter, control panel with key start and stop button, oil pressure, temperature, and amp indicator lights, analog electronic tachometer, warning buzzer for low oil pressure, and a color-coded electrical harness with quick disconnect block. Each shipment includes a spare parts kit containing an air filter, fuel filter, two impellers, and a flange fitting. Each sheet presents a photo and drawing of one engine, plus specifications and a chart of the engine's capabilities.

BENNETT MARINE, INC.
550 N.W. 12th Avenue
Deerfield Beach, Florida 33441
(305) 427-1400

Brochure, 4 pages; Informational sheets (6). Free.

Bennett's "electro-hydraulic trim planes, aircraft-type planing control, engineered in correct designs and sizes for boats 16 to 80 feet in length are guaranteed to enable you to trim your boat in seconds for maximum speed and efficiency, regardless of the load of fuel and passengers aboard." The brochure presents the virtues of trim planes, describes the composition of the planes, standard and optional equipment (controls, indicators, power units), and gives ordering and installation instructions in brief. Three more sheets furnish detailed illustrations and directions for installing the planes; another sheet gives operating instructions; and yet another states Bennett's three-year limited warranty. A final sheet, a reprint from *Pleasure Boating Magazine,* explains the fuel savings that trim tabs make possible.

*BERKELEY PUMP COMPANY
829 Bancroft Way
Berkeley, California 94710
(800) 227-1088; (415) 843-9400

Catalog, 144 pages. Free.

The Berkeley catalog is composed of an eight-page color brochure explaining the jet-drive packajet marine propulsion unit using an inboard; twenty-two pages of technical bulletins depicting and describing in detail

Beacon Plastic and Metal Products, Inc. The Mini 3 Sole Marine Diesel Engine, imported from Spain, is a one-cylinder, 12 horsepower engine and weighs only 12 pounds.

several jet-drive models, the packajet, a jet-drive repair parts kit, and jet-drive accessories and installation fixtures; forty-six pages of well-illustrated installation instructions for various models and parts; nine pages of operation and maintenance instructions for Model 12J; and fifty-five pages of illustrated parts and price lists. T-shirts, pit caps, and belt buckles with the Berkeley logo may be purchased.

BOAT LEVELER MANUFACTURING COMPANY

7305 Natural Bridge Road
St. Louis, Missouri 63121
(314) 385-7470

Brochure, 6 pages; Form letter; Installation instructions. Free.

Readily adaptable to any size or shape hull and easily installed, "Insta-Trim" electric hydraulic boat levelers allegedly produce a fuel-efficient, smooth, and level ride, eliminating squatting and listing, and reducing the wake. The brochure offers color photos of boats using and not using the levelers, provides testimonials from satisfied customers, lists features and specifications, and furnishes photos and brief descriptions of boat leveler parts.

Kiekhaffer Aeromarine Motors, Inc.   K-planes, heavy duty cast aluminum verisions of trim-planes now engineered for boats as small as 21', are used to compensate for varying wind, water, power, and loading conditions.

FEDERAL MARINE MOTORS COMPANY

3033 - 47th Avenue N.
St. Petersburg, Florida 33714
(813) 522-1522

Brochure, 4 pages; Information sheet. Free.

Federal Marine offers flexible couplings which, placed between the propeller shaft and engine of a boat, counter misalignment, reduce noise, absorb vibration, and by isolating iron engine parts from the bronze shafting and propeller, prevent electrolysis. The brochure explains in detail the usefulness and composition of the coupling, charts the models available, lists their recommended loads, and partially lists models to be used with certain diesel and gas engines. Couplings with standard bore and keyways are available for most gas engines not exceeding 500 hp ratings and diesels to 900 foot-pounds torque; all necessary bolts, nuts, and set screws are supplied. Also described and pictured is a marine universal joint coupling for use on propeller shafts coupled to V-drives (engines up to 400 hp) where space is limited; blank models can be supplied for local machining to size.

Kiekhaffer Aeromarine Motors, Inc.   KAM propellors for the racing enthusiast, manufactured from high quality stainless steel investment castings, are available in pitches from 23″ to 34″ and in four different rake angles.

KIEKHAEFFER AEROMARINE MOTORS, INC.

P.O. Box 1458
Fond du Lac, Wisconsin 54935
(414) 921-5330

Catalog, 15 pages; Order form; Price lists (10). Free.

Photos, specifications, and detailed descriptions of uses and features are provided in the catalog and on an extra sheet for two competition engines (454-495 cu. in., 670-700 hp, 5800 rpm) and electro-hydraulic K-plane kits. Pictured, but too briefly described, are various engine assembly parts: yo-yo blocks, a heavy-duty hydraulic cylinder, pump, and valve, universal drivelines, water-cooled power-tuned exhaust headers, flywheel housing, a high capacity fuel filter, fuel tank fuel pick-up, electric high-pressure fuel pump, heavy-duty marine offshore gear case, aluminum oil pan, stainless steel propellers with short or long hubs for III SSM, steering tie-bars, throttle and shift box, heavy-duty inner transom plate for Mercruiser III, one-piece velocity stacks, and a dual engine low-level water pick-up kit. The price catalog lists additional parts (adapters, alternator assemblies, spark plug and distributor lead kit, fuel selection valve, etc.) and outlines the costs of several services offered: dual engine installation in a new hull, engine rebuilds, and blueprint rebuild and conversions for Mercruiser III SSM stern drives. It is not clear if the engines described are available without installation.

LAND & SEA PERFORMANCE CENTER

P.O. Box 96
10 Manor Parkway
North Salem, New Hampshire 03073
(603) 893-8093

Catalog, 50 pages; Price lists. $3.

Devoting nine pages to Land & Sea's custom engine modification services, the catalog offers photos and often lengthy descriptions of the high-performance engine parts available: big bore carbs, drag-on pipes, exhausts and exhaust plates, an exhaust extension ring, float bowls and stuffers, fuel injection systems, an afterburner injection system, fuel jets, an electric fuel pump, flywheel, and a gas octane booster. You will also find gear cases and conversion shafts, competition gauges and switches, high-performance heads, a nose cone kit, various manifolds and manifold kits, rigid motor mounts, forged pistons, custom reworked propellors, a propellor exhaust hub, locking prop nuts, a trim and tilt bushing kit, power trim lines, trim tabs (afterplanes), velocity stacks, a water brake kit, water pick-up kit, wristpins, repair compound and sealer, an automatic transom drain, bucket seats, racing jackets, T-shirts, and decals. Orders for racing parts are not recommended unless the customer possesses mechanical and technical ability to tune and adjust the engine properly to compensate for the new parts.

LEHMAN POWER CORPORATION
800 East Elizabeth Avenue
Linden, New Jersey 07036
(201) 486-5700
Catalog, 57 pages. $2.

Manufacturing marine power equipment since 1932 under the "Econ-O-Power" copyright, Lehman sells Ford and Peugeot-based marine diesel engines, marine conversion parts for Ford and Peugeot engines, a variety of engine options, exhaust and fuel accessories, transmissions, controls and accessories, propellors, drive and steering accessories, marine electrical instruments, and special accessories such as a generator, voltage regulator, bilge pumps, zincs, strainers and seacocks, thru-hull fittings, water hose and hose clamps. A photo, scale drawings, specifications and abundant technical description is provided for each engine. Photos, solid descriptions, recommended uses, and sometimes additional illustrations and technical data and special ordering instructions are given for the other items listed. A very detailed index prefaces the catalog. As a special service, Lehman engines are offered with installation kits assembled to the builder's requirements; every engine comes with a comprehensive manual covering proper engine care and operation. A three- to four-hour orientation course for diesel engine owners is offered at the plant the first Wednesday of each month. A Lehman engine requires a left-hand propellor.

*MARINE DRIVE SYSTEMS
519 Raritan Center
Edison, New Jersey 08837
(201) 225-3300
Catalog, 35 pages; Supplement, 4 pages. $5. Series 100 Comprehensive Manual, 131 pages. $10 to $12. (No charge for catalog or manual to serious inquirers.)

The "Stern Powr Propulsion Equipment" catalog furnishes photos, illustrations, specifications, longish descriptions, and recommended uses for the variety of equipment offered: several models of stern drives for gas or diesel marine engines, cushion and solid hub propellors, major sterndrive assemblies, a shaft extension kit, manual hydraulic steering systems and parts, electro-hydraulic lifts, hydraulic drive systems, housing extensions, engine bell housings, damper plates, water pick-ups, transom platforms and cowl, coatings and finishes, and some old-to-new model and other-to-Stern-Powr conversion kits. Also provided are a table of general sterndrive specifications, drawings showing sterndrive dimensions and internal parts, a detailed guide to sterndrive model and propellor selection, and advice on converting engines to marine use. Other literature available, including the Series 100 manual, is briefly described. All old style major assemblies and parts and complete replacement drives of older types may be obtained. Other services include design and production of special private label forms of sterndrives, and incorporation of special features and new technology in custom work. The catalog supplement covers "Speed Powr" and "Super Speed Powr" sterndrives and assemblies. The manual, complete with detailed table of contents and numerous diagrams of various assemblies and components, covers "the principle aspects of application, installation, maintenance, parts identification, and service" for a series of sterndrives which can be attached to most marine engines, gas or diesel, for propulsion of medium-sized vessels.

Land & Sea Performance Center   Besides high-performance engine parts, this company also offers a custom engine modification service.

MARINE ENGINE CENTER, INC.
P.O. Box 649
568 E. Elizabeth Avenue
Linden, New Jersey 07036
(201) 486-5758
Catalog, 70 pages; Ordering instructions. $2.50.

This "Original Marine Power Catalog" presents only a selection of the Center's vast inventory of marine engines, transmissions, parts, accessories, and related drive-train, electrical, exhaust, cooling, and fuel system components, controls, instruments, and hardware. Marine components and accessories are listed for several models of base engines (Chevy V-8, Ford 6 and V-8, Olds V-8). Photos, general specifications, and features are given for the Lehman, Chris Craft, and Crusader marine engines the firm distributes. Pictured and described sometimes at length are varieties of marine transmissions, special gear drives, exhaust manifolds, systems, fuel system parts, heat exchangers and kits, keel coolers, carburetor wedges, various small engine parts, marine gasket kits, propellors, rudders, shafts, bearings, couplings, zincs, related parts and equipment, Kobelt controls, Morse controls, cables, and steering systems, Wagner hydraulic steering and accessories, some instruments, panels, alternators, and electrical components, water system parts and a variety of bilge and other pumps. Additional catalogs on drive components, controls, exhaust systems, fuel systems, cooling systems, electrical components, instruments, and hardware are available at $1 each.

NATIONAL MAGNETIC SENSORS, INC.
P.O. Box 439
141 Summer Street
Plantsville, Connecticut 06479
(203) 621-6816/6817
Informational sheets (4); Price sheet. Free.

National Magnetic Sensors' time-operated pump control systems "reliably automate any electric bilge pump for efficient pumping in larger, deeper bilges as found in sailing vessels, and deep "V" cruisers… Model SSR-1 is for offshore racing and has a time delay control to eliminate inertial actuation." One sheet furnishes photos of the equipment, installation diagrams, and lists of features. Additional sheets answer questions to common pumping problems and discuss the prevention of avoidable sinkings by using automatic pump controls and alarm systems. Prices are shown for only one 12-volt DC sensor/timer, a 12/32-volt DC sensor, 12-volt DC timer, alarm panel, and selector panel. Other models may be available. An easy wiring diagram is furnished with each order.

PENNSYLVANIA DEVELOPMENT COMPANY
3810 Crooked Run Road
North Versailles, Pennsylvania 15137
(412) 471-4181
Informational sheet. Free.

A photo, specifications, a list of features, and some additional description are given for a 6 hp direct-electric or manual start long-shaft diesel "Carniti" one-cylinder outboard. The engine is to be used for displacement and auxiliary power (on fishboats, workboats, pontoon boats, houseboats, sailboats, inflatables) but not for planing.

*ROSS MANUFACTURING
916 Second Street
Snohomish, Washington 98290
(206) 568-3888
Informational sheets (2). Free.

The easily-installed Ross oil changer removes oil from a marine engine by using the oil pump, fitting into the pressure system. The transfer valve maintains a safe level of oil pressure. One sheet shows a photo and illustration of the pump, describes its operation and virtues briefly, and answers common questions asked about it. The other sheet provides a larger illustration and outlines both installation and oil change procedures.

S & A INDUSTRIES
442 Statler Building
Boston, Massachusetts 02116
(617) 426-7382
Informational sheets (2). Free.

These sheets provide a photo, brief description, and installation instructions for a "rock n' roll" bilge pump which operates solely on the motion of the boat, pumping harder the rougher the water. The self-priming pump can pump over 500 gallons a day and it will lift or push over 6 feet. Tested, proven, built to last of the finest non-corroding materials, the pump can be used for any kind of boat and it is fully guaranteed as long as the customer owns the boat.

SEAAIR INC.
Route 302, Box 365
Raymond, Maine 04071
(207) 655-7800
Information sheet; Order form and price list. Free.

SeaAir offers easy-to-install disc-brake and indexing types of "PropLock" in manual or automatic versions which will stop sailboat propellors from rotating under sail, will safely allow shutting down one engine on dual engine powerboats, and on racing sailboats will correctly locate a two-blade prop behind the deadwood or keep a folding prop blade from hanging down. The sheet shows photos and illustrations and describes the features of the types of PropLock, giving warranty and ordering information. The price list indicates options (neutral switch, solenoid

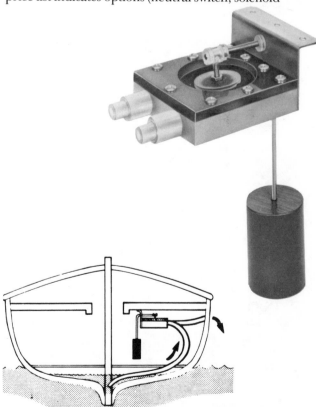

S & A Industries   The Rock 'n Roll Bilge Pump runs on natural energy. It needs no hand or electric power, but operates solely by motion of the boat. The rougher the water, the more it pumps.

shut-off valve, extra hydraulic hose or control cable, spare brake pads, stainless steel disc) and parts available. PropLocks are stocked to fit almost all available marine transmissions; units can be modified rapidly for special installations.

*VERNAY PRODUCTS, INC.
Yellow Springs, Ohio 45387
(513) 767-7261

Two brochures, 4 pages each; Informational sheets (2); Price list. Free.

Furnishing selection procedures, installation instructions, specifications, photos and several line drawings, each piece of literature describes and illustrates one of Vernay's 4 marine products—marine wet exhaust tubing and 3 mufflers composed of fiberglass and fire-retardant polyester resins which will not rust, corrode, or deteriorate from contact with exhaust gases, fresh or salt water. The "Super Vernatone" marine muffler, built longer than the "Vernatone" muffler, improves silencing with the same minimum of back pressure and associated power loss that the Vernatone offers. The "Vernalift" muffler, very effective in reducing engine exhaust noise and preventing water return to the exhaust manifold (important in engine

Vernay Products, Inc.   The Vernalift Wet Marine Muffler will not rust, corrode, or deteriorate. No metallic parts are used, except the drain plug, so electrolysis is eliminated.

installations at or below the waterline), is available in vertical cannister and in-line configurations to lift the exhaust cooling water for overboard discharge.

See also, under:

Small Open Boats
North Shore
Porta-Bote
Specialty Craft
Hal Kelly's
Yachts
P & M
Materials and Supplies
Aircraft Supply
Soundown
Steering Systems
Edson
Sailing Hardware
Beckson
Lange

Merriman
Navtec
Tuna Tournament
Cabin and Water Heaters
Allcraft
General Catalogs
Airborne
Cabela's
Chartroom
Defender
E & B
Fore and Aft Marine
Goldberg's
M & E
M.M.O.S.

Manhattan
Marine Center
National Marine
Nautical Boatique
Overton's
Port Supply
Sears
Stone Harbor
Transmar
Turner's
Warehouse

Battery Chargers

AMPAIR PRODUCTS
76 Meadrow
Godalming
Surrey GU7 3HT   England
Phone: Godalming (04868) 4769
Aston House
Blackheath
Guildford
Surrey GU4 8RD England
Phone: Guildford (0483) 893413

Two pamphlets, 6 pages each; Form letter; Export price list and order form. Free.

Designed for permanent installation on cruising yachts, the Ampair 50, a wind-driven alternator, and the Aquair 50, a wind- or water-driven alternator especially suited for smaller cruising boats, are capable of producing up to 50 watts of 12- or 24-volt DC electricity. Built up to a standard rather than down to a price, of marine-grade materials, mainly aluminum alloy and stainless steel, the alternators are sealed and incorporate permanent-magnet direct-drive rotors and double-sealed grease-packed ball bearings; the front bearing is protected further by a special V-seal. The pamphlets provide photos of the equipment, explain its performance and composition in some detail, and offer lengthy testimonials of satisfied owners. Special mounting bracket kits for the Ampair 50, an optional voltage limiter, and optional read-out unit are available.

ENVIRONMENTAL STABILITY SYSTEMS CORPORATION OF AMERICA (ESSCOA)
3035 Route 23N
P.O. Box 318
Newfoundland, New Jersey 07435
(201) 697-6448
Catalog, 12 pages. Free.
ESSCOA's "mini-windtap" with "antifurl," based on a "very high efficiency rotating venturi concept," begins output at 5 knots and builds to full output by 25 to 40 knots. The smallest of the 5 models charges 6- and 12-volt batteries up to 100 amp hours and the largest can be used to charge large deep cycle marine batteries over 100 amp hours; multiple generator operation is possible with the 3 largest models; the smallest models are portable and can be flown from the mast rigging or mounted permanently. The rotor is built of aircraft-strength heavy-gauge tempered coated aluminum and the frame of heavy-gauge welded undercoated steel; for double the cost, any model can be built entirely in stainless steel. The catalog furnishes photos and illustrations of the windtaps, charts their performance characteristics and features, and provides general information about the generators, their construction, and applications. Also briefly described are some wind-speed indicators and alternate energy publications available for purchase.

HAMILTON Y. FERRIS II
P.O. Box 129
Dover, Massachusetts 02030
(617) 785-0745
Informational sheets (4). Free.
Ferris offers water- and wind-powered generators for bluewater sailors, 3 models of heavy-duty generators, and components for people who prefer to assemble the power plants themselves. The effective operational range of the water-powered generator is 4 to 8 knots; of the wind-powered variety, 10 to 20 knots; 5 or more amps are generated continuously at 6 or 15 knots respectively until the battery approaches a fully charged state. The generators, equipped with grease-sealed ball bearings and composed of anodized aluminum, stainless steel, and other marine-grade materials, are spray- and poop-proof but not immersion-proof. The literature describes the operation and composition of the two units, providing specifications, photos, and power curves, and listing uses for the water-powered generator. Power curves and specifications are furnished for the heavy-duty generators, and parts available independently are listed and priced.

PDC LABS INTERNATIONAL, INC.
P.O. Box 603
El Segundo, California 90245
(800) 227-1617, ext. 136; (800) 772-3545, ext. 136 (CA); (213) 374-7992
Pamphlet, 8 pages; Order form; Price list. Free.
Listing features and presenting testimonials from satisfied customers, the pamphlet provides photos and brief descriptions of 3 models of "Solarcharger" long-lasting, low-profile, teak-frame, solar panels composed of high-density high-efficiency, single-crystal silicon cells, sealed by heat and pressure lamination, bottom-vented for efficiency and drainage, containing no moving parts and

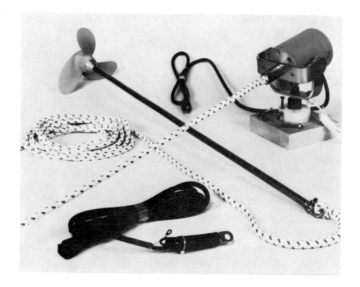

Hamilton Y. Ferris II   The Neptune Supreme (above), a water-powered generating system for bluewater sailors, is a husky, dependable unit which will prove invaluable on long coastwide and ocean passages. The Neptune Supreme (left) is a wind-powered generating system designed for usage when anchored or moored.

demanding no maintenance. Designed for 12-volt systems, the smallest model (9.2″ × 24″) produces 10 watts, the medium-size model (17.7″ × 18.7″) 18 watts, and the largest one (two 14.5″ × 25.5″ panels) 34 watts, under standard conditions. All models can be stepped on, they can be permanently mounted even on curved surfaces (or remain portable), and they can be connected in parallel to multiply current. A battery-condition indicator, dual battery adaptor, and rail mount may also be purchased. Quantity discounts and occasional sales prices are offered.

SUNWATT CORPORATION
P.O. Box 1396
Carbondale, Colorado 81623
(303) 963-0149

Two pamphlets, 6 pages each; Brochure, 4 pages; Informational sheets (2). Free.

SunWatt "offers a broad line of photovoltaic devices, systems, and manufacturing equipment and know-how to businesses, professionals, institutions, hobbyists, and the general consumer public internationally." Promoting the book *Practical Photovoltaics*, one pamphlet answers common questions regarding the composition, use, performance, cost, durability, installation, maintenance, and safety of boat and r.v. solar modules. An accompanying sheet lists features and charts capabilities of recreational solar battery chargers (16-volt, 6-10 watts, 9″ × 9½″, 12″ × 14″, 7″ × 28″); prices are available on request. Another sheet describes photovoltaic module kits using solar cell seconds offered to participants in workshops sponsored by one of SunWatt's dealers, Skyheat Associates, Route 2, English, Indiana 47118; (812) 338-3163. *Practical Voltaics* and some other solar energy literature are also described and available for purchase from Skyheat. In the remaining literature, a solar hot water/electricity module is described in detail, and SunWatt's international franchise system for the manufacture of low-cost solar cell equipment is presented.

WEB CHARGER INCORPORATED
P.O. Box 586
Provincetown, Massachusetts 02657
(617) 487-2294

Pamphlet, 5 pages; Informational sheets (7). Free.

Using the same permanent-magnet generator with permanently sealed and lubricated ball bearings that the Ferris chargers do, the "Web Charger" is handcrafted of "go-to-sea" clear Douglas fir, aluminum, stainless steel, brass, and bronze. Easily stowed and re-rigged, requiring no maintenance, the wind-powered unit puts out an average of 4 to 6 amps per hour in tradewinds. The pamphlet provides photos of the equipment, lists features, and compares it briefly with other generating systems. Five sheets give technical details concerning the construction and features of Web Charger parts. Remaining sheets present the new three-year warranty and a testimonial from *The Practical Sailor* (March 1, 1982). A water-powered model is being developed.

PDC Labs International, Inc.   The SC 10, a solar panel, is an excellent source of 12 volt power for the yacht on a mooring and for the weekend sailor. Panels mount on curved surfaces and may be stepped on.

WESSON PEDAL POWER
Mr. Bob Wesson
667 Jessie Street
Monterey, California 93940

Pamphlet, 6 pages. Free.

Wesson sells a highly efficient, low-rpm, high-output pedal generator (complete, or in major parts) composed of a galvanized frame with zinc-coated pulleys and bearings and rubber-capped ends. Measuring 10″ × 15″ × 17″ and weighing 22 lbs., the unit is easily portable and stowable; when it is pedalled at 60 rpm, its output is 5 amps or more. The pamphlet presents a photo, brief description, and suggestions based on Wesson's experiences using the equipment on his boat. The unit comes with belt tension adjustment and 25′ power cord with polarized connectors.

WINCO
Division of Dyna Technology, Inc.
7850 Metro Parkway
Minneapolis, Minnesota 55420
(612) 853-8400

Brochure, 6 pages; Pamphlet, 6 pages; Informational sheet. Free.

Manufacturing and selling "Winchargers" since the 1930s, Winco currently makes more than 100 models of generators and generator sets. The pamphlet gives a history of the company and brief descriptions of the company today, its line of products and their uses. The brochure presents more historical and general descriptive information about winchargers, furnishes photos, dimensions, and specifications for six models, describes their features, and offers numerous windspeed charts and maps for selecting the right system. Models listed put out 12 to 48 volts, 200 or 450 watts maximum, at 23 to 25 mph. Sizes may be prohibitive for use on small boats—the tower is 10' high, propellor 6' to 8' in diameter, and tail between 6' and 7' long. The lone sheet provides photos, specifications, description, and a selection guide for the DC/AC inverter.

See also, under:

Engines and Transmissions
Aquabug
Lehman

Nautical and Outdoor Clothing
Wind in the Rigging

Winco Dynamight light-weight, portable generators operate appliances and hand tools and charge batteries at the same time. The powerful Maxi-Watt motor provides unequaled motor starting ability.

Steering Systems

CASTLE ELECTRONICS
651 South State Street, Suite 17
Fullerton, California 92631
(714) 992-0342

Brochure, 4 pages; Pamphlet, 5 pages; Informational sheets (4). Free.

Castle Electronics offers a CS-1 autopilot in four configurations to match the specific boat's requirements (up to 98 lbs. of force and up to 0.48 inches per second response), and, for sailboats between 35' and 70', a CS-10 autopilot (172 lbs. force, .30 inch per second response). Both feature marine-grade construction throughout, a watertight heavy ABS case, stainless steel leadscrew, Delrin A. F. follower with Teflon for low friction, large isolated 12-volt gear motor, large sealed ball bearing, I C controlled solid-state circuits, adjustable sensitivity control, modified Ritchie compass card in liquid-fill enclosure with light-emitting diode, internal mechanical feedback, reverse-polarity protection, accessible fuse protections, convenient polarized connector, and adjustable bracket. A lifetime guarantee covers the motor, gearbox, and leadscrew drive assembly. The pamphlet and one sheet treat the CS-1, the brochure and another sheet the CS-10, and the two additional sheets both models, furnishing illustrations of the equipment, ample specifications, and explanations of features and parts.

COEPILOT MANUFACTURING COMPANY
Division of Thermocraft International Corporation
P.O. Box 463
Dana Point, California 92629
(714) 830-4518

Informational sheet; Form letter. Free.

Designed mainly for tiller-controlled racing boats, the non-hunting "Coepilot" is a multicontrol portable electronic automatic pilot system for any size sailboat with 12-volt battery and a tiller; a special fitting adapts the system to destroyer-type steering systems. Furnished with adjustable brackets to fit most cockpit sizes, the device features a $1/10$th hp permanent-magnet type motor, $5/8$th diameter acme-threaded screw drive shaft, bronze or lock assembly tiller car (yoke), three-position switch control module integrated in a solid-state circuit board, fiberglass cover designed to prevent water from directly entering the unit, and a sealed magnetic compass with two sensors for accurate and instant course keeping. Since the unit does not use power unless a course correction is necessary, power consumption varies with weather conditions. The remote control can be used as a dodger or course changer. A windvane plug-in may be available. Several guarantees, described in the form letter, cover the equipment, and include an upgrading program for incorporating improvements and new developments in older units. The sheet provides a photo of the unit and explains its operation and composition.

EDSON INTERNATIONAL

The Edson Corporation
460 Industrial Park Road
New Bedford, Massachusetts 02745
(617) 995-9711

Catalog, 59 pages; Form letter; Price list and order form. $2.

Edson's catalog "represents over 123 years of experience in the design and production of Marine Steering Systems and Bilge Pumps." Two helpful indexes are provided along with photos, illustrations, brief descriptions, dimensions, weights, and other specifications for: hand-crafted and destroyer steering wheels and accessories, numerous steerers, racing/cruising, radial-drive, pull-pull, and autopilot steering systems, pedestal idlers, wire rope sheaves, cable chain and fittings, quadrants, rudder accessories, pedestal guards, accessories, and engine controls, instrument displays and housings, compasses and accessories, permanent and portable "lever-action" bilge pumps, marine deck pumps, pump accessories, cockpit tables and teak holders. In addition, the catalog is filled with detailed selection guides, special ordering instructions, installation and maintenance guides, and general introductory descriptions for most equipment. Questions about specific products, help with orders, and factory visits are welcomed. The form letter lists sales representatives worldwide and upcoming boat shows where customers may consult with Edson representatives.

HYDROVANE YACHT EQUIPMENT LTD.

117 Bramcote Lane
Chilwell
Nottingham NG9 4EU
England
Phone: Nottingham (0602) 256181

Booklet, 18 pages; Price list. Free.

Hydrovane's current models represent fourteen years experience in the design and manufacture of windvane self-steering units which have the effect of making a yacht's rudder act like a trim tab, adding significantly to the stability of the boat. Using its own rudder to steer the boat, the hydrovane unit is totally independent of the yacht's main steering, is always ready for use, and is rapid in its response to the smallest deviation from set course. Compact, lightweight, "robust," and made of corrosion-resistant marine-grade materials, the system is easy to install on any transom, simple and safe to operate in any wind, and useful as an emergency back-up system. The booklet explains the hydrovane system and its operation in detail, describes and pictures the 2 models available (one for boats up to 28' to 32', the other for boats from 32' to 50'), gives their dimensions, specifications, and installation instructions, illustrates typical transom-mounting brackets, describes a compass-autopilot option, and shows photos of sailboats in action, fitted with the equipment. Some spare parts are available. Direct sales to America.

Coepilot Manufacturing Company   The Coepilot is a multicontrol portable electronic automatic pilot system for any size sailboat.

MADEIRA MARINE AND MANUFACTURING, INC.

P.O. Box 1218
Pinellas Park, Florida 33565
(813) 546-4358

Brochure, 4 pages; Price list. Free.

Measured and fabricated for the specific boat and ruggedly "overbuilt" of the highest quality materials, the Riebandt windvane steering system, "RVG," acts totally independently of a ship's steering arrangement, steers a straight track, works in any sea condition, and engages/disengages with a single lever. The brochure offers photos and illustrations of the equipment, describes the construction of its components, the operation and principle of the system, and gives measuring and ordering instructions. Models are available for boats from 39' and 20,000 lbs. to over 45' and 38,000 lbs. A spare parts kit comes with each unit; additional kits, spare parts and spare sails are also available.

TILLER MASTER

P.O. Box 1901
Newport Beach, California 92663
(714) 675-1668

Brochure, 6 pages; Instruction manual, 8 pages. Free.

Developed over a twenty-year period, tested extensively, and built of the highest-quality materials to stand up under exposure and use little enough current to be practical on sailboats with limited battery capacity, the non-hunting Tiller Master can steer in a variety of conditions and temperatures under power or sail. Easy to install, service, disengage, and stow, the unit features a liquid-filled, photocell-actuated magnetic compass, fiberglass-printed solid-state electronic circuit board protected against moisture, a permanent-magnet high-precision motor with reduction gear of continuous rating, a precision-ground acme-threaded jackscrew drive, and a simple mechanical feedback system to prevent oversteering. The brochure

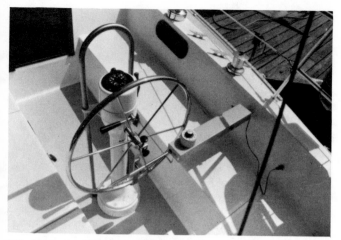 

Tiller Master   A side-mount auto-pilot, with its own magnetic compass, the tiller master is compact, non-hunting, and can steer in a variety of conditions.

provides illustrations and photos of the equipment, a wheel adapter and a remote course dodger, describes the Tiller Master parts and features in detail and related equipment in brief, and presents a list of stock boats which use the unit. An illustrated synopsis of instructions for

adapting the unit for wheel steering systems is also included. The instruction manual presents in detail installation, maintenance, and operating instructions, and discusses common problems.

See also, under:

Engines and Transmissions
Lehman
Marine Drive
Marine Engine
Sailing Hardware
Clark
Follansbee

Merriman
Rickborn
General Catalogs
Commodore
Defender
E & B
Golden Fleece

M & E
M.M.O.S.
Manhattan
National Marine
Nautical Boatique
Sears
Stone Harbor
Warehouse

Electrical Equipment, Marine Electronics, Navigation Instruments, Charts and Charting Tools

AMERICAN MARINE ELECTRONICS
   1082 Post Road
   Darien, Connecticut 06820
   (800) 243-0264; (800) 243-4204 (AK, HI);
   (203) 655-1409
Catalog, 40 pages. Free.
American Marine endeavors to give the best possible prices on the marine electronics offered, and the best advice on the value, delivery, installation, and service of equipment. Representing less than one-fourth of the products available, the catalog lists eighty-six manufacturers whose electronics equipment is kept in stock, and furnishes a photo or illustration, short list of features, sometimes additional description, and a comparison of list with American Marine prices for each item presented in the various sections: Loran, Satellite Navigation, Radar, Autopilots and Accessories, Radio Direction Finders,

Depth Recorders, Radiotelephone, Antennas and Mounts, Loudhailers, Sailboat and Powerboat Instruments, Binoculars, and Miscellaneous Items (stereos, tape decks, EPIRBs, refrigeration devices). American Marine services what it sells. Most products are covered by manufacturer warranties, copies of which are available free upon written request.

***AQUA METER INSTRUMENT
   CORPORATION**
   465 Eagle Rock Avenue
   Roseland, New Jersey 07068
   (201) 228-3600
Catalog, 30 pages. Free.
Aqua Meter "produces the most complete line of compasses, tachometers, speedometers, engine gauges, gas detectors, depth/fish finders, radio direction finders, and

graph recorders available in the marine industry." The catalog offers large color photos, small scale drawings, and generous descriptions of the individual models available. Substantial, instructive descriptions introduce each type of equipment listed above.

Bartell Marine Electronics   The Monitrol Corrosion Control System enables you to detect and correct stray current corrosion.

BAKER, LYMAN, AND COMPANY, INC.

308 Magazine Street
New Orleans, Louisiana 70130
(800) 535-6956; (504) 522-0745; (713) 864-2502

Catalog, 125 pages; Price list; Order forms. Free.

Baker, Lyman, and Company manufactures binnacles and other navigational instruments and aids, distributes, imports, and services the navigational equipment of other manufacturers, adjusts compasses, and acts as chart agents. The catalog provides photos and sometimes brief, sometimes long descriptions of the variety of meteorological instruments, clocks and timers, binnacles, compasses, binoculars, glasses, and scopes, charting equipment, sextants, brass sounding rods, peloruses, small portable tools, chart maps, charts, tables, plotting sheets, light lists, coast pilots, navigation rule manuals, marine educational textbooks, chart tubes and covers, reading glasses, cotton or nylon flags (U.S., Louisiana, International code, foreign merchant code, novelty), plaques, globes, table lamps using nautical parts or motifs, lanterns, hailers, and heaving line. Service repairs are usually completed within 48 hours of the receipt of the instrument, and they are guaranteed for a year. Estimates are provided upon request prior to repair.

BARTELL MARINE ELECTRONICS

1577 Monrovia
Newport Beach, California 92663
(714) 645-7040

Pamphlet, 6 pages; Price list. Free.

Working completely independently of a boat's electrical system, the electronic "Monitrol" operates constantly to detect and correct stray current corrosion and to tell when to replace zincs. The pamphlet presents a photo and description of the device and explains corrosion, the usefulness of the Monitrol, and the easy installation procedure. Monitrol systems, including zincs, for wood and fiberglass sail or powerboats and boats with aluminum outdrive and jet-pump-equipped hulls are listed.

Mounting pads furnished with zincs make zinc replacement easier and protect wooden hulls from "burning."

BETTER BOATING ASSOCIATION, INC.

P.O. Box 407
Needham, Massachusetts 02192
(800) 225-8317; (617) 449-3314 (MA)

Brochure, 4 pages; Information sheet; Order form. Free.

Described and depicted in color in the brochure, BBA's chart kits, available for eleven regions, contain a complete collection of regional harbor, coastal, and offshore charts printed of fade-resistant inks and furnishing Loran-C, longitude and latitude, detailed insets, point-to-point distances and plottings of most used courses, definitions of symbols and abbreviations used, and a listing of marine weather services. The additional sheet offers color photos and description of a portable chart kit plotting machine. Chart kit covers, a plotter carrying case, a Ritchie hand-bearing compass, Chapman's *Piloting*, and Reed's West and East Coast nautical almanacs may also be purchased.

"Time Bowl"—Chattanooga, Inc.   The Quartz-Z, Mark III, is a 24-hour marine chronometer, affectionately called the "Time Bowl." It will withstand spray, storm, and shock and comes with quick detach mounting.

*CABLE ASSEMBLERS INC.

Division of Cablecraft, Inc.
P.O. Box 11372
Tacoma, Washington 98411
(206) 475-1080

Brochure, 4 pages; Price sheets. Free.

The brochure explains part number codes, illustrates parts (threaded and grooved conduit end-fittings, twist-lock, micro-adjust, and non-locking control heads, conduit clamps, ball joint connectors, clevises and pins) and assemblies, gives instructions for selecting and measuring the cables, and briefly describes the features of the

Equipment for Boating and Sailing **99**

push-pull controls, a moisture and dust-proof knob cover, friction lock, and heavy-duty control lever. Locally-assembled control head cables come with a flexible armored inner member while the "trim-to-length" varieties come with a stainless steel wire inner member.

CELESTAIRE
416 S. Pershing
Wichita, Kansas 67218
(316) 686-9785
Catalog, 32 pages; Price list and order form. Free.

Offering low prices and a selection of navigation equipment that includes rare pieces, Celestaire is staffed by experienced marine and air celestial navigators. The catalog provides photos for most items, technical specifications for larger pieces, and descriptions that cover the equipment's merits and recommended uses. Besides a wealth of marine sextants and some astrolabes, aviation sextants, several kinds of compasses, navigation calculators and computers, plotting aids, chronometers, weather instruments, direction finders, optical instruments, some interesting emergency equipment, government publications and other navigation books are available.

"TIME BOWL"—CHATTANOOGA, INC.
P.O. Box 8202
Chattanooga, Tennessee 37411
(615) 624-5528
Brochure, 2 pages; Order form. Free.

Designed and constructed mainly for offshore cruisers and racers of smaller boats who take their navigation seriously, the watertight, corrosion-proof, floatable, and easily removable Quartz-Z Mark III marine chronometer is also used on larger and U.S. Navy vessels. Guaranteed to keep time within one minute per year, the chronometer's quartz movement is manufactured by Kienzle of West Germany. The unit features a 24-hour dial with additional time track graduated in decimal hours, constructed of easy-to-read white polished Mylar. The high-impact black ABS plastic case will be replaced free if it breaks. The brochure provides photos of the "time bowl" and describes its features, operation, and the construction of its parts in detail.

CREATIVE CONSULTANTS
McKenzie Maps
37 Providence Building
334 West Superior Street
Duluth, Minnesota 55802
(800) 346-0089; (800) 232-0069 (MN);
(218) 727-2113
Map Index; Sample Map; Order form. Free.

Creative Consultants produces and markets a series of 21 Boundary Waters Canoe Area Wilderness maps for McKenzie Maps. Providing for the first time a reliable, navigable chart of the travel areas, each map comes in an easy-to-read scale of 2″ to the mile, covers 144 square miles, and measures 25″ × 30″. Coded in three colors to depict water areas, contours, legal campsites, portages, and hiking trails, the maps are printed with waterproof ink on totally waterproof, floatable, tear-, crumple-, and fold-resistant, acrylic-impregnated paper. The maps are updated annually and reviewed by the U.S. Forest Service for accuracy. The map index describes the maps and shows the areas for which they are available. Each map costs $3.95 plus $2 for postage and handling for the first map and 50¢ per map thereafter.

ELECTRA YACHT, INC.
3 Yacht Haven Marine Center
Stamford, Connecticut 06902
(203) 323-1163
Handbook, 191 pages. $5.95.

Electra Yacht, an authorized dealer for the equipment covered in its *Marine Electronics Handbook,* services and, upon request, installs what it sells: VHF/FM radiotelephones, HF single sideband, Telex, communication receivers, weather facsimile recorders, intercom systems, EPIRBs, radio direction finders, Loran C, Omega, satellite navigation, Omni, radar, automatic pilots, depth sounders, sonars, instruments, and antennas. While the equipment included in the handbook is becoming outdated, it is highly informative and designed to allow the customer to make an informed selection of marine electronics. Enhanced with a good table of contents, the handbook describes Electra Yacht's philosophy, provides good photos, specifications, and descriptions of each model offered, and furnishes a wealth of general and technical information regarding the capabilities, operation, and installation of the various kinds of equipment. Marine distress communication and ship radio station license application forms are included.

GREAT CIRCLE PRODUCTIONS
P.O. Box 122
Southwest Harbor, Maine 04679
(207) 244-3615
Informational sheet; Price list. Free.

At present Great Circle offers only a 2′ × 6′ color "explorer's map and directory of the New England coast" (New London, Connecticut, to Passamaquoddy Bay, Canada), available rolled or folded for $9.95 plus $2 for postage and mailing tube. The map shows 380 recreation and education centers, natural areas, public beaches, shellfish areas, town boundaries, bathymetry, and panoramic photos; it also provides directories of museums, nature centers, aquariums, and environmental agencies, and calendars of whale cruises, field trips, boatbuilding festivals, and yacht races. The sheet briefly describes the map but gives no idea of what it looks like. Ordering information and discount rates for dealers and retailers are given on an additional sheet.

HARBOR ELECTRONICS, INC.
365 Main Street
Winthrop, Massachusetts 02152
(800) 343-3602; (800) 732-3730 (MA);
(617) 846-7132
Catalog, 28 pages. Free.

New England's largest marine electronics dealer, with over twenty year's experience in the marine electronics

Kane Marine Just a turn of the MK PBC Plotter's patented red grid brings virtual instant position, bearing, course, or distance off. Grease penciled computations may be erased or transposed to the chart.

business, Harbor Electronics services what it sells, offering the best possible products at fair prices. The newsprint catalog furnishes fair photos and lists features or gives brief descriptions for marine VHF radios, CBs, loudhailers, antennas, small sounders, chart recorders, weather facsimile recorders, navigation and sailing instruments, Loran, satellite navigation and radar equipment, EPIRB, autopilots, radio direction finders, chart kits and paper, power supplies and battery chargers, often presented within sections according to manu-facturer. Other information is presented to help with selection: Loran coverage charts, explanations of Loran C and chart recorder instructions for some equipment, and listings of marine weather service stations and marine telephone operators. Copies of any written warranty regarding any product in the catalog may be obtained free upon written request.

HOWARD COMMUNICATIONS
P.O. Box 205
1 Pear Street
Boothbay Harbor, Maine 04538
(207) 633-3167
Pamphlet, 6 pages. Free.
In order to offer superior back-up service with complete and regularly updated instrumentation, a radio-equipped mobile service van, an extensive spare parts inventory, and personnel with on-going training, Howard Communications, in the marine electronics business for thirty-five years, services only the top-of-the-line brands that it sells for prices higher than most competitors. The pamphlet, which briefly describes the firm's services and orientation, lists a full range of electronics equipment and

related subjects for which the firm offers free information: VHF, SSB, radar, Loran, Omega, satellite navigation, RDF, fathometers, sonar, autopilots, weather fax, yacht instruments, commercial leasing, consulting, and more.

KANE MARINE
P.O. Box 5421
100 S. Ellsworth, Suite 402
San Mateo, California 94402
(415) 342-4781
Pamphlet, 6 pages; Informational sheets (2); Reprints; Order form. Free.
Kane Marine offers the MK III PBC protractor-plotter, which circumvents the awkwardness of using parallel rules, and a related chart roller kit, instant navigation book, illuminated handbearing compass, time/distance/speed computer, and a tote bag especially designed to carry this navigation equipment; the items may be purchased in a complete navigation kit including dividers and grease pencils. The pamphlet explains four charting methods using the equipment, furnishes photos of the device in use, and describes the chart roller kit and tote bag—both of these items are shown and described more fully on the additional sheet. The reprints from several boating magazines review Kane's *Instant Navigation* and detail the use and practicability of the plotter.

KLEID NAVIGATION, INC.
443 Ruane Street
Fairfield, Connecticut 06430
(203) 259-7161
Catalog, 22 pages. Free. Book, 13 pages; Supplement sheets (3). $1.
Offering several sextants, related accessories, a few compasses, plotting tools and aids, sight log reduction forms, several navigating books (including *Choosing a Marine Sextant*), and government publications, the catalog provides good descriptions for all items, photos for most, and detailed specifications for the sextants. Items no longer stocked are minimally described and listed at bargain prices; they are sold with the standard guarantee of satisfaction. Also covered are weekend coastal or celestial navigation courses, offered in major cities across the U.S.; a form is provided for signing up. Kleid's *Choosing a Marine Sextant,* a buyer's guide, discusses sextant features, compares certain models, showing diagrams of their optical geometry, and gives recommendations.

*MARINETICS CORPORATION
P.O. Box 2676
Newport Beach, California 92663
(800) 854-4601; (714) 646-8889 (CA)
Portfolio, 23 pages. Free.
Marinetics manufactures a variety of marine control, instrument, and distribution panels, some modular. Sheets included in the portfolio offer photos, specifications, and detailed descriptions of several double module and "offshore cruiser" master power control panels, main breaker and battery monitor "mini" panels, single module load center, alarm, accessory control, instrumentation, and gas control panels, specialized

controls, electrical hardware, and interior light fixtures.
Circuit breakers, ammeters and voltmeters, and more
electrical components are listed on the price sheet. Legend
plate indexes are provided for electrical and alarm panels.
Another price sheet briefly describes the number of
instructional and "documentary" publications and
diagrams available. A business reply card is provided for
requesting equipment recommendations.

MAXIMUM

42 South Avenue
Natick, Massachusetts 01760
(617) 785-0113; 653-3820

Catalog, 13 pages; Order form. Free.

Sporting 6½" solid brass casings and brushed aluminum
faces, Maximum's weather instruments (wind direction,
speed, gusts, temperature, relative humidity, barometric
pressure) and quartz-movement clocks allegedly achieve
an extreme degree of accuracy. The catalog provides
gorgeous color photos, good descriptions, and technical
specifications for this equipment. Also shown and
described are complete weather stations, panels and
plaques separate of instruments, and system components.

NATIONAL MARINE ELECTRONICS

263 Kelly Street
Lake City, South Carolina 29560
(800) 922-3618 (SC); (800) 845-5927 (U.S., Puerto
Rico, Virgin Islands); (800) 845-0695 (AK, HI)

Catalog, 48 pages. Free.

The largest direct marketer of marine electronics today,
National Marine is designed to offer expert advice and
service, and the widest possible selection of electronics at
the best possible prices. The catalog furnishes photos, lists
of features, and some description for depth sounders and
recorders, Loran C and radar systems, autopilots, sailing
instruments, direction finders, loudhailers,
radiotelephones, hand-held VHF radios, antennas and
mounts, and emergency equipment (EPIRBs, battery
chargers, power supplies); the various models of each type
of equipment are arranged a bit haphazardly within
sections. Also featured is much helpful information: charts
of equipment features, selection guides, technical
glossaries, installation and operation tips, listings of marine
weather service stations, and so on. Manufacturers'
warranties may be requested in writing in advance of
purchase.

RIEKER INSTRUMENT COMPANY

P.O. Box 52
Sycamore and Mill Streets
Clifton Heights, Pennsylvania 19018
(215) 622-4545

Informational sheet; Distributor list; Order form. Free.

Rieker offers a pair of "trim-heel-list indicator" clinometers
for medium to large sailboats, a heel-angle clinometer for
small to medium sailboats, a model combining fore-and-aft
level for large sailboats and medium to large powerboats
and heel-angle clinometer for medium to large sail- and
powerboats, and another model for determining the heel
angle of medium to large sailboats and the time angle of

Maximum   A variety of weather instruments, with 6½" solid brass
castings and brushed aluminum faces, are offered by this firm.

powerboats. All models give instant, accurate angular position readings; they neither lag nor lead the motion. The damping fluid prevents the build-up of inertial forces; it does not freeze nor impede the ball travel. A photo, the dimensions, scale, range, marking intervals, and purpose of each model are presented.

Rieker Instrument Company   By using two Clinometers (port and starboard), with reversed markings, the skipper has a useful range of 40°, with readability and accuracy doubled.

RUSSELL'S PROFESSIONAL SHOPPER
779 Bush Street
San Francisco, California 94120
(800) 227-3416; (415) 433-7540
Catalog, 16 pages; Order form. Free.

Pictured and described amid a host of novelty, mostly electronic or electrical equipment are a few items that might be of interest to boaters: a quartz-movement brass clock or barometer/thermometer as separate or combined instruments, a pocket altimeter/barometer, weather/storm alarm, rangefinder, telescope/magnifier/ microscope, monoscope, binoculars, and a power converter kit. Interesting travel accessories include a shaver, universal five-way lantern, small vacuum cleaner, digital dashboard clock, vertical car compass, mini-clock radio, quartz-movement carriage alarm clock, travel iron, and chess-game computer.

SEANAV INC.
142 Ferry Road
Old Saybrook, Connecticut 06475
(203) 388-0705
Catalog, 30 pages; Price list. Free.

A full service dealer, Seanav provides reliable repair service (even for equipment purchased elsewhere) and professional installations at reasonable prices. Purchasers of Seanav equipment receive operator training, and mail-order customers get all necessary installation instructions over the telephone. Most parts can be supplied for skilled do-it-yourselfers to service their own equipment. Often reproducing manufacturers' literature, the catalog provides photos and lists of features for VHF and SSB radiotelephones, antennas, hailers, Loran C and radar equipment, depth indicators and recorders, sailing and powerboat instruments, autopilots, and accessories; within sections, models are listed in order of manufacturer, and over twenty-six manufacturers are represented. Also included are a Beaufort scale, listings of

VHF marine channels and marine telephone operators, charts showing marine SSB band frequency ranges, international Morse code and the phonetic alphabet, and explanations of the Loran C system and screen interpretation. Information on satellite navigation equipment is available on request. Copies of manufacturers' warranties for products offered may be obtained free upon written request.

SKIPPER MARINE ELECTRONICS, INC.
180 North LaSalle Street
Chicago, Illinois 60601
(800) 621-2378; (312) 726-1721
Five buyer's guides, 8 to 67 pages each. Free.

Self-proclaimed as America's largest genuine factory authorized marine electronics dealer, Skipper offers several guides for purchasing various kinds of marine electronics equipment. In addition to presenting in some detail the important features to consider when choosing specific kinds of equipment, the fully-indexed guides furnish photos, prices, descriptions or lists of features, and sometimes comparison charts, for the brand-name models of each kind of electronics available; special note is made of the outstanding features of certain models. The navigation instruments guide covers Loran C, radar, Omega, and Satellite systems, autopilots, radar detectors, on-board computers, radio direction finders, and facsimile recorders. The sailboat instrument guide covers knotmeters, logs, sounders, wind instruments, digitals, data systems, and remote compasses. The powerboat and fishing instrument guide covers depth sounders, speed instruments, graph recorders, flashers, fish locators, sonar, digitals, and fishing aids. One guide is devoted solely to VHF marine radios, and the shortest manual includes hailers, intercoms, CB radios, stereo systems, and battery chargers.

Weems and Plath Fine Nautical Instruments   Solid cast and tooled brass yacht lamps, available as oil, 110V or 12V electric.

WEEMS AND PLATH FINE NAUTICAL INSTRUMENTS
222 Severn Avenue
Annapolis, Maryland 21403
(301) 263-6700

Catalog, 48 pages; List price sheets. Free.

Continuing in the tradition of its founders, Weems and Plath, now in its fifty-first year, supplies the finest instruments and navigation aids available. Complete with a table of contents, the catalog provides nice, large photos, lengthy descriptions, and specifications for the equipment available: sextants and accessories, navigation computers, several compasses, binoculars and rangefinders, timers and barographs, clocks, chronometers, marine logs, locator and vecta radio direction finders, portable chart tables, a chart lamp, various rules, plotters, dividers, and other plotting tools, rescue and search lights, strobes, beacons, EPIRBs, and yacht lamps. Descriptions are also given for the navigation, piloting, weather, and other books, dictionaries, cruising guides, and chart books that may be purchased; available government publications are listed. Classroom instruction and home study courses in celestial navigation, piloting and chartwork are also described.

WESMAR
Western Marine Electronics
801 Dexter Avenue N.
Box C19074
Seattle, Washington 98109
(206) 285-2420

Brochure, 8 pages; Price sheets. Free.

Wesmar's "Buyer's Guide" presents photos and short descriptions for the firm's full line of offerings, representing Coastal Navigation, Dirigo, International Marine, Nelco, Offshore Marine, Panasonic, Regency Polaris, Unimetrics, and Wesmar's own products: marine radiotelephones and transceivers, depth sounders, Loran C receivers, satellite navigators, fish scans, sonars, color radars, video sounders, chart recorders, flasher recorders, autopilots, compasses, rudder angle indicators, marine alternators, fresh water markers, a stereo system, and portable TVs to be used in connection with radar and other equipment. The order form can be used to request free literature on the individual models. Wesmar makes available detailed color brochures on its digital color radar, digital color sonar, satellite navigator, and autopilot systems. Briefer, less dazzling sheets may be had for a digital compass and console digital depth sounder.

ROBERT E. WHITE INSTRUMENTS, INC.
51 Commercial Wharf
Boston, Massachusetts 02110
(617) 742-3045

Catalog (two parts), 10 pages; Price lists (2). Free.

Presenting small photos and good descriptions, one part of the catalog covers a selection of windspeed and direction, barometric pressure, temperature, humidity, and precipitation instruments, clocks and chronometers available, while the second part includes sextants,

handbearing compasses, general navigation aids (binoculars, standard compass, clinometer, timer, log), and chartroom aids (rules, plotters, dividers, forms, computers, kits, etc.). Lists of brand names and other equipment (charts, weather shelters, custom instrument panels) carried but not shown are also provided. Manufacturers' brochures are available for new digital weather stations and wind chill indicators.

1.

2.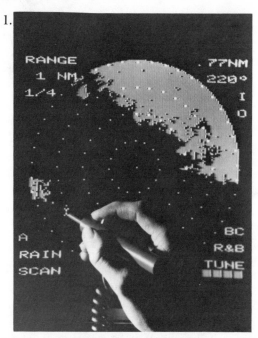

3.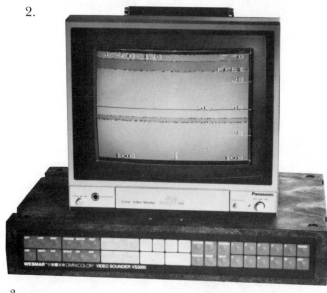

Wesmar   From Wesmar's product guide: 1) Digital Color Radar provides a full-color display of targets, for a full 360-degree picture that stays on the screen without fading, 2) Omnicolor Video Sounder, 3) Omnicolor Radar SR1000—console, antenna, and video marker.

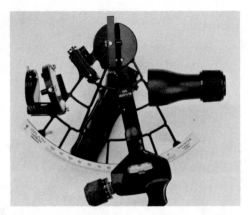
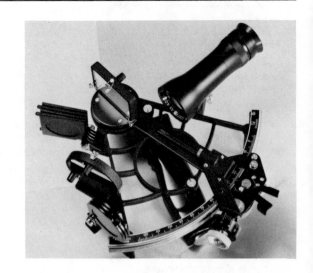

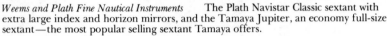

Weems and Plath Fine Nautical Instruments   The Plath Navistar Classic sextant with extra large index and horizon mirrors, and the Tamaya Jupiter, an economy full-size sextant—the most popular selling sextant Tamaya offers.

See also, under:

Yachts
Roberts
Materials and Supplies
Aircraft
Chesapeake
Tools
Shopsmith
Engines and Transmissions
Lehman
Marine Engine
Steering Systems
Edson
Sailing Hardware
Alexander-Roberts
Go
H & L
Merriman
Offshore
Rickborn
Sailing Specialties
Troy

Refrigeration
Raritan
SpaCreek
Nautical and Outdoor Clothing
Afterguard
Bean
Recreational Equipment
Wind in the Rigging
Gifts
Captain's Emporium
Mystic
Preston
General Catalogs
Airborne
Cabela's
Cal
Chartroom
Commodore
Cuttysark
Defender
E & B

Fore and Aft Marine
Goldberg's
Golden Fleece
Haft
International Sailing
M & E
M.M.O.S.
Manhattan
Marine Center
Murray's
National Marine
Nautical Boatique
Overton's
Port Supply
Sears
Stone Harbor
Transmar
Turner's
Warehouse
Books
Armchair
Yankee Whaler

Sailing Hardware

Rigging, Sailing, and Deck Hardware

*ALEXANDER-ROBERTS COMPANY
1851 Langley
Irvine, California 92714
(714) 540-2141
Catalog, 36 pages; Price list. $2.
The Alexander-Roberts catalog features the company's Arco USA winches—single-speed, mid-range, larger, self-tailing, halyard—handles, and parts, furnishing large color photos, ample specifications and description,

installation and maintenance information, and guides to the selection of proper size. Photos, descriptions, and some technical data are also provided for the Howard rope clutch, Servo cleats, IYE travellers, Sheerline mast sections, Arco swage terminals, eyes, and backstay insulators, Yale cordages, Trevco plow anchors, Austral fixed and folding props, Vaassen deck hatches, and Swann marine electronics switches, panels, and accessories. The full range of individual items is specified on the extensive price list.

ANNAPOLIS MAST STEP COMPANY
226 Haverton Road
Arnold, Maryland 21012
(301) 647-8846

Informational sheets (6). Free.

Made of 304 stainless steel, the nesting mast steps offered are completely detachable, guaranteeing no windage from mast protrusions, no added weight aloft, no snagging or chafing of lines or sails, no corrosion from dissimilar metals, and no obstacles to cleaning or refinishing. Also offered are mast tangs and deep hooks which will fit into the slots created in the mast for the steps. The sheets provide illustrations of these items, describe their features at length, and explain the installation procedures. A set of installation instructions and a marking template for holes to be cut in the mast are sent with each step order. Detachable mast steps for wooden masts are in the works.

*AVIBANK MANUFACTURING, INC.
210 South Victory Boulevard
Box 391
Burbank, California 91503
(213) 843-4330
East Coast:
975 Jericho Turnpike
Smithtown
Long Island, New York 11787
(516) 979-8045

Brochure, 4 pages; Price list. Free.

Avibank manufactures non-corrosive, aircraft-quality stainless steel "Ball-Lok Quick Release Marine Pins" in three styles (deluxe, ring, and detent), lengths from ¼″ to 4″ in ¼″ increments, and diameters from ³/₁₆″ to ¾″ in ¹/₁₆″ increments (other sizes are available on request). No taping and no cotter pins are required. The pins can be used as tack pins, and on stay and shroud adjustors, jib furling gear, blocks, and shackles. The literature furnishes photos, illustrations, and brief description of the pins and uses, and lists available sizes.

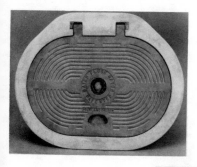

L.S. Baier & Associates   With only two moving parts, these aluminum, bronze, or galvanized steel hatches are tamper proof and never iced in as the t-wrench is removable.

L. S. BAIER & ASSOCIATES
7527 N.E. 33rd Drive
Portland, Oregon 97211
(503) 287-8885

Catalog, 21 pages; Price list. Free.

Guaranteed watertight at 25 foot head, psi, Baier hatches meet the highest standards of U.S. and British Coast Guards, the American Bureau of Shipping, U.S. Navy, U.S. Corps of Engineers, and the Canadian Department of Transport. Manufactured from corrosion-resistant aluminum, bronze, and galvanized steel, and fitted with neoprene oil-resistant gaskets, the hatches are available in round or oval, flush plain or flush hinged models; coamings are also available. Photos, illustrations, and features of the hatches, and a list of businesses using them, are presented on a few introductory pages. The majority of pages consist of large, detailed scale drawings of the various models, complete with specifications and bills of materials.

*BARLOW MARINE U.S.A. INC.
3899 Ulmerton Road
Clearwater, Florida 33520
(813) 576-3920
West Coast:
889 Production Place
Newport Beach, California 92663
(714) 631-4004

Barlow/Gibb catalog, 40 pages; Barlow catalog, 16 pages; Goiot catalog, 20 pages; Catalog supplements; Price lists. There may be a fee if ordered direct.

Barlow's larger catalog treats the firm's line of winches (offered in aluminum alloy, polished bronze, chrome, stainless steel) and the Gibb line of yacht fittings (winches, handles, a variety of blocks and stainless shackles, track and sliders, stainless thimbles, rigging screws, swage and T-ball terminals, lifeline fittings, safety hooks and stanchions, aluminum cleats and fairleads, and deck, ventilator deck, and spar fittings), furnishing a detailed index, large color photos of all items, good descriptions of the features of most items, a selection guide for winches, and extended discourses on self-tailing winches and winch efficiency. The smaller Barlow catalog presents much the same information on winches alone. Distributors for Goiot yacht hardware and furling systems, Barlow also offers a Goiot catalog which presents color photos, specifications, and good descriptions of hand and electric windlasses, a variety of port lights and hatches, genoa tracks, cars and sliders, main sheet tracks and travellers, foot blocks, fairleads, toe rails, stanchion bases, end-fittings, and rail connectors, which are composed almost entirely of black or silver anodized aluminum alloys.

*BECKSON MARINE, INC.
165 Holland Avenue
P.O. Box 3336
Bridgeport, Connecticut 06605
(203) 333-1412

Catalog, 20 pages; Form letter; Price list. 50¢

Featuring Beckson-designed plastic marine products, this

catalog provides small photos and mostly brief but sometimes lengthy descriptions of all items offered—a variety of all-plastic pumps including several models of bilge pump, a variety of plastic hoses and fittings, plastic deck plates and ventilators, plastic opening and fixed ports with Lexan windows with or without rain drains or shields, flexible PVC winch handle and other holders, plastic holding clips, chart holders, self-adhesive step pads and window track, self-locking vinyl trim, accessory hardware such as barrel nuts, pry bars, risers, tie downs, port and deck plate chain, and special drills for plastic, and miscellany like plastic or vinyl-covered log books, and a vinyl-sheathed aluminum boat hook.

BREMER MANUFACTURING COMPANY, INC.
Route 2, Box 100
Elkhart Lake, Wisconsin 53020
(414) 894-2944

Catalog, 7 pages. Free.

The catalog furnishes photos, brief descriptions, and occasionally specifications for Bremer's line of aluminum products cast from sand or production molds: several models of stern davits and related brackets, several outboard motor brackets including one for canoes, an anchor hoist, a stowable motor lift, an extension handle, transom steps, large cleats, a fishing rod holder, and galley accessories such as a swinging stove, double griddle, square skillet, stove-top toaster, shark-shaped bottle opener, and whale-boat ash tray. Navy-type and "new-type" anchors of high tensile cast iron with white enamel finish may also be purchased.

Beckson Marine, Inc. This small ventilation hatch provides ventilation where installation of a larger hatch is not permitted. Ideal for the head, galley, main, or aft cabin.

CLARK CUSTOM BOATS
Bronze Hardware Division
3665 Hancock Street
San Diego, California 92110
(714) 297-2795

Catalog, 36 pages; Price list; Order form. $3.

Providing a large photo and some specifications for most

of the 272 items offered, this catalog presents a wide range of traditional bronze hardware. Available are belaying pins, blocks, boom bails and bail plates, boom jaws, bow rollers, chocks, cleats, eye straps, fairleads, gallows parts, goosenecks, crance and gammon irons, mast bands, pad eyes, pedestals, pole fittings, rope clamps, stanchion bases, sway hooks, tangs, solid thimbles, and track slides; deck filler keys and pipes, hatch hinges, lifting rings, fasteners, and adjusters, ladder hardware, round, eliptical, oval and rectangular port lights, deck prisms, dead lights, cowl and mushroom ventilators, and decorative stars, letters, and numbers. Also offered are bronze oarlocks, an anchor windlass, a fog bell, teak cleat bars, a galley pump with teak handle, teak steering wheels, brass commissioning plaques, brass interior lamps and dome lights, and a variety of brass and bronze fixtures such as handrails and brackets, handles, hinges, and door hooks, hasps, bolts, catches and fasteners.

Freeman Marine, Inc. Steel hatches with dog mechanisms are available in round, oval, or square with aluminum rings.

THOMAS DAHLKE
RD 3, Box 199
Bill Hill Road
Lyme, Connecticut 06371

Informational sheets (2). Free.

Dahlke offers only a few items for which photos and brief descriptions are given: 1½" or 2" diameter red bronze stars, red bronze offset oarlocks, and a cockpit box/helmsman seat hand-crafted of teak and marine plywood (17" × 15" × 15").

A. L. DON COMPANY
Division of Steelstran Industries, Inc.
Foot of Dock Street
Matawan, New Jersey 07747
(201) 541-7880

West Coast:
Robertson and Schwartz Sales Company, Inc.
722 Folger Avenue
Berkeley, California 94710
(415) 845-9336

Informational sheet; Price list. Free. Technical literature on request.

An illustration and detailed description of A. L. Don's new improved pilot ladder with easily replaceable steps are provided on one side of the sheet. The other side furnishes smaller pictures and very brief descriptions including dimensions of the other marine wood products available: round rung ladders, ladder rungs, hearts for flat steps, oval-sided Jacob's ladder steps, bosun's seats and chairs, hatch boards, pyrotechnic chests, boat poles and oars, hand and standing fids, and wood plugs. Not pictured but listed on the catalog and price sheets are chain and wire rope ladders, a variety of other kinds of ladders and ladder steps, ladder replacement parts, hatch wedges, deck and condenser tube plugs, serving and round hickory mallets.

DWYER ALUMINUM MAST COMPANY
P.O. Box 201
Branford, Connecticut 06405
(203) 481-0122

Catalog, 28 pages; Spar extrusion price list. Free.

Dwyer's major products, of course, are clear anodized aluminum custom-fabricated mast and boom assemblies or bare tubes. Major portions of the catalog provide illustrations of various size masts, booms, and their cross-sections, listing section properties and furnishing photos and prices for assembly components. Also available separately are clear anodized aluminum round tubing of various sizes, and the full range of assembly components including tangs, eyes, bails, vang plates, rudder fittings, connecting hardware, chain plates and covers, cleats, hinges, goosenecks, blocks, rope, rigging tape, stainless rigging hardware and cable, and several rigging kits. Most of the hardware appears to be composed of aluminum, but some items are offered in stainless steel. Prices not listed will be quoted on request.

JOHN EGGERS, INC., SAILMAKERS
1000 Highway 35
South Amboy, New Jersey 08879
(201) 721-4667

Informational sheets (2). Free.

Pictured and offered in various diameters are wire-to-rope tail splices, stainless steel wire for standing and running rigging, a heavy-duty aircraft thimble, heavy-duty nicopress loop with thimble, compression sleeve, marine eye, ball with one shank, fork and eye straps with balls, eye, fork/jaw, and stud ends, all of stainless steel, and white vinyl-coated lifeline wire and galvanized wire. Complete halyard assemblies including shackles, splices, and line made up to specifications are also available. Also furnished on the sheets are illustrations of lifeline layouts and terminals, measuring and ordering instructions for standing and running rigging, guides to the selection of cable, sheaves, drums, and hardware, and specifications for wire, rope, and terminals. Lifeline fittings, turnbuckles, and their replacement studs, parts, and toggle forks, as well as other items from Merriman, Sail Line, Navtec, and Ronstan catalogs can also be shipped from stock.

*D. B. FOLLANSBEE INC.
12 Marshall Lane
Middleton, Rhode Island 02840
(401) 846-4358

Manufacturers' literature: Enkes, 13 pages; Holland Yacht Equipment, 1 page; Stazo, 4 pages; Zwaardvis, 9 pages; Price sheets. Free.

Follansbee distributes "Dutch Marine Products"—Enkes custom-engraved winch handles, and guaranteed-for-life winches, some with patented self-tailing clutches; Holland Yacht Equipment's stainless stanchions (18″ to 30″) and bases with "ingenious" gate brace systems; Stazo all-teak or teak and stainless/aluminum steering wheels; and Zwaardvis helmsman's seats, and chair and table gas-spring pedestals of anodized aluminum. The Enkes catalog presents winch selection guides and a chart of winch specifications together with small photos and lists of features and specifications for each winch; more photos, promotional descriptions, and an illustrated explanation of the composition of winch components are provided on additional sheets. Holland's stanchions and bases are pictured and minimally described on one sheet. The Stazo brochure offers photos only of 17 models of steering wheel, and the price list indicates the materials and sizes in which many of these wheels can be obtained. The Zwaardvis catalog furnishes photos, descriptions, and some specifications for some seats and mostly for parts for fixed or adjustable table and chair pedestals.

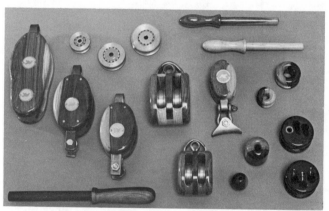

Golden Dove Marine   Traditional boating hardware.

FREEMAN MARINE, INC.
P.O. Box F
Hunters Creek Road
Gold Beach, Oregon 97444
(503) 247-7078

Catalog, 24 pages; Annual newsletter, 4 to 8 pages. Free.

Freeman Marine's products, constructed of special corrosion-resistant, high-strength marine alloys and other quality materials, are thoroughly tested, and built to withstand harsh and abusive conditions. The catalog presents large photos, good building drawings, specifications, lengthy descriptions, and special ordering instructions for round, oval, square, and steel hatches with dog mechanisms; insulated weathertight doors with dogs; fabricated steel, aluminum standard, ABS, or custom doors, hatches, manholes, and scuttles; aluminum or steel-framed windows; and anchor winches. Frame and shutter-style freeing ports, Dover funnels, "spinner" windows, and portlights/fixed lights are also shown and more briefly described. Other available products listed are cleats, locksets, dog assemblies, bow rollers, hinge blocks, custom castings, and aluminum cleaning supplies. The newsletter describes the firm, various products and experiences with them in greater depth, and presents "Freeman's Funnies" and proven facts about the products. Custom work is welcome.

GO INDUSTRIES, INC.
629 Terminal Way
Costa Mesa, California 92627
(714) 642-1194
Informational sheets (6). Free.

GO manufactures lightweight, strong, leakproof, extruded vinyl frame windows which, according to the literature, are impervious to weathering, resistant to many chemicals and solvents, flexible enough to conform to some cabinside curvature, and are easy to install and clean. They are available with white- or teak-colored frames and clear or tinted panes; heavy duty frames come in white only. GO carries few windows in stock, preferring to manufacture *quantities* of them to customer specifications. Quotes are furnished upon submission of sketches and dimensions of the required windows; a form is supplied for this purpose and another sheet describes the windows and the procedure for ordering them. Remaining sheets offer photos and explain the features of sample windows as well as instrument panel boxes.

GOLDEN DOVE MARINE
Traditional Blocks
14492 Sunrise Drive, N.E.
Bainbridge Island, Washington 98110
(206) 842-7250
Brochure, 4 pages; Price lists (4). Free.

This small company is dedicated to providing the finest traditional hardware at affordable prices. The brochure shows nice photos and illustrations and gives good descriptions of the firm's manufactures: blocks with lignum vitae cheeks and bronze roller sheaves and straps, lone bronze roller sheaves, bronze span shackles, belaying pins of balau, locust or lignum vitae, and lignum vitae deadeyes, lizards, and parrel beads. Special purpose blocks and custom sheaves and bow rollers can be made to specifications.

H & L MARINE WOODWORK INC.
2965 E. Harcourt Street
Compton, California 90221
(213) 636-1718
Catalog, 30 pages; Price list; Order form. Free.

Representing the combined efforts of experienced yachtsmen and skilled woodworkers, the mostly teak and mahogany accessories presented, handcrafted in the U.S.A. of the best materials obtainable, have been tested for durability and practicability. Good photos and descriptions are furnished for laminated mahogany and ash tillers, teak tiller extensions, mahogany rudders and

boards, Sabot parts including spruce booms, winch and other pads, wedges, and spinnaker pole holders; deck planking, teak treads, moldings and matching corners, plugs and thru-hull plugs, and trim rings; hatches and sectional hatch boards, cockpit grates, light-duty gratings, swimsteps, folding and fixed ladders and hardware, hand and pin railings; control panel, dorade, first aid, instrument, and winch handle boxes. Also included are cabinets, doors, drawers, frames for ship's papers, louvers, mirrors, table legs, and racks and holders for tools and equipment, fishing rods, kitchen utensils, toiletries, magazines, books, and charts; and switch and plug covers, flag poles, coasters and trivets. Used in the construction of these items are silicone bronze, stainless steel, or galvanized steel fastenings, chromed brass, polished white manganese bronze or stainless steel hardware, and resorcinol or plastic resin glues.

*HARKEN YACHT FITTINGS
1251 E. Wisconsin Avenue
Pewaukee, Wisconsin 53072
(414) 691-3320
Catalog, 40 pages; Price list. Free.

The self-proclaimed world leader of small boat ball-bearing blocks for 14 years, Harken has recently entered the field of big boat hardware. The catalog presents large photos or illustrations, specifications, construction details, recommended uses, and comparative data for the variety of fittings, organized into the following well-marked sections: Bullet Blocks, Wire Bullet Blocks, Big Bullet Blocks, 2.25″ Racing Blocks, 3.00″ Racing Blocks, Fiddle Blocks, Hexa-Cats, Low Profile Triple Ratchet and Cam System, Hexaratchet II, Little Hexaratchets, Little Hex-Cats, Ball Bearing Furling Gear, Ball Bearing Magic Boxes, Cam-Matic Cam Cleat, Low Profile Recirculating Ball Bearing Travelers, Accessories, New Big Boat Hardware, Big Boat Sheaves, 3.00″ Big Boat Blocks, Big Boat Foot Blocks, Big Boat Traveler.

THOMAS HORNBLOWER YACHT EQUIPMENT
P.O. Box 798
Mukilteo, Washington 98275
(206) 743-1285
Informational sheet; Order form. Free.

Pictured and offered in 316L stainless steel are "Herreshoff style" hollow base cleats (5″ to 12″), "banana style" four hole cleats (8″ and 10″), "stanchion style" two hole cleats (4½″ and 6″), and bow and stern chocks (5″). Quotes are invited on all yachting hardware and accessories.

CECIL M. LANGE & SON, INC.
Route 3, Box 202
Port Townsend, Washington 98368
(206) 385-3412
Brochure, 4 pages. Free.

At the time that I received this brochure from Mr. Lange, he was planning to publish, eventually, a full catalog of the imported marine hardware that he has been selling at much lower prices, he vows, than his major competitor.

The current brochure shows small photos of a selection of the stainless steel, brass, bronze, or chromium-plated hardware available: blocks, chocks, cleats, shackles, and terminals; deck plates, port lights, vents, and windows; door hooks, hatch adjusters, fasteners, hinges, lifting handles, and ring pulls; pipe-to-hose adapters, seacocks, and thru-hull connections; anchors, anchor windlasses, and boat hooks; bilge, cabin oil, and galley pumps, and water heaters. Lange also offers custom boatbuilding services.

MARINE ISLAND PRODUCTS, INC.
P.O. Box 2806
1639 Old Dixie Highway
Vero Beach, Florida 32960
(305) 567-3420

Pamphlet, 8 pages; Brochure, 6 pages; Informational sheets (3); Price lists. Free.

Manufacturing all types of rails for boating and marine use, using the highest quality materials and Heli-arc/tungsten-inert gas welding method, Marine Island offers tuna towers, half towers, folding towers, Tee tops, stainless steel rails, radar arches, boarding ladders, swim platforms, boat davits and lifts, dock hardware, and aluminum dock ladders. Custom work in aluminum, stainless and galvanized steel is also available. The pamphlet provides photos or illustrations and some description of the majority of stock items offered. The brochure furnishes ordering information for most items and additional photos, illustrations, and lists of features for the variety of towers available. The additional sheets treat individually the boat lifts, boat davits, and dock ladders, listing features, some specifications, presenting illustrations and photos, and giving ordering information.

MARLIN RIGGING SUPPLY
864 Napa Street
Morro Bay, California 93442
(805) 772-1375

Catalog, 18 pages; Order form. Free.

A mail-order business only, Marlin Rigging Supply keeps prices at a minimum for the traditional hardware, equipment, and tools offered. A small photo and appropriate description accompanies each listing in the catalog; recommendations and bits of advice appear throughout. The mostly rigging and sailmaking tools listed include a nicopress hand tool, wire cutters, pliers, and nippers, punches, a canvas plier, awls, prickers, push pins, needles, shears, bench hooks, cutting guns, marlin spikes, fids, caulking tools and mallets, a rope-forming vise, grommet hole cutters and dies, tool buckets, bosun's chairs, ditty bags, and leather palms. The supplies available include swaging and wire rope terminals, nicopress sleeves, stainless and galvanized wire rope, wire-to-rope halyard kits, galvanized and heavy duty plow steel thimbles, nylon anchor, dock, and mooring lines, galvanized chain, ash battens, wooden cleats, polyester twine, tarred yacht marlin, beeswax, pine tar, leather, and manila rope. The remaining finished items and hardware shown include shroud rollers, wood sail hanks, wood mast hoops, bronze hoop sail fasteners, lignum vitae deadeyes, parrels, and

blocks, ash blocks, Greenheart belaying pins, bronze snaps and snap hooks, nickle-silver or stainless slides and track, stainless D-rings, brass swivels, shackles, rings, and grommets, bronze and stainless thimbles, and sail cover hooks and rivets. Many other items not shown, standard or custom-made, can also be supplied. Help with custom rigging can be obtained if the customer sends accurate specifications, sketches, and proposed uses of the item(s). Wire rope splicing is available on request.

H & L Marine Woodwork, Inc. This Dish, Cup and Towel Rack holds up to six 10″ plates, 10 cups or tumblers, utensils, and a large roll of paper towels.

MEACHAM MARKETING
7842 Commerce Place
Sarasota, Florida 33580
(813) 355-3130

Brochure, 4 pages; Price list; Installation instructions. Free.

This brochure furnishes good photos and describes the features of Meacham's "disappearing" retractable cleats and chocks, a universal flush-deck hasp, and a low-profile hinge that opens 120 degrees, all made of strong but light corrosion-resistant impervium; the related springs and hinge pins are stainless steel. The disappearing cleat or chock must be set into a rectangular cut-out in a boat's gunwale or deck. All items are available in standard tumble finish; chrome, high-polished, or black finish options are possible with the cleats and chocks.

*MERRIMAN/AIM
(AMERICAN INTERNATIONAL MARINE CORPORATION)
P.O. Box 405
215 Najoles Road
Millersville, Maryland 21108
(800) 638-5012; (301) 987-0916

Seven catalogs: Merriman, 82 pages; Merriman/AIM, 28 pages; AIM, 40 pages; AIM/RWO, 44 pages; Barton, 44 pages; Plastimo, 50 pages; Y. S. Fittings, 68 pages; Price and distributor lists. (There may be a charge for each of these catalogs, but they also may be available free from local marine suppliers.)

The Merriman catalog contains a detailed table of contents, general information about hardware materials and finishes, detailed steering system selection and layout guides, installation instructions for steering systems and autopilots, and specifications, photos, and good descriptions for the variety of sailing hardware, steering systems, and components available: numerous blocks (including wooden ones), jiffy reefing blocks and kits, boom vangs, cam cleats, deck and spar fittings, eye straps, halyard organizers and lifeline fittings, sail battens, a sheet stopper/mainsail feeder, various shackles, stay adjusters, track and slides, turnbuckles and components, wire rope terminals, centerboard winches and handles; steering systems, parts, pedestals, steerers and wheels, packing glands, instrument housings, autopilot drive units, quadrants, steering hardware, clevis pins and kits; tables, beverage caddies and an outboard motor bracket.

The Merriman/AIM "product selection book," not exhaustive in coverage or description, contains a brief index, and photos or illustrations, some specifications and technical information, and lists of some features for Plastimo compasses, deck, cabin, and navigation lights, small cruising sailboat hardware, bullseyes and bushes, rope clutches and cleats, furling gear, shackles, vang systems, rudder hardware, tiller extensions, marine locks, PVC ventilators, holders, spreader boots, and inspection ports.

The AIM catalog contains a fairly detailed index, and photos, brief descriptions, and some specifications for Sail Speed bearing and ball bearing blocks, Y. S. fittings (deck cleats, door latch assembly, fairleads, hinges, bow rollers, stanchion bases, running lights), Sprint Speed Stay luff tape jib attachment systems, cleats, clips, drain plugs, fairleads, hinges, lacing hooks, mast steps, pintles and gudgeons, rigging adjusters, shackles, sheet jammers and stoppers, spar and gooseneck fittings, spinnaker poles and accessories, stemhead fittings, swivel bases, tiller extensions

and connections, thru-hull fittings, nylon and poly webbing, nylon and dacron cordage, and pumps. Some items receive elaborate explanations of their materials and features.

The AIM/RWO catalog includes a table of contents, an illustration fittings guide, and good photos, some illustrations, and good descriptions, including specifications for bailers, bungs, inspection ports, lifting rings, ventilators, life vests, pennants, related signs, and penknives, in addition to a full range of hardware: a wide variety of blocks, bullseyes and bushes, cam and other cleats, fairleads, furling gear, kicking strap systems, rigging adjustors, screws, pins, and rings, strip and bar shackles, spinnaker gear, track, slides, travellers, clips, trapeze gear and harnesses, turning blocks and jammers, U and eye bolts, hull and stemhead fittings, mast and boom fittings, mast steps, rudder and tiller fittings, tiller extensions, sail fittings, thimbles, and oarlocks.

The Barton yacht equipment catalog contains a brief index, photos, specifications, and descriptions for blocks, cam, clam, and other cleats, fairleads, a halyard clutch, reefing gear and sliding goosenecks, a slab reefing kit, nylon and stainless steel rudder fittings, stainless steel shackles, deck clips, rigging links, and adjusters, steering pulleys, thimbles (nylon), travellers, track and slides, outhaul, sheet, and snubbing winches, bailers, nylon bungs, and hatch covers.

The Plastimo catalog offers a good index, some illustrations and operating instructions for magnetic compasses, and large color photos, specifications, and very brief descriptions for the magnetic compasses, spare parts and accessories, handbearing compasses, marine quartz clocks, an aneroid barometer, a thermometer-hygrometer, wind indicators, and electrical equipment and lights; flexible water tanks, pumps and bailers; cam and other cleats, fairleads, hooks, shackles, nylon thimbles and other fittings; drain sockets, nylon door catches and hinges,

Meacham Marketing   Made of strong but light corrosion-resistant impervium are: 1) Meacham's "disappearing" retractable cleats and chocks, 2) universal flush-deck hasp.

1.

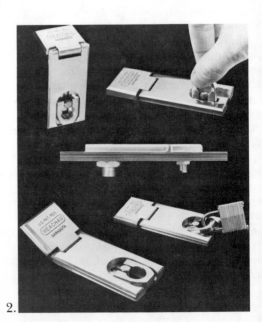

2.

hatches, PVC holders and covers, thru-hull connections, ventilators; grapnel anchors, buoys, shock cords, plastic guard rails and oarlocks, outboard motor brackets, and safety harnesses.

The Y. S. Fittings catalog contains a detailed index and provides a large photo, drawing, and specifications for each product: hooded sheave and turning blocks, bollards and bollard cleats, chain pipe, claw rings, deck and mast cleats, deck filler, eyes and hooks, fairleads, flagpole sockets, handles, hand/grabrail ends and brackets, hatch and other hinges, furniture locks and clasps, navigation lights, drop-nose pins, round open port lights, bow and stemhead rollers, spinnaker pole end fittings, stanchions, bases, joints, and tiller fittings. Composed of strong and lightweight aluminum alloy, these fittings are available in "galvanized-look" and black finishes in addition to the normal polished and anodized finish.

MOONLITE MARINE CORPORATION
776 West 17th Street
Costa Mesa, California 92627
(714) 645-0130

Brochure, 4 pages; Price list. Free.

Moonlite Marine's main offering, the "automatic" hatch holder, springs into a shape when a hatch or lid is raised, which supports the hatch and lid until moderate side pressure bends the spring out of column and allows the hatch to be closed. Several big hatch and small hatch stainless steel holders, with chrome-bronze fittings or hard black anodized aluminum end fittings, are shown and described in the brochure, along with a special "hatch latch," an Aladdin cleat shroud mounting, and a stern anchor roller. Not described but listed on the price sheet are several sizes of anchor hangers, anchor saddles, and mast stairs.

NASHMARINE
32906 Avenida Descanso
San Juan Capistrano, California 92675
(714) 493-4260

Informational sheet; Order form. Free.

Available equally through mail order as through dealers and distributors, Nashmarine's yacht fitments, pictured and described on the sheet, include trigger cleats, synchro-grip cam cleats, mini-stopper cleats, angle brackets, fairleads, teak riser pads, and for Harken and Schaefer blocks, trigger cleats and adapting brackets. A diagram shows how the trigger cleat works. Also presented for sale are rigging labels, a race flag label, a racing trim guide, a sanding block, and a scraper/squeegee.

*NAVTEC INC.
527 Great Road
Littleton, Massachusetts 01460
(617) 486-3163

Catalog, 26 pages; Distributor lists. Free.

Navtec's contributions to the rigging and hardware field include development of the headed rod system, the use of Nitronic 50 stainless steel for standard application rod rigging and of MP35N nickel-cobalt rod material, and development of reliable and easily operated hydraulic

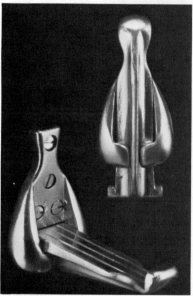

PB Nautical Innovations Inc.   A practical alternative to the Bosun's chair, mast walkers can be mounted to flat, oval, or round masts, and are perfectly suited for the singlehander.

systems for often unique purposes. In addition to providing large photos and ample specifications for the products offered, the catalog bursts with helpful, lengthy technical descriptions of the firm's solid rod rigging and fittings, hydraulic systems, controls, accessories, plumbing, and cylinders, cylinder terminals, integral and ratchet backstay adjusters, turnbuckles, tie rods, associated parts, chainplate systems, and backstay insulators.

NEW FOUND METALS
Route 2, Box 922-A
Chimacum, Washington 98325
(206) 385-3315

Catalog, 28 pages; Price list; Order form. $2.

Richard Walcome and Steve Johnson design and build the patterns for the marine hardware they offer, which they cast with ASARCO no. 500 silicon bronze, or when high strength and toughness are required, with ASARCO nos. 421 and 423 manganese bronze. The team maintains metal quality and consistency by using only new ingot, careful moulding practices, and up-to-date feed systems. Photographed and often illustrated with building drawings are bobstays, boom gallows and bases, chocks, cleats, deck irons, deck tangs, gammon and kranz irons, a gooseneck strap, hawse holes and cleats, pad eyes, port windows, rollers, stanchions, bases, and other parts, trim rings, whisker stays, and New Found Metal's universal rudder fittings assembly. More complex illustrations present full assemblies of bow, cockpit, and rudder fittings in place on the boat. More items will be presented in upcoming editions of the catalog. Drilling, tapping, and machining of desired hardware may be performed upon request.

OBERT MARINE SUPPLY INC.
3441 2nd South at Spokane Street
P.O. Box 3992
Seattle, Washington 98124
(800) 426-0986 outside Washington; (206) 623-7822
Catalog, 74 pages. Free.

Maintaining one of the largest inventories of heavy marine rigging, hardware, and wire rope in the U.S.A., Obert supplies quality products at the best prices to the fishing, marine, offshore marine, logging, construction, industrial, and trucking industries. Enhanced with a detailed index, discussions of wire rope, cordage, nylon slings, and block reeving, and information on selecting anchors, chain, and wire rope slings, the catalog provides photos, detailed specifications, and often working drawings and test results for the various products presented: anchors, anchor chain and attachments, mooring systems and buoys, welded and weldless chains, chain slings and components, heavy-duty fittings (shackles, turnbuckles, sockets, hooks, snaps, clips, thimbles, links and rings, swivels, eyes and eye bolts), blocks of and for various materials, block connections, wire rope and slings, cordage (polypropylene, polyester/polypro, nylon, polyester, manila), nylon slings, trucker equipment (load straps, winches, binders, bars and irons), winches and hoists, cargo-securing systems and lashing gear, and rope accessories (cutters, stoppers, grips, marlin spikes, fids and pushers). Rope measuring devices, and miscellaneous items such as rust and corrosion preventive dressings, chocks, cleats, toggle pins, boat fenders, boarding ladders, Bayley exposure suits, flying forks, safety nets, tarps, various bars and clamps, and log-rafting tools are also listed. Not all products available are presented in the catalog, so inquiries are welcome regarding desired but unlisted items.

OFFSHORE SPARS
22930 Industrial Drive East
St. Clair Shores, Michigan 48080
(313) 772-4010
Two brochures, 2 pages and 4 pages. Free.

Offshore sells a "trim-lite," pictured and briefly described in one brochure, for illuminating telltales with a strong, steady, 8-inch spot beam. The firm also manufactures tapered, aerodynamically-shaped custom or production aluminum mast, boom, and spreader extrusions. Navtec rod rigging, hydraulics, and hardware, and flush fittings for shroud attachments are offered too along with headsail control, jib furling, and mainsail furling systems. The

longer brochure explains the design and construction of these products, furnishing illustrations. Prices will be quoted upon submission of specific measurements of the equipment desired.

PB NAUTICAL INNOVATIONS INC.
262 Cardinal Leger
Pincourt, Quebec J7V 3Y7
Canada
(514) 423-7096
Informational sheets (4); Order form. Free.

Peter Buche, president of this firm, makes available "Mast Walkers," mast steps, cast of non-corroding aluminum, which may be fastened to flat, oval or round masts and other surfaces of wood, carbon and glass fibers, aluminum alloy, or other materials. Guaranteed for the life of the boat, tested for strength, designed and fabricated for safety, the steps open and close without hinges, present a low profile against the mast when retracted, and can be adjusted against the mast after installation. Sheets provide photos of the walkers in place and in use, list features and specifications, and give directions for determining the type and number of mast walkers needed.

PERT LOWELL COMPANY
Lane's End
Newbury, Massachusetts 01950
(617) 462-7409
Informational sheet; Price list. Free.

With over forty years of hoop-making experience, this firm manufactures mast hoops from clear straight-grain oak laminated for extra strength, parrel beads and hand-made cleats of black locust or other woods, and sail hanks. Stock hoops, 2″ to 12″ in diameter in ½″ increments or 13″ to 24″ in diameter in 1″ increments, are bolted with brass machine screws; the smaller sizes can be riveted with copper instead. Other sizes and shapes may be specially ordered. The sheet furnishes photos and brief explanations of the gear. An accompanying brochure offers home and boat furnishings and decorative items, most of which incorporate mast hoops (see entry under *Seats, Bedding…Lighting,* page 135).

RANDOLPH BOATWORKS
27 Pine Island Road
Mattapoisett, Massachusetts 02739
(617) 758-4270
Pamphlet, 2 pages. Free.

Specializing in masts, booms, gaffs, clubs, spreaders, sprits, and such, Randolph can build spars for existing boats or boats under construction, using architectural drawings, old spars, or even storm remains as guides. Solid laminated spars or hollow-box rectangular masts are available, in Sitka spruce, as a rule, or in vertical-grained fir for certain large spars. Desired hardware can be supplied by the customer or obtained through the boatworks, and it can be installed by the customer or the boatworks staff. The brochure simply explains the kind of work the firm does, the construction and finishing techniques used, and the general procedure for placing orders. Price quotes and more detailed information must be requested.

RICKBORN FLYING BRIDGES
175 Atlantic City Boulevard
Bayville, New Jersey 08721
(201) 349-4545

Pamphlet, 6 pages; Informational sheet; Price list. Free.

Rickborn "self-fitting" one-piece fiberglass flying bridges are available in several models, economy and deluxe, large and small, in any degree of completion from basic unit to a complete factory-installed outfit with or without various controls and accessories. The pamphlet offers photos and brief descriptions of the various models, of several boats equipped with them, and of some of the seats, ladders, steering wheels, and instrument panels available. Deck and storm railings, bridge covers, windscreens, bimini tops, steering systems, bridge kits (economy, standard, and deluxe) and an installation manual, runabout and cruiser hardtops and kits, a fishing pulpit, tuna tower, center consoles, and small bridge accessories, listed on the price sheet, may also be purchased. An additional sheet explains installation of a bridge and some of its accessories.

ROSTAND MANUFACTURING COMPANY
33 Railroad Avenue
Milford, Connecticut 06460
(203) 874-2547

Catalog, 37 pages; Price list (upon request), 13 pages. Free.

Established in 1902, Rostand offers its marine hardware in solid bronze or aluminum cast from certified ingots. High tensile manganese bronze and ALMAG 35 aluminum are used where greater strength is required. The catalog provides several detailed indexes, and pictures and specifications for the many items offered. Included are blocks, chocks, cleats, eye plates and straps, shackles, toggles, solid cast bronze rigging thimbles, turnbuckles; hatch and casement adjusters, handles, hasps, hinges, locks and clasps, lift and drop rings; bits, floor flanges, rope deck and hawse pipes, flagpole sockets, lifeline stanchion bases and eyes; hatches, deck and manhole plates, opening, fixed, and heavy-duty port lights of various shapes, ventilators; hinged tiller fittings, a throttle control, stern bearing, stuffing boxes, thru-hull fittings, and strainers; cabin lights and fixtures, a ship's bell, and boat hook. Some aluminum items such as chocks and cleats are also available with epoxy coatings of any color; other custom finishes are available, and all are hand-polished.

Rickborn Flying Bridges   A "self-fitting," one-piece fiberglass flying bridge, one of several models.

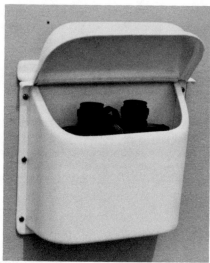

Sailing Specialties, Inc.   Binocular Case, made from especially molded flexible white TPR® rubber, can be attached to bulkhead or cockpit surfaces for safety and convenience.

*SAILING SPECIALTIES, INC.
P.O. Box 527
Route 235 South of U.S.N.A.S.
Lexington Park, Maryland 20653
(301) 863-8196

Catalog, 12 pages; Form letter. Free.

A small photo, sometimes a working drawing, dimensions, and some description are provided for each item in this catalog: plexiglas view-vent louvers, ventilating hatches, and skylights; TPR rubber port hoods, mast boots, winch handle holders, and binocular cases and racks; ABS plastic coaming, deck, and dorade boxes, vertical anchor wells, storage compartments, utility boxes, toiletry holders, recessed control panels, electric box and wiring covers; PVC and vinyl rubrails and polyethylene end caps. Samples of vinyl rubrails are available upon request at $2 for 2 and $3 for 5.

*SCHAEFER MARINE, INC.
Industrial Park
New Bedford, Massachusetts 02745
(617) 995-9511

Catalog, 108 pages. $2.

A good half of this catalog covers Schaefer's several series of high-strength lightweight blocks made of various combinations of materials (aluminum, bronze, plastic, stainless steel, titanium), furnishing large photos of the blocks, specifications, good descriptions of block components and performance, and providing an illustrated, lengthy introduction to block types, materials, uses, and operation. The table of contents lists in some detail, alphabetically, the array of general hardware available, while the index goes by part number. The hardware is grouped in the following sections, which provide photos and specifications for individual items, and good sometimes lengthy descriptions of them in general: backstay adjuster kits, boom vangs, cam cleats, cleats, gudgeons and pintles, jib furling gear, systems, and accessories, quick reefing systems, shackles, slides, snap shackles, spinnaker poles, equipment, and tie-down gear, tangs, track, traveller blocks and control systems, turnbuckles, and miscellaneous items (various eyes and hooks, exit and other small blocks, rudder heads, mast steps, reefing hooks, utility rings, chain plate covers, stanchions, boom bails).

*SEA MATE PRODUCTS COMPANY
P.O. Box 3
West Pittston, Pennsylvania 18643
(717) 655-2537

Informational sheets (4). Free.

Sea Mate's sheets furnish photos of the curved and straight transom platforms, cockpit and transom ladders, and a mini-transom deck with optional drop steps offered, providing construction details, mounting information, and recommendations for use. The platforms, some of which must be custom fit, are composed of pressure-laminated teak, with stainless steel support beams and fasteners. Folding and fixed ladders in general are composed of stainless steel tubing and laminated teak steps; some ladders can be made instantly removable.

SEABRITE STAINLESS STEEL MARINE PRODUCTS
63 Morris Avenue and Highway No. 35
Neptune City, New Jersey 07753
(201) 988-8818

Catalog, 34 pages. $2.25 (deductible on first purchase).

Prefaced with a good index, Seabrite's catalog offers photos, some specifications, and brief descriptions for its range of marine hardware and fixtures using types 304 and 316 stainless steel: arches, hardtops, bimini frames, tuna towers, radar installations, one-piece welded bow, bridge, center console, pulpit, and stern rails, hand and grab rails, lifeline stanchions and parts, bridge and swim platform ladders with teak steps, footrests, fender, rod, and boat hook holders. Other hardware and fixtures include: flagpoles, furniture and a variety of fish fighting chairs, fish hooks, lights, bases, bits, braces, brackets, clamps, cleats, elbows, endcaps and fittings, exhaust ports, flanges, guides, hatch trim, hinges, locks, loops, plates, pulls, rings and spinnaker rings, rubrail, scuppers, support stanchions, bearing struts, propellor shafting and shaft logs, a rudder, rudder port, tiller head assemblies, and stainless steel tubing, strip, sheet, plate, bar, and threaded specialties. A nylon shaft log and rubber hose kit is also available.

SEATTLE SHIPWRIGHTS CO-OP
938 N.W. 49th
Seattle, Washington 98107
(206) 782-1724

Pamphlet, 6 pages. Free.

The five craftsmen who formed this cooperative offer repair, restoration, refinishing, design, custom new construction, consultation, surveying, rigging, pattern making, cabinet making, and equipment installation services. Additionally they build custom masts and spars to 70', using Sitka spruce and epoxy glues. Contract prices for piece work and services can be provided; and all work is insured. The craftsmen also operate a mobile outfitting unit to cut costs. The brochure furnishes photos of some of the co-op's work, and briefly describes the firm's services and orientation.

SHEWMON, INC.
P.O. Box 755
Dunedin, Florida 33528
(813) 447-0091

Brochure, 4 pages; Price list. Free.

Shewmon offers self-opening sea anchors from 2' to 15' in diameter, and self-opening drogues from 2' to 4' in diameter, which when attached to a boat's bow or stern, respectively, greatly reduce the vessel's chances of broaching, pitch-poling, or breaking up. Sea anchors can also be used for drift fishing, squid jigging, for holding down upwind ends of surface longlines, and for reducing vessel roll while laying over at sea anchor. The brochure furnishes photos of the equipment, detailed explanations of its make-up, handling, uses, and performance, and charts and calculations for determining the proper size anchor or drogue for a specific boat.

SIDEWINDER INTERNATIONAL, LTD.
125 Cardinal Drive
Wilmington, North Carolina 28403
(919) 392-4649

Informational sheets (2). Free.

Sidewinder offers its new marine fender-ladder, which is composed of non-marking polypropylene wheels, stained and oiled hardwood rungs, and nylon-coated galvanized aircraft cable. Lightweight, flexible, and "self-fending," the ladder fits any curvature, attaches instantly to any cleat or winch, and stows easily. Measuring 12″ between rungs and 16″ between cables, the ladder is available in custom or in 4' (3-step), 5' (4-step), and 6' (5-step) standard lengths. Teak rungs are also available. The sheets provide a photo, specifications, and description of the ladder.

SOUND SPARS INC.
29 Sagamore Hill Drive
Port Washington, New York 11050
(516) 883-3550

Catalog, 10 pages; Various informational sheets. Free.

Sound Spars designs, engineers, and fabricates spar systems for sailing yachts up to 80'. The catalog shows illustrations and photos of the extruded aluminum spar and spreader sections, booms, and sail track kept in stock as well as the custom, mostly aluminum hardware fabricated—mastheads, mast collars, steps, and stairs, winch pads, exit pads and entrance sheave boxes, scored sheaves, spreaders and spreader bases, track gate, boom assemblies, a full line of spinnaker gear, light fixtures, and type 304 and 316 stainless steel tangs, toggles, link plates, and spreader clips. Quotations on spars or fittings for a particular yacht will be furnished upon submission of the sail plan, displacement weight, measurement of the beam at the chain plates, righting movement of the hull, and other individual requirements. An additional sheet describes the firm's replacement spreaders, giving prices and furnishing a measurement form for ordering the spreaders. Another sheet lists some further extrusion specifications. Additional services include rigging (using Navtec rod rigging), fabricating custom stainless steel or aluminum fittings, repairing and altering spars, repairing damaged hardware, and painting spars with Awlgrip polyurethane paint.

SOUTH COAST MARINE

788 W. 16th Street
Costa Mesa, California 92627
(714) 646-5445

Informational sheets (2). Free.

This literature provides illustrations, long descriptions, and some specifications for only a few of the custom products—a teak dorade box with plexiglas top, boom gallow arch supports and deck bases, laminated wood davits with bronze fittings and various options, teak light covers, and doors and drawers—which have been developed as the result of South Coast's builders' experiences building custom boat interiors and exteriors. Custom sizing and styling of these items and custom woodwork of other kinds are available on request. References can be furnished for custom work.

SPAR TECH

15230 N.E. 92nd Street
Redmond, Washington 98052
(206) 883-2126

Brochure, 4 pages. Free.

Designer and developer of aluminum spars for the Olympic class one-designs, "Star" and "Thunderbird," developer and manufacturer of spars and rigging for San Juan 24s and 28s, and manufacturers of spars and rod rigging for Nordic 40s and 44s, Valiant 40 and 47 cruising yachts, Spar Tech provides custom spars, fittings, hardware and rigging for medium-sized dinghies to 55′ custom cruising and racing yachts throughout the country. The brochure explains the firm's services and offers a chart of stock extrusions which, made of marine grade aluminum alloy (6061-T6511), are available in any stage of completion from bare tubes to complete rigs. Various finishes are offered: mill, clear lacquered, clear anodized, black anodized, and painted. Besides the extensive extrusion inventory, sheet, plate, tubing, Navtec rod rigging and components, wire, swage fittings and terminals, yacht braid, wire and shackles for halyards, lifeline hardware, and associated hardware, castings, spreaders, and goosenecks are kept in stock. Since all orders are custom, inquiries are always welcome.

SPARTAN MARINE PRODUCTS, INC.

160 Middleboro Avenue
East Taunton, Massachusetts 02718
(617) 823-6779

Catalog, 26 pages. Free.

Complete with a fairly detailed table of contents, this catalog furnishes large photos of the items available, giving good descriptions which include illustrations and information regarding the appropriate use of the particular product. Included are aluminum spar extrusions, spar systems, mast and boom assemblies and parts, stainless steel pins, shackles, and components for masthead parts, bowsprit assembly parts, a bow stemhead with anchor roller, jib club pedestal assembly, traveler bridge assembly, winch stand assembly, a variety of bronze chain plates, chocks, cleats, deck plates, drain plugs and scupper drains, exhaust flanges, fairleads, drawer handles and pulls, hasps and hinges, lift rings and straps, opening port lights of various shapes, round fixed ports, quarterknees, rod bases and flagpole sockets, seacocks and handles, rudder and prop shafts, struts, shaft tiller and caps, stuffing boxes and parts, tank vents, thru-hull fittings, and an outboard motor mount. The firm also offers a complete range of rigging services and sells rigging kits and wire-to-rope halyards.

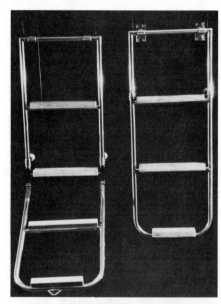

Tops-In-Quality, Inc.   Straight and folding ladders, available in various sizes, with and without teak steps.

STANDARD EQUIPMENT COMPANY, INC.

75 Beauregard Street
P.O. Drawer G
Mobile, Alabama 36601
(205) 432-1705

Catalog, 63 pages. Free.

Standard Equipment's marine doors, hatches, scuttles, manholes, port lights, and lights, kevels, and pipe bends are used almost exclusively on steel or aluminum hulled boats over 35′ in length. The catalog, complete with an index, provides large scale drawings and often specifications and schedules of materials for the stock items available. Custom configurations can be negotiated.

TOPS-IN-QUALITY, INC.

P.O. Box 125
Marysville, Michigan 48040
(313) 364-7150

Catalog, 20 pages; Price and ladder sheets. Free (with self-addressed stamped, envelope—postage $1.50).

Manufacturing marine rails since 1962, this firm makes available for sailboats several models of stock pulpits and lifelines in kit form, lifeline parts, custom-bent adjustable and fixed stern rails, as well as custom-made welded pulpits, lifelines, stern rails, and boarding ladders. For power boats, stock stern rails, several models of bow rails and handrails, hinged flybridge ladders, and custom-made flybridge rails, powerboat and platform ladders are offered. Stock rails are made with type 304 stainless steel tubing and welded rails with 16 gauge stainless tubing, both in ⅞″ and 1″ diameters. Bases for welded rails are composed of cast T-316 alloy stainless steel, and those for stock rails are chrome-plated bronze or stainless steel castings. Available separately are numerous bases, bow forms, deck anchors, elbows, flagstaffs, handrail parts, hinges, jaw inserts, teak steps, tees, tubing, cable assembly parts, Johnson lifeline fittings, machine and set screws, bolts, nicopress tool and stop sleeves, and pulpit and stern rail lights. All items are pictured in photos or illustrations, and construction details, some installation information, and measurement instructions for custom rails are given. An additional sheet presents photos, specifications, descriptions, and installation instructions for swinging and folding type transom or amidship ladders.

Troy Brothers Marine Gear.

TROY BROTHERS MARINE GEAR
   P.O. Box 71
   810 Electric Ave.
   Seal Beach, California 90740
   (213) 596-7434
Informational sheets (3); Order form. Free.
Entirely made in the U.S.A., Troy Brothers' hand-assembled traditional blocks consist of hand-selected teak cheeks, bronze sheaves with stainless steel roller bearings or custom-made micarta sheaves with self-lubricating oilite bronze roller bearings, stainless steel straps and pins, and bronze endcaps, screws, fasteners, and deck fittings. Singles, doubles, triples, fiddles, 6″, 8″, and 10″ blocks are available; options include a bottom

becket with clevis pin, bronze diamond base deckplate, bronze swivel eye, bronze circular swivel deckplate, and sheaves scored for wire. Blocks can be specially designed, made of other woods, and built for special applications, upon request. The sheet provides nice large photos, a diagram of block parts, and quite a bit of information regarding the composition and construction of the blocks. Since the firm makes about 400 block variations, parts are assembled upon receipt of an order. The firm also offers imported rubber-armored, ruggedly-constructed 7 × 50 IF marine binoculars with fully coated lenses; an additional sheet explains their features at length and provides a photo and illustrations.

TUNA TOURNAMENT PRODUCTS
   Box 471 Center
   Shelter Island, New York 11964
   (516) 749-1015
Brochure, 4 pages; Informational sheets (3); Price list. Free.
Tuna Tournament provides the components for making safety rails and lifelines: 1″ stainless steel tubing and interchangeable, triple-chrome-plated bronze fittings which allow adjustments for height, width, rake, and contour; some pre-cut rail lengths are offered. Also available are some fiberglass outrigger poles, triple-chrome-plated bronze pole holders, stainless steel boat hook rod holders, paddle holders, fender hooks, stainless steel and teak foot rests, folding steps, folding and straight ladders, swim platforms, and a power actuator kit for reverse gear. These items are pictured and described in the literature, along with flying bridges, harpoon pulpits, and lookout towers that are no longer available. Since the brochure and price list are substantially out of date, it is difficult to determine precisely what items are available and what their prices are: questions regarding the availability and pricing of specific items should be submitted with the request for literature.

*UNITED YACHTING MANUFACTURING
   23230 Tireman Avenue
   Dearborn Heights, Michigan 48127
   (313) 274-4589
Catalog, 8 pages; Supplemental sheet; Order form. Free.
The catalog provides large photos, some illustrations, and descriptions of a variety of sailing paraphernalia: quick-release, easy-lock line holders, a line tensioner, Delta ocean and mini-series, vertical and horizontal line stoppers, high-strength cheek lead blocks, a rudder lock, kick-up rudder control, heavy-duty nylon snap hooks for ¼″ line or shock cord, self-adhesive telltales, and a deep molded multipurpose rack of polypropylene copolymer.

WINCH TAILER
   Division of Declercq Marine Systems Inc.
   7144 South Shore Drive, South
   St. Petersburg, Florida 33707
   (813) 347-8882
Pamphlet, 6 pages; Form letter; Order form. Free.
The winch tailer, a safe lock-in device, expands the performance of any winch by providing both self-tailing and instant cleating capabilities; the tailers require little

maintenance, reduce the amount of effort needed to crank a winch, and allow lines to be released and relocked from a distance. Available in five models, adaptable to any winch and any size line, winch tailers are rugged precision machines weighing 2½ pounds and made of the best non-corrosive materials. The complete mounting kit includes instructions, spacers, and fasteners to simplify installation. The pamphlet furnishes photos of the equipment and describes its features and the mounting kit.

Clark Custom Boats   Traditional bronze hardware is among the 272 items offered by this company.

YACHT RIGGERS, INC.
4448 - 27th Avenue W.
Seattle, Washington 98199
(206) 282-7737

Brochure, 4 pages. Free.

A retail and wholesale firm, Yacht Riggers manufacturers masts, standing and running rigging, and lifelines, mainly for cruising and racing sailboats, providing custom or production spars for numerous well-known cruising hulls and successful boats, which are listed in the brochure. Other work has included building spars for sailing fishing boats and radar and stabilizing spars for power boats. Yacht Riggers also carries one of the largest stocks of turnbuckles and lifeline fittings in the country, and distributes Super Spar, Sheerline, Navtec, Schaefer, and Merriman Holbrook lines of fittings and hardware, as well as Hyde's roller reefing and furling systems. In addition to showing photos of the plant and of boats fitted out by Yacht Riggers, the brochure indicates the firm's services, terms and conditions, and provides a form for the customer to fill out and submit for a price quote.

ZEPHYR PRODUCTS, INC.
P.O. Box 152
Wareham, Massachusetts 02571
(617) 295-2240

Pamphlet, 10 pages; Price list. Free.

Affiliated with Cape Cod Shipbuilding, Zephyr maintains a large inventory of aluminum spars (masts and booms), roller reefing goosenecks, spinnaker poles, reaching struts, outhauls, spreaders, lights, winches, hinges, fittings, terminals, turnbuckles, and stainless steel wire rope. The pamphlet furnishes cross-sections and recommended uses for several mast shapes, and provides small photos of the many mast fittings and several swage terminals. A tapering service is offered for certain sizes of masts.

See also, under:

Small Open Boats
    Swanson Baggins

Yachts
    P & M
    Roberts

Multihulls
    Myers

Materials and Supplies
    Quality

Fasteners
    Berco

Tools
    Dingo
    Morty
    Wooden Boat Foundation
    Wooden Boat Shop

Engines
    Marine Engine

Sailing Hardware
    Knotted Line
    Vandermeer
    Waterfront Equipment

Sails and Canvas Goods
    Bohndell
    Hild
    Sailrite
    Wilson

Seats, Bedding...Lighting
    EACCO

Nautical and
    Outdoor Clothing
    Afterguard

General Catalogs
    Cal
    Chartroom
    Cuttysark
    Defender
    E & B
    Fore and Aft Marine
    Goldberg's
    Golden Fleece
    Haft
    International Sailing
    M & E
    M.M.O.S.

(continued)

Winch Tailer   Self-tailing and instant self-cleating, Winch Tailers are available to fit any size winch.

Docks, Dock Hardware, Mooring and Waterfront Equipment

FOLLANSBEE DOCK SYSTEMS

Follansbee Steel Corporation
State Street
P.O. Box L
Follansbee, West Virginia 26037
(800) 624-6906; (304) 527-1260

Catalog, 12 pages; Price list. Free.

Exclusive distributor of the "Dayton Float Drum," Follansbee offers, invarious sizes, swim float kits, unassembled floating and stationary dock sections (which include drums, decking, and hardware), and indivdual components and accessories for these systems. The catalog provides color photos of the docks and swim floats, and specifications for and illustrations of the components of both floating and stationary dock sections. Also described are non-rusting float drums which, molded of tough, durable, permanently-fused polyethylene, are resistant to fresh and salt water, gasoline, oil, and other contaminants. Some advice regarding planning and installing a stationary dock is also proffered. Complete engineering and layout services are available. There may be Follansbee representatives in some areas.

HMS MARINE, INC.

904 West Hyde Park Boulevard
Inglewood, California 90302
(213) 674-4540

Information sheet. Free.

Pictured and briefly described on this sheet are boarding steps made of hand-laid fiberglass with a non-skid top surface. Available in 2-step, 3-step, and 4-step models with optional heavy gauge stainless steel handrails, the steps double as large lockable storage compartments with raised marine plywood floors.

HEMISPHERE MARINE INC.

1900 Southeast 15th Street
Fort Lauderdale, Florida 33316
(305) 523-8507

Brochure, 4 pages; Drawings (4); Various manufacturers'
literature. Free.

Hemisphere Marine offers free advice, sample dock drawings, and price quotes along with the brochure "Choosing a Floating Dock," which discusses the features of the full range of floating dock components, and provides a guide for determining floating dock costs. The additional manufacturers' literature presents photos and descriptions of Zarn polystyrene-filled polyethylene "poly-floats" and Marine Docks' aluminum and wood decks, ramps, and related hot-dip galvanized dock hardware, which Hemisphere Marine sells.

Hemisphere Marine Inc. You supply the bare lumber, Hemisphere supplies the necessary hardware and the floating dock components. *Photo:* Donald M. Schwarm.

THE KNOTTED LINE

Dennis Armstrong
9908 - 168th N.E.
Redmond, Washington 98052
(206) 885-2457

Sheet and card listing services. Free.

Sometime in the future Dennis Armstrong may put together a catalog advertising his marlin spike work. For the time being, he attends regional boat festivals, giving demonstrations of his craft and displaying samples and an album full of photographs of his work. Quite willingly he will sell rope fenders and service mats through the mail, or negotiate with prospective customers to make fancy handrail, tiller, or wheel coverings. He also offers marlinspike instruction, splicing services, and minor rigging repair. You might be able to goad some color photos of his work out of him.

MONARCH MOOR WHIPS

P.O. Box 6
Normandy Beach, New Jersey 08739
(201) 793-3833

Pamphlet, 6 pages; Informational sheets (2). Free.

Monarch's moor whips keep boats up to 50' in length away from docks or seawalls in spite of boat wakes or storms. The tapered poles are made of solid fiberglass, and the corrosion-resistant "tenzaloy" mounting bases mount vertically or horizontally on wood, cement, or metal. The pamphlet provides a brief description of the whips

embellished with photos of them and illustrations of their
correct use. An additional sheet describes mini-moor
whips for small boats up to 18' in length docked in
moderately turbulent areas, and another sheet presents
"mooring line mates" with fiberglass rods, stainless steel
hooks, and "tenzaloy" mounts, for easy docking in strong
winds.

MOORING WHIP SALES OF FLORIDA

1554 North Federal Highway
Pompano Beach, Florida 33062
(305) 941-9200

Informational sheets (3); Price sheet; Order form. Free.

Since 1956 this firm has manufactured mooring whip
systems that hold boats up to 60' and 60,000 pounds a safe
distance from the dock, counteracting wind, boat wakes,
and tides, and eliminating the need for boat fenders. The
standard kit includes two corrosion-protected cast
aluminum base assemblies, two solid fiberglass tapered
whips, two $5/16''$ braided nylon whip lines with tension
adjusters, stainless steel mounting hardware for wood or
concrete, and complete installation instructions. Also
available are a whip for keeping a dinghy/tender away
from a yacht underway or at the dock, and
specially-designed flexible fiberglass-core dock fenders
with polyurethane mounts (4'-10'). The sheets provide
photos/illustrations, and list the features of these items.

SCHUYLER'S BUMPERS, INC.

P.O. Box 326
Woodinville, Washington 98072
(800) 426-3917; (206) 488-2255
East Coast:
P.O. Box 87
Staten Island, New York 10303
(212) 727-9697

Two brochures, 8 pages and 4 pages; Price list. Free.

Schuyler's bumpers are custom-manufactured of
shock-absorbent fabric-reinforced laminated rubber
sections to fit and protect any boat's bow or stern.
Ready-to-mount side fenders are also available, as are trawl
net "grommet guards" (bottom rollers, footrope discs),
pushing knees and cylindrical pilothouse fenders for
workboats, and special bumpers for piers, docks, loading
docks, and oil rigs. The bumpers are unaffected by
temperature changes, moisture, or salt water, and they are
resistant to oil and corrosion. The longer brochure shows
and briefly describes various bumper types and
applications, while the shorter brochure focuses on loading
dock bumpers and their features. Footrope discs are
priced economically in 100 pound sacks.

SHELTER SYSTEMS

P.O. Box 308
5680 Carmel Valley Road
Carmel Valley, California 93924

Information sheet. Free.

Shelter Systems' "Big Cave," with patented arch forms and
rectangular floor plan, is large enough to store or build a
boat or use as an on-site workshop. The tough, woven and
laminated polyethylene skin is UV- and tear-resistant,

Schuyler's Bumpers, Inc.   Upper bow and side fenders.

should last up to three years with normal exposure, and
can be easily and cheaply replaced. The support structure
incorporates strong patented clips that will not puncture or
weaken the fabric at point of attachment. Measuring 11'6"
wide, 19' long, 7' high at center, and 6'2" high 2' from
extreme edges, the Cave has end closures, and units can be
clipped together to form any length of desired shelter.
The sheet furnishes photos and a description of the
shelter.

STAMFORD PACKAGING COMPANY

P.O. Box 3091
Stamford, Connecticut 06905
(203) 322-2131

Informational sheets (2); Fabric swatch; Price sheet; Order form.
Free.

Stamford specializes in boat covers for winter storage.
Available in 34 sizes from 8' × 14' to 40' × 60', the covers
are made of a puncture and tear-resistant, UV-treated,
temperature-stable, waterproof, non-absorbent,
lightweight, oriented, woven 8 × 8 substrate, high-density
polyethylene coated with 1½ mils of blue polyethylene on
both sides. Tie-down plastic grommets, rolls of no. 675
blue waterproof pressure-sensitive repair tape and 100'
rolls of the fabric in 10' to 40' widths are also available.
One sheet describes these products and provides photos of
the covers and grommets. A smaller sheet illustrates steps
for attaching the tie-downs to the fabric.

SUPER DOCK PRODUCTS

R.R. 1, Box 56A
Center Harbor, New Hampshire 03226
(603) 253-4000

Catalog, 8 pages; Price list; Order form. Free.

Super Dock offers ruggedly constructed docking that anyone can assemble and afford: light, middle, and heavy weight modular dock sections, permanently-fused tough and durable linear polyethylene float drums, dock-building components (galvanized pipe, finishing and driving caps, brackets and braces, bracer and joiner kits), accessories/options (mooring bars, mooring whips, cleats, polypropylene rope, vinyl dock padding, ladders, driving boards, slides, cement anchors, aquatherms, thin ice signs), and various preservatives and maintenance supplies and equipment (deck scrubber, dock leveling jack). Each item is pictured and described; procedures are outlined for installing a pipe dock without working in the water.

TOPPER INDUSTRIES INC.
P.O. Box 1587
Vancouver, Washington 98668
(206) 694-9261

Information sheet. Free.

Topper's three complete dock kits (6′ × 10′, 8′ × 10′, 10′ × 10′) utilize the firm's special floats—used tire casings filled with expanded polystyrene. Conditionally guaranteed for 25 years, each float weighs 25 pounds and floats in excess of 180 pounds.

*UNITED MCGILL CORPORATION
United Flotation Systems
2400 Fairwood Avenue
P.O. Box 820
Columbus, Ohio 43216
(614) 443-0192

Brochure, 4 pages; Price list; Order form. Free.

Distributed nationwide but evidently available also directly from the manufacturer, "Water Walks," fixed or floating modular docks, can be purchased in several easily assembled kits or in parts—exterior plywood modules with galvanized steel frames, pressure-molded polystyrene foam flotation billets, and optional galvanized steel encasements, anchor guides, fixed pier leg attachment assemblies, yellow pine rubrail, anti-scuff black vinyl bumper stripping, pine-vinyl bumper posts, dock cleats, and standard or anti-skid ramps. A color photo and some description is provided for each component and kit model; some layout and assembly information is also given.

RAY VANDERMEER—BOAT FENDERS
3305 South "G" Street
Department D
Oxnard, California 93033
(805) 483-2945

Two brochures, 4 pages each; Price list. Free.

Vandermeer offers hand-made manila rope side and bow fenders in five standard sizes with either manila or polypropylene interiors. Tri-sided fenders are also available. Fenders may be made to specifications and the brochure provides charts of possible sizes along with photos or illustrations of sample fenders. Some Seapower and Crosbie Laboratories boat care products, pictured and described in the brochure, are also available. Additionally

Topper Industries Inc.   A true do-it-yourself dock kit, this single kit can be hauled in a pickup and easily assembled in four hours by one person.

Vandermeer distributes Dutch-made Vemefa bv stainless steel deck ventilators, portholes, bollards, and pull rings, for which photos and specifications are furnished in the second brochure. All products are unconditionally guaranteed.

THE WATERFRONT EQUIPMENT AND HARDWARE STORE
104 Annapolis Street
Annapolis, Maryland 21401
(301) 268-8802

Catalog, 156 pages; Order form. $3. Design service available.

This catalog furnishes a wealth of information—illustrations, photos, specifications, features, installation procedures, and more—for each of the many, many items offered: boat houses, storage buildings, covers, related equipment and hardware, boat lifts, elevators, and railways, truck, boat, and dinghy davits, winches and trailer accessories (loaders, carriers, ties, trailer parts), motor and trailer locks, mooring and dock equipment (anchors, chain, shackles, links, swivels, buoys, floats, anchor line, chafe-guards, cleats, fenders, bumpers, dock mats, matting, boxes, carriers and stands, mooring arms and whips), dock and pier fittings (brackets, posts, deckings, dock sections, systems, kits, handrails, ladders, benches, dock wheels, floats, float drums, swim float accessories). Other items are: ladders, stairs, and ramps, lighting and wiring devices, de-icing equipment, electric insect control devices, lawn and pier furniture, and power tools and equipment (pumps, compressors, air hose). Manufacturers' literature for any catalog product is available on request. Each order submitted is carefully checked to insure that all proper parts have been ordered. Design packages including product literature, sketches, bills of materials, available options, installation instructions, and a price quotation good for 30 days, can be prepared to the customer's requirements for a $10 to $25 fee which will be credited towards the customer's order.

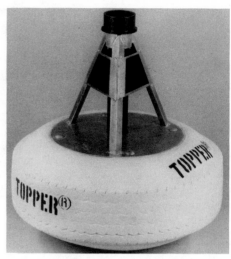

Topper Industries Inc.   With galvanized disc on both top and bottom, this buoy is available in either white or orange.

Ray Vandermeer —Boat Fenders   Manila rope side fenders come in five standard sizes with manila or polypropylene interiors.

See also, under:

Specialty Craft
  Rotocast
Trim
  Wefco
Tools
  Wooden Boat Shop
Sailing Hardware
  Marine Island
  Obert
Sails and Canvas Goods
  Sailor's Tailor
General Catalogs
  Defender
  E & B

Fore and Aft Marine
Goldberg's
Golden Fleece
M & E
M.M.O.S.
Manhattan
Marine Center
Murray's
National Marine
Nautical Boatique
Overton's
Sears
Stone Harbor
Warehouse

Sails and Canvas Goods—Awnings, Biminis, Dodgers, Covers, Cushions

ANDERSEN & VINING SAILMAKERS, INC.
  155 Derby Street
  Salem, Massachusetts 01970
Catalog, 12 pages. Free.
Featuring accuracy, dependability, and craftsmanship backed by a decade of experience, Andersen & Vining's sails are built meticulously by hand, one at a time, to the individual boat owner's specifications, using the best sailcloth and hardware, and incorporating individually-shaped, triple-stitched, and broad-seamed panels for lasting performance. The catalog describes the sails in general and provides a form for obtaining a sail quote. Most of the space in the catalog is devoted to the firm's nicely illustrated and generally described sea and travel bags, totes, shoulder bags, book, ski, and tennis bags,

a backpack, hammock, apron, log carrier, bosun's chair, rigger's bag, and covers for steering wheels, tillers, sailboards, and sailboard masts and sails, all handcrafted of rugged 100% heavy duty cotton water- and mildew-resistant canvas. The canvas and 100% heavy duty cotton webbed handles used on some items are available in a variety of mix-and-match colors. Also offered are a sailor's duck shirt, T-shirts, D-ring belts, and sailboards.

BIERIG SAILMAKERS
  11092 Freeport Lane
  North East, Pennsylvania 16428
  (814) 459-8001
Two pamphlets, 4 pages and 6 pages; Brochure, 4 pages. Free.
Bierig's letterhead indicates that the firm offers innovative

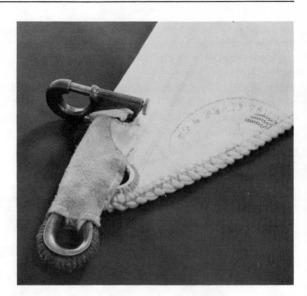

Thomas Clark & Company Sailmakers, Inc. Example of the quality of sail reinforcements provided by this company.

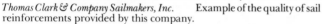

custom sails for racing, cruising, and voyaging, for yachts, multihulls, iceboats, and workboats. The pieces of literature available illustrate and describe in detail the workings of only a few of the firm's more innovative products. One pamphlet covers the "Tri-Miter" multipurpose storm sail used as a storm jib, main trysail, or in some cases, as a storm staysail, foresail, or mizzen. The second pamphlet explains the "CamberSpar" jib control which produces an acceptable draft and twist on all points of sail, controls headstay sag, and allows the jib to be self-tacking, controlled with a single sheet, and quickly rigged and stowed. The brochure elaborates on a single luff spinnaker which requires little gear, can be handled on mono- and multihulls up to 40′ by a crew of two, and can be used for cruising; instructions for obtaining a quote are given.

E. S. BOHNDELL & COMPANY, INC.
Sails and Rigging
U.S. Route 1
Rockport, Maine 04856
(207) 236-3549

Informational sheets (3). Free.

Bohndell's services are briefly explained on one sheet. The firm builds all types of sails for all kinds of boats, repairs, recuts, rebuilds, and converts sails, offers a fall and winter wash-check and repair service with free storage, provides hand-splicing, swaging, and complete lifeline services using Merriman terminals, produces custom canvas boat and sail covers, awnings, dodger recoverings, mast coats, pipe berths, cabin tops, chafing gear, windscoops, boom slings, and accessories such as cushions, mattresses, curtains, and three sizes of tote bags. The additional sheets provide forms for obtaining sail estimates and ordering sail covers.

C & G MARINE/LEE SAILS
P.O. Box 6686
San Diego, California 92106
(619) 226-2131

Brochure, 4 pages. Free.

This firm offers custom-built sails as well as sails cut to the original designer's specifications for production boats and one-designs. The brochure describes the features of Lee sails: highest quality stainless steel slides, gun metal bronze hanks, standard fiberglass battens, sail bag, and fully stitched insignia and racing numbers on mainsails included in the price; no. 1 grade sail cloth of proper weight tailored to the best fullness for the customer's locale; chafe protection installed behind all jib hanks; a leech draft adjustment for maximum efficiency in varying wind conditions; "three ton" type grommets and heavy reinforcements used at head, tack, and clew; leather reinforcement at corners and at headboard; triple stitching used on large and storm sails, hand roping on large mainsails, and vinyl-coated stainless steel wire or rope luffs on headsails. Also provided are detailed forms for submitting information necessary to obtain a free quote.

THOMAS CLARK & COMPANY SAILMAKERS INC.
37 Pratt Street
Essex, Connecticut 06426
(203) 767-0512

Five pamphlets, 4 pages to 8 pages each. Free.

Clark's sails and other products, built to be strong, neat, and seamanlike, combine quality old-time craftsmanship with modern materials and design principles. One pamphlet shows photos of the firm and people at work making the sails. After consultation with the customer and selection of suitable sail cloth, sails are laid out on a full-size pattern, cut from narrow-paneled unresinated cloth, joined with contrasting thread, reinforced at stress points with patches, tablings, and tapes, fitted with brass rings sewn in by hand, hand-roped along spar edges (if a mainsail), fitted with a hand-tapered rattail, and reinforced with a hand-spliced stainless steel luff wire and bronze thimbles (if a headsail). Another pamphlet illustrates and describes one aspect of the dying art of sailmaking—hand-sewing headboards; yet another pamphlet explains in greater detail the components and methods used in making Clark sails. A full line of sails and canvas goods is available including canvas dodgers, cockpit cushions, awnings, and covers for sails, hatches, wheels and binnacles. A fourth pamphlet presents the firm's "spinnacher," an inexpensive, simple, light-air headsail for the cruising sailor which can be used with or without spinnaker gear. The fifth and final pamphlet describes Clark's custom dodgers, listing features and giving an illustration. The company also offers a variety of services such as repair, recutting, conversions, inspection and surveying, cleaning, and storage.

COOK MARINE PRODUCTS, INC.
101 Rowayton Avenue
Rowayton, Connecticut 06853
(203) 866-0164
Brochure, 6 pages. Free.

Cook offers the hand-operated, dual-purpose, domestic, portable, all-metal, 42 pound, Reads "Sail Maker" sewing machine with 110- or 220-volt electric motor options. The machine will sew, in zigzag or straight stitch, sail cloth up to 80 ounces, spinnaker material, nylon, reinforced PVC, cotton or terylene sail cloth; additionally it will make buttonholes, sew on buttons, darn, and do rolled hemming, quilting, freehand embroidery, and overcast seams, on materials from fine synthetics to thick leather. The brochure shows the machine, explains its features at length, and lists parts and briefly described accessories (thread, thread stand, needles, cover and sail fabrics, repair tapes, nylon webbing, velcro, Delrin zippers, shears, grommet and snap kits, hotknife) and "canvas work" books.

DEWITT SAILS
1230 Brickyard Cove Road
Point Richmond, California 94801
(415) 234-4334/8192
Pamphlet, 8 pages; Various technical bulletins. Free.

With the longest record of championship sailmaking in the San Francisco area, DeWitt combines the latest in computer design and sail cloth technology with a personable staff of experts dedicated to helping every customer meet his or her objectives. The pamphlet shows photos of the shop, briefly explains the firm's philosophy and services, and provides a glossary of useful and often misused sail terms and phrases. The firm furnishes a variety of technical bulletins (1-3 pages each) written as new information or research data turn up, to keep sail buyers well informed. Recent issues include a more up-to-date glossary of useful and often misused sail terms and phrases, plus "Kevlar in Sailmaking," "To 'Ply' or Not to Ply," "Rollerfurling Systems," "Sails for Rollerfurling Systems," "Poleless Spinnakers," "Use Telltales and Tell Tale Window, Become a Better Sailor," "Easy Reefing," and "Mylar in Spinnakers???" Featuring a guest dock, the firm offers sail repair and inspection services, on-the-boat or roof-top sail testing, and custom covers and awnings for power- or sailboats. Phone calls and loft visits are preferred

to negotiations by mail. Tours are available by appointment; sailing seminars are offered at the loft from time to time.

HAARSTICK SAILMAKERS INC.
100 Pattonwood Drive
Rochester, New York 14617
(716) 342-5200
Newsletters, 8 pages to 12 pages each; Reprints; Various informational literature; Price list. Free.

Haarstick's sails are completely designed according to a computer design program, and sail panels are meticulously glued together before they are sewn to insure a near perfect seam every time; additionally, spinnaker panels are precision-cut by Gerber computer. Upon request, interested persons can be put on the mailing list to receive the firm's newsletters and technical publications. The 1981 newsletter explained the evolution of owner Steve Haarstick's sail design career, his computer design system, the quilt-cut genoa innovation, sail development programs for the STAR and J/24, spinnaker gybe technique, and the backgrounds and special abilities of two Haarstick staff members. The fall supplement described the firm's present new facility, discussed new mainsail materials, compared mylar and dacron, and explained a mainsheet and genoa system developed for a particular boat. Additional, more in depth papers are available, some at a cost, regarding sail cloth, the computer cut, sail design, the quilt cut, and genoas. The "C & C Racing Price Schedule" gives prices, ranges, cloth weights, and square footages for genoas, main, jib, tri, and stay sails, triradials, and sail options. Cleaning, repair, and storage services, as well as offseason sail handling lectures are offered.

DeWitt Sails   Photo: Rita Gardner.

DeWitt Sails   *Photo:* Rita Gardner.

HILD SAILS/ISLAND NAUTICAL, INC.

225 Fordham Street
City Island, New York 10464
(212) 885-2255

Three brochures, 4 pages to 6 pages each; Pamphlet, 4 pages; Informational sheets (2). Free.

The Hild Sails branch of the business custom builds sails; its literature includes two brochures, embellished with photos and illustrations, which explain at length a cruising spinnaker, a multi-shaped all-purpose headsail, and a roller furling main that can be used in winds as light as 10 knots and as high as 40. Another brochure furnishes photos and descriptions of Island Nautical's custom-made offerings: dodgers, hatch dodgers, awnings, biminis, cushions, and sail covers. The pamphlet duplicates some of this information and lists other canvas products available: wheel and winch covers, windscoops, duffle and ice bags, and vang and halyard straps. One sheet discusses the awning again, giving prices for stock designs, while the other sheet provides instructions for ordering a dodger.

KOLL CANVAS PRODUCTS

P.O. Box 262
Rumson, New Jersey 07760

Information sheet; Order form. Free.

Described and shown is Koll's bimini boat top, available in 2 kits for boats or flybridges from 40″ to 80″ in beam. The top, available in white or tan and in 4′, 5′, or 6′ lengths, is constructed of an easily cleaned, waterproof, sun- and fire-resistant superior dacron polyester vinyl-laminated fabric, sewn with high quality dacron polyester thread. the ¾″ heavy-wall, bright-dipped anodized aluminum tubing

features preformed bows and adjusts up to a maximum of 52″, 47″, and 41″, for the 4′, 5′, and 6′ tops respectively. Understandable directions and drawings are supplied with all necessary parts to make installation quick and easy. A replacement parts list and prices are available on request.

MARE COMPANY SAILS

4080 Lincoln Boulevard
Marina del Rey, California 90291
(213) 822-9344

Brochure, 12 pages. Free.

The largest sail loft in Marina del Rey, Mare Company provides, for cruising and racing sailboats, new custom sails including roller furling headsails and mainsails using the finest grade domestic dacron sail cloth and hardware, and for racing and cruising multihulls, well-built, strong custom nets and trampolines. Full services for new and seasoned sails are also available. Offering a sail quote form and some tips on sail care, the literature focusses mostly on trampolines and nets, describing them, their constructions, and components in some technical detail, comparing the characteristics of various synthetic fibers, furnishing fabric samples, illustrating related lacing and net fastening hardware, giving detailed illustrated order forms, and listing prices for stock trampolines, options and parts, webbing, mesh fabric, tape, velcro, and thread. There are no obligations or charges for estimates.

NORTH AMERICAN NAUTICAL
INDUSTRIES, INC.

10801 Endeavour Way
Largo, Florida 33543
(813) 546-4671

Pamphlet, 6 pages; Two sheet sets (9 pages each); Informational sheets (3); Ordering instruction sheet. Free.

The pamphlet furnishes general specifications and several small color photos for the firm's cushions and covers, and briefly describes the firm's markets; an accompanying sheet lists some of the custom work the firm has been selected to do. Bimini tops for sail- or powerboats, constructed of Weblon with nylon webbing and bonded polyester dacron thread, are available in widths from 60″ to 120″, and lengths from 90″ to 120″; three- or four-frame models with split or single mounts are available featuring 1″ O.D. stainless steel tubing and type 316 stainless steel fittings, or cheaper anodized aluminum tubing and fittings; heights reach from 40″ to 56″. Interior cushions feature polyurethane foam, bonded polyester dacron thread, and nylon, olefin vectra, herculon, and marine naugahyde covers in decorator colors; cockpit cushions come in 2″ closed cellular flotation foam covered in marine grade expanded vinyl; zippers for both types of cushion are composed of molded nylon with polyester tape. One set of sheets furnishes elaborate measuring/ordering instructions, prices, and specifications for the bimini tops, while the other does the same for the cockpit/flybridge cushions. Remaining sheets promote new hinged cockpit chairs and sailboat sofas made of the same materials as the cockpit cushions.

THE SAILORS' TAILOR
191 Bellecrest
Bellbrook, Ohio 45305
(513) 848-4016

Informational sheets (9). Free.

The Sailors' Tailor makes and stocks marine-sewn items including covers for 99 classes of one-designs, racing sails for some of them, duffle and ditty bags, and sail/boom covers. The one-design cover price sheet briefly describes the kinds of covers (trailering, mooring, skirted, cockpit, bottom, envelope) and cloths ("yachtcrillic," canvas, napbac canvas, polyester, nylon) available; the sail price sheet indicates prices for custom sails, one-design racing sails, sail repair, numbers, windows, tails, and fiberglass battens. A list of covers presently in stock, and illustrations, photos, and fabric swatches of the covers are available upon request for a specific boat model. Additional sheets furnish photos or illustrations, some description, and sometimes order blanks for the variety of waterproof coated nylon ditty bags and caddies, the sail/boom cover, and the firm's monogramming service.

SAILRITE ENTERPRISES
Route 1
Columbia City, Indiana 46725
(800) 348-2769; (219) 244-6715

Catalog, 46 pages; Order form. Free.

Embellished with a handy index, small photos or illustrations, and often long descriptions of the offerings, this well-ordered "Sailmaker's Catalogue" features a variety of sail fabrics, trampoline mesh, nylon bag and flag cloth, insignia material and precut numbers, several sewing machines, attachments, and accessories, sailmaking tools, sewing supplies, lines and tapes, sailmaker's hardware, finishing supplies, some rigging hardware, accessory kits (boom covers, bosun's chairs, various bags, dodgers, awnings, telltales, windows), sail repair kits, instruction manuals, and a sailing game. A detailed explanation of sail kits and how to order one, a brief guide to sailmaking procedures using the kit, a cloth selection guide, a long discussion of sewing machines for sailmakers, descriptions of sailmaking data and computer programs available, and full explanations of a series of home-study courses for sailmakers round out the catalog.

SAILS BY SMYTH
15628 Graham Street
Huntington Beach, California 92649
(714) 898-2434

Information sheet; Price sheets (7); Order form. Free.

Specialists in high-performance racing and cruising sails, including world champion catamaran sails, Smyth offers a "Fun Line" of sails for the recreational sailboarder, high-aspect ratio "Surf Line" sails for wind/big surf sailors, 2 open-class racing "Regatta Line" sails cut for the specific mast, mainsails and "Black Magic" composite battens for the Prindle 15, and mainsails, vertical seam jibs, and the composite battens for the Prindle 16, Prindle 18, and Tornado. Illustrations, brief descriptions, and dimensions are provided on the sheet for the Fun, Surf, and Regatta lines; some photos and descriptions are also given for several accessories available: a medium-size nylon duffle bag, a special sailboarder tote, two styles nylon sail/mast cover, racer or cruiser back harnesses, harness lines and boom straps, several harness hooks, mast extensions, sweatshirts and T-shirts. Price sheets for the Prindle and Tornado sails list sail features.

Hild Sails/Island Nautical, Inc.
Besides building sails, Hild offers various other canvas products—awnings, biminis, and sail covers to name a few.

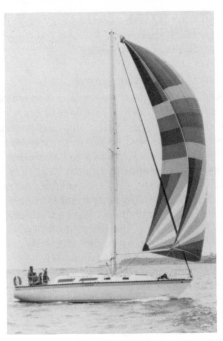

V.F. Shaw Company, Inc.   The Chutescoop® furls or unfurls a cruising spinnaker with ease, requiring only two people.

SAILS U.S.A.
Silver Street
P.O. Box 542
Portland, Maine 04112
(800) 341-0126; (207) 772-4335

Pamphlet, 12 pages. Free.

By keeping a low overhead, Sails U.S.A. can charge low prices and deliver a quality product. Illustrations, and lists of standard and optional features are furnished for the firm's main sails, genoas, drifter-reacher or cruising spinnakers, and sail covers. Prices are listed for options; prices and dimensions only are shown for storm jibs (25-100 sq. ft., 6-10 oz. dacron); and quotes for other sails are available upon request. If the customer does not like the sail, or if the sail is found to be defective in material, cut, or workmanship within the first year of ownership, the sail will be adjusted or made anew at company expense. Sails U.S.A. offers 50% of the original purchase price for one of its sails traded in for a new one.

V. F. SHAW COMPANY, INC.
P.O. Box 605
Bowie, Maryland 20715
(301) 262-5266

Brochure, 4 pages. Free.

V. F. Shaw's "Chutescoop," available in standard sizes for boats up to 40′ or in custom sizes and colors, furls or unfurls a cruising spinnaker with ease, requiring only two people and taking away worries about accomplishing jibes or dropping the sail in the water; partially pulled down, the scoop effects a reefed spinnaker. The brochure provides photos of the scoop, illustrates its operation, lists its features, describes its virtues, and furnishes testimonials from satisfied users.

STOKER MARINE FITTINGS
P.O. Box 1063
Norcross, Georgia 30091

Information sheet; News release; Reprint; Price list. Free.

Stoker offers a "Neetsheet" 12″ × 18″ yachtcrillic sheet and halyard bag which attaches to sailboat travelers and winches with two rugged snaps, allowing the sailor to stuff the loose trailing ends of working sheets and halyards in the bag and retrieve the line (up to 100′ of ⅜″) from the bag smoothly without knots or snags. The sheet provides a photo and description of the bag; the news release duplicates the description. The reprint touts the virtues of such a bag in aiding sailboat "housekeeping" and the sailor's peace of mind.

THURSTON SAILS, INC.
406-408 Water Street
Warren, Rhode Island 02885
(401) 245-5145

Brochure, 11 pages. Free.

Built on over seventy-five years of experience and dedication to quality, integrity, and craftsmanship, Thurston's custom sails are the most popular throughout the Narragansett Bay. Racing sails are constructed from stiffer, resinated cloth for greater drive, and are triple-stitched for durability. Cruising sails are made of softer, heavier cloth for durability and easier setting and stowing. The brochure, a sail selection guide, spells out basic inventories of both racing and cruising sails, then illustrates each sail listed, specifying its purpose, cut and design, fabric, features, and options. Custom accessories available are also pictured: halyard bags, canvas tote bags, a spinnaker turtle, and covers for sails, tillers, winches, and binnacles. Sail inspection and repair services are offered.

Prices as well as cloth samples will be sent upon submission of the completed sail quote form.

WEDEKIND SAIL AND CANVAS COMPANY
101 Surf Avenue
Port Jefferson
Long Island, New York 11777
(516) 928-6840
Brochure, 4 pages; Information sheet. Free.

Established in 1973 and serving Port Jefferson and the surrounding community with high quality custom work, Wedekind offers good design, the best of materials, painstaking care in manufacture, a fair price, and good old-fashioned service. The brochure briefly describes the firm's orientation and offerings, and provides photos of sailbuilding in process. The sheet presents a photo of the firm's "Long Islander Dodger" and lists its features: zip-out sides, a roll-up center window, optically clear vinyl windows, zipper pockets for quick removal from frames, anodized aluminum frames, chrome brass mounting hardware, and acrylic or a new vinyl-coated fabric. Call or write for sail quotes, repairs, modifications and further information regarding the firm's dodgers, tops, cushions, and covers for power- and sailboats.

NATHANIEL S. WILSON, SAILMAKER
P.O. Box 71
Lincoln Street
East Boothbay, Maine 04544
(207) 633-5071
Informational sheets (2). Free.

With experience ranging from square-riggers to small prams, Wilson's specializes in custom dacron, cotton, or flax sails for vessels of all sizes and rigs. Brass rings, cringles, internal headboards, and bolt ropes are sewn in by hand; cotton and flax sails are roped with hemp imported from England; and custom designed and built hardware is available. Sail repair, alterations, and cleaning, wire splicing, swaging, and nicopress services are offered. Rope-to-wire halyards, slings, and straps are available. Items in stock include a wide variety of cordage, yacht braid, three-strand dacron, hemp bolt rope, cotton rope, and no. 10 wide duck canvas from 36″ to 120″ wide. One sheet explains the firm's services and furnishes photos of the shop, sails, and sail detail. A smaller sheet provides photos, prices, and ordering information for a hand or shoulder bag (10″ × 12″), cruising duffle bags (10″ × 23″, 12″ × 29″), and a lined tote bag (14″ × 16″), all offered in many colors of canvas.

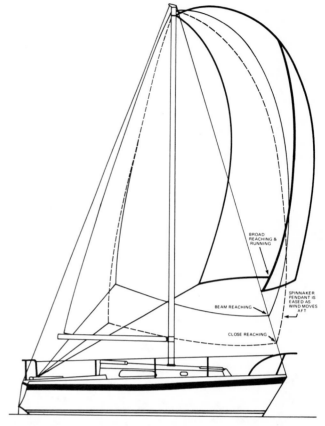

Thurston Sails, Inc. The Thurston Thrasher, with a sail area only 15% less than a conventional spinnaker, is a downwind sail that can be set and trimmed much like a genoa.

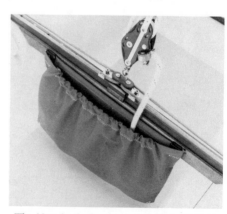

Stoker Marine Fittings The Neetsheet allows you to stuff the loose tailing ends of working sheets and halyards in the pouch and retrieve the line without knots or snags.

See also, under:

4. FURNISHINGS FOR BOATS

Flags
Pennants
Windsocks
Graphics
Nameboards
Seats
Bedding
Racks and Holders
Tableware
Lighting
Cabin and Water Heaters
Stoves
Lamps
Fire Extinguishers
Refrigeration Equipment
Air-Conditioning Systems
Water Systems

Ted Brewer Yacht Designs, Ltd.   The Chappaquidick catboat.

Flags, Pennants, Windsocks

Flags! Some of Jeanne Sillay Roberts' designs for flags, windsocks, and other sculptural pieces.

ART FLAGS UNLIMITED
P.O. Box 222B, RD 1
Oley, Pennsylvania 19547
(215) 689-9240

Pamphlet, 4 pages. Free.

The artists at Art Flags are intent upon incorporating both tradition and creativity into their six basic designs and custom flags made to complement the name of a boat, club, or business. Pictured and described are 16″ × 24″ dolphin, ying-yang, solar, and 2 fishes pennants, a 12″ × 36″ striped streamer, and 18″ × 24″ striped rectangle. Constructed of ripstop nylon with brass grommets and nylon headings, each flag is built piece by piece without the use of any silkscreen process. Price estimates for custom designs are furnished upon submission of size, color, and design specifications.

FLAGS!
P.O. Box 1776
Lincoln, Massachusetts 01773
(617) 369-8137

Pamphlet, 6 pages. Free.

Jeanne Sillay Roberts fashions her flags and three-dimensional flying fish, windsocks, and other sculptural pieces from 3.9 ounce dacron sail cloth (heavier weigor special projects) or from 100% nylon ripstop spinnaker fabric specially treated to withstand the stresses of wind, sun, and water, and available in ten vibrant colors. She uses solid brass grommets and nylon hoist binding, machine-appliqués each flag on both sides with zig-zag stitches, and specially reinforces hems. Her outdated pamphlet provides color photos of some of her work and lists and describes stock designs: a 12″ × 15½″ martini flag, 13″ × 18″ brew flag, 14″ × 18″ unicorn flag, 12″ × 18″ friendship/ rainbow pennant, 11″ × 37″ streamer, 14″ × 20″ rainbow flaps, and an "after hours kit" of six 12″ × 16″ special-design flags. A custom design service is offered whereby the customer, business, or club may design the flag, banner, burgee, wallhanging, windsock, or fish, or can have Roberts design it to specifications.

FLYING COLORS
2160 N. Cypress Road
Pompano Beach, Florida 33060

Brochure, 10 pages. Free.

Pictured, briefly described, and offered in Annin-Nyl-Glo 100% heavyweight nylon with white canvas headings and brass grommets are sets of international code signals, individual code flags, U.S. storm signals, U.S. power squadron flags, sewn or dyed U.S. yacht ensigns, yacht club officer flags, sewn race committee flags, private and yacht signals, personal bow pennants, and absent, meal, guest, skin diver, fun and fish flags. Dimensions are listed for all flags. A form is provided for furnishing specifications for custom flags or banners. Additional literature is available on a limited basis concerning the business's complete line of state, territorial, and foreign flags, as well as custom burgees, swallowtails, and such.

OLMSTED FLAG

P.O. Box 666
Woods Hole, Massachusetts 02543
(617) 548-7631

Pamphlet, 6 pages; Order form. Free.

Olmsted Flag provides custom-designed flags, burgees, spinnaker turtles, instrument, sail, and hatch covers, steadying sails, special foulweather gear, and one-of-a-kind contraptions. Sail repair and recutting services, and a good supply of repair materials are available. The brochure briefly describes these services and custom products, illustrating the spinnaker turtle, furnishing detailed ordering instructions for flag reproductions and new designs, and elaborating on flag construction and materials (4 oz. nylon in 9 colors, hard-twist dacron sail thread, woven nylon or dacron boltape, brass spur grommets). Estimates are furnished for custom work upon submission of the proper information (a flag estimate/order form is provided).

Ed Rich, "The Bean Hill Whittler"   A retired mechanical engineer, Ed Rich displays the trail boards he carved in his studio for the yacht *America.*

See also, under:

Electrical Equipment
Baker and Lyman
Sailing Hardware
Merriman
Boat Names
Landa
Nautical and Outdoor Clothing
Seattle Fabrics

Gifts
Mystic
General Catalogs
Commodore
Cuttysark
E & B
Goldberg's
Golden Fleece
Haft

M & E
M.M.O.S.
Manhattan
Marine Center
National Marine
Stone Harbor
Warehouse
Books
Yankee Whaler

Boat Names, Graphics, Nameboards

A TO Z SIGNS AND GRAPHICS

4635 Cabrillo
San Francisco, California 94121
(415) 752-1071

Form letter; Order form. Free.

A to Z offers custom-designed boat names made of "dry paint," a quality dry transfer outdoor adhesive material combining paint, adhesive, and a mylar base, which provides a tough, sun-, salt-, and weather-resistant surface that, guaranteed for as long as the hull finish lasts, looks bright and sharp three times as long as ordinary paints. Each order is hand-drawn and hand-cut to preserve that quality of individuality missing in machine-made products. Twenty-six letter styles and colors, and arc, straight, flair, and custom layouts are available, shown on the order form. Signs are priced per inch of the width or the longest dimension. Duplicates ordered at the same time cost half the price. Hailing ports and registration numbers are available in matching styles and colors, and special artwork is produced on request. Signs come pre-spaced on transfer paper, ready to apply; an instruction sheet gives step-by-step application technique.

BOAT GRAPHICS

21080 Concord
Southfield, Michigan 48076
(313) 358-3150

Brochure in poster format; Order form. Free.

For its boat names, Boat Graphics uses 3-M's durable, dimensionally-stable, adhesive-backed glossy vinyl films which allow incredibly tight detail, withstand severe weather and handling conditions, and by guarantee, retain their gloss and color for at least six years. The Boat Graphics staff works with the customer to select the best colors and type styles, develop the correct size sign, and design an appropriate layout. Three levels of design service—standard type styles, creative layouts, custom design—are offered to suit the pocketbook. Seven type styles, nineteen colors, and many photos and illustrations of the firm's work are provided in addition to explanations of the firm's design philosophy, its three design services, the materials used, the application method, prices, and conditions and guarantees regarding the refund and possible foul-ups in applying the name. Hailing ports, state registration numbers, proper federal documentation letters and numbers, and "exciting, colorful" graphic images can also be prepared.

CWA INC.
1906 Ebony Drive
York, Pennsylvania 17402
(717) 741-2129

Information sheet; Order form. $1 (refunded with first order).
CWA offers, in teak marine plywood, a winch handle holder, a binocular/ cruising guide holder, louvered screened drop boards, and machine-carved nameboards, bent to conform to curved transoms and attached with contact cement. All items are available in solid teak at prices 30% higher. Quotes may be requested for low-priced hand-carved nameboards. Estate nameboards and commercial signs are available in 1″ pine or stained maple. Showing photos only of five letter styles for the nameboards, the sheet briefly describes each item (giving dimensions), the teak marine plywood used, and the firm's reasons for offering low prices.

FULL SAIL
P.O. Box 720076
Atlanta, Georgia 30358
(404) 992-3548

Brochure, 8 pages; Price list; Order form. Free.
Full Sail's boat letters and numbers are made with 3-M brand self-adhesive vinyls guaranteed for five to seven years. Twenty-six standard colors are shown in the brochure, but the firm offers custom mixes. Pricing is the same for custom designs, stock styles, or oversizes; duplicates ordered at the same time are half the price of the original. Proper documentation letters and numbers, and custom and standard striping designs in vinyl or custom materials are also available. The brochure briefly describes Full Sail's services, the materials used, and the application procedure. The price and ordering sheets show thirty-three stock letter styles to which the customer is not limited, since skilled artists custom craft all of the firm's lettering.

LANDA PRODUCTIONS
2119 Unicorn Lane
Richmond, Virginia 23235
(804) 320-4949

Brochure, 4 pages; Supplemental sheet; Price sheet and order form. Free.
Fred Landa designs boat name layouts in any style desired, putting the design on a flexible plastic sheet with adhesive backing which, when Landa cuts out the letters, provides a stencil for the customer to attach to the boat and paint the name himself. Landa will help the customer as little or as much as the customer likes. He offers advice about what paint to use, how to apply it, and how to obtain it. He will send a sample layout in black and white, free of charge if the customer puts in an order for it, or $5 otherwise. The brochure explains Landa's service and shows some sample letter styles. An extra sheet illustrates the stencil procedure; complete instructions are provided with orders. Logo and hailing port stencils, custom-designed flags in cloth or printed appliques, custom-designed

T-shirts and La Coste shirts printed to match boat names are also available.

MULLER MARINE DISTRIBUTORS
1022 Canter Road, N.E.
Atlanta, Georgia 30324
(404) 233-8892

Brochure, 4 pages; Informational sheets (7); Order form. $2.
Muller Marine offers five "Namepak" plans for ordering pressure-sensitive letter and number decals. The brochure briefly explains the service and shows the ten colors available. Each plan is briefly described on an additional sheet and more sheets present letter styles available for each plan: plan 1, eleven styles of plain letters; plan 2, five styles of shadowed letters or outlines; plan 3, four styles of documentation letters; plan 4, oversize letters of any style; and plan 5, custom designs. Duplicates are offered at lesser prices. Remaining sheets describe a special offer and present instructions for applying the decals. Price lists, order forms, and only a few illustrations may be obtained for personalized T-shirts, cotton duck sailing jackets, and totes, canvas bags, pouches, seat cushions, totes and other products, and for T-Graphics' custom hand-screen-printed clothing, bags totes, aprons, and visors. Other items may be custom printed with a boat name, yacht logo, or special design. Muller Marine also fabricates cockpit cushions.

PRISM CREATIVE BOATNAMES
Mariner's Square
1900 N. Northlake Way
Seattle, Washington 98103
(206) 633-5848

Brochure, 4 pages; Price sheet; Order form. Free.
Offering clean, crisp workmanship and design excellence, Prism's designers hand-cut boat names and graphics from the finest pressure-sensitive, self-adhesive vinyl, so thin it produces virtually no edge and allows a positive, secure bond. Four design plans are available: one where the customer chooses among ten stock letter styles and twenty colors; a second where the designers offer a choice of three well-researched customer-specified letter styles; a third where the designers create a one-of-a-kind type; and a fourth where the designers produce a custom graphic design. Estimates are given for a customer's own design. The brochure explains the firm's services and shows photos, some in color, of its work. The price and order brochure present the twenty colors, the ten letter styles, explains ordering procedures in detail, and briefly lists documentation letter style guidelines. A second form is furnished for ordering one of four stock styles in common sizes. Files are kept on orders filled so that quick repairs and later duplicates are possible. A photographic reprostat of the name can be made for silk-screening it on shirts and visors.

ED RICH, "THE BEAN HILL WHITTLER"
East Hebron Turnpike
RD 1
Lebanon, Connecticut 06249
(203) 642-6008

Brochure, 6 pages; Various informational sheets; Reprints. $1 (deducted from order).

Ed Rich hand-carves classic yacht and estate nameboards, quarter and trail boards, figureheads, and other pieces of mahogany, teak, and pine. His brochure provides many photos of his work, and illustrations to help customers order nameboards. Another sheet shows how two nameboards are priced. Customers can save 17% by sealing, priming, and finishing the boards themselves. Scale sketches and price quotes are available upon submission of the proper data. Rich occasionally offers discounts during slack times. He supplies maps to his "Peaceful Acres" and welcomes people to stop by for coffee when in the vicinity. The reprints furnish tales and good photos of the character and some of his work.

See also, under:

Materials and Supplies	**General Catalogs**	National Marine
Aircraft	Commodore	Turner's
Marine Development	M & E	Warehouse
	Manhattan	**Books**
	Marine Center	Tamal Vista
	Murray's	

Seats, Bedding, Racks, Holders, Tableware, Lighting

C CUSHIONS
313 North Bronte
Rockport, Texas 78382
(512) 729-1244
Brochure, 2 pages; Quote form; Informational sheet; Price list. Free.

The brochure provides photos, one in color, and full description of the firm's custom boat cushions composed of 1½" closed-cell ensolite which will not absorb water but will retain its buoyancy in spite of punctures and mildew attacks. The flexible vinyl coating is chemically bonded to the foam to ensure extended weatherability, abrasion-resistance, and toughness. The cushions can be used as floats and as safety devices. The sheet offers photos and descriptions of cockpit cushions, hinged squares, throwable cushions, ice chest cushions, and pool floats; pads, squares, can/bottle wrap coolers, key floats, back rest wedges, stadium cushions, horseshoe buoys, knee pads, and helmsman's saddles are also available, listed on the price sheet. Quotes are provided on cushion sets upon submission of the proper information.

CANVAS TAILORS, INC.
Building 21
Hingham Shipyard
Hingham, Massachusetts 02043
(617) 749-6980
Pamphlet, 4 pages; Price list. Free.

Canvas Tailors produces hand-made "Anderson Boat Seats," back-to-back boat seats which open out to form a lounge, and which provide storage space beneath. Three stock sizes are available to fit boats in the 13' to 15', 16' to 18', and 18' and larger ranges; the seats weigh 65, 100, or 110 pounds, respectively. Custom heights, widths, and colors are available at extra cost. The pamphlet furnishes

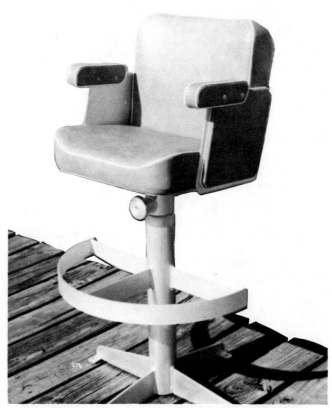

EACCO Marine Seating, Inc.   Standard Offshore Pilot Chair/Swivel.

photos of the seats, dimensions of each model, and lists seat components: heavy dacron thread, stainless steel staples, treated wood, heavy-duty hinges, and finest-grade Nautelex Gold Coast marine vinyls in eight colors, swatches of which are included.

CURTAIN LOFT

Patterson Road at Linto Creek
P.O. Box 1339
Willow Creek, California 95573
(916) 629-3430

Informational sheets (2); Order form; Quote form. Free.
"Boatique yacht curtains" are made to order of durable, machine-washable, drip-dry, mildew-resistant fabric available in many colors, and easily installed non-corrosive maintenance-free hardware and tracks suited to the specific interior. Color photos of several installed curtains are shown on one sheet. The other sheet lists standard features, optional extras (trims, lining, matching privacy curtains, shower curtains, use of the customer's fabric, design, or already installed track and hardware), frequently asked questions, and testimonials from satisfied customers. Information regarding each order filled is kept on file for future replacements. Quotes are furnished upon submission of the form provided.

EACCO MARINE SEATING, INC.

P.O. Box 423
Metairie, Louisiana 70004
(504) 835-7201

Brochure, 4 pages; Form letter. Free.
EACCO specializes in heavy-duty inland and offshore pilot house chairs, multiple-passenger seating (reclining, standard, convertible bunk bench), and aluminum electronic (radar) display pedestals and water and weathertight cabin and bulkhead doors. The brochure provides photos and specifications for these items, and scale drawings for the multiple seatings. All products are manufactured on a custom basis; inquiries are welcome to discuss requirements or to receive a bid.

HOLDARVAN

4058 New Castle Avenue
New Castle, Delaware 19720
(800) 441-7554; (302) 571-8575

Catalog, 12 pages; Supplement sheet; Price list; Form letter;
Sample imprinted drinkware. Free.
Holdarvan's catalog and supplement provide photos, some in color, of the clear plastic tumblers and wine glasses, tan plastic mug cups, white china-finish styrofoam cups and can coasters, white plastic souvenir cups, glass tumblers and mugs, napkins, napkin holders, matches, stirrers, and playing cards which can be personalized with a special silk-screened design in one color; plastic drinkware can also be gilded. Stock emblems and letter styles are shown, but Holdarvan can work from the customer's logo, letterhead, photograph, or other special design.

KENDALL PLASTICS, INC.

P.O. Box 787
Kendallville, Indiana 46755
(800) 348-2398; (219) 347-5235 (collect in IN)

Brochure, 6 pages; Two area samples; Trial offer form. Free.
Guaranteed for a minimum of five years from date of shipment, available in black, red, green, yellow, dark blue, tan, or any combination of the colors, "Dri-Dek" polyvinylchloride 12″ × 12″ × ⁹/₁₆″ tiles can be snapped

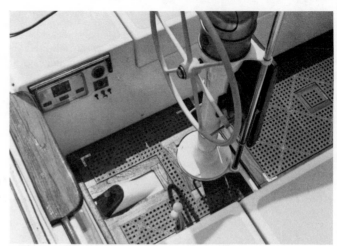

Mopco   This nautically styled yacht mat is a skid-resistant plastic grid framed in genuine teak. The Teak-Tile mat is kit supplied and comes in various sizes.

together and trimmed to non-rectangular shapes to form a floor system that will not rot, splinter, flake, soil, fade, mildew, tear, unravel, burn, melt, or dissolve. Dri-Dek trimmers, optional adhesive bond, 12″ × 2″ edging, a sample Dri-Dek coffee coaster (4″ × 8″), as well as pre-assembled flooring and factory installations are available. The brochure provides color photos, full specifications, and general description of the tiles.

MOPCO

Moffitt Products Company
P.O. Box 99
Radnor, Pennsylvania 19087

Informational sheets (4). Free.
Mopco's "teak-tile yacht mat," a nautically-styled, skid-, weather-, UV-, flame-, and fungus-resistant tan plastic grid framed in genuine teak to resemble the traditional nautical grate, is available in kits of various sizes for almost any application (29″ × 29″ to 41″ × 65″), complete with assembling instructions and all necessary materials. The literature shows a color photo of one installation, illustrates the various sizes of mats and recommended layouts, lists specifications and available spare parts, and provides fairly detailed, illustrated installation instructions.

WIND AND SEA

4479-G 122nd Avenue N.
Clearwater, Florida 33520
(813) 576-2580

Pamphlet, 6 pages; Form letter; Price list. Free.
Wind and Sea offers a line of tested yacht furnishings, featuring meticulous joinery, in teak, Honduras mahogany, or blond ash: racks or holders for navigation tools, binoculars, flashlights, dishes, bottles, cups, cans, glasses, knives, spices, paper towels, toilet tissue, magazines, paperbacks, and cassette tapes; radio, tape player, medicine or toothbrush cabinets; mirrors and step pads. The firm also distributes Amazon golden teak oil and mills veneers and mouldings for the do-it-yourselfers. The outdated brochure provides small photos, dimensions, and descriptions of most items.

PERT LOWELL COMPANY
Lane's End
Newbury, Massachusetts 01950
(617) 462-7409

Brochure, 4 pages; Price list. Free.

Known for its mast hoops (see entry under *Sailing Hardware,* page 112), Pert Lowell also hand-crafts boat and home furnishings and decorative items using traditional methods and materials, and authentic nautical detailing. Coffee tables, a tray and coasters, a towel holder, napkin rings, bracelets, and a mobile incorporate mast hoops in their designs. Also offered are a wooden rudder-shaped coffee table, a signal flag signboard, several sizes of "old time bailers" to be used as scoops, toys, or serving trays, wooden snow shovels, and a cedar reproduction of a Portsmouth trellis. Garden benches and mast hoop mirrors are available but not shown.

SAND CANYON RECREATION PRODUCTS
23452 Peralta Drive, Suite A
Laguna Hills, California 92653
(714) 855-1239

Catalog, 8 pages. Free.

Sand Canyon supplies a range of special beddings for boats, recreational vehicles and other purposes: custom sleeping "Superbags," custom mattress pads for bedding and heavily upholstered cushions, custom woven-terry-cloth covers, and custom sheets, "duo-sheets," sleeping bag inserts, and pillowcases of Wamsutta ultracale or Dura-blend flannel. Polarguard-filled comforters, nylon pack-cloth-covered foam furniture, and flannelette sheet/blankets are available in standard or custom sizes. Utility wool blankets, Pendleton virgin wool blankets, and a variety of Cordura nylon gear bags may be procured in standard sizes only. Photos, many in color, and full descriptions are furnished in the catalog.

SEASAFE DEVICES
Department SM
P.O. Box 444
Wilmington, Massachusetts 01887

Information sheet; Order form. Free.

SeaSafe makes available a portable "Shower Mate" shower with easy-grip handle, water-efficient shower nozzle, water-pressure regulator, corrosion-resistant pump assembly, and rugged, lightweight, one-piece, three-gallon capacity, sun-resistant, high-density polyethylene tank (23¼″ × 8½″). The sheet provides photos and illustrations of the unit and its parts, lists features, and suggests several uses.

*YACHTING TABLEWARE COMPANY
P.O. Box 546
Wilmington, Delaware 19899
(302) 655-9168

Catalog, 7 pages; Order form. Free.

Yachting Tableware's non-skid, dishwasher-safe, melamine dinnerware and mug sets for six or eight, designed exclusively for boats, are available in five patterns with the customer's boat name, flags, burgee, drawings or designs

Pert Lowell Company.

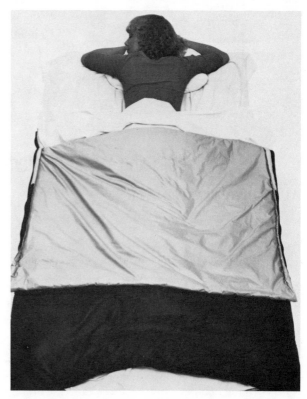

Sand Canyon Recreational Products   A superbag sleeping bag.

molded in. Non-personalized open stock dinnerware (dinner and salad plates, platters, soup bowls, serving dishes, stacking cups, mugs), nautical-design paper plates, non-skid wicker paper plate holders, and non-skid galleyware (ashtrays, shakers, rings for the bottoms of cans, jars, and drinkware, double-wall insulated cups and other items) should be purchased from local marine dealers, when possible. The catalog provides good descriptions and photos, many in color, of the items available. The order form is for personalized dinnerware and mugs only.

Yachting Tableware Company   Melamine dinnerware and accessories are non-skid and won't slide even at 25° angles. All items are dishwasher safe and break-resistant.

See also, under:

Cabin and Water Heaters, Stoves, Lamps, Fire Extinguishers

ALLCRAFT CORPORATION
  55 Border Street
  West Newton, Massachusetts 02165
  (617) 969-7743
Brochure, 4 pages; Informational sheets (3); Price list; Order form. Free.

Allcraft distributes Viking catalytic safety heaters, Seafarer stainless steel hot water heaters with heat exchanger or 120-volt electric heating element, Seafarer stainless steel hydro-silencer marine mufflers, and stainless steel pressure fuel tanks for cook stoves and cabin heaters. Photos, generous descriptions, a long list of features, and a chart of fuel consumption and operating costs are given for the Viking heaters. Photos, descriptions including some specifications, scale drawings and installation

instructions are furnished for the mufflers, water heaters, and fuel tanks; the water heaters and fuel tanks come in vertical or horizontal models.

ENVIRONMENTAL RESEARCH ASSOCIATES
  P.O. Box 531
  Vineyard Haven, Massachusetts 02568
  (617) 693-4402
Informational sheets (8); Form letter. Free.

Tom and Jane Counter of E.R.A. sell and distribute a line of tankless water heaters including the British compact "Nymph" instantaneous gas water heater (1.4 pounds gas per hour), the British Thorn "Homemaster" with a flow rate of ¾ to 2 gallons per minute approved by the American Gas Association, and the complete line of

1.

2.

Allcraft Corporation   1) Made in Britain, the flameless Viking catalytic heater is silent, with no disturbing hiss, and provides a moist heat. 2) These stainless steel water heaters produce hot water in a very short time and are built to withstand the corrosion of a salty atmosphere.

European-certified French Saunier-Duval tankless heaters (0.7-2 gal./min. models). The Nymph literature provides photos of the unit, a spout and tap kit, and a shower head assembly, illustrations of common installations, general description, and some specifications. More specifications, full description, lists of features, scale drawings, and cost comparisons with traditional tank heaters are given along with a representative photo for the Saunier-Duval line; the largest, most expensive model, thermo-statically controlled, is compatible with solar collectors. All of the heaters operate on propane or natural gas and are available with non-electric Piezo ignitions. No literature is available for the "Homemaster."

FAIRE HARBOUR LTD.
44 Captain Peirce Road
Scituate, Massachusetts 02066
(617) 545-2465
Catalog, 24 pages. Free.

Incorporating or reproducing much manufacturers' literature, Fair Harbour's "catalog" offers photos, some in color, some description and specifications for a variety of Aladdin kerosene-electric table, hanging, and mantle lamps and parts, Aladdin kerosene heaters, a Dickinson "Chesapeake" cabin heater, Junkers gas-fired tankless water heaters, Eastham Maxol gas ovens, cook tops, grills, and combinations, and Stanley unbreakable thermos bottles. Lengthy specifications for kerosene oil for Aladdin

lamps and heaters are included. Inquiries are welcome regarding parts, models, or sizes not shown. Faire Harbour also collects, sells, repairs, and trades old Aladdin lamps.

FATSCO
251 N. Fair Avenue
Benton Harbor, Michigan 49022
(616) 926-7795
Informational sheets (3); Price list. Free (with self-addressed, stamped envelope).

Fatsco puts out a line of small, sturdy, efficient heat and cook stoves which will burn almost anything like coal, charcoal, wood, cobs, pressured fuel, or waste paper. They are available in four sizes (11¾" to 25½" high, 13 to 55 lbs.), in non-marine cast iron or all-purpose stainless steel, with or without cooking top, sea rails, and galvanized or stainless steel shield. Kits for converting the plain heating stoves to cook stoves may also be obtained as well as stove parts and stainless steel pipes and exhaust fittings, extension pipe, deck plates with standard and custom pitches, and weather tops with long or short collars. Photos, dimensions, and descriptions of the various stoves, a woodsman barrel-stove kit, and some stove fittings, plus tips on burning fuel in the stoves, are provided.

SEA-FIRE EXTINGUISHING MARINE PRODUCTS
Metalcraft, Inc.
718 Debelius Avenue
Baltimore, Maryland 21205
(301) 485-0882
Two brochures, 4 pages to 6 pages each; Information sheet; Price list. Free.

Metalcraft's Sea-Fire extinguishing systems, sized according to the volume of the engine compartment (75 to 1000 cu. ft.), automatically discharge the fast-acting

Fatsco   Combination stoves that both heat and cook are ideal for boat cabins and will burn most anything as fuel.

Halon 1301 extinguishant when necessary, whether the boater is on board or not. Each model is fitted with a thermal sensor and protective guard; more deluxe models feature pressure gauges and charged/discharged indicator lights. The literature provides photos and specifications of the extinguishers and a new portable model, lists their features, explains their operation, gives installation instructions, and discusses at length the properties of the extinguishant.

SHIPMATE STOVE DIVISION

Richmond Ring Company
P.O. Box 375
Richmond Road
Souderton, Pennsylvania 18964
(215) 855-2609

Brochure, 4 pages; Informational sheets (3); Price list. Free.
Shipmate offers two-burner and three-burner stainless steel stoves with ovens which operate on kerosene, alcohol, or gas. The three-burner gas stove and oven is available with a broiler; this model as well as the three-burner kerosene and alcohol stoves also come in coppertone enamel. In addition to brass pressure alcohol or kerosene tanks with pump and gauge and refillable steel gas cylinders, a cast-iron coal or oil-burning cabin heater, a stainless steel kerosene cabin heater, a stainless steel and brass coal/charcoal/ wood-fired bulkhead-mounted heater, and an enameled cast-iron, stainless steel, and a bronze open-fireplace cabin heater are available. Photos,

illustrations, dimensions, and good descriptions are provided for these stoves and heaters. More literature may be had on request for wood/coal/oil- burning cast-iron ranges in eight sizes, and bottled gas stainless steel and aluminum ranges with various numbers of hot plates or surface burners.

Shipmate Stove Division   This 3-burner stainless steel gas stove is fully insulated and especially engineered to fit the limited space available in most galleys.

See also, under:

Yachts
Roberts
Electrical Equipment
Baker and Lyman
Sailing Hardware
Lange
Water Systems
Raritan

Nautical and Outdoor Clothing
Bauer
Bean
Gleason
General Catalogs
Chartroom
E & B
Goldberg's
Haft
M & E

M.M.O.S.
Manhattan
Marine Center
National Marine
Port Supply
Sears
Transmar
Turner's
Voyager
Warehouse

Refrigeration and Air-Conditioning Systems

CROSBY MARINE REFRIGERATION SYSTEMS, INC.

204 - 2nd Avenue S.
St. Petersburg, Florida 33701
(813) 821-3325

Two brochures, 5 pages and 13 pages; Price list. Free. Marine Refrigeration Guide Book, *103 pages. $11.*
Crosby's marine refrigeration systems feature low-amperage draw, maximum holdover capacity, low maintenance, low cost, reliability, and efficiency.

Component flexibility allows for custom-engineered systems to fit individual requirements; holdover components can be easily installed to convert existing ice boxes into refrigerators, freezers, or combinations. The small brochure provides photos, specifications, some description or lists of features, and operating diagrams for four systems: one engine driven, a 110-volt AC water-cooled system that runs off the generator or shore power, a 12-volt water-cooled DC unit that runs off the battery, and a combination engine-driven/ 110-volt AC water-cooled system. The larger brochure, Howard M. Crosby's "How to Compare Marine Refrigeration," succinctly defines marine refrigeration, describes the requirements of different kinds of users, discusses compressors, condensers, and eutectic holding plates, and provides some advice regarding the selection of a refrigeration system. Complete with cold plate and wiring schematic diagrams and illustrations of parts, Crosby's *Guide Book* goes into greater depth comparing marine with home refrigeration, providing information on boxes, insulation, heat leaks, types and adjustments of temperature controllers, the selection of holdover plates and condensing units, the pump-down and start-up of field charged systems, giving installation instructions for condensing units and cold plates, offering general operating data, and explaining common problems and their solutions. Phone calls are suggested for discussing which system would be most appropriate.

HYDRAGON CORPORATION
1326 South Killian Drive
Lake Park, Florida 33403
(305) 848-1066

Brochure, 4 pages; Informational sheets (2); Folder, 2 pages; Price lists. Free.

Hydracool's compact thermo-electric, water-cooled cooling unit with solid-state electronic controls and sealed magnetic-drive water pump, needs no locker space, has only one moving part, and uses no high-pressure gases, compressor, or cooling fan. The rugged finned aluminum unit mounts inside an existing ice box up to 12 cubic feet; the system withstands shock and vibration and is not affected by motion or angle of heel. The folder provides an illustration of an installed system and briefly explains the unit's features, operation, and installation. The brochure goes into greater depth, explaining the system's features, capabilities, 3 models, and their specifications. Additional sheets duplicate much of this information in describing and depicting 2 models. Price sheets list the equipment supplied with each model. Sales prices are occasionally offered.

KING MARINE AIR-CONDITIONING
14525 - 62nd Street North
Department 12
Clearwater, Florida 33520
(813) 536-5170

Two brochures, 2 pages and 4 pages; Update sheets (2); Color photo; Price and ordering brochure. Free.

King began building custom marine air-conditioning systems for discriminating yachters in 1947. Designed for salt-water use, of aluminum, copper, and stainless steel, with finned cupro-nickel coils, efficient, quiet, powerful squirrel-cage blowers, dependable compressors and sea pumps, King's standard and custom water-cooled systems are engineered to the smallest size for any BTU rating. Production models are rated from 7,000 to 16,000 BTUs; even 18,000 and 20,000 BTU systems operate on 115 volts. Special orders up to 60,000 BTUs or using 230 volts are available. Completely precharged and prewired, the units are easy to install, and they can be ducted to serve several

Crosby Marine Refrigeration Systems, Inc.   Components of the Crosby
"Engine Driven" system.

areas. The two brochures describe the features and installation of the units, and the firm's sales policy and limited warranty. The ordering brochure presents illustrated guides to ordering the right duct kit for the desired air conditioner. Specifications for all air-conditioning models, lists of duct kit contents, dimensions and other helpful descriptive information regarding duct kit components, a seawater pump, strainer, and other accessories, are provided in the price brochure. Prices and contents of seawater kits and additional duct kits are given on the update sheets.

SAILOR BOY PRODUCTS, INC.
120 Stadium Drive East
Arlington, Texas 76010
(817) 274-6938

Portfolio, 16 pages; Form letter; Order form; Price list. Free.

Sailor Boy's literature lists in detail the parts included in the one-plate, two-plate, and three-plate mechanical and/or 110-volt refrigeration systems for cooling areas up to 8 to 10, 15 to 20, and 24 cubic feet, respectively. Illustrations show typical installations, suggested box arrangements, mounting positions and inlet/outlet connections on stock holding plates, typical rubber hose-to-tubing fittings, and the various compressors. Heat loss data and plate dimensions and features are listed; standard systems come with 24′ of hose and use a 2-ton capacity cast iron compressor. Custom plates and hose assemblies are available. Each system package includes all necessary components except a drive belt and seawater hose. A trial fit kit is available as well as a complete systems with stock or custom plates cost for a 110-volt, for a mechanical, for a combination one-plate system, and for a three-plate combination system.

SPACREEK
616 Third Street
Annapolis, Maryland 21403
(301) 267-6565

Brochure, 3 pages; Informational sheets (5); Booklet 15 pages; Reprint; Order form. Free.

SpaCreek offers several refrigeration systems which will convert a sailboat icebox to a refrigerator, freezer, or both: a fast, efficient, engine-driven system powered directly by the engine; a very quiet, compact, completely separate and independent shore-power system; and a modified system for use with onboard generators. The brochure explains these systems, their features, and the stainless steel cold plates; three additional sheets discuss heat leaks and cold holding data and describe further the engine drive system and cold plates, illustrating them and the tubing layout of the electrical system. The reprint compares the marine refrigeration systems of several major manufacturers, including SpaCreek. The booklet, *Much Practical Advice from SpaCreek Electricians*, briefly discusses, with diagrams, symptoms of and solutions to typical electrical problems aboard. Two small sheets briefly present two of the firm's books, available for $15 each: *The 12-Volt Doctor's Practical Handbook for the Boat's Electrical System* and *39 Ways to Improve Your Ice Box*. While the firm sells directly only, the order form provided covers only the books and related diagnostic electrical equipment offered. Prices should be requested.

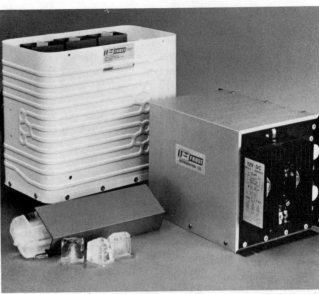

Hydragon Corporation   This marine refrigeration system cools up to 12 cubic ft. and can be mounted almost anywhere, including a hot engine room. *Photo:* Maximilian Kaufmann.

See also, under:

Electrical Equipment
American Marine

Water Systems
Raritan

General Catalogs
Goldberg's and National Marine for air conditioners, most of the catalogs for refrigerators.

Water Systems—Heads, Tanks, and Accessories

MARINE AND MOBILE WATER SYSTEMS
6400 Marina Drive
Long Beach, California 90803
(213) 598-9000

Two brochures, 6 pages each; Tank material sample; Order form. Free.

The literature provides some photos, many scale drawings, and dimensions for numerous sizes and shapes of the one-piece water and holding tanks available (7 gals. to 99 gals.), composed of taste- and odor-free, thick-walled, baffled, high-density polyethylene. Custom placement of three fittings, also illustrated and their dimensions listed, is included in the tank price. Tubing, plastic rocker pumps, and a Peters and Russell automatic demand multi-fixture pump, may also be purchased. Tanks, tubing, and fittings are all made of non-corrosive materials; fuel should not be used in the tanks, but alcohol is O.K. Brief installation instructions and recommended marine usages are indicated.

*MICROPHOR, INC.
452 East Hill Road
P.O. Box 490
Willits, California 95490
(707) 459-5563

Four brochures, 4 pages each; Informational sheets (2). Free.
Microphor offers compact Microphor/Taiko oily water separators in light to heavy weight models, floor-mounted

Microphor, Inc.   This stainless steel toilet, with only two quarts of water per flush, conserves water and helps protect the environment.

two-quart marine toilets in vitreous china or stainless steel, and 18 sizes of marine sanitation devices for overboard discharge to suit crews of 3 to 100. The water separator brochures present specifications, lists of features, operating principles, installation instructions, and illustrations of sections, plumbing connections, and a typical installation. The toilet literature provides large photos, illustrations of typical installations, general descriptions, some specifications, and comparative data. The marine sanitation device literature offers photos and specifications of various models, lists features, and describes operating principles using schematic diagrams.

RARITAN ENGINEERING COMPANY, INC.
1025 North High Street
Millville, New Jersey 08332
(609) 825-4900
Catalog, 39 pages. Free.
Raritan has over twenty years experience designing and servicing marine equipment. An 8-page brochure provides good photos, descriptions, and some specifications for the majority of products available: several self-priming or automatic, compact to deluxe, head models, flexible and molded holding tanks, sewage treatment units, water pressure systems and pumps, raw and fresh water strainers, hot water heaters, ice cube makers, converters, some electrical and plumbing components, rudder angle indicators, and air and electric horns. Additional sheets furnish larger photos, greater descriptions, more specifications, as well as scale drawings and illustrations of installations for most of the items and some new models. Price sheets detail head, treatment unit, water heater, pressure system, and rudder angle indicator (replacement) parts available separately. The firm's customer service team willingly answers questions regarding product features and installation.

See also, under:

Engines and Transmissions
  Marine Engine
Sailing Hardware
  Navtec
Nautical and Outdoor Clothing
  Gleason

General Catalogs
  Defender
  E & B
  Goldberg's
  Haft
  M & E
  M.M.O.S.
  Manhattan
  Marine Center
  National Marine
  Port Supply
  Sears
  Stone Harbor
  Warehouse

5. CLOTHING AND RELATED NAUTICAL ACCESSORIES

Soft Luggage
Outdoor Fabrics
Nautical Clothing
Gifts
Jewelry
Trophies
Plaques

The Apprenticeshop   In full sail, a recently completed Peapod.

Nautical and Outdoor Clothing, Soft Luggage, Outdoor Fabrics and Equipment

AFTERGUARD MARINE
254 Kimberly Avenue
New Haven, Connecticut 06519
(203) 562-4430
Catalog, 12 pages; Order form. Free.

Dedicated to providing excellent products and service, Afterguard's staff of racers has filled the catalog with the best in sailing gear, chosen after extensive research and water testing. Presented in photos and descriptions that include guidelines and recommendations for clothing selection, are one-piece and two-piece suits, body warmers, polypropylene thermal underwear, Chuck Roast pile jackets, socks, a vest and suit, wet suits, sailing jackets, sailing, hiking/trapezing, and deck boots, sailing and cold weather gloves, life vests and jackets, and safety, trapeze, and windsurfing harnesses. Also shown and briefly described are a few clothing accessories, a sailing watch, a few compasses, some rudder fittings, tiller universals, a windsurfer dagger board, W.E.S.T. system materials and supplies, and Laser accessories. The firm also carries a full line of small boat hardware representing Harken, Holt Allen, RWO, Proctor, Laser, Windsurfer, Windex, Schaefer, Nicro Fico, Samson, Kenyon, Barient, and Z-Spar. An authorized dealer, Afterguard also sells Windsurfer, Laser, Topper, and AMF boats; quotes are available on request.

Afterguard Marine   One piece foul weather gear: (left) a sprayproof Dinghy Suit to wear over a wetsuit, (right) an Inshore One Piece Suit to keep you dry in a small boat.

EDDIE BAUER
Fifth and Union
P.O. Box 3700
Seattle, Washington 98124
(800) 426-6253/8020; (206) 885-3330
Seasonal and holiday catalogs, 70 pages to 124 pages; Order forms. Free.

The spring and summer editions of Bauer's outdoor equipment catalog, especially, feature items of interest to boaters and fishers: Atlantis foulweather jackets, pants, and sou'westers, Gore-Tex and Storm Shed rain suits, anoraks, and hats, a variety of fishing and sports hats, watch caps, a wool pea coat, fleece thermal wear, cotton and wool sweaters, many shorts, pants, and shirts, boating shoes and sandals, waders, waterproof gear bags and pouches, Sea Eagle and Hike inflatables, soft luggage and totes, kerosene space heaters and lamps, folding camp chairs, and travel accessories. Good color photos and good descriptions are provided for these products and a full range of recreational clothing, equipment, and accessories.

L. L. BEAN, INC.
Freeport, Maine 04033
(207) 865-3111
Seasonal and holiday catalogs, 72 pages to 136 pages; Order forms. Free.

L. L. Bean offers a wide variety of outdoor and casual sportswear and related equipment, seasonal selections of which are shown in color and fully described in each catalog. Of particular interest to boaters, sailors, and fishers are boating moccasins and boat sole sandals, rubber pacs, waders and hip boots, neoprene-coated nylon rain suits, rugged outdoor garments including wool and cotton sweaters, knit shirts, and sturdy shorts and pants, soft luggage and totes, bedding, folding chairs, kerosene lamps, galley accoutrements, navigation instruments, field watches, binoculars, all-weather cameras and equipment, flashlights, and a guide to the outdoors which covers canoes and navigation.

CHANNEL ISLAND IMPORTS
P.O. Box 517
Little Compton, Rhode Island 02837
Portfolio, 12 pages; Price list; Order form. Free.

Channel Island offers a variety of traditional sweaters knitted in the British Isles of native wools. Good photos and descriptions are provided for four styles of Guernseys sporting fisherman's designs, tightly hand- and machine-knit to order of 100% pure English wool; a traditional island Guernsey hand-finished and tightly machine-knit of a lightly-oiled, pure worsted English wool; Shetland Isle pullovers machine-knit of 100% native Shetland yarn in natural wool colors; Shetland Isles gloves with nordic snowflake designs in natural Shetland wool colors; a zipper-front Guernsey, classic V-neck vest, boat-neck Welsh Mountain Fair Isle sweater patterned in natural wool colors; and Guernsey socks, gloves, and a hat.

CHUCK ROAST EQUIPMENT, INC.

P.O. Box 1006
31 Odell Hill Road
Conway, New Hampshire 03818
(603) 447-5492

Catalog, 10 pages; Order form. Free.

Chuck Roast manufactures several lines of outdoor wear made from varying kinds of pile: jackets, pants, mitts, and a hat in the original 65% polyester, 35% acrylic pile which absorbs very little moisture, passes excess body heat and moisture away from the body, and even if wet, keeps the body warm; a vest, watch cap, booties, covered mitts as well as jackets and pants in a new "offshore" 100% polyester pile which provides the same insulation as original pile but with less bulk; a jacket, vest, pullover and pants in 100% polyester Polarfleece which is more wind and water-resistant yet lighter and less bulky still; and a jacket and hat in the Polarfleece covered with a wind shell. Other Chuck Roast garments pictured in color and briefly described are wind- and water-resistant wind-shell anoraks and wind pants. Also available in water-repellent ripstop cordura nylon are flip-top gear bags, a small "club" bag, a computer data "brief case," and a carryall. Each Chuck Roast item is sewn from start to finish by one person. Odlo polypropylene underwear, Acorn Downeaster slippers, and a floating fly wallet may also be purchased.

COFISH INTERNATIONAL, INC.

P.O. Box 13
East Haddam, Connecticut 06423
(203) 873-9500/9266

Four brochures, 4 pages to 12 pages; Information sheet; Fabric swatches. Free.

The largest supplier of foulweather clothing in the U.S., Cofish mainly offers Grundens of Sweden rainwear—trousers, jackets, ¾ coats, "seven seas" suits, aprons, hats, hoods, yachting garments and slickers, ladies coats, children's garments—in mildew-resistant, washable, drip-dry, freezer-tested cotton or synthetic backed PVC, guaranteed against all defects in workmanship and materials for the life of the garment. Three brochures give prices and descriptions, list the features, and show color photos of these garments. An additional brochure provides large photos, good descriptions, and detailed lists of features and "benefits" for 4 pair of work gloves—a PVC, nylon-foam-insulated pair, and American-made synthetic and plasti-grip models. Full hip, ¾, and regular Ranger plain-toe felt-lined boots, designed for commercial fishermen, are shown on the single sheet. Quantity discounts are available; cases and standard packs can be broken sometimes at additional cost. A "Commercial Fishermen Help You Live Better" bumper sticker is available.

*COLUMBIA SPORTSWEAR COMPANY

P.O. Box 03239
6600 North Baltimore
Portland, Oregon 97203
(503) 286-3676

Catalog, 30 pages; Price list; Order form. Free.

Supplying outdoor people with quality clothing and accessories since 1938, Columbia Sportswear offers a range of ruggedly-tested, quality-constructed, outdoor garments made of the finest materials, and designed and engineered for protection, practicality, and style. Boaters and fishers may find the rain and storm pants, wind shirts, 100% cotton dirigible shorts, many hats, and a fascinating variety of fishing-hunting vests interesting, as well as the many coats, parkas, jackets, and other vests. All items are shown in color and they and some of the materials of which they are made are well described.

Chuck Roast Equipment, Inc.   Pilot jacket.

DREAMWEAVER NEEDLEWORKS

Division of the Next Event, Inc.
P.O. Box 781
Newport, Rhode Island 02840
(401) 849-3380

Catalog, 10 pages; Informational sheets (2). Free.

Dreamweaver specializes in custom-embroidered (block or script letters) "offshore" sportswear, including pile jackets, Creslan V-neck sweaters, cotton crew-neck sweaters, authentic 100% heavyweight cotton rugby jerseys, and 100% cotton or cotton-polyester La Coste knit shirts. Photos, brief descriptions, sizing and embroidery information are given on the sheets. The catalog covers a full line of men's and women's apparel (shirts, sweaters, jackets) and accessories (T-shirts, sweatshirts, ties, wallets, bags) available, in quantities only, custom-monogrammed or embroidered with a corporate/commercial/group logo.

EARLY WINTERS, LTD.

110 Prefontaine Place South
Seattle, Washington 98104
(206) 622-5203; 624-5599

Spring and fall catalogs, 132 pages; Various seasonal catalogs; Order forms. Free.

Early Winters specializes in unique outdoor equipment

which indeed includes many novel clothing, travel, and galley accessories in addition to more standard outdoor garments (including rain and storm suits, fishing vests, pile and polypropylene underwear), luggage, sleeping gear, and tents. Besides providing lengthy descriptions and good color photos of the many items offered, the tenth anniversary "big" catalog included a 34-page magazine section sporting eleven articles about outdoor practices and adventures, complete with gorgeous color pictures. The big catalogs show the firm's entire line of manufactured gear (parkas, tents, rain gear) along with a seasonal selection of other goods, while the smaller catalogs offer smaller, seasonal selections of all products available.

*FORE 'N' AFT
Sir/Gal Footwear, Inc.
Main Street
P.O. Box 101
Bowdoinham, Maine 04008
(207) 666-8811
Catalog, 8 pages; Price list. Free.

The suppleness, proper fit, and durability of Sir/Gal's boating and casual shoes are guaranteed by their hand-sewn constructions using special leathers obtained from a select group of tanners, finest quality specially-formulated rubber soles with built-in arch supports, and dye-repellent, unstretchable white polyester thread. The catalog provides brief descriptions of the many styles of boating and casual moccasins, boots, oxfords, slip-ons, loafers, and sandals available for men, women, and children, showing small color photos of each style in the colors offered. A few eastern stores that offer repairing and resoling services are listed.

FROSTLINE KITS
Frostline Circle
Denver, Colorado 80241
(303) 457-4484; 451-5600
Catalog, 36 pages; Order form. Free.

Among the many kits offered for various kinds of coats, parkas, outdoor jackets, ski wear, booties, bathrobes, packs, totes, comforters, sleeping bags, and tents, are some

Land's End   Leather and nylon stretch Sailing Gloves come in sizes for both men and women.

for Gore-Tex anoraks, pants, parkas, and storm suits, coated nylon rain parkas and pants, polyester fleece jackets and vests, sportsman/fisherman vests, and cordura duffle and travel bags and other soft luggage. Color photos and good descriptions are furnished of the finished products. Some kits include a monogram option; some items are offered completely sewn. All kits are complete, ready-to-sew packages including pre-cut quality fabric, all sewing notions, and step-by-step instructions. Help with sewing problems can be had by calling the experts at the Customer Service number: (303) 457-4484.

DON GLEASON'S CAMPERS SUPPLY, INC.
Pearl Street
P.O. Box 87
Northampton, Massachusetts 01061
(413) 584-4895
Catalog, 80 pages; Order form. 75¢.

Packed with small photos or illustrations and good descriptions of the offerings, Gleason's "complete catalog of camping and backpacking equipment" contains many items among the tents, backpacks, and sleeping bags that might be of interest to boaters, namely, a variety of cotton duck or waterproof nylon gear bags, rainwear, underwear, wool socks and caps, outdoor cloth, accessories, and hardware, canvas tarps and treatments, shock cord, portable toilets, tanks, sinks, and showers, coolers, camp stoves, lanterns, propane tanks, parts and accessories, a broad range of cooking utensils, kits, freeze-dried food and camping/travel miscellany, folding chairs and tables, and car-top carriers.

LANDS' END
Lands' End Lane
Dodgeville, Wisconsin 53533
(800) 356-4444; (608) 935-9341
Seasonal catalogs, 80 pages to 90 pages; Order forms. Free.

Lands' End stocks a full line of reasonably-priced, fine-quality outdoor and fashionable sportswear, pictured in color and well described in the catalogs. Available are a variety of wool, oiled wool, wool ragg, and cotton sweaters, 100% cotton rugby jerseys, soccer shirts, sailor's shirts, turtlenecks, Lisle knits, shorts, jeans, canvas hats, coveralls, nylon or cotton anoraks, cotton fisherman and sailing smocks, wool pea coats, wool watch caps, a nylon fisherman's cap, cotton-backed PVC day-sailing raingear, Sperry topsiders, deck shoes, sandals, and boat boots, stretchable sailing gloves, water-resistant watches, galley gadgets, a lockspike knife and brass foghorn, portable shower, floatable gear bag, wool blankets, soft luggage of cotton duck or nylon pack cloth, sports bags, duffles, and totes, and dress jackets, trousers, slacks, skirts, shirts, ties, shoes, socks, gloves, hats, scarves, sleepwear, parkas, slickers, jackets, and coats.

MCKENZIE OUTFITTERS
780 Willamette Street
Eugene, Oregon 97401
(503) 485-5946
Catalog, 32 pages. Free.

McKenzie Outfitters produces a newsprint catalog

furnishing illustrations, photos, and good descriptions of a variety of outdoor gear including heavy-duty inflatables, inflatable frames, waterproof ammo cans, Atlantis Ultimate foulweather gear and SeaBags, and Columbia Sportswear fishing-hunting vests and hats.

OUTDOOR WILDERNESS FABRICS
2511 Latah Drive
Nampa, Idaho 83651
(208) 466-1602

Informational sheets (2); Fabric swatches; Order form. Free.

Samples, dimensions, descriptions, recommended uses, and prices per yard are furnished on one sheet for the outdoor fabrics available: nylon ripstop, pack cloth and cordura, camouflage nylon twill, Oxford and ballistic nylons, heavy nylon lock mesh, Taslan Klimate and taffeta Gore-Tex multilaminates, 100% polyester knit no-see-um netting, 60/40 early warning fabric with Scotchlite finish, and downproof polyester-cotton cloth. Pictured and described on the second sheet are Fastex buckles and Fastabs, a Progresco fine little cord lock, and YKK zippers and components. Other listed items include nylon braid rope, velcro fasteners, D-rings, nylon webbing, thinsulate, and ensolite and beva-lite padding. Inquiries regarding other fabrics and colors, and requests for samples are welcome. Unstocked fabrics, hardware, and notions can be located and special-ordered at little or no extra charge.

PACIFIC/ASCENTE
P.O. Box 83761
1766 N. Helm
Fresno, California 93747
(800) 344-7428; (209) 252-2887

Catalog, 15 pages; Supplement sheet; Price list; Order form. Free.

Pacific/Ascente has been in the business of manufacturing no-nonsense, well-made, useful, long-wearing, comfortable, trouble-free, and reliable outdoor gear since 1895. Today's outerwear and sleeping bags feature clean and functional designs, thorough workmanship, the best fabrics and materials, double-stitching, bar tacks, and brass grommets. A number of the Storm Shed jackets and a Gore-Tex storm suit, anorak, parka, and pants may be of interest to boaters, sailors, and fishers. Photos or illustrations of these items, and full descriptions of them and the fabrics of which they are constructed are given.

PATAGONIA SOFTWARE
Division of Great Pacific Iron Works
P.O. Box 150
Ventura, California 93002
(805) 648-3386

Catalog, 38 pages; Dealer list; Order form. Free.

The catalog provides good color photos and descriptions of all offerings, gorgeous color photos of people wearing Patagonia garments, and detailed discussions of the famous pile, bunting (polar fleece), and polypropylene materials used with or without integral or separate wind-shells for a broad range of outdoor wear including jackets, sweaters and cardigans, vests, pants, gloves, mitts, socks, balaclavas and face masks, underwear, turtlenecks,

and sleeping shells. Also available are wool sweaters, cotton-polyester sweatshirts, cotton rugby shirts, cotton-nylon rugby shorts/swim trunks, cotton web belts, cotton T-shirts, and heavy-duty canvas shirts, pullovers, and many kinds of shorts and pants for men and women; a canvas walking skirt for women is also shown.

PORT CANVAS COMPANY
Box H - Beachwood Avenue
Kennebunkport, Maine 04046
(800) 341-9674; (207) 967-5570

Catalog, 32 pages. Free.

The Port Canvas staff designs and manufacturers all of its canvas products, mostly luggage and clothing, using 100% cotton minimum grade A no. 8 canvas duck vat-dyed to specifications, heavy-duty industrial 100% cotton webbing for bag handles and strapping, double-stitched sailmaker's dacron thread, heavy-duty rustless, non-sticking, non-corroding YKK sailmaker's zippers, hand-set spur-type no. 2 brass grommets, and brass and stainless steel snaps. Nice photos, many in color, and brief descriptions often including dimensions are presented for sea duffles, one-piece construction ice bags and totes, specialty sport bags, shoulder bags, garment bags and other travel bags, Breton canvas shirts, canvas jackets, British- and American-made wool sweaters, belts of cotton webbing, Greek sailor's caps, wool masks and watch caps, fishing hats and sou'westers, slickers, wind- and waterproof storm suits, storm boots and wet weather mocs, director's chairs, replacement covers, and a log carrier. Cleaning procedures are indicated and monogram letter styles and nine of the ten canvas colors are shown.

Land's End   Drifters, cotton sweaters for the whole family, come in a variety of colors and can be worn all four seasons of the year.

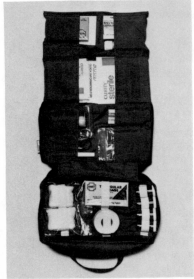

Recreational Equipment, Inc.   The 1st Essential First Aid Kit, packed in a durable, nylon carrying case, and a variety of parkas and down jackets (next page) are among the many and varied items offered by REI.

RECREATIONAL EQUIPMENT, INC.

P.O. Box C-88125
Seattle, Washington 98188
(800) 426-4840; (800) 562-4894 (WA);
(206) 433-0771

Seasonal and holiday catalogs, 48 pages to 100 pages; Order forms. Free.

REI has expanded in recent years to include some boating and fishing clothing and gear besides the traditional back-packing and mountain-climbing equipment, for example, REI-brand offshore rain suits, Helly Hansen dry and rain suits, neoprene wetsuits, a sportsfishing vest and some fishing equipment, canvas deck shoes, hand-sewn boating moccasins, inflatables, waterproof gear bags, life vests, car-top carriers and tie-downs. Other items of special interest, also fully described and shown in color, are Patagonia pile garments, a wide range of rain suits, soft luggage, binoculars and camera equipment, galley and travel accessories, outdoor fabrics and sewing supplies.

SEATOGS

P.O. Box 912
Newport, Oregon 97365

Catalog, 10 pages; Fabric swatches. There may be a charge.

Kay and Bruce MacQuaid have recently opened shop to provide reasonably-priced, hand-made, sturdy, practical, natural-fiber clothing that combines durability and function with a bit of uniqueness and style. Nicely illustrated and described are a hooded pullover in 24 oz. wool or water-repellent 10 oz. cotton canvas, a pullover in the 10 oz. canvas, a British fishing smock in 6 oz. drill or 10 oz. chamois, double-seated, kneed, and thighed pants of 6 oz. cotton drill or deck pants of 10 oz. water-repellent canvas with or without suspenders, a sea parka of the 10 oz. canvas lined with lightweight cotton, a wool vest, and earwarmers, a watch cap, and a kon-tiki helmet knitted using Fair Isle techniques and design and Navajo wool in natural or dyed colors. Double-stitched, clean-finish seams

and bar-tacked stress points are standard on all sewn items; cotton-polyester thread, polyester zippers, and brass snaps and grommets are used. Washing and care instructions are indicated.

SEATTLE FABRICS

3876 Bridge Way N.
Seattle, Washington 98103
(206) 632-6022

Price list-catalog, 6 pages. Free.

A retail and wholesale store, Seattle Fabrics specializes in recreational fabrics (uncoated and coated nylon taffetas, pack cloth, Oxford, cordura), acrilan ("yachtcrillic" or "sunbrella"), natural untreated canvas in various weights and widths, dyed and treated cotton duck in many colors, insulating fabrics for thermal roman and roll-up shades, hard-to-find fabrics, webbing, and hardware for the outdoorsperson. Ready-made items for sailors such as bulkhead bags, duffels, and signal flags are kept in stock. The price sheets present the fabrics and some hardware, giving their prices and dimensions, and listing their features, uses, and the colors in which they are available. Small fabric swatches will be sent upon request. No custom sewing services are offered.

TILLEY ENDURABLES

39 Beveridge Drive
Don Mills, Ontario
Canada M3A 1P1
(800) 883-1000; (800) 252-2300 (NY);
(416) 444-2291

Catalog, 8 pages. Free.

Alex Tilley's floatable, machine-washable, bleachable hat, offered in three styles, is constructed of tough, pre-shrunk natural-color 10 oz. cotton duck, lockstitched with polycore thread and fitted with a foam-filled sweatband (to absorb perspiration), four brass eyelets, four brass ventilation grommets, and an effective tie-down cord. Tilley also hand-crafts comfortable, sturdy, double-seated shorts with

many practical pockets and D-rings. They are made of nearly unrippable wash-and-wear pre-shrunk poly-cotton (navy, tan, or white), double-seamed, lockstitched, and reinforced with many bar tacks. The catalog provides good photos and explains in detail the features and virtues of the hats and shorts. Glorious testimonials are included.

MILTON G. WALDBAUM COMPANY
501 N. Main
Wakefield, Nebraska 68784
(800) 228-8176; (402) 287-2211
Pamphlet, 6 pages; Information sheet. Free.
The largest egg-processing plant under one roof in the U.S., Waldbaum's produces a dried whole egg mix packaged in 6 oz. foil-lined pouches (30 to a case, 11.25 #, net) each of which makes the equivalent of 12 eggs when added to 12 oz. of water; the mix can be used to make scrambled eggs and omelets, or to replace eggs in cakes, french toast and such. The sheet explains the mix, ideal for camping, boating, and sailing, and the pamphlet describes the company, its range of products and their specifications.

WIND IN THE RIGGING
P.O. Box 323
125 E. Main Street
Port Washington, Wisconsin 53074
(414) 284-3494
Catalog, 12 pages; Order form. Free.
Emphasizing fitting out gear in the spring/summer edition, and gift items for the sailor and home in the fall/winter edition, the catalog provides good-size photos, some in color, and good descriptions of a variety of sailboat equipment and sailing accessories. The catalog covers a New Zealand wool sweater, monogrammed wool/acrylic sweater, embroidered poly-cotton knit shirts, T-shirts, deckhand shorts, a windproof sailing cap, an authentic Greek fisherman's cap, deck hat, watch cap, sou'wester, sandals, web belts personalized or with sailing motifs, Oxford nylon duffles, a canvas ditty bag, cotton duck shoulder bag, collapsible buckets, totes and aprons, a V-berth sleeping bag, galley accessories, a bosun's chair, folding boat ladder, heaving line with monkey fist, solar energy battery charger, folding radar reflector, signaling mirror, single-hand dividers, compass corrector, Rieker clinometer, a few maintenance devices, an anchor spanker sail, a portscoop, windscoop, high-quality sail stops, rawhide rigging ties, personalized sail ties, brass and roped teak block key rings, a personalized camera strap, personalized dog leash, log book, seaside note cards, and jewelry, mobiles, and doorknockers in nautical shapes.

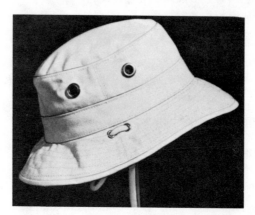

Tilley Endurables   The standard Tilley floatable hat.

See also, under:

Sailing Hardware
  Obert
Sails and Canvas Goods
  Anderson & Vining
  Bohndell
  Hild
  Sailors' Tailor
  Sailrite
  Smyth
  Thurston
  Wilson

Flags
  Olmsted
Boat Names
  Landa
  Muller
Seats, Bedding...Lighting
  Sand Canyon
Gifts
  Center for Environmental
  Education
  Mystic
  Preston

General Catalogs
  All catalogs except
  Haft, Pastime,
  Transmar, Voyager
Books
  Cruising World

Gifts, Jewelry, Trophies, and Plaques

ARTEK, INC.
Elm Avenue
Antrim, New Hampshire 03440
(603) 588-6825

Catalog, 12 pages; Form letter; Price list; Order form. $1.

Artek's "Save the Whale Collection," scrimshaw reproductions hand-crafted of polymer ivory, is intended to encourage the appreciation and practice of scrimshaw with the use of a non-whale product, while discouraging the slaughter of whales and publicizing the plight of the whale and other endangered species. Each reproduction is carefully made to preserve the weight, feel, detail, and finish of the original, down to the cracks, nicks, and chips. A note on the price list explains Artek's philosophy, and the form letter provides a brief history of whaling and an introduction to scrimshaw. Furnishing historical information on noted pieces, the catalog presents good color photos of the items available: sperm whale tooth scrimshaw, engraved miniature boxes, thimbles, buckles, buttons, pendants, coasters, and napkin rings, carved bodkins, napkin rings, and figurines, carved or engraved knife and barware handles, plaques, cribbage boards, ditty boxes, letter openers, and desk accessories containing engravings, and blanks for carving and engraving.

THE CAPTAIN'S EMPORIUM, INC.
331 Kedzie Street
Evanston, Illinois 60202
(312) 475-0180

Catalog, 8 pages; Form letter; Price list. Free.

The Captain's Emporium was started to provide a more complete source of sailing trophies, gifts, and related services for today's sailors and clubs. The staff of experienced craftsmen, consultants, and buyers, who are also active racing sailors, will give sailors and clubs helpful suggestions and new ideas to save on trophy budgets. The catalog furnishes color photos and brief descriptions of stock items offered: wire sculpture reproductions of racing designs, nautical design plaques, plates, medals, medallions, and buckles, sail/nautical- equipment-shaped trophies, nautical design book ends, desk accessories, mugs, and pitchers, lamps, fog horns, ash trays, bar sets, a sextant box, clock, and other accessories. Variations of stock designs, custom designs for special classes of boats, and custom design and manufacture of one-of-a-kind permanent or class trophies are available.

CENTER FOR ENVIRONMENTAL EDUCATION
Whale Gifts
P.O. Box 37422
Washington, D.C. 20013
(800) 228-2606; (800) 642-8777 (NE);
(202) 723-0511

Catalog, 32 pages; Annual report; Order form. Free.

The Center for Environmental Education sponsors the Whale Protection Fund, Seal Rescue Fund, and Sea Turtle Rescue Fund, among other enterprises, aiming "to maintain the biological diversity and ecosystem integrity of the Earth's marine environment." The annual report explains progress made on the center's various programs. The Whale Gift collection is made available to help support these programs financially while publicizing their purposes. The catalog provides color photos and brief descriptions of a host of items picturing whales, sporting whale motifs, or taking the forms of whales and other marine life: sculptures, prints, photos, mobiles, toys, games, books, calendars, address books, stationery, desk accessories, clothing, accessories and jewelry, totes, duffles, pillows and quilts, toiletries, cookie cutters and tableware, candy and more.

The Captain's Emporium, Inc.   Nautical design bookends and other desk accessories along with trophies and related sailing gifts can be found at the Emporium.

A. G. A. CORREA
P.O. Box 401
Wiscasset, Maine 04578
(800) 341-0788; (207) 882-7873

Jewelry catalog, 32 pages; Trophy catalog, 24 pages; Order forms. Free.

Correa's jewelry catalog shows lovely color photos of a variety of exquisite jewelry—necklaces, bracelets, pins, tie tacks and bars, earrings, brooches, pendants, charms, cuff links—in nautical shapes and 14 or 18 karat gold. Also pictured but not in color are a necktie, card set, book ends, plaques, trays, and gift boxes bearing nautical motifs, a 100% rag paper log book, personalized mugs and sailplan glasses, a jewelry box, tung oil, a cedar bucket, and in color, a tinned copper captain's kettle. The trophy catalog presents large photos and some description of personalized trays, sailplan plaques, trophies, boxes, desk and other accessories, glassware, mugs, and a full line of fine pewterware. The Correas offer a free home-cooked meal to customers who arrive at their home by boat, according to reservations made in advance.

DESIGNER'S MANUFACTURING, INC.

1545 Mission Street
San Francisco, California 94103
(415) 346-0922

Informational sheets (4); Price list. Free.

This firm provides custom-engraved solid brass nameplates in many forms: plates and plaques, badges, key/luggage/dog/ bag tags, door knockers, and desk accessories (some solid oak and walnut) containing the engraved plaques. Most items are pictured in color and their dimensions are given.

MYSTIC SEAPORT MUSEUM STORE

Mystic, Connecticut 06355
(203) 536-9957

Catalog, 36 pages; Order form. Free.

The Mystic Seaport Museum Store offers a wealth of handsome nautical accessories and items sporting nautical motifs or shapes. Pictured in color and fully described are weather, navigation, and charting instruments, bells and horns, lanterns and lamps, flags, folding deck chairs, chart tables, mirrors, a hatch cover table, galleyware, New England taste treat delights, clothing, jewelry, totes, desk accessories and stationery, some toys, boat model kits, polymer ivory scrimshaw kits, pillow and hooked rug kits, carvings, sculptures, figurines, plaques, glass panels, prints, and more.

S. T. PRESTON & SON, INC.

Main Street Wharf
Greenport, Long Island
New York 11944
(516) 477-1990

Catalog, 112 pages; Order form. Free.

Preston's catalog presents a representative selection of nautical items that can be found in the firm's store, in business for more than a century. Photos, often in color, brief descriptions, and dimensions are furnished for the extensive array of offerings: ship's bells and fog horns, weather and navigation instruments, weathervanes, lamps and lanterns, tables, interior furnishings, galleyware and glassware, doorknockers, brass plaques, book ends, ships in bottles, sculptures, figurehead replicas, carvings, polymer ivory scrimshaw, prints, paintings, stained glass scenes, wallhangings and decorations, many model boat and ship kits, decoy and string art kits, books, some clothing, jewelry, and nautical novelties.

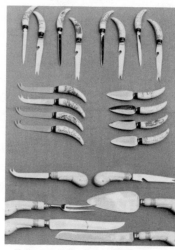

Artek, Inc. Knives and barware with scrimshaw handles made of hand-crafted polymer ivory, a non-whale product.

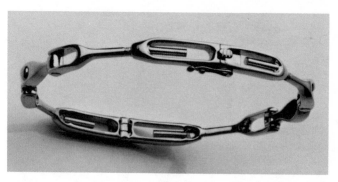

A.G.A. Correa Turnbuckle bracelet.

RAINBOWS UNLIMITED

P.O. Box 1644
Alameda, California 94501

Pamphlet, 6 pages. Free.

Stephen Barlow practices the art of ivory engraving on an ecologically-sound modern medium, recreating the delicate beauty and fine detail of original engravings on plaques, buckles, pendants, and coasters. The pamphlet provides photos of the available items and classic engravings—fishing and hunting quarries, nautical and outdoor scenes.

See also, under:

Electrical Equipment
Baker and Lyman
Sailing Hardware
Clark
Nashmarine
Sails and Canvas Goods
Sailrite
Nautical and Outdoor Clothing
Wind in the Rigging

General Catalogs
Commodore
Golden Fleece
Haft
International Sailing
M & E
Manhattan
Marine Center
National Marine
Nautical Boatique

Port Supply
Sears
Warehouse
Books
Armchair
Bluewater
Chesapeake
Cruising World
International Marine
Yankee Whaler

6. CATALOGS OF GENERAL BOATING EQUIPMENT

Sanford Boat Company, Inc.

General Boating Equipment Catalogs

AIRBORNE SALES COMPANY, INC.

P.O. Box 2727, Department C-82A
8501 Steller Drive
Culver City, California 90230
(213) 870-4687

Catalog, 92 pages; Order form. $1.

This newsprint catalog provides a limited index, photos and brief descriptions, sometimes including specifications, of a vast array of haphazardly arranged items: aircraft instruments, a navigation kit, clinometers, indicators, gauges, meters, compasses and correctors, sextants, binoculars, watches and clocks, radar reflectors; magnets, electrical equipment (control cables and fittings, actuators, generators, inverters, DC and permanent-magnet motors, gear and starter motors, solenoids, transformers, voltage regulators), components, relays, switches, and circuit breakers. The catalog also lists a great variety of water and air pumps and compressors, blowers and fans, ventilators, gas and air tanks; a Paragon hydraulic transmission and Briggs and Stratton 3 to 8 hp gas engines; hydraulic cylinders, filters, and other components, hydraulic, pneumatic, and solenoid controls, marine hose assemblies and fittings; aircraft fittings, "famous mixes" of nuts, bolts, screws, washers, drill bits, furniture hardware, electrical terminals and switches, pulleys, shafts and couplings, universal joints, winches, windlasses; hand and power tools, clamps, drill bits, hydraulic jacks, some welding tools; an inflatable raft and collapsible oars, sea anchors, life preservers, emergency lights and flares; boat accessories such as rope, cushions, buckets and lights; backpacks, duffles, flight and military clothing, and goggles. Additional engineering and research data can not be provided. If a desired item is not listed in the catalog, Airborne may carry it or may be able to procure it. Warehouse and surplus store visits are encouraged.

AUSTAD'S

4500 East 10th Street
P.O. Box 1428
Sioux Falls, South Dakota 57101
(800) 843-6828; (605) 336-3135

Seasonal catalogs; Order forms. Free.

Offering equipment primarily for sports and leisure activities, golf in particular, Austad's summer catalog (64 pages) does make available some items of interest to boaters: besides athletic clothing, camping and outdoor gear, and waterskiing equipment, a few Condor and Sea Eagle inflatables and accessories, life vests and buoyancy jackets, and some fishing equipment including a fillet knife and board, at prices well below list. Color photos and brief descriptions are provided for these items, and a list of features prefaces the descriptions of Condor inflatables.

BART'S WATER SKI CENTER

Highway 13
North Webster, Indiana 46555
(800) 348-6016; (219) 834-7666

Catalog, 36 pages. Free.

Bart's full line of waterskis, related equipment and gear, includes a Tube-In-It inflatable, quite a variety of wetsuit brands and types, much sports and beach wear, and a few tote bags, all allegedly at the lowest prices in the country. Brief descriptions and color photos present the firm's products.

CABELA'S INC.

812 - 13th Avenue
Sidney, Nebraska 69162
(308) 254-5505/8800/7032

Five catalogs: Spring, 132 pages; Summer, 80 pages; Fall, 100 pages; Christmas, and Mid-Winter, 64 pages; Order forms. Free.

While all of Cabela's catalogs represent the firm's full range of fishing, hunting, and outdoor gear, the spring and summer catalogs especially emphasize the fishing equipment, and the fall catalog, hunting gear. Good color photos and solid descriptions are furnished for the tremendous variety of offerings. The fishing and boating items include: reels, rods, rodbuilding kits, components, cases, rod holders, downriggers, a tremendous variety of lures, jigs, flies, weights, spoons, hooks, swivels and snaps, lines, molds and equipment and supplies for making jigs, lures, and sinkers, spinner and lure-making parts and supplies, fly-tying tools and supplies, fly and tackle boxes, creels, bait containers and entrapments, dip nets, scales, scalers, skinners, many filleting knives, cleaning boards, fishing pliers, sharpening devices and stones, and fish cleaning gloves. The catalog continues with a list of small electronics fish finding equipment including depth sounders, chart recorders and conversion units; a variety of binoculars, a fishing barometer, small compasses; a battery charger, Minnkota gas outboards, trolling motor props, handle extensions, a variety of boating and trolling accessories such as anchors, motor mounts, brackets, car top carriers, boat trailer accessories, boat seats and chairs, float tubes and cushions, and an ABS plastic "bass chaser" boat with wood crossbracing (79″, 96″; 60#, 85#). Outdoor gear such as duffle bags, travel cases, waterproof packs, flashlights and lanterns; outdoor wear such as wading shoes, boots, and socks, fishing suits and shirts, angler's and life vests, flotation jackets, waterproof rain suits, fishing hats and gloves can also be found.

CAL-MARINE DISCOUNT

6317 Seaview Avenue N.W.
Seattle, Washington 98107
(206) 789-4640

Sales brochure, 8 pages. Free.

Furnishing color photos and brief descriptions, the brochure features a broad selection of the firm's goods: marine electronics (VHF radios, radio direction finder, depth sounder), sailing instruments (wind and knot meters, depth sounders), navigation equipment (compasses, binoculars, chart kit), emergency equipment (life rafts, life jackets, boat cushions, flares, strobes, EPIRBs), hardware (winches, anchor packages, bow rollers, dock lines and fenders, outboard brackets), signal flags, a fog bell, interior amenities (propane range, tableware, towel bars and toilet seat, heaters), maintenance equipment and supplies (cleaners, finishes, lubricants, mops, brushes, pails), some foulweather and outdoor gear, deck boots and shoes, duffle bags and a waterproof watch.

THE CHARTROOM AT CHASE-LEAVITT
10 Dana Street
Portland, Maine 04112
(207) 772-7989
Catalog, 18 pages. Free.

Growing in less than ten years from a small chart supplier to a complete marine store, the Chartroom presents in the catalog small photos or illustrations and brief descriptions of only a small selection of the items in stock: Avon and Achilles inflatables, Atlantis, Helly Hansen, and Line 7 foulweather gear, boots and shoes, Imperial survival suits, Atlantis, Extrasport, and Stearns life vests, safety gear (distress signals, poles, harnesses and bosun's chairs, lights, flares, radar reflectors), weather instruments and ship's clocks, sextants, navigation computers, compasses and binoculars, a ship's log, chart room instruments, galley stoves, heaters, and lamps, and a variety of boating accessories (bosun knives, rope palms, clinometers and wind indicators, outdoor showers, binocular holders). The firm also offers a complete selection of quality hardware, up-to-date charts, publications, piloting tools and bridge equipment, Drascombe and Howmar boats, Givens, Switlick, and R.F.D. life rafts, and Universal, Volvo, Westerbeak, Perkins, Yanmar, Warner and Parigon marine transmissions. The firm services the inflatables, life rafts, and marine transmissions that it sells. Additional information on any item may be procured upon request.

Cal-Marine Discount   The Ocean Racer set, hi-fit pant and jacket in red, yellow, green, and navy, is one of a broad selection of goods available from this firm.

COMMODORE NAUTICAL SUPPLIES
Division of Commodore Uniform Company, Inc.
396 Broadway
New York, New York 10013
(800) 824-7888; (800) 852-7777 (CA), operator 79;
(212) 226-1880
Guide, 100 pages; Sales flyer; Order form. Free.

Commodore aims to offer the latest in boating fashion and design while still maintaining the classic look of traditional uniforms, caps, insignia, flags, and other products. Fortunately armed with several detailed indexes, the catalog provides small photos and descriptions of various lengths for an incredible array of items, a bit haphazardly arranged: novelty and marine flags, race and private signals, decals, plaques, and name plates; foulweather gear, outdoor wear and sweaters, Sperry top-siders and boots, Sir/Gal footwear, gloves, nautical uniforms, blazers and coats, whites, khakis, caps, belts, buckles, ties, scarves, socks, sunglasses, cap, sleeve, and collar insignia, shoulder tabs, emblems, brass buttons, and jewelry. Also offered are emergency equipment including life vests, flashlights and strobes, first aid kits, gaffs and boat hooks; ship's wheels, marine fastener kits, repair materials and tools; plotting and navigation instruments, sailing instruments, clocks, chart cases and instrument covers, boating books, log books, ocean survey charts; sleeping bags, blankets, sheets, pillows, garment and gear bags, folding chairs and tables, lamps, boat mats, galley utensils and equipment, glass and tableware, towels, soaps, travel accessories, racks, holders and other fixtures; model kits, games, LPs and cassettes of sea songs, carvings, figurines, and stained glass reproductions.

CUTTYSARK
Cuttysark of Bellevue
10235 Main Street
Bellevue, Washington 98004
(206) 453-1265
Personal letter; Occasional mailings upon request. Free.

Cuttysark carries a constantly shifting and growing inventory of items saved from dismantled ships from all over the world (flags, brass bells, binnacles, fixtures, horns, lanterns, portholes, windows, and so forth). Some telescopes, sextants, navigation tools and charts, documents, new flags and quality hats are also available. Requests by phone for specific items are most welcome; after some discussion Audrey and Dennis Wood-Gaines will send photos of a selection of offerings to help the customer make a decision.

DEFENDER INDUSTRIES, INC.
P.O. Box 820
255 Main Street
New Rochelle, New York 10802
(914) 632-3001
Catalog, 166 pages. $1.25 (free to boat owners).

In order to offer the largest selection of marine goods in the U.S.A., at the lowest prices, Defender does not produce a "highly-polished, slick" catalog, and its staff is instructed *not* to make recommendations to customers regarding the selection of merchandise. Complete with index, the newsprint catalog is packed with small photos and minimal to expansive descriptions of the vast assortment of brand-name products available: fiberglass and polyester cloths, polyester and epoxy resins, related materials, Airex and other foams, Thai teak plywood and lumber, trims and rubrails, maintenance and repair products and equipment, paints and finishes, basic tools, fasteners and fittings, ropes, lines, rigging tools and hardware, sail and utility fabrics, and a full line of yachting hardware (anchors, chain, catches, cleats, oars and oarlocks, winches, blocks, and the rest). Other items listed are deck hardware (ventilators, lights, hatches), boat top frames, rails, ladders and fittings, fishing and other chairs, dock hardware (davits, fenders), outboard engines, motor brackets, props, steering wheels and systems, engine controls, tanks and filters, pumps and hoses, mufflers, batteries, gauges and instruments, clocks and watches, compasses, navigation equipment, charts and charting tools, marine electronics, binoculars, lights and signals, first aid kits, life vests and harnesses, inflatables, covers for boats and other equipment. Supplies and materials for mattresses and cushions, galley appliances, equipment and accessories, sanitation systems and components, lamps, trolling and fishing equipment, foulweather gear, boots, shoes, hats, gear bags, and boatbuilding, sailmaking, and seamanship books can also be found.

E & B MARINE SUPPLY, INC.
150 Jackson Avenue
P.O. Box 747
Edison, New Jersey 08818
(201) 442-3940

Spring, Summer, and Christmas catalogs, approx. 116 pages; Order forms. Free.

In business for twenty-five years, E & B is self-proclaimed as the nation's leading discount marine supply company. Containing condensed and full indexes, the mostly newsprint catalog jams together small photos and brief descriptions of a broad range of brand-name and E & B's own sail and powerboat goods arranged haphazardly and confusingly: dinghies and inflatables, outboard brackets, trailer accessories, fuel accessories and tanks, mufflers, trim planes, steering equipment, controls, marine electronics, marine instruments, navigation instruments and charting tools, navigation lights, electrical components, batteries, rescue lights, flares and strobes, horns, boat covers, dock hardware, fenders, rails, ladders and fittings, anchors, chain, rope and accessories, deck and yachting hardware, sail and rigging fittings, flags, folding tables and chairs, galley fixtures, appliances and equipment, lamps and racks, heaters, sanitation devices, pumps, hose and strainers, waterskiing equipment, trolling and fishing equipment and accessories. Other items include filleting knives, fishing chairs and boat seats, maintenance and repair supplies and equipment, books, life vests, safety harnesses, swim wear, foulweather gear, shoes and boots, and gear bags. A few special pages furnish descriptions and color photos of sale items. Staff members will help customers select proper equipment. Copies of manufacturers' warranties, if they exist, will be sent upon written request.

E & B Marine Supply, Inc.

FORE AND AFT MARINE
12055 Seminole Boulevard
Largo, Florida 33540
(813) 391-3559

Catalog, 96 pages. $1.

Another newsprint catalog offering discount marine supplies, it furnishes a brief index, larger than usual photos, and the usual brief descriptions (not quite as crammed together as is common) for a great variety of items crazily arranged: porta-botes, Achilles inflatables, outboard engines, trim planes, outboard brackets, trailer accessories, fuel accessories and tanks, pumps and strainers, lights and electrical equipment, gauges, weather instruments and clocks, navigation instruments, compasses and charting tools, maintenance and repair supplies, some fasteners, rigging and yachting hardware, rigging knives, sail accessories and repair kits, anchors, chain, rope, deck hardware, rails and fittings, ladders, swim platforms, fenders, boat covers, folding chairs and tables, racks and holders, galley appliances, utensils and equipment, life vests, horns, flashlights, foulweather clothing, shoes and gloves.

GOLDBERG'S MARINE
202 Market Street
Philadelphia, Pennsylvania 19106
(800) 523-2926; (215) 627-3700/3719

Summer sales catalog, 108 pages; Order form. Free. Discount catalog, 224 pages. $2 (free with order only).

This newsprint catalog, complete with index, features a less confusing format than most catalogs of its kind, presenting its vast array of offerings in well-defined columns and somewhat within appropriate sections. Photos and brief descriptions are given for an 8' ABS foam-filled dinghy, inflatables, competition racing boat models, outboards, outboard brackets and carriers, trailer accessories, fuel tanks and components, bilge and other pumps and accessories, electrical power supplies, fire safety equipment, navigation lights, marine electronics, navigation and marine instruments, gauges, clocks, compasses and binoculars, charting tools and kits, books, charts, calculators, emergency equipment, horns, bells, distress signal kits, lights, life vests, harnesses, life rings, winches, whisker and spinnaker poles. Further listings include some sailing hardware, anchors, windlasses, chains and accessories, deck hardware, convertible tops and hardware, ladders, fenders, rope, dock hardware, boat and equipment covers, storage lockers, marine finishes, maintenance and repair supplies and materials, some tools, rigging knives, and fasteners, marine fabric, sail needles, flags, folding tables and chairs, boat and fishing seats, interior racks and lights, galley appliances, equipment and utensils, heaters, fans, air conditioners, marine sanitation devices, sleeping bags, bed linens, and gear bags. Several color pages present mostly foulweather and nautical clothing, shoes and boots, fishing lures and rods, and sailboard and waterskiing equipment and clothing. Factory descriptions and consumer advice are available on request.

*GOLDEN FLEECE DESIGNS, INC.

441 South Victory Boulevard
Burbank, California 91502
(213) 848-7724; 849-1901

Catalog, 128 pages; Price lists. $2.

Presenting a good index, nice large photos, many in color, and brief descriptions of the items offered, the catalog features quite a variety of marine fabric goods: sails, sail covers and bags, instrument and equipment covers, boat tops and covers, canopies, awnings, dodgers and biminis, car covers, tarpaulins, umbrellas, windscoops, bunk boards, bosun's chairs, tool bags, cases and pouches, gear and tote bags (many of which are waterproof, some of which will float), sea anchors, bait tanks, trapeze harnesses, catamaran and raft accessories, hammocks, blankets, towels, pillows, boat cushions, curtain sets, pilot seats, many hats, shirts, sweaters, aprons, belts, and flags. Additional offerings include first aid kits and emergency supplies, bells and horns, European marine hardware (rings, hooks, grommets, snaps, curtain fasteners, webbing slides, links, furniture hardware, chocks, cleats, shackles, turnbuckles, eye and U bolts, thimbles, guides and straps, ventilators, louvers, port lights, deck plates, rod holders, boat top fittings), marine fabrics, webbing and tape, maintenance and repair supplies and equipment, some tools, navigation and charting instruments, rigging knives, cutlery, steering wheels, diving helmets and equipment, sea sponges, and nautical jewelry.

JAY STUART HAFT COMPANY, INC.

P.O. Box 11210
57th Street Branch
Bradenton, Florida 33507
(813) 753-6446

Catalog, 114 pages; Order form. Free.

Devoting eleven pages to the virtues and specifications of C-Q-R anchors, eighteen pages to a variety of anchor windlasses and winches, and another five pages to anchor chain and related accessories, the newsprint Haft catalog provides large, good photos, some illustrations, good descriptions, and often specifications for the variety of products. Offered in addition to the anchors and related equipment are sea anchors, solid brass boat hooks,

Simpson davits, port and deck lights, ventilators, ventilating systems, anti-skid deck covering, wire terminals and insulators, turnbuckles, shackles, and hooks, compasses, navigation and weather/sailing instruments, clocks, watertight navigation lights, waterproof plugs and sockets, interior electric and oil lamps, door and cabinet hardware, galley appliances, heaters, sanitation devices, holding tanks and seacocks, fuel filter/water separators, a variety of canvas goods, signals, code flags, radar reflectors, horns, bells, brass signs, and trophies.

E & B Marine Supply, Inc. From their catalog, Sport Duffle Bags, Garment Bags, and Sea Bags all made of 100% heavy-duty cotton with nylon coil zippers and white, cotton webbing for straps and handles.

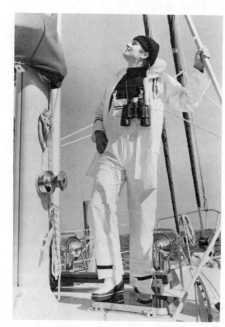

E & B Marine Supply, Inc. From their catalog, foul weather gear and boots. This jacket and chest-high trousers have electronically welded seams for complete protection.

INTERNATIONAL SAILING PRODUCTS
P.O. Box 355
Oyster Bay, New York 11771
(516) 922-5182
Catalog, 30 pages. $1.
The exclusive importer of Proctor small boat spars and representative for seven leading sailmakers, ISP provides state of the art spars and sails. Various spar and rigging parts are priced and described briefly in a special section in the catalog. Other items in the catalog receive small but good photos and descriptions: Lindsay sailboards, rudders, tillers, other boardsailing equipment, sails, covers, envelopes, and roof racks, inshore and offshore hardware (self-bailers, battens, cam cleats, fastpins and adjusters, inspection ports, shackles, sheet stoppers, extension tillers, turnbuckles), line and shock cord, lights, compasses, binoculars, watches, foulweather gear, wetsuits, footwear, gloves, warm wear and bunting, flotation devices, water bottle jackets, trapeze harnesses, a few maintenance and repair materials, and sailing games. Several pages explain ISP's special Barient and Lewmar winch exchange program. A dealer for the complete hardware lines of most quality marine manufacturers, ISP will send at no charge catalogs for Clam Cleats, Forespar, Harken, Merriman/RWO, Navtec, Nicro Fico, Ronstan, Samson, Schaefer, Seaway, Sherman Johnson, and Wichard. The firm also is a full service dealer for Elvstrom and Vanguard boats, and furnishes information on request for the classes shown in the catalog. Further, the firm carries a full line of sailboards, offers unbiased advice on the equipment, holds daily classes, and provides rentals.

M & E MARINE SUPPLY COMPANY
P.O. Box 601
Camden, New Jersey 08101
Marine Dept.: (609) 858-1010
Dive Shop: (609) 962-8719
Orders: (609) 858-2307
Catalog, 358 pages; Price list; Order forms. $2.
Often reproducing manufacturers' literature, this catalog provides a necessary detailed index, small photos/illustrations, and descriptions varying in length and coverage, for tons of marine goods, somewhat arranged in appropriate sections: a light 71" "Sportyak" dinghy with sail and motor mount options, inflatables, oars, paddles, related hardware, Mercury outboards, outboard brackets, trailer hitches, winches, and accessories, Sen-Dure off-engine kits, strainers, oil coolers, engine gaskets, disc drives, trim planes, mufflers, fuel tanks and accessories, pumps, hose and fittings, controls, cable systems, steering systems, rudders, collars, shafts and shaft logs, stuffing boxes, zincs, props, anchors, buoys, windlasses, ropes and shock cord, and deck and dock hardware. Other sections list several full lines of brand-name sailing hardware, furniture hardware, marine electronics, nautical instruments, gauges, meters, clocks and watches, navigation and charting instruments, compasses, binoculars, maintenance and repair supplies and equipment, fasteners, trims, flooring, planking, and decking, yachting knives and kits, rigging tools, folding chairs and tables, racks and holders, sleeping gear, galley

accessories, heaters, fans, water and holding tanks, sanitation systems, extinguishers, life vests, foulweather gear, nautical clothing, waterskis and equipment, gear bags, travel accessories, flags, signals, plaques, boat name letters, books, log books, games, figurines and figureheads. A marine engine cooling pump reference guide, and illustrated rigging and splicing guides are included. A copy of any manufacturer's warranty may be obtained free upon written request.

M.M.O.S. INC.
15219 Michigan Avenue
Dearborn, Michigan 48126
(313) 582-9480
Catalog, 108 pages. Free.
Accompanied with a detailed index, this partly newsprint catalog presents small photos, some in color, and mostly very brief descriptions of the variety of products available, arranged in well-defined sections: inflatables and sailboards, marine electronics and instruments, clocks, compasses, navigation and charting instruments, binoculars, navigation lights, searchlights, flares, horns, safety and emergency equipment, rope, anchors, accessories and windlasses, fenders, mooring equipment, paddles, oars, and various lines of yachting and sailing hardware. Further items include rigging tools and supplies, boat hooks, ladders, cabin hardware, rail fittings, windshield accessories, ventilators and port lights, cabin lights, power supplies, wiring and switches, pumps, sanitation systems, stoves and heaters, steering wheels and engine controls, fuel tanks, outboards, motor bracket accessories, trim tabs, a few winches and fishing rod holders, chairs, tables, boat seats, lamps, interior teak racks and holders, tableware and galley equipment, flags, tarps, marine vinyls, maintenance and repair materials and supplies, lifevests and jackets, warm wear, footwear, hats, some foulweather gear and gear bags. Copies of any written warranty relating to any product illustrated may be obtained free upon written request.

MANHATTAN MARINE AND ELECTRIC COMPANY
116 Chambers Street
New York, New York 10007
(800) 221-1924; (212) 267-8756/8759
Catalog, 434 pages; Discount sheets; Order form. Free.
One of the largest marine supply warehouses in the world, Manhattan Marine has been putting out a catalog for nearly sixty years. Complete with a detailed index, the latest catalog presents small photos, some in color, and fairly lengthy descriptions of the offerings, arranged somewhat comprehensibly: inflatables, life rafts, sailboards and equipment, various outboards, motor brackets and carriers, Sen-Dure on/off engine kits, mufflers, trim tabs, fuel tanks, fittings, and filters, pumps, hose, props, shaft logs, stuffing boxes, steering systems and wheels, controls, rope and shock cord, anchors, windlasses and accessories, dock hardware, davits, bumpers, fenders, rubrails, deck hardware, rails and fittings, hatches and port lights, vents, boat seats, ladders, outrigger equipment, sailing hardware, cabin and furniture hardware, fasteners, flooring,

planking, and decking and finishes. Also presented are items like maintenance and repair supplies and materials, rigging and sail repair tools, navigation, safety, and interior lights and lamps, horns, power supplies and electrical components, marine electronics, navigation instruments, gauges, and meters, compasses, clocks and watches, binoculars, navigation and charting instruments, folding chairs and tables, racks and holders, galley appliances, equipment, and accessories, heaters, fans, sanitation and water systems, emergency equipment, flags, plaques, letters, life vests and harnesses, flotation jackets, foulweather gear, nautical clothing, shoes and boots, gear bags, waterskis and equipment. Various services such as rigging and swaging, and advice regarding marine related problems, are available. Manufacturers' warranties for catalog items may be obtained upon written request.

Goldberg's Marine.

MARINE CENTER
2130 Westlake Avenue N.
P.O. Box 9968
Seattle, Washington 98109
(206) 284-3906/1405

Catalog, 195 pages; Seasonal sales flyers; Extensive ordering information; Order form. $1 (deducted from next order).

The Marine Center's catalog offerings are regularly stocked items whose manufacturers have good records of backing up their products, shipping on time, and maintaining good attitudes toward consumers. A detailed index is provided along with small photos and usually brief descriptions of products, pleasingly arranged in well-defined sections: Avon and Sea Eagle inflatables and accessories, polyethylene "Polywog" boats, boat hooks, oars, paddles, and accessories, Tanaka outboards, motor brackets, trailer accessories, engine accessories, fuel tanks, fittings, trim planes, pumps, strainers, filters, hose and fittings, anchors, windlasses, and accessories, cleats and chocks, ropes and shock cords, fenders, bumpers, buoys and snubbers, boat steps, ladders, transom platforms, dinghy davits, boat seats and chairs, and deck chairs and tables. Additional items include fishing equipment and traps, sailing hardware, deck hardware, hatches and port

lights, cabin and furniture hardware, fasteners, finishes, repair and maintenance supplies and equipment, navigation, safety, and cabin lights, electrical components, marine electronics and instruments, clocks, navigation and charting instruments, compasses, charts, log books, texts, cabin and head racks, holders, and accessories, galley appliances, equipment and accessories, heaters and dehumidifiers, sanitation devices, water makers, and caddies, life vests, emergency and safety equipment, horns, bells, and whistles, flags, pennants, plaques, letters and numbers, foulweather gear, nautical clothing, shoes, boots, hats, boat bags, travel accessories, and nautical gifts and novelties. Copies of any written manufacturers' warranties rgarding catalog offerings may be obtained upon written request.

*MURRAY'S MARINE
P.O. Box 490
601 Maple
Carpinteria, California 93013
(805) 684-8393/5446

Catalog, 50 pages. Free (bulk rate). $2 (first class). Sailboard equipment supplement, 16 pages. Free (bulk rate); $1 (first class).

In this catalog the Murray staff attempts to present a broad spectrum of the finest quality catamaran sailing equipment available. Embellished with comments and recommendations, the catalog offers small but good photos and reasonable descriptions of the products available, arranged in proper categories: dry suits, jackets, hats, gloves and accessories, wetsuits and boots, life vests, trapeze harnesses, buckles, handles, rings and kits, hiking sticks and paddles, trampolines and accessories, boomvangs, downhauls, mainsheet systems, marine hardware, wire, shock cord, and rope, a full line of Hobie parts, kits, sails, systems, and accessories, Prindle catamaran kits, parts, and systems, accessory parts for Nacra, Sol Cart, Freestyle, and Laser cats, sailboarding equipment, sail and hull repair and maintenance supplies and equipment, rigging, riveting, splicing, and swaging tools, multi-stripe, pin-stripe, and non-skid tapes, watches, compasses, wind and speed meters, wind indicators, safety equipment, boat covers and tents, trailer accessories, mast supports and tie downs, books, and manufacturers' catalogs.

NATIONAL MARINE SUPPLY CORPORATION
P.O. Box 010870
Main Post Office
Miami, Florida 33101
(800) 645-2565; (305) 864-2600

Catalog, 242 pages; Order form. $2.

Featuring powerboat equipment, National Marine's newsprint catalog provides a detailed index and clearly presents photos and often substantial descriptions of its offerings, arranged in well-marked, well-defined sections: inflatables, life rafts, outboard motors, trailer winches, boat hooks and paddles, marine exhaust systems, engine parts, shafts, bearings, couplings, trim tabs, fuel tanks and accessories, pumps and hoses, steering systems, controls, cables, stuffing boxes and rudder fittings, zincs, shaft logs, struts and tiller parts, marine electronics, electrical components and power supplies, navigation, safety, and interior lights, bells and horns, meters and gauges, weather instruments and clocks, navigation and charting instruments, binoculars, and compasses. Shock cord and ropes, fenders, dock and mooring equipment, anchors, windlasses and related equipment, boat steps and storage lockers are offered as well as rails and hardware, davits, ladders and platforms, deck hardware, cabin and furniture hardware, trim, fasteners, decking material, maintenance and repair supplies and equipment, boat chairs and yacht furniture, racks, holders, lamps, lanterns, brass accessories, galley appliances, equipment and accessories, air conditioners, heaters, sanitation devices, holding tanks, and emergency equipment. In addition flags, plaques, letters and numbers, life vests and jackets, foulweather gear, deck shoes, hats, insignia, belts, nautical bags and sleeping gear, log books, chart cases, nautical books, waterskis and equipment, fishing rod holders, outriggers, downriggers, gaffs, and fishwells are available. The firm services what it sells.

NAUTICAL BOATIQUE
El Capitan Sport Center
1590 N.W. 27th Avenue
Miami, Florida 33125
(800) 327-6457; (800) 432-5406 (FL);
(305) 633-6660

Fall and Spring catalogs, 32 pages and 80 pages. Free.
This newsprint catalog affords poor quality photos and little or some description (often the manufacturer's) for a host of discount marine goods, arranged a bit haphazardly: Avon and Sevylor inflatables, outboards, outboard brackets, trailer equipment, fuel tanks and accessories, mufflers, pumps, steering components, marine electronics, lights, clocks and weather instruments, navigation instruments, compasses, binoculars, anchors, deck hardware, rails, ladders, fittings, platforms, boat seats, dock hardware, maintenance and repair supplies and equipment, galley equipment and accessories, racks and holders, lamps, emergency equipment, life vests, foulweather gear, nautical clothing, boots, shoes, belts, boat covers, quite a bit of fishing gear and equipment, filleting knives, waterskiing and diving equipment, and novelties. The only warranties available on catalog products are the manufacturers', copies of which may be obtained upon written request.

OVERTON'S
211 Jarvis Street
P.O. Box 8228
Greenville, North Carolina 27834
(800) 334-6541; (800) 682-8263 (NC)
(919) 758-7600

Catalog, 72 pages. Free.
Devoted mostly to waterskiing equipment, including two competition ski boats and promotional accessories, Overton's catalog provides good color photos and usually brief descriptions of its offerings. In addition to beachwear, gear bags, wetsuits, rope and accessories, other products that might be of interest to boaters in general include sailboards, inflatables, marine electronics and instruments, binoculars, boat lights, electrical switches, outboard props, gas tank accessories, pumps, some marine hardware, boat seats, boat covers, mooring equipment, anchors and line, trailer accessories, safety equipment, maintenance and repair supplies and equipment, and deck shoes.

PASTIME PRODUCTS, INC.
1035 S. 11th Street
Philadelphia, Pennsylvania 19147
(800) 228-2028, ext. 715; (215) 755-7733

Marine Accessory catalog, 5 pages; Tool brochure, 8 pages. Free.
Pastime's catalog offers good photos/illustrations and descriptions/lists of features for a handful of apparently regularly stocked items: a ventilating sail, rainwater catcher, stabilizers for boats at rest, a safe deposit box for boats, Voss rolling cam cleats, boat hooks, deck mops and brushes, a tool bag, tie-downs, water/windproof matches. The brochure furnishes small photos and minimal descriptions for a host of items, mostly tools, available while quantities last: clamps and vises, hand trucks, hammers, a hoist, jacks, knives, drill, plier, punch-and-chisel, riveter, screwdriver, socket, tin snip, and wrench sets, tool kits, a tool bag, and a safe deposit box.

PORT SUPPLY
2245 S. Michigan Avenue
Chicago, Illinois 60616
(312) 842-2704

Pamphlet, 8 pages. Free. Catalog, 427 pages. $8.50 (credited to first $50 purchase).
While the large photos and often lengthy descriptions, usually reproductions of manufacturers' literature, are not well printed on the pages, Port Supply's catalog contains a detailed index and presents the wealth of products in well-defined, well-marked chapters, outlined in a table of contents—Finishing Products (including marine grade lumber and plywood, fiberglass cloth, polyester and epoxy resins), Fasteners, Pumps, Deck Hardware, Compasses, Lights and Horns, Electrical, Propulsion, Chemicals and Toilets, Appliances, Gifts and Accessories, Navigational Aids and Radios, Safety Equipment, Instruments, Ropes and Anchors and Wire Chain Fittings, Winches, Miscellaneous Hardware (including whisker and spinnaker poles), Merriman, Kenyon Hardware (including masts and fittings), Schaefer, Nicro-Fico Hardware, and Clothing (including the largest variety of foulweather gear in the area). A fiberglass racing class/family sailboat (14'), and a fiberglass canoe/kayak (15') are pictured and described on a final page. The pamphlet shows pictures of Port Supply's store and waterless yacht yard, explains the personal interest that the Peterson family and their staff take in their customers, specifies briefly the kinds of equipment offered, and mentions the fiberglass and wooden boat repair and refinishing, rigging, swaging, splicing, and nautical lending library service available. The Petersons and staff will do their utmost to obtain any item not in the catalog or not in stock.

SEARS, ROEBUCK AND COMPANY
Boating and Fishing Specialog
Sears Tower
Chicago, Illinois 60684
(312) 875-6816

Catalog, 60 pages. Free.

In the usual Sears catalog format, this catalog provides usually small photos, many in color, and good but brief descriptions of Sears' boating offerings, reasonably arranged and fully indexed: many varieties of inflatables, aluminum, fiberglass, and polyethylene (Coleman) canoes (12' to 17') some with keels, some with square sterns, ABS plastic sailboats (11'), a sailboard, fiberglass "tri-hull" fishing boat (12' and 14'), "semi-vee" aluminum fishing boat (12' to 14'), several sizes and shapes of aluminum Jon boat (11½' to 14'), rails, seats, covers, tops, trailers and accessories, oars and hardware for these and other boats, electric fishing motors, gas outboards, motor accessories, steering kits and accessories, fuel tanks and accessories, power supplies and pumps, anchor, line, mooring, docking, and boarding equipment. Other items indexed are: marine electronics, lights, horns, instruments, compasses, portable toilets, repair materials, finishes, some marine hardware, life vests and emergency equipment, down/siderigger equipment, some fishing gear (rods, reels, lures), storm suits, waders, hip boots, boots and deck shoes, sunglasses, waterskis and equipment, lamps, brass gifts, nautical prints, and a few basic boating books. Free copies of manufacturers' warranties for items offered are available upon written request.

STONE HARBOR YACHT CORPORATION
Stone Harbor Marina
Stone Harbor Boulevard
Box 397
Stone Harbor, New Jersey 08247
(609) 368-1141

Catalog, 368 pages. $2.95.

Furnishing a detailed index and a partial list of companies represented, this catalog provides small photos and generally brief descriptions, usually reproductions of manufacturers' literature, for an immense variety of items not that clearly arranged: inflatables, oars, paddles, boat hooks, and hardware, trailer accessories, motor brackets and carriers, trim tabs, fuel tanks, fittings, filters, pumps and hose, holding tanks and marine toilets, steering components, systems, controls and cable, marine and interior lights, horns, electrical components, marine electronics, instruments, and clocks, compasses, binoculars, and Barlow winches. Represented are Forespar, Harken, Johnson, Merriman, Nicro Fico, and Schaefer marine hardware and fittings, cabin and deck hardware, anchors, windlasses, chain and fittings, other mooring and docking equipment, ladders and platforms, boat tops, covers, and fittings, chairs and seats, folding tables, racks and holders, storage compartments, galley appliances, equipment and accessories, outrigger equipment, waterskis and equipment, life vests and safety equipment, flags, pennants, foulweather suits, gear bags, canvas accessories, fasteners, finishes, maintenance and repair supplies and equipment, and books.

TRANSMAR MARINE HARDWARE
P.O. Box 462
Highland Park, Illinois 60035
(312) 432-7210

Informational sheets (4). Free.

Transmar, a direct importer and distributor, offers a small selection of marine goods at attractive prices: a sextant, quartz-movement ship's bell clock, horns, stainless steel rigging knives, a field knife, an adjustable wrench/tool set, an aluminum locking winch handle, bilge pumps, a stainless steel heater, and brass oil lamps. A large photo, brief description and sometimes a list of features is provided for each item.

TURNER'S SPORTING GOODS
810 W. Collins Avenue
Orange, California 92667
(800) 854-8690; (800) 422-7419 (CA);
(714) 771-2852

Marine/Fishing catalog, 355 pages; Price list; Order form. $4 (credited toward first order over $25).

A good two-thirds of this catalog, complete with detailed index, is devoted to fishing equipment—rods, reels, rod-building components and materials, trolling equipment, flies, lures, baits, spoons, sinkers, hooks, snaps, swivels, floats, components and tools for making them, line, tackle boxes, creels, ice-fishing shanties and drills, nets, traps, and knives. Presented in well-marked sections, pictured and described briefly in the rest of the newsprint catalog are: ABS plastic bass hunter boats (6½' to 9½'), an aluminum sailboat (11'), a sailboard, inflatables, oars, motor brackets, boat carriers and tie-downs, boat seats, anchors and accessories, some marine (deck) hardware and fittings, electronic instruments, meters, compasses, marine lights and horns, pumps, electric fishing motors, throttles, props, weed guards, battery chargers and boxes, gas outboards, buoys, life rings and vests, boat cushions, waterproof clothing, waders and hip boots, fishing vests, sunglasses, gear bags, knapsacks and other camping and outdoor equipment including camp stoves and lanterns, waterproof letters and numbers, waterskis and equipment, and some sporting goods and clothing.

VOYAGER MARINE
P.O. Box 123
1296 State Street
Alviso, California 95002
(408) 263-7633

Introductory brochure, 6 pages. Free.

Voyager Marine, a marine hardware distributor and boatbuilding center serving independent boatbuilders (mostly amateurs), provides a full range of marine goods in addition to high quality cruising type hardware often imported directly from Australia, England, and Holland. The firm does not publish its own catalog, but instead, for $12.95, furnishes manufacturers' brochures and catalogs assembled into an expanding 5" to 7" post-type binder, complete with a comprehensive cross-reference index and discount schedule. Catalog updates are sent out quarterly, and a complete annual update is available to catalog subscribers for $5.95. The introductory brochure provides a partial list of the manufacturers represented in the catalog, and partly explains the catalog, discounts, and ordering procedures. Copies of the cross-reference index and discount schedule provide more specific information regarding prices and the manufacturers represented.

WAREHOUSE MARINE

316 N. Capitol Way
P.O. Box 2575
Olympia, Washington 98507
(800) 426-8666; (206) 754-9353

Catalog, 179 pages; Order form. $2.

For a newsprint catalog, this one provides good photos and descriptions of the many offerings: Avon inflatables, oars, hardware, outboards, brackets and carriers, fuel accessories, pumps, seacocks, strainers, steering systems and components, stuffing boxes, marine lights and horns, electrical components, marine electronics and instruments, clocks, watches, navigation and charting instruments, compasses, binoculars, shock cord, lines, anchors, chain, windlasses, trailer winches, mooring and docking equipment, boat seats and chairs, davits, ladders, deck hardware, winches and a variety of sailing hardware, cabin and furniture hardware, fasteners, maintenance and repair supplies and equipment. Rigging knives, tools, and supplies, racks and holders, oil lamps, galley appliances, equipment, and accessories, heaters, fans, dehumidifiers, water and sanitation systems, survival suits, life vests, harnesses, buoys, safety equipment, flags, windsocks, plaques, boat letters and numbers, some fishing equipment, books, foulweather gear, nautical clothing, deck shoes, gear bags, sleeping gear, buttons and jewelry are also offered. While the catalog is embellished with a detailed index and ample ordering instructions, unfortunately, the arrangement of products is rather confusing. Copies of manufacturers' warranties pertaining to catalog items are free upon written request.

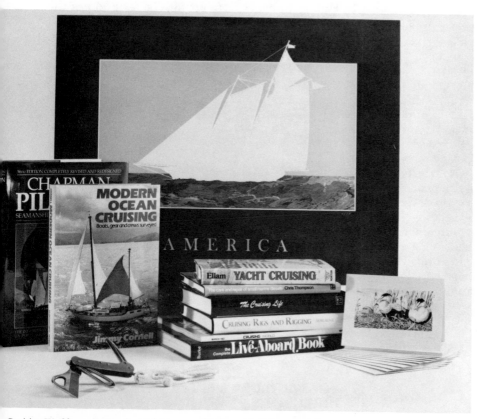

Cruising World   A sampling of the many books, practical gear, and unique gifts selected especially for the yachtsman to be found in the Cruising World Catalog.

Books

ANTHEIL BOOKSELLERS
2177 Isabelle Court
N. Bellmore, New York 11710

Quarterly catalogs, 35 pages each; Order form. $3.

Antheil's naval-maritime-military book catalog lists available new and used books alphabetically according to author, and magazines and government publications according to title. Some publication data and information regarding the condition of used books are provided. Boating, sailing, boatbuilding, and ship-modelling guides, historical and descriptive works regarding ships, boats, fishing and sailing, accounts of seafaring experiences, and journals such as the *American Neptune* are included.

ARMCHAIR SAILOR BOOKSTORE
Lee's Wharf
Newport, Rhode Island 02840
(401) 847-4252

Navigation Instrument catalog, 14 pages; Order form. Free. Book catalog, in 2 volumes, 212 pages; Order forms. $4 (deductible from first order of $25).

Embellished with a very detailed subject index and table of contents, and perhaps offering the most comprehensive and diverse bibliography of in-print marine-related books in the U.S., the two illustrated book catalogs together list, in over 50 sections, more than 3,500 titles including "how-to" books, cruising guides, maritime histories, imported books, hard-to-find historical and technical books, professional and license-study texts for commercial fishers, shippers, and seamen, sea books for children and teenagers, marine games, sea chanty cassettes and records. The price and a short review of each book is furnished; the second volume additionally provides each book's publication date and number of pages. The well-indexed navigation instrument catalog features small photos and good descriptions of the plotting instruments, barograph, sextants, chronometers and computers, hand-bearing compasses, log books, and yachtsmen's knives offered; government and commercial charts and publications are also listed and described. The firm also offers a worldwide chart and cruising guide service, a book search service for used and out-of-print twentieth century maritime literature, a book trade-in service, and lists of current marine paperback titles, boatbuilding study plans, used and out-of-print literature, and study texts for marine licenses and professional titles.

BAYVIEW BOOKS & BINDERY
P.O. Box 208
Northport, New York 11768
(516) 757-3563

Catalog, 42 pages to 54 pages; Order form. $2 (deductible from first purchase).

Bayview Books carries between 1,000 to 1,500 used books, mostly nautical, some travel. The maritime catalog lists about 400 offerings alphabetically according to author or editor, or by title if neither is named. Included are diaries, fiction, first-hand accounts, government publications, guides, histories, magazines, manuscripts, registers, and books about circumnavigation, coastal matters, cruising, explorations, navigation, oceanography, racing, restoration, rigging, sails, sailing and yachting, vessels of all kinds, sizes, and materials. Publication data and a brief review of each book's content and condition are provided. A list of 100 special marine books should also be available soon.

BLUEWATER BOOKS
109 Mariner's Square
1900 N. Northlake Way
Seattle, Washington 98103
(206) 632-6657

Catalog, 32 pages. Free.

Bluewater's newsprint catalog furnishes prices, some photos and illustrations, and short reviews of the new books in stock. The titles are listed alphabetically within the following sections: Boat Building, Design, Maintenance, Marine Electrical, Sails and Rigging, Marlinspike, "How To," Canoeing and River Running, Sailing and Cruising, Racing Navigation, Weather Sense, Boater's First Aid, Fishing, Commercial (Shipping), Sea Life and Diving, Nautical History, Boating Cuisine, Log Books, and Kid's Korner. Bluewater also handles at the shop a collection of Dutch brass lamps, scrimshaw jewelry, carvings, and sculpture, salty notecards, and a collection of William Ryan prints.

Armchair Sailor Bookstore.

BOATBUILDER'S INTERNATIONAL DIRECTORY
512 Viewmont Street
Benicia, California 94510
(707) 745-1627

Catalog, 140 pages. $6.50.

This directory, not a traditional catalog from which items may be ordered through the mail, is instead a source book listing over 2,000 addresses of businesses in the United States, Canada, the United Kingdom, Australia, New

Clymer Publications To keep boats and marine engines in top condition, Clymer offers this series of maintenance/repair handbooks.

Zealand, South Africa, Belgium, Holland, Scandinavia, Italy, and Switzerland, that offer boat kits, plans, building materials, tools, keels, masts and spars, rigging, sails, steering gear and systems, engines and motors, marine supplies and hardware, used equipment, docks, and marine-related books, publications, or instructional programs. Coverage includes canoes, kayaks, dinghies and small craft, cruising and racing sailboats, one-designs, multihulls, powerboats, commercial craft, specialty craft and houseboats. The addresses, interspersed with many display ads of the listed businesses, are prefaced with several articles about amateur boatbuilding, plans, kits, building materials and tools.

CARAVAN-MARITIME BOOKS

87-06 168th Place
Jamaica, New York 11432

Catalog, 36 pages. $5.

The Caravan catalog lists, alphabetically arranged according to author, over 400 used books, many of them quite old and rare. Topics covered include naval architecture, ship-modeling, yachting, navigation, oceanography, maritime history, the merchant marine, piracy, steamships, whaling, and more. A brief review, price, and some publication data are provided for each book along with information regarding its condition. Prices are quite high. An international search service is maintained at $1 per title, including advertising.

CHESAPEAKE BAY MARITIME MUSEUM

P.O. Box 636
Department A
St. Michaels, Maryland 21663
(301) 745-2916

Brochure, 4 pages. Free.

The Museum makes available a "Chesapeake Bay Indigenous Craft Series" of publications, currently two Chapelle reprints, a Gillmer book on sloops, and a history of the last log-bottom bugeye still sailing today, briefly described in the brochure. Signed and numbered John Mecray prints of "A Chesapeake Passing" are also available. Additional literature briefly describes the Museum's offerings, memberships, and occasional tours.

CLYMER PUBLICATIONS

12860 Muscatine Street
P.O. Box 20
Arleta, California 91331
(213) 767-7660

Information sheet; Order form; Price list. Free.

Clymer offers a series of owner-oriented maintenance and repair handbooks covering sailboat maintenance, powerboat maintenance, stern drive units, and various outboards (British Seagull, Chrysler, Evinrude, Johnson, Mercury). The sheet lists the available boat maintenance books and provides photos of them. The order form and price sheet lists in addition Clymer's entire line of do-it-yourself books involving automotive, motorcycle, bicycle, and recreational vehicle maintenance and repair, automobile history and restoration.

THE COX LISTING

Suite 1014
1301 20th Street, N.W.
Washington, D.C. 20036

Catalog, 7 pages. $1.

This "independent guide to boating catalogs" briefly reviews 81 of the better-known mail-order catalogs (most but not all of which are covered in this catalog), presented in the following sections: Boatbuilding (plans, patterns, kits, semi-completed boats), Canoes/Kayaks/ Inflatables, Comforts/Gifts/Gadgets, "Everything" Catalogs, Hardware, Instruments, Miscellaneous, and Sail.

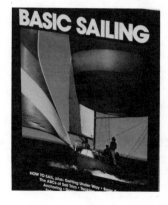

Hearst Marine Books.

CRUISING WORLD
**524 Thames Street
Newport, Rhode Island 02840
(401) 847-1588**

Catalog, 16 pages; Order form. Free.

Cruising World's catalog offers an exclusive line of gear carefully selected for quality, practical worth, and uniqueness, with the cruising sailor in mind. Well described and sometimes pictured in color are a few gift items, often sporting the *Cruising World* sailboat in silhouette—tie, apron, custom log book, calendars, canvas briefcase, heavy canvas tool bag, knit sport shirt, wool ski hat, T-shirt, candies, and notecards—and 70 books grouped into four categories—Boatbuilding and Design, Boatkeeping and Maintenance, Voyages and Cruising Narratives, and Boat Handling and Navigation.

HEARST MARINE BOOKS
**151 River Road
Cos Cob, Connecticut 06807
(203) 629-1880/1881**

Plans catalog, 43 pages; Book pamphlet, 9 pages; Order form. Free.

Hearst publishes a select number of well-known books on marine subjects, notably Chapman's *Piloting* and *Log and Owner's Manual*, a yachtsman's emergency handbook, and books on basic, practical, storm, and Hobie Cat sailing, windsurfing technique, boat living, and marine electrical systems. All of the books receive brief to long reviews in the catalog; photos are provided of most of the books, and sometimes information about authors is presented. Perhaps more interesting is the boat plan catalog, Hearst's effort to make available the best of the boat plans published in *Motor Boating and Sailing* over a sixty year period. Specifications, a sailplan/profile, and an illustration of the interior layout are provided for 94 boats including dinghies, prams, sailing and utility skiffs, a sailing canoe, dories, a Norwegian Hardangersjekt, sloops, catboats, knockabouts, a catamaran, skip jack, cutters, schooners, ketches, yawls, launches, runabouts, a scow, outboard, cabin, and sternwheel cruisers, a tug, dragger, and houseboat. Each plans package consists of a full set of plans including five to six pages of blueprints, offset tables, and a copy of the original article that accompanied the plans in the magazine. Plans are returnable within ten days.

INTERNATIONAL MARINE PUBLISHING COMPANY
**Camden, Maine 04843
(207) 236-4342**

Catalog (monthly), 16 pages. Free.

International Marine's newspaper format catalog contains reviews and occasionally photos of about 500 titles, fluctuating monthly as new titles are added and older ones deleted. New books are covered on the front and last pages; sandwiched in-between are descriptions of cookbooks, cruising guides, nautical prints, marine reference works, records, books about boats, boat design, maintenance, boatbuilding, commercial fishing, cruising adventures, electricity, engines, fish farming, marine art, maritime history, marlinspike seamanship, modeling, navigation, racing, sea life, seamanship, sportfishing, tools and methods, and underwater salvage.

THE ISLAND HUNTER BOOKSTORE
**1559 Spinnaker Drive, #106
Ventura, California 93001
(805) 644-5827**

Catalog, 30 pages. $2.

Pleasantly illustrated with pictures of boats, equipment and boating scenes, the catalog comes with a table of contents and includes prices and brief reviews of marine-related books listed nonalphabetically according to topic—boatbuilding and design, repair and maintenance, cruising guides, racing and sailing, seamanship, navigation, weather, first aid, reference, fishing and sealife, diving, sea and true cruising stories, cookbooks, photography, people and places, odds and sods.

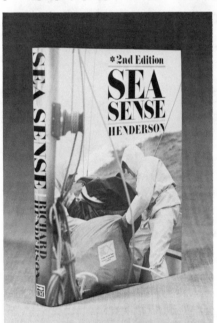

International Marine Publishing Company.

MULTIHULLS MAGAZINE
**421 Hancock Street
North Quincy, Massachusetts 02171
(617) 328-8181**

Book catalog, 14 pages; Back-Issue catalog, 10 pages; Order forms. $1 (free to subscribers of Multihulls *magazine).*

Multihull's Book Catalog is provided as a service to subscribers to present a good source of books about multihulls and related topics. Arranged roughly according to topic—multihull types and design, boatbuilding, sail and motor power, boat handling and navigation, boat housekeeping, tales of voyages and races—but not arranged alphabetically, the books receive short to extensive reviews; each is preceded with a small photograph of the book cover. The second catalog lists the contents of each back issue; copies of articles in sold-out issues are available for $1.

JOHN ROBY

Aerospace/Nautical/Technical Books
3703 Nassau Drive
San Diego, California 92115

Catalog, 82 pages. $3.

Roby's Nautical Book List presents, in alphabetical order by author or title, almost 1,900 out-of-print and in-print used books dealing mostly with ship/boat design and building, seamanship, cruises, model building, or canoeing. In addition to some publication data, information about the book's condition and sometimes a brief description of the contents are given. Inquiries for

TAMAL VISTA PUBLICATIONS

222 Madrone Avenue
Larkspur, California 94939

Pamphlet, 6 pages. Free.

Tamal Vista sells Hazen's *Stripper's Guide to Canoe Building,* reviewed at length in the pamphlet, and offers single and twin large-scale decals of Pacific Northwest native American salmon eye, eagle, or whale designs to decorate the wood-strip canoes. Printed in black ink on clear mylar, the decals are durable and easy to apply, and they will bond to metal. The designs are illustrated and their dimensions given.

J. TUTTLE—BOOKS

1806 Laurel Crest
Madison, Wisconsin 53705
(608) 238-3668 after 6 p.m.

List, 13 pages. Free.

Tuttle's "Maritime Book List" presents 242 used books arranged alphabetically by author. Titles regarding maritime history, museums, vessels, ship models, boating, sailing, yachting, fishing and whaling, voyages and more are included. A brief review and some publication data are given for each book along with information about the book's condition.

WOODENBOAT CATALOG

P.O. Box 78
Brooklin, Maine 04616
(207) 359-4651

Catalog, 34 pages; Order form. Free.

The Woodenboat Catalog presents in pleasant format small photos and good reviews of a good selection of books on boats (mostly boat types), design, boatbuilding and repair, ship models, woodworking and tools, seamanship, and cruising around. Contents of available *Woodenboat* magazine back issues are listed, and the covers of all back issues are shown in color. Binders, hardbounds, and an index for the issues are also presented. Color photos and descriptions are provided for half models for which plans and kits are available, and for the ship model for which plans and instructions may be purchased. A description and small profile are given for 25 boats (tenders, skiff, sailing dinghy, canoe, and other small craft, yawls, sloops, schooners, a cutter, a launch) for which plans may be obtained. Fuller data on these boats and plans are presented in two plans catalogs ($2 each). T-shirts, shop aprons, and hats with the *Woodenboat* logo, and the wooden boat calendar are also available.

THE YANKEE WHALER

201 5th Avenue S.
Edmonds, Washington 98020
(206) 775-6757

Catalog, 43 pages; Order form. Free.

Illustrated with reproductions of old engravings of nautical scenes, the Yankee Whaler catalog furnishes a good table of contents and an index of the 301 books listed—the most popular of the store's more than 1,000 titles—arranged alphabetically by title. Topics represented include navigation and seamanship, sailing and cruising, Northwest cruising, sails and rigging, racing, voyaging, canoeing, sailor's arts, nautical history, boatbuilding and repair, design, marine life, poetry and fiction, regional Northwest, Alaska, children's titles, and cookbooks. Some publication data and a brief description are provided for each book. Information will be sent to interested persons upon request regarding the store's one-of-a- kind marine antiques ranging from telescopes, ships' lights, binnacles, compasses, microscopes, clocks and instruments, flags and Royal Navy fingerbowls. The shop boasts no reproductions. Scrimshaw, marine prints, and engraved brass pieces are also kept in stock.

See also, under:

Battery Chargers
SunWatt

Electrical Equipment
Baker and Lyman
Better Boating
Celestaire
Creative Consultants
Kane
Kleid
Weems

Sails and Canvas Goods
Cook
Sailrite

Refrigeration
Crosby
SpaCreek

Nautical and Outdoor Clothing
Bean

Gifts
Center for Environmental
Education
Preston

General Catalogs
Chartroom
Commodore
Defender
E & B
Goldberg's
M & E
Marine Center
Murray's
National Marine
Port Supply
Sears
Stone Harbor
Warehouse

COMPANY INDEX

SUBJECT INDEX